DOROTHY WORDSWORTH

A Longman Cultural Edition

DOROTHY WORDSWORTH

Edited by

Susan M. Levin

PEARSON
Longman

New York   San Francisco   Boston
London   Toronto   Sydney   Tokyo   Singapore   Madrid
Mexico City   Munich   Paris   Cape Town   Hong Kong   Montreal

Editor-in-Chief: Joseph P. Terry
Marketing Manager: Joyce Nilsen
Production Manager: Ellen MacElree
Project Coordination and Electronic Page Makeup: TexTech International
Cover Designer/Manager: John Callahan
Cover Illustration: Waterhead Windermere, anonymous chromolithograph
    owned and provided by Susan M. Levin
Title page: Silhouette of Dorothy Wordsworth as a Young Woman
    (The Wordsworth Trust United Kingdom)
Manufacturing Manager: Mary Fischer
Printer and Binder: R.R. Donnelley/Harrisonburg
Cover Printer: Phoenix Color Corp.

Library of Congress Cataloging-in-Publication Data

Wordsworth, Dorothy, 1771–1855.
    [Selections. 2009]
    Dorothy Wordsworth / edited by Susan M. Levin. — A Longman
cultural ed.
        p. cm. — (Longman cultural editions)
    Includes bibliographical references.
    ISBN-13: 978-0-321-27775-6
    ISBN-10:   0-321-27775-9
    1. Wordsworth, Dorothy, 1771–1855.   2. Authors, English—19th
century—Biography.   I. Levin, Susan M., 1950–   II. Title.
    PR5849.A3 2009
    828'.703—dc22   2007052443

Please visit us at http://www.ablongman.com.

ISBN-13: 978-0-321-27775-6
ISBN-10:   0-321-27775-9

2 3 4 5 6 7 8 9 10—DOH—11 10 09 08

Contents

List of Illustrations

About Longman Cultural Editions

Reading always vibrates with the transformations of the day—now, yesterday, and centuries ago when presses first put printed language into circulation. So too, literary culture is always open to change, with new pulses of imagination confronting older practices, texts transforming under new ways of reading and new perspectives of understanding, canons shifting and expanding, traditions reviewed and renewed, recast and reformed. Inspired by the innovative *Longman Anthology of British Literature,* Longman Cultural Editions present key texts in contexts that illuminate the lively intersections of literature, tradition, and culture. In each volume, a principal work gains new dimensions from materials that relate it to its past, present, and future: to informing traditions and debates, to the conversations and controversies of its own historical moment, to later eras of reading and reaction.

The series is designed for several kinds of readers and several situations of reading: the cultural editions offer appealing complements to the *Anthology,* as well as attractive resources for a variety of coursework, or for independent encounters. First-time readers will find productive paths to investigate, while more-seasoned readers will enjoy the fresh perspectives and provocative juxtapositions. The contexts for adventure vary from volume to volume, but the constants (in addition to handsome production and affordable pricing) are an important literary work, expertly edited and helpfully annotated; an inviting introduction; a table of dates to track its composition, publication, and reception in relation to biographical, cultural, and historical events; and a guide for further study. To these common measures and uncommon enhancements, we invite your attention and curiosity.

Susan J. Wolfson, General Editor
Professor of English, Princeton University

About This Edition

In assembling selections from her work across a history of its production for the first time, this Longman edition provides an account both of Dorothy Wordsworth's writings and of how readers at different times have experienced them. As the sister of William Wordsworth and a member of his household, Dorothy Wordsworth was, until the 1980s, regarded more as an adjunct to the literary energies of Romanticism than as an independent authorial presence. Yet her writing so fascinated so many people that it was circulated both in manuscript and in publications. The texts presented here, many of which have not been readily available to the reading public, offer a record of a woman organizing her world and of how that record achieves public awareness.

Dorothy Wordsworth copied and recopied her journals and poems and sent them to family and friends all over England. To the Clarksons, for instance, she sent a version of the Green Narrative that is printed here for the first time. She wrote poetry, some of which William Wordsworth included in his collections of 1815, 1836, and 1842. Many poems, however, remained in manuscript until the 1980s when I collected them in *Dorothy Wordsworth and Romanticism*, texts reprinted here.

Her preferred mode of expression was the journal. In her hands this form becomes a powerful narrative of emotional, domestic, and artistic life sustained among a group of extraordinary people. In 1851, her nephew Christopher Wordsworth published excerpts from her work in his *Memoirs of William Wordsworth, poet laureate*, some of which are included here. Not until 1875 did a journal receive conventional publication, when Principal Shairp put out *Recollections of a Tour Made in Scotland a.d. 1803*, my basis for selections from the Scottish tour. So successful was Shairp's endeavor (he received many fan letters) that scholars such as William Knight and Ernest de Selincourt turned to the manuscripts preserved at

Dove Cottage in Grasmere to create fuller editions of her other journals. Knight's late nineteenth- and early twentieth-century editions are my basis for selections from both her journals and letters.

Both personal and cultural, her perennially resonant concerns gain focus through the contextual material presented here. A table of dates provides orientation to literary, political, and cultural events of her time. As descriptions by her contemporaries Samuel Taylor Coleridge, Thomas De Quincey, and Maria Jane Jewsbury demonstrate, she was a woman who impressed and puzzled those around her. William Hazlitt, Samuel Rogers, and Thomas De Quincey portray her daily life in the Wordsworth circle—the walking, the talking, the writing, the family dynamic. Considered strange, perhaps incestuous, the Wordsworths' life generated an investigation by the Home Secretary, described in letters presented here for the first time since the 1930s.

With other women of the household, Dorothy was responsible for daily cuisine and home management. Cookbooks provide important insights into cultural norms—one thinks of *The Settlement Cookbook or The Way to a Man's Heart* that from 1901 helped integrate so many Jewish immigrants into the American way, or of how Julia Child's work developed American tastes. Hannah Glasse's *Art of Cookery* served a similar function in Dorothy's day, and so a brief excerpt is included. A chart explaining monetary values and units of measure helps clarify her daily concerns.

A selection of William's poems and De Quincey's narrative of the Green tragedy illuminate Dorothy Wordsworth's place in a community of writers. As she and her circle registered their local world and traveled abroad, they produced accounts influenced by theories of the picturesque as well as by the culture of travel writing. Selections from William Gilpin, Mary Russell Mitford, Ann Radcliffe, Henry Crabb Robinson, and Mary Wordsworth that parallel her work establish a context for Dorothy's views of her world.

Illustrations also illuminate. Three portraits of Dorothy-Wordsworth reveal her changing appearance. The silhouette suggests the slim young woman who wrote to her friend Jane in a letter of May 6, 1792, of gaining two pounds. "I now reach *eight stone.*" A stone is 14 pounds. At 112 pounds, Dorothy stayed trim by walking miles every day. An effect of her illness was loss of mobility and weight gain, reflected in Crosthwaite's formal portrait of her at 62. Nine years later, John Harden sketched her in a kind of wheelchair.

And finally, the importance of social and political activities in Dorothy Wordsworth's life cannot be overstated. The school she helped create, part of a movement to allow women some education, drew on the work of educator Sarah Trimmer, from whose *Œeconomy of Charity* I provide a short excerpt. Dorothy's writing gives an account of a changing world as people are thrown off their land, partly owing to enclosure, the redistribution and fencing off of private and public property to create large, private holdings. Her concerns are those of a country farmer whose 1786 pamphlet *Cursory Remarks on Inclosures* illuminates issues of the Grasmere journals and the Green narrative. Often cited by economists and cultural historians, this pamphlet has been out of print since the early nineteenth century, but is presented here.

In all the texts of this edition, annotations are mine, unless otherwise noted. Dealing with many Wordsworths can be confusing, so for clarity I identify them by first name. I also use the following abbreviations: DW—Dorothy Wordsworth; WmW—William Wordsworth; STC—Samuel Taylor Coleridge; MW—Mary Wordsworth.

Because Dorothy Wordsworth's writing appears in many different forms in many different places, collecting it presents particular challenges. In the 1940s and 1950s, Helen Darbishire and Mary Mooman produced further editions of the journals and arranged for copies of all the Dove Cottage material to be brought to North America. One tradition maintains that during the Cold War, Darbishire became convinced that the Russians would head to the Lake District to bomb Dove Cottage and the national treasures it held. The manuscripts would have to be photocopied for safekeeping. But then what? George Healey, the director of libraries at Cornell University, convinced her to give Cornell the reproductions. But worried that Ithaca, in a location sometimes called "The American Lake District," might also be vulnerable to attack, she took out a map of Canada, closed her eyes, and put her finger down on a random spot, which turned out to be Winnipeg. A second set of copies was sent to a bank vault there.

Working with such a variety of material has indebted me to many people and institutions. The Cornell Wordsworth collection has been invaluable, as have library resources at Drew University, Columbia University, and Stevens Institute of Technology. As holder of copyright to the works of William and Dorothy Wordsworth, the Wordsworth Trust has kindly supported this project. Dorothy's *Narrative of George and Sarah Green* and material from her late journals are published here with permission of The Wordsworth Trust, Cumbria, United Kingdom. My transcription of the Green narrative is from a manuscript preserved in the British Library and printed here with its permission: © The British Library Board. All rights reserved. Permission to print material from the late journals has also been given by Marilyn Gaull, founding editor of *The Wordsworth Circle,* in which Carl Ketcham's texts used here first appeared. My transcriptions from manuscripts of the poems and of *Mary Jones and her Pet-lamb* in the archive at Dove Cottage Library, Grasmere, first published in *Dorothy Wordsworth and Romanticism,* appear here again with the kind permission of The Wordsworth Trust, Cumbria, United Kingdom. Specific manuscript information about each poem appears in the footnotes. The selection from the *Harvard Library Bulletin* containing Richard Woodhouse's *Cause Book* appears by permission of Houghton Library, Harvard University. For some texts no copyright holder could be found, despite an extensive search; we apologize for any omission. We mean to credit all those, from Dorothy Wordsworth's day to our own, who have sustained a community of interest in her writing.

Three great Wordsworthians who have been my teachers have enabled my investigations of Dorothy Wordsworth's life and work: Steven Parrish, Carl Woodring, and M. H. Abrams. Rachel Brownstein, Margaret Homans, and Susan Wolfson, my partner in this Longman project, have been crucial to my involvement with Dorothy. Without the technical assistance of Eric Rosenberg and his staff at Stevens, the proofreading skills of Eleanor Wedge, and the help in every way of my husband, Robert Ready, this edition would not exist.

Susan M. Levin
Stevens Institute of Technology, 2008

Introduction

The name "Dorothy" means "gift of god," and Dorothy Wordsworth (1771–1855) was born on Christmas day in Cockermouth, Cumberlandshire, the third child and only daughter of John Wordsworth, an attorney, and Anne Wordsworth. Dorothy Wordsworth's work and life would be bound to the writing community of the Lake District, one that included Samuel Taylor Coleridge, Thomas De Quincey, and her brother William. Her authorship and sistership converged to create writing—journals, poems, stories, travel narratives, and letters—that have come to be valued as the work of a distinct, intimate sensibility.

John Wordsworth earned his living as scribe and agent to one of the principal landlords of the region, Sir James Lowther. The Wordsworth children occupied a comfortable place in Cockermouth society, but then, in 1778, Anne Wordsworth died. The family disintegrated; the boys were sent away to school, and six-year-old Dorothy was sent to live with Elizabeth Threlkeld Rawson of Halifax, an arrangement Anne had made before her death. With the blessing of her husband, "Aunt" Rawson started Dorothy on a fine education, giving her the classics of England, Greece, and Rome to read and encouraging her to write stories and compositions. Though Dorothy missed her brothers terribly, she seems to have found consolation in literature and in a friendship with Jane Pollard that endured for a lifetime.

At age nine, Dorothy went to boarding school in nearby Hipperholme. Her father's sudden death in 1783 left the Wordsworth children in a difficult financial position. Dorothy had to continue her education at Miss Mellin's Day School, near the Rawson home, and then leave school altogether to go live with the

Cooksons—her maternal grandparents and an uncle—at Penrith. These grim relatives, her legal guardians, discouraged her literary inclinations and were especially upset when William arrived to take his sister on long country walks. Luckily, another uncle, the Reverend Dr. William Cookson, captivated by her intelligence and industry, arranged for Dorothy to live with him and his wife at Forncett. He taught his niece French, Latin, Italian, math, and geography; Dorothy helped with the housework and with five children. With the Cooksons, she established a Sunday School and then planned for a School of Industry for girls.

Always sustaining her was the plan she and William had of living and writing together. A bequest from William's college friend Raisley Calvert and income from tutoring a friend's son finally made this project possible. Over the protests of their relatives, who considered it "a very bad wild scheme,"[1] William and Dorothy moved to Racedown in 1795 and then, to be near Samuel Taylor Coleridge, to Alfoxden House in 1797.

Viewed as morally and politically dangerous because of their unconventional life, they were asked to leave Alfoxden House. They decided to go to Germany, and having written *Lyrical Ballads* to help finance the trip, Coleridge and the Wordsworths embarked in 1798. The mud and rain of a German winter made the Wordsworths happy to return home in April 1799.

In December, William and Dorothy took up residence at Dove Cottage in Grasmere. William's wife, Mary, joined their household in 1802, and as the family grew they moved to more commodious houses: Allan Bank in 1808 and Rydal Mount in 1813. They lived in the Lake District for the rest of their lives.

Several events were particularly disturbing to Dorothy Wordsworth's precarious balance of art and domesticity: the death at sea in 1805 of her brother Captain John Wordsworth; the falling out with Coleridge in 1810; and, in 1829, her own illness, perhaps a stroke, perhaps arteriosclerosis. Even so, that same year, when nephew Jonny faced a professional and emotional crisis, Aunt Dorothy, almost fifty-eight, was dispatched to see him through. Traveling to his dreary parsonage in Whitwick, she described in a journal entry, departing day: "On new Terrace—Sun bursts out/before setting—unearthly and/ brilliant—calls to mind the change to another world—Every/leaf a golden lamp—every twig/bedropped with a diamond. The/splendour

---

[1] De Selincourt, *Biography,* 59.

departs us rapidly—." At Whitwick, the light left her. For the next 30 years, she moved in and out of sanity, at times refusing to recognize her world, at times a fervent participant in life around her.

DOROTHY WORDSWORTH'S WRITING

If she did not write for publication, Dorothy Wordsworth did write to be read, circulating manuscripts to friends and family. Her journals were kept partly to be consulted by William and other writers. William published some of her poetry with his own; a number of people urged her to publish various writings, and she entered into publication projects.

Her work raises many issues of writing and reading. What does it take for a woman to become a writer? What were the cultural pressures and prejudices that nineteenth-century women faced as they wrote? How does Romanticism define Dorothy Wordsworth's work, and how does Dorothy Wordsworth help define Romanticism? What kind of writer is Dorothy Wordsworth?

The process of defining herself, her community, and her perspective on her world emerges in the Alfoxden notebook (1798), an account of her life in the country with her brother and Coleridge. Both used her ways of seeing and her words in their poems. Her Grasmere journals (1800–1803) relate William's courtship of and marriage to Mary Hutchinson, a narrative reflecting repeated anxiety about being replaced as her brother's companion. Rather than marry, Dorothy remained in the household of her brother, to write, to help him write, and to contribute to the domestic labors. Aunt Dolly did laundry, baked gingerbread, wrote poems for William's five children, and copied and edited her brother's work. Her Grasmere journals, written to organize her own emotions and "to give William pleasure," provide material for some of his best-known poems. These notebooks also detail the life of the village and the movements of beggars, vagrants, and gypsies, of people displaced in the changing economy of the early nineteenth century. Recording and reflecting on the stories of the men and women who pass her door, Dorothy registers her own center in Grasmere.

Nineteenth-century economics, especially the handling of support for the poor, figure in *A Narrative Concerning George & Sarah Green of the Parish of Grasmere* (1808). Telling of the Greens's death in a snowstorm and of the way the parish organized to support their orphaned children, Dorothy Wordsworth explains a system of charity under attack by advocates of the workhouse system. The Poor Law Amendment Bill of 1834 helped replace the individual parish care Dorothy extols with, in the words of Dr. John Kay, one of its enforcers, "workhouse humiliations."

Complementing her commitment to her domestic life in the Lake District are travel narratives in which Dorothy Wordsworth represents herself as the woman who goes out to seek experience in the company of family and friends. Her *Journal of Visit to Hamburgh and of Journey from Hamburgh to Goslar* (1798) provides the group account of her first trip abroad and begins the blending of tourism, landscape description, comparative sociology, and chronicles of memory and change that would animate all her travel writing. Her *Journal of a Tour on the Continent, 1820,* visits the scenes of William's youth to create her own myth of the mind, nature, and memory. In the Alps, as at home, the stakes are high, as the power of her writing reveals. Many people wrote travel journals; many people wrote diaries—but both Dorothy and her readers recognize the distinguishing force of her vision, of her ability to see and place the details of her world in a unique narrative.

Recollections of a Tour Made in Scotland A.D. 1803 has little to do with conventional descriptions. Poet Samuel Rogers was so impressed with Dorothy's manuscript that he offered to find a publisher. The circumstances surrounding this possible publication demonstrate much about Dorothy's life as a writer. In 1822, nearly twenty years after the tour, publication was still being discussed. William, referring to Rogers's "skill and experience in these matters," writes to him in a letter of September 16 about finally bringing the book to press. Dorothy would like, William adds, to publish a series of her travel writings. Glad to be of service, Rogers advises Dorothy not to sell the copyright, but to "enter the Lottery oneself and not sell the ticket for little or nothing to the bookseller." He continues: "The bookseller I should go to myself in such a case would be Murray. He will consult Gifford, who will certainly be charmed with a talent such as hers. . . ."[2] Replying to Rogers on January 3, 1823, Dorothy says she prefers a "middle course," and suggests that a bookseller might be convinced to pay for the right to

[2] Hill, *Letters,* 3, 1, p. 155*n.* John Murray was the publisher of choice for many writers, including Byron, to whom in 1816 he paid £2000 for canto III of *Childe Harold's Pilgrimage* and *The Prisoner of Chillon.* Jane Austen sold the copyright of *Pride and Prejudice* for £110. William Gifford was a founding editor of the *Quarterly Review,* also published by Murray.

publish a certain number of copies. She would, however, need to receive at least £200 to make relinquishing her privacy worthwhile. By 1837, when her health and mind had disintegrated, William put an end to the possibility of her publishing and wrote of the Scottish tour project: "I *had* hoped that my carrying my Sister's journal thro' the press might prove a salutary interest to her—but as I no longer can cherish that hope, I must defer the publication—we find that the work perhaps would not interest her at all, or if it did, like every thing that excites her, it would do her harm."[3]

The Green narrative also generates one of many discussions Dorothy had about publication and about the profession of authorship. The Clarksons urge that this extraordinary work be given larger circulation through publication. Dorothy writes to Catherine Clarkson: "My dear Friend, I cannot express what pain I feel in refusing to grant any request of yours, and above all one in which dear Mr. Clarkson joins so earnestly, but indeed I cannot have that narrative published." She then makes a statement which is often taken to mean that she did not see herself as a publishing writer: ". . . I should detest the idea of setting myself up as an author." If we look at the full context of the statement, however, its meaning is not so clear-cut. She writes: "I cannot have that narrative published. My reasons are entirely disconnected with myself, much as I should detest the idea of setting myself up as an Author. I should not object on that score as if it had been an invention of my own. It might have been published without a name, and nobody would have thought of me. But on account of the family of the Greens I cannot consent." She then goes on to write of her fears that publication might "bring the children forward to notice as Individuals, and we know not what injurious effect this might have upon them."[4]

Dorothy focuses on avoiding notoriety, both for herself and others. Hers is an anxiety many women feel about the prospect of becoming public figures, an anxiety enhanced by the ambivalence she must have felt about treading on her brother's turf. Her objections to publication also raise a general question about works drawn "from real life": what effect will the text have on the subject? For a Romantic writer, who often takes herself and those nearest to her as the best subject available, the concern is typical.

[3] Hill, *Letters,* 6, pp. 505–506.
[4] Knight, *Letters,* I, p.351.

But as she aged, Dorothy's own writing, especially her poetry, became her focus. Her poetry underscores her relationship to the writers around her even as it emphasizes her need to distinguish herself from them. Analyzing her life as a Lake District woman, the poems set past fantasies against present realities. Speaking to some of William's most famous poetry, they show the "violet betrayed," and "consciousness no longer hidden." She continually recited her verse, and when a gift was required, Dorothy often sent some of her poems.

Table of Dates

Dorothy Wordsworth and Her Time

Boldface indicates key events in the life and writings of Dorothy Wordsworth (**DW**).

1766   John Wordsworth marries Ann Cookson and becomes law-agent to Lord Lowther at Cockermouth, Cumbria.

Anthony Benezet, *A Caution and Warning to Great Britain on the Calamitous State of the Enslaved Negro;* Oliver Goldsmith, *The Vicar of Wakefield.*

Bonnie Prince Charlie claims British throne; Stamp Act of 1765 repealed.

1767   Laurence Sterne, *Tristram Shandy* (first installment).

British Parliament passes Townshend Acts, taxing everyday products such as lead, paper, paint, glass, and tea.

1768   **DW's brother Richard born.**

Thomas Gray, *Poems.*

John Wilkes imprisoned for attacking George III in an article published in the *North Britain;* rioting in London ensues; Royal Academy founded with Sir Joshua Reynolds as president; Captain Cook's first voyage to Australia and New Zealand.

1769   Elizabeth Montagu, *An Essay on the Writings and Genius of Shakespeare.*

Richard Arkwright patents a spinning frame driven by the water wheel.

1770   **DW's brother William (WmW) born.**

Beethoven born; Thomas Chatterton commits suicide. Oliver Goldsmith, *The Deserted Village.* Boston Massacre; fireworks at wedding of Marie Antoinette and Louis the Dauphin cause death of approximately 800; Joseph Priestley introduces the rubber eraser to remove pencil marks.

1771   **DW born 25 December, Cockermouth, Cumbria.**

Walter Scott born. Henry Mackenzie, *The Man of Feeling.*

Spain cedes Falkland Islands to Britain; James Cook sails *Endeavor* back to Downs, England.

1772   **DW's brother John born.**

Samuel Taylor Coleridge born. Tobias Smollet, *Humphry Clinker.*

Morning Post founded.

1773   Goldsmith, *She Stoops to Conquer;* first edition of *Encyclopaedia Britannica.*

Boston Tea Party protests "Tea Tax."

1774   **DW's brother Christopher born.**

Johann Wolfgang von Goethe, *Sorrows of Young Werther.*

Edmund Burke's orations in House of Commons on *American Taxation.*

1775   Jane Austen and Charles Lamb born. Mary Robinson, *Poems.* Harriett Abrams debuts at Drury Lane in David Garrick's *The Little Gypsy.*

1776   Thomas Paine, *Common Sense;* Adam Smith, *The Wealth of Nations.*

American Declaration of Independence; Concert of Ancient Music Series established.

1777   Mrs. H. Cartwright, *Letters on Female Education, addressed to a Married Lady.*

First London production of *School for Scandal* by Richard Brinsley Sheridan.

1778   **After her mother dies, DW goes to live with her mother's cousin, Elizabeth Threlkeld, at Halifax.**

William Hazlitt born. Frances Burney, *Evelina.*

French join Americans in war against England; Cook discovers Sandwich Islands (Hawaii).

1779   Samuel Johnson, *Lives of the Poets.*

Mary Robinson's Perdita in *Winter's Tale* captivates the Prince of Wales, with whom she begins an affair.

1780   Richard West, *Guide to the Lakes* (expanded second edition).

Gordon Riots against toleration of Catholics; Robert Raikes opens first Sunday School.

1781   **DW sent to boarding school at Hipperholme (two miles from Halifax).**

Fuseli paints "The Nightmare"; British surrender at Yorktown.

1782   J.-J. Rousseau, *Confessions* (Part One); William Cowper, *Poems.*

James Watt patents steam engine.

1783   **DW's father dies.**

William Blake, *Poetical Sketches.*

Treaty of Paris ends American Revolution.

1784   **For economic reasons, DW leaves boarding school and goes to local Miss Mellin's School with her close friend Jane Pollard.**

Charlotte Smith, *Elegaic Sonnets and Other Essays.*

Britain begins to import American cotton.

1785   Thomas De Quincey born. Marquis de Sade, *Les 120 journées de Sodome;* William Paley, *The Principles of Moral and Political Philosophy.*

Edmund Cartwright invents the power loom; Pitt initiates financial reform.

1786   Robert Burns, *Poems Chiefly in the Scottish Dialect;* William Gilpin, *Observations of Picturesque Beauty in Cumberland and Westmorland;* William Beckford, *Vathek;* W. A. Mozart, *Marriage of Figaro.*

1787   **DW sent to live with Cookson grandparents over their shop in Penrith. Tutored by her uncle, Rev. William Cookson.** WmW enters St. John's College, Cambridge.

After Joseph Farington, *Views of the Lakes;* Mary Wollstonecraft, *Thoughts on the Education of Daughters.*

Formation of Society for Effecting the Abolition of the Slave Trade.

1788   **DW accepts invitation to live at Forncett with Rev. Cookson and his new wife, Dorothy.**

Byron born. Charlotte Smith, *Emmeline, The Orphan of the Castle;* Thomas Clarkson, *Impolicy of the Slave Trade.*

1789   **DW begins teaching Sunday School. Works with Cooksons on the idea of creating a School of Industry for young girls.** Abolitionist William Wilberforce visits Forncett; Jane Pollard teases **DW** about possible romantic involvement with Wilberforce.

J.-J.Rousseau, *Confessions* (Part Two); Blake, *Songs of Innocence;* Erasmus Darwin, *Botanic Garden;* Olaudah Equiano, *The Interesting Narrative of the Life of Olaudah Equiano.*

Storming of the Bastille; revolution in France.

1790   WmW tours France and the Alps with Robert Jones.

Burke, *Reflections on the Revolution in France.*

1791   WmW receives B.A. and returns to France.

James Boswell, *The Life of Samuel Johnson LL.D;* Paine, *The Rights of Man.*

Birmingham Riots—attack on supporters of French Revolution.

1792   **DW travels to London with Cooksons.**

WmW becomes involved with Annette Vallon, returns from France; their daughter, Caroline, born; Percy Bysshe Shelley born.

Mary Wollstonecraft, A *Vindication of the Rights of Woman.*

Corresponding Societies formed in London and Sheffield for the purpose of bringing about *"Parliamentary Reform"*; Paine charged with sedition and sentenced to death; *Rights of Man* banned.

1793   Felicia Hemans born, Liverpool.

William Godwin, *An Enquiry Concerning Political Justice.*

Process of "enclosing land" begun in the 1760s increases as over 2000 local enclosure acts are passed between 1793 and 1815; Louis XVI and Marie Antoinette guillotined.

1794   **DW reunited with WmW; they visit Grasmere and The Lakes;** WmW nurses college friend Raisley Calvert.

Blake, *Songs of Innocence and of Experience, Europe, First Book of Urizen*; Uvedale Price, *Essay on the Picturesque*; Ann Radcliffe, *The Mysteries of Udolpho*; Paine, *The Age of Reason.*

Treasonable Practices Act passed.

1795   **Legacy from Raisley Calvert allows DW and WmW to set up housekeeping at Racedown Lodge in Dorset. Care for Basil Montagu, age three. They meet Samuel Taylor Coleridge (STC).**

John Keats born. Matthew Gregory "Monk" Lewis, *Ambrosia or the Monk.*

Two bills outlawing unlawful assemblies and treasonable practices passed into law; Speenhamland system of poor relief implemented to relieve rural poverty through wage supplements.

1796   Mary Hays, *Memoirs of Emma Courtney.*

Edmund Jenner's first smallpox vaccination.

1797   **DW and WmW move to Alfoxden House, which is near Coleridge's home at Nether Stowey. DW manages housewarming party for fourteen with John Thelwell "the agitator" as guest of honor. Investigation by Home Office identifies "the inhabitants of Alfoxden House as a Sett of violent Democrats."**

Mary Godwin (Shelley) born. Thomas Bewick, *History of British Birds;* Hannah Webster Foster, *The Coquette.*

Naval mutinies at Spithead and Nore protesting insufficient pay, living conditions aboard ships, and the longer periods at sea allowed by coppering the bottom of hulls.

1798   **DW's *The Alfoxden notebook.* In September, DW, WmW, and STC travel to Germany. DW's *Journal of Visit to Hamburgh and of Journey from Hamburgh to Goslar.***

WmW and STC anonymously publish *Lyrical Ballads.* Jeremy Bentham, *Political Economy;* Joanna Baillie, *Plays on the Passions* with *Introductory Discourse* (published anonymously); Thomas Malthus, *An Essay on the Principle of Population as it Affects the Future Improvement of Society.*

Pitt introduces income tax, first levied in 1799; French invade Switzerland, horrifying British liberals; Irish Rebellion.

1799   **Wordsworths return from Germany and move to Dove Cottage.**

WmW completes 1799 version of what becomes *The Prelude.*

Thomas Campbell, *The Pleasure of Hope.*

Act of Parliament to suppress radical societies.

1800   **DW begins** *Grasmere Journal* **(1800–1803), helps prepare second edition of** *Lyrical Ballads.* **Forms lasting friendship with Catherine and Thomas Clarkson.** Mary Jane Jewsbury born. WmW begins courting Mary Hutchinson.

Mary Robinson, *Lyrical Tales* (**DW annoyed at title**).

Act of Union joins Ireland and Britain.

1801   **DW becomes subject to headaches and stomach problems, "bilious sicknesses."**

Maria Edgeworth, *Belinda.*

Preliminary peace treaties with France signed, allowing correspondence with Annette Vallon. First General Enclosure Act.

1802   **DW and WmW go to France to settle matters with Annette Vallon.**

Return to London, visit Charles and Mary Lamb. WmW marries Mary Hutchinson.

William Paley, *Natural Theology.*

Edinburgh Review and Cobbett's *Weekly Political Register* founded. Treaty of Amiens brings cessation of hostilities between England and France.

1803   **DW takes six-week tour of Scotland with WmW and STC; begins writing** *Recollections of a Tour Made in Scotland.* WmW and MW's son John born.

Jane Porter, *Thaddeus of Warsaw.*

England and France resume war.

1804   **DW's eyes become inflamed; begins losing her teeth; her goddaughter Dorothy, called Dora, born.** STC at Dove Cottage where he is frequently ill; sails for Sicily via Gibraltar and appointed Acting Public Secretary in Malta.

William Lisle Bowles, *The Spirit of Discovery.*

Napoleon crowns himself emperor.

1805   **DW, *Excursion on the Banks of Ullswater.* Brother John dies in shipwreck.**

Mary Meeke, *The Wonder of the Village.*

Nelson dies at Battle of Trafalgar.

1806   **Wordsworths stay at Coleorton for eight months as guests of Lord and Lady Beaumont. DW keeps "Coleorton Notebook." WmW and MW's son Thomas born. STC returns from Malta; visits Wordsworths at Coleorton; WmW recites thirteen-book *Prelude.***

Jane and Ann Taylor, *Rhymes for the Nursery.*

First gas-lighting of cotton mills.

1807   **DW and family return to Grasmere. De Quincey comes to Dove Cottage.**

WmW *Poems in Two Volumes;* Lambs's *Tales from Shakespeare.*

Great Britain abolishes slave trade.

1808   **DW's *Narrative Concerning George and Sarah Green of the Parish of Grasmere* to raise money for the couple's orphaned children. DW and family become first tenants of Allan Bank, a drafty building that fills with smoke from the chimneys. STC and De Quincey join household at Allan Bank where WmW works on *The Convention of Cintra* and STC works on *The Friend.* WmW and MW's daughter Catherine born.**

Charlotte Smith, *Beachy Head;* Goethe, *Faust* (Part One).

United States abolishes slave trade.

1809   **DW oversees renovations at Dove Cottage for De Quincey.**

Byron, "English Bards and Scotch Reviewers" (published anonymously); Hannah More, *Coelebs in Search of a Wife.*

1810   **DW visits Coleorton with WmW and continues on her own to Cambridge. Visits the Clarksons; Henry Crabb**

Robinson escorts her to London where she stays with Charles and Mary Lamb. WmW and MW's son William born. Wordsworths break with STC, largely over his drinking and drug habits.

Mary Pilkington, *Parental Care Producing Practical Virtue.*

1811   **Wordsworths move to Grasmere Rectory.**

Mary Tighe, *Psyche, with Other Poems.*

The Regency begins; Luddite riots in Nottingham.

1812   **DW stays in Grasmere with children while WmW and MW travel; Her niece Catherine dies; DW buries her. Dorothy visits Jane Marshall; her nephew Thomas dies.**

Byron, *Childe Harold's Pilgrimage,* cantos I & II.

Napoleon's retreat from Moscow.

1813   **Gift from Lord Lonsdale allows Wordsworths to move to Rydal Mount.**

WmW becomes Distributor of Stamps for Westmoreland.

Jane Austen, *Pride and Prejudice* (anonymous).

Monopoly of East India Company ended.

1814   **DW spends three months at Keswick helping Mary Barker nurse Basil Montagu.**

WmW, *The Excursion.*

Trial of Leigh and John Hunt for seditious libel against the Regent. Pope Pius VII restores the Inquisition after being released from Napoleonic imprisonment.

1815   **DW's plans to attend Caroline's wedding in France scrapped when Napoleon returns from Elba. In his *Poems,* WmW publishes three "By My Sister."**

Mary Pilkington, *Celebrity: or The Unfortunate Choice.*

Battle of Waterloo; Corn Law raises prices on corn.

1816   **DW visits foster mother, Elizabeth Threlkeld Rawson, at Halifax for five months.** Caroline marries but no members of the Wordsworth family attend the ceremony. Names her daughter Louise Dorothée after her Aunt Dorothy. De Quincey and Peggy Simpson marry, having had a child the year before; the Wordsworths disapprove. Brother Richard dies.

Lady Caroline Lamb, *Glenarvon;* Coleridge, *The Statesman's Manuel.*

Income Tax abolished.

1817   John Keats, *Poems;* STC, *Biographia Literaria.*

Blackwood's Magazine founded. Suspension of habeas corpus.

1818   DW climbs Scawfell Pike with Mary Barker. Lord Lonsdale's sons in Parliamentary election for Westmoreland even though their opponent is William Brougham, the abolitionist. Keats visits Rydal Mount.

Mary Shelley, *Frankenstein* (anonymous).

Habeas corpus restored.

1819   *Blackwood's* publishes Hemans's prize-winning poem "The Meeting of Wallace and Bruce on the Banks of the Carron." Peterloo Massacre; Lord Liverpool and Tories respond in part by passing "Six Acts" to suppress radical meetings and publications.

1820   DW goes to London to have eight remaining teeth removed and is fitted with false teeth. Stays to nurse brother Christopher in Lambeth. Sees first collected edition of WmW's poems to press. Visits France, Belgium, Germany, Switzerland, and Italy in July to October with a group of family and friends. The Wordsworths visit Caroline and Annette. DW visits brother Christopher, now master of Trinity College, Cambridge. DW writes *Journal of a Tour on the Continent.*

P. B. Shelley, *Prometheus Unbound.*

George IV attempts to divorce Queen Caroline; becomes king on the death of George III.

1821   **DW revises manuscript of first Scottish tour for publication at urging of Samuel Rogers.**

Keats dies; De Quincey, *Confessions of an English Opium-Eater.*

Mechanics Institutes formed in Glasgow and London.

1822   **DW tours Scotland for one month with Joanna Hutchinson; writes *Journal of My Second Tour in Scotland.* Caring alone for Jemima Quillinan as she dies of burn injuries.**

P. B. Shelley drowns in Italy. Lamb, *Essays of Elia.*

Famine in Ireland.

1823   **DW visits Edinburgh.**

P. B. Shelley, *Posthumous Poems.*

Charles Macintosh develops water-resistant raincoat fabric.

1824   **DW visits London, southern England, and Cambridge. Begins journal that continues for eleven small volumes until 1835.**

Byron dies in Greece. Mary Russell Mitford, *Our Village* (first of five volumes).

National Gallery opens.

1825   Hazlitt, *The Spirit of the Age.*

Trade unions legalized.

Darlington railway opened.

1826   **DW visits Hutchinson farm at Brinsop with Joanna, walking tour of Wye valley, visits Coleorton, and returns to Rydal nine months later. More than a year after De Quincey had pleaded with her to visit his wife, Peggy, DW complies.**

Mary Shelley, *The Last Man.*

Peel, as Home Secretary, reforms Penal Code.

1827   DW visits Halifax. Dora's illness begins.

Letitia Elizabeth Landon (L.E.L.), *Poetical Works.*

England, France, and Russia defeat Ottoman Navy at Navarino Bay.

1828   DW tours Isle of Man with Joanna Hutchinson; writes *Journal of a Tour in the Isle of Man.* Visits M. J. Jewsbury in Manchester. Helps nephew John set up his parsonage at Whitwick.

Hemans, *Records of Woman, with other Poems.*

Duke of Wellington becomes prime minister.

1829   DW becomes ill at Whitwick, perhaps a gall bladder attack. Returns to Rydal Mount. Beginning of chronic bowel illness.

STC, *On the Constitution of Church and State.*

Catholic Emancipation Act.

1830   Hemans visits Rydal Mount for two weeks and then moves to nearby Dove Nest for several months.

Jewsbury, *The History of the Enthusiast;* Tennyson, *Poems Chiefly Lyrical.*

William IV becomes king.

1831   Second edition of Mary Shelley's *Frankenstein.*

"Swing Riots" in which agricultural workers demand higher wages and an end to use of threshing machine.

1832   Scott, *Castle Dangerous* and *Count Robert of Paris.*

Formation of the Liberal Party from the Whigs; Great Reform Act.

1833   DW thought to be on verge of death.

Death of Jewsbury in India. Lamb, *Last Essays of Elia.*

Shaftesbury's factory act limits hours children can work.

1834   Deaths of STC and Charles Lamb. Thomas Carlyle, *Sartor Resartus.*

Fire in Westminster Palace destroys much of the Houses of Parliament.

1835   **DW receives letter from Annette Vallon, begging her to intercede with WmW about continuing Caroline's annuity. DW's mental acuity and physical condition vary; her handwriting deteriorates.** Sara Hutchinson dies.

Mary Shelley, *Lodore*.

Muncipal Corporations Act allows men only to vote for local governments.

1836   **DW is able to withdraw from opium; health fluctuates.**

Charles Dickens, *The Pickwick Papers*; Hans Christian Andersen, *The Little Mermaid*.

London University formed; Newspaper Tax reduced; Second General Enclosure Act.

1837   Carlyle, *The French Revolution, A History*.

Queen Victoria ascends throne. Samuel Morse invents the telegraph.

1838   John Audubon, *The Birds of America*; Elizabeth Barrett Browning, *The Seraphim and Other Poems*.

Opening of London to Birmingham railway.

1839   Charles Darwin, *The Voyage of the Beagle*.

Custody of Infants Act allows a woman separated from her husband to apply for custody of children under seven. First Opium War.

1840   Penny Post introduced.

1841   Niece Dora marries Edward Quillinan.

Punch Magazine begins publication. First National Census taken.

1842   Burney, *Diary and Letters* published posthumously. Founding of *Illustrated London News*.

1843   WmW becomes poet laureate.

Catherine Gore, *The Banker's Wife;* Thomas Hood, *The Song of the Shirt.*

First tunnel built under the Thames.

1844   Friedrich Engels, *Condition of the Working Class in England.*

In an unpublished 250-page essay, Charles Darwin outlines his theory of natural selection.

Mines Act prohibits using women and boys in mines.

1845   Alexandre Dumas, père, *The Count of Monte Cristo.*

Third (and final) General Enclosure Act; Irish potato famine begins.

1846   Brother Christopher dies.

Dickens edits *Household Words,* first inexpensive English newspaper. Corn Laws repealed.

1847   Niece Dora dies. John Ruskin visits Rydal Mount.

Emily, Jane, and Anne Brontë publish *Wuthering Heights, Jane Eyre,* and *Agnes Grey;* William Makepeace Thackeray, *Vanity Fair.*

Major emigration from Ireland; Ten Hours Factory Act.

1848   Marx and Engels, *Manifesto of the Communist Party.*

Revolutions throughout Europe.

1849   Dickens, *David Copperfield.*

Bedford College for Women founded.

Cholera epidemic.

1850   **William Wordsworth dies.**

The Prelude published posthumously; Tennyson becomes poet laureate.

Public Libraries Act enables local councils to provide free libraries.

1851	**DW's nephew Christopher, Bishop of Lincoln, publishes passages from DW's journals and letters in his** *Memoirs of William Wordsworth, Poet Laureate.*
	Herman Melville, *Moby-Dick.*
	Great Exhibition held in Hyde Park.
1852	Harriet Beecher Stowe, *Uncle Tom's Cabin.*
	Victoria and Albert Museum opens.
1853	**DW writes last known letter.**
	Elizabeth Gaskell, *Cranford* and *Ruth.*
	Founding of Cheltenham Ladies College. Smallpox vaccination made compulsory.
1854	Henry David Thoreau, *Walden, or, Life in the Woods.*
	Crimean War begins as Britain and France declare war against Russia.
1855	**Dorothy Wordsworth dies.**
	Charlotte Brontë dies. Walt Whitman, *Leaves of Grass.*
	Repeal of stamp duty on newspapers.
1859	Mary Wordsworth dies.
1874	Principal Shairp publishes **DW's** *Recollections of a Tour made in Scotland A.D. 1803.*
1889	William Knight publishes excerpts of **DW's journals** as part of his *Life of William Wordsworth.*
1894	Shairp publishes third edition of **Recollections.**
1896	Knight publishes a few of **DW's poems** in *The Poetical Works of William Wordsworth.*
1897	William Knight publishes excerpts from **DW's journals** in two volumes.

DOROTHY WORDSWORTH

TEXTS

THE ALFOXDEN NOTEBOOK

When Dorothy and William Wordsworth moved to Alfoxden House in Somersetshire, mostly to be near Coleridge at Nether Stowey about three miles away, Dorothy began keeping a journal. This text not only initiates a characteristic weaving of countryside, her brother, and poetry, but with its reflection of William's poetry demonstrates Dorothy's participation in a community of writers. William copied the first four sentences into a notebook, but Dorothy's manuscript has disappeared. Luckily, William Knight transcribed her original, our text here, including his ellipses and hanging date-markers.

Alfoxden, January 20*th* 1798.—The green paths down the hill-sides are channels for streams. The young wheat is streaked by silver lines of water running between the ridges, the sheep are gathered together on the slopes. After the wet dark days, the country seems more populous. It peoples itself in the sunbeams. The garden, mimic of spring, is gay with flowers. The purple-starred hepatica spreads itself in the sun, and the clustering snow-drops put forth their white heads, at first upright, ribbed with green, and like a rosebud when completely opened, hanging their heads downwards, but slowly lengthening their slender stems. The slanting woods of an unvarying brown, showing the light through the thin net-work of their upper boughs. Upon the highest ridge of that round hill covered with planted oaks, the shafts of the trees show in the light like the columns of a ruin.

21*st*. Walked on the hill-tops—a warm day. Sate under the firs in the park. The tops of the beeches of a brown-red, or crimson. Those oaks, fanned by the sea breeze, thick with feathery sea-green moss, as a grove not stripped of its leaves. Moss cups more proper than acorns for fairy goblets.[1]

22*nd*.—Walked through the wood to Holford. The ivy twisting round the oaks like bristled serpents. The day cold—a warm shelter in the hollies, capriciously bearing berries. Query: Are the male and female flowers on separate trees?

23*rd*.—Bright sunshine, went out at 3 o'clock. The sea perfectly calm blue, streaked with deeper colour by the clouds, and tongues

---

[1] Similar phrases appear in "The Thorn," especially verses II–IV. William wrote the poem at Alfoxden (cf. March 19).

or points of sand; on our return of a gloomy red. The sun gone down. The crescent moon, Jupiter, and Venus. The sound of the sea distinctly heard on the tops of the hills, which we could never hear in summer. We attribute this partly to the bareness of the trees, but chiefly to the absence of the singing of birds, the hum of insects, that noiseless noise which lives in the summer air. The villages marked out by beautiful beds of smoke. The turf fading into the mountain road. The scarlet flowers of the moss.

24th.—Walked between half-past three and half-past five. The evening cold and clear. The sea of a sober grey, streaked by the deeper grey clouds. The half dead sound of the near sheep-bell, in the hollow of the sloping coombe,[2] exquisitely soothing.

25th.—Went to Poole's after tea.[3] The sky spread over with one continuous cloud, whitened by the light of the moon, which, though her dim shape was seen, did not throw forth so strong a light as to chequer the earth with shadows. At once the clouds seemed to cleave asunder, and left her in the centre of a black-blue vault. She sailed along, followed by multitudes of stars, small, and bright, and sharp. Their brightness seemed concentrated, (half-moon).[4]

26th.—Walked upon the hill-tops; followed the sheep tracks till we overlooked the larger coombe. Sat in the sunshine. The distant sheep-bells, the sound of the stream; the woodman winding along the half-marked road with his laden pony; locks of wool still spangled with the dewdrops; the blue-grey sea, shaded with immense masses of cloud, not streaked; the sheep glittering in the sunshine. Returned through the wood. The trees skirting the wood, being exposed more directly to the action of the sea breeze, stripped of the net-work of their upper boughs, which are stiff and erect, like black skeletons; the ground strewed with the red berries of the holly. Set forward before two o'clock. Returned a little after four.

27th.—Walked from seven o'clock till half-past eight. Upon the whole an uninteresting evening. Only once while we were in the wood the moon burst through the invisible veil which enveloped her, the shadows of the oaks blackened, and their lines became more strongly marked. The withered leaves were coloured with a

---

[2] A deep, narrow valley.

[3] Thomas Poole, Coleridge's friend, arranged for the lease of Alfoxden House. "Tea" is a substantial refreshment, "taken" late afternoon or as "high" tea in the early evening. "Dinner" is a midday meal; "supper" an evening meal.

[4] See William's "A Night-Piece" and STC's "Christabel," written in April 1798.

deeper yellow, a brighter gloss spotted the hollies; again her form became dimmer; the sky flat, unmarked by distances, a white thin cloud. The manufacturer's dog makes a strange, uncouth howl, which it continues many minutes after there is no noise near it but that of the brook. It howls at the murmur of the village stream.

28*th*.—Walked only to the mill.

29*th*.—A very stormy day. William walked to the top of the hill to see the sea. Nothing distinguishable but a heavy blackness. An immense bough riven from one of the fir trees.

30*th*.—William called me into the garden to observe a singular appearance about the moon. A perfect rainbow, within the bow one star, only of colours more vivid. The semi-circle soon became a complete circle, and in the course of three or four minutes the whole faded away. Walked to the blacksmith's and the baker's; an uninteresting evening.

31*st*.—Set forward to Stowey at half-past five. A violent storm in the wood; sheltered under the hollies. When we left home the moon immensely large, the sky scattered over with clouds. These soon closed in, contracting the dimensions of the moon without conceal-ing her.[5] The sound of the pattering shower, and the gusts of wind, very grand. Left the wood when nothing remained of the storm but the driving wind, and a few scattering drops of rain. Presently all clear, Venus first showing herself between the straggling clouds; afterwards Jupiter appeared. The hawthorn hedges, black and pointed, glittering with millions of diamond drops; the hollies shin-ing with broader patches of light. The road to the village of Holford glittered like another stream. On our return, the wind high—a vio-lent storm of hail and rain at the Castle of Comfort.[6] All the Heavens seemed in one perpetual motion when the rain ceased; the moon appearing, now half veiled, and now retired behind heavy clouds, the stars still moving, the roads very dirty.

February 1*st*.—About two hours before dinner, set forward towards Mr. Bartholemew's.[7] The wind blew so keen in our faces that we felt ourselves inclined to seek the covert of the wood. There we had a warm shelter, gathered a burthen of large rotten boughs blown down by the wind of the preceding night. The sun shone clear, but all at once a heavy blackness hung over the sea. The trees

[5] See "Christabel," 1.17.

[6] Inn on the road to Nether Stowey.

[7] The Wordsworths sublet Alfoxden House from John Bartholemew, the renter.

almost *roared,* and the ground seemed in motion with the multitudes of dancing leaves, which made a rustling sound, distinct from
that of the trees. Still the asses pastured in quietness under the hollies, undisturbed by these forerunners of the storm. The wind beat
furiously against us as we returned. Full moon. She rose in uncommon majesty over the sea, slowly ascending through the clouds. Sat
with the window open an hour in the moonlight.

    2nd.—Walked through the wood, and on to the Downs before
dinner; a warm pleasant air. The sun shone, but was often obscured
by straggling clouds. The redbreasts made a ceaseless song in the
woods. The wind rose very high in the evening. The room smoked
so that we were obliged to quit it. Young lambs in a green pasture in
the Coombe, thick legs, large heads, black staring eyes.

    3rd.—A mild morning, the windows open at breakfast, the red-
breasts singing in the garden. Walked with Coleridge over the hills.
The sea at first obscured by vapour; that vapour afterwards slid in
one mighty mass along the sea-shore; the islands and one point of
land clear beyond it. The distant country (which was purple in the
clear dull air), overhung by straggling clouds that sailed over it,
appeared like the darker clouds, which are often seen at a great distance apparently motionless, while the nearer ones pass quickly
over them, driven by the lower winds. I never saw such a union of
earth, sky, and sea. The clouds beneath our feet spread themselves
to the water, and the clouds of the sky almost joined them. Gathered sticks in the wood; a perfect stillness. The redbreasts sang
upon the leafless boughs. Of a great number of sheep in the field,
only one standing. Returned to dinner at five o'clock. The moonlight still and warm as a summer's night at nine o'clock.

    4th.—Walked a great part of the way to Stowey with Coleridge.
The morning warm and sunny. The young lasses seen on the hill-tops,
in the villages and roads, in their summer holiday clothes—pink petticoats and blue. Mothers with their children in arms, and the little ones
that could just walk, tottering by their side. Midges or small flies spinning in the sunshine; the songs of the lark and redbreast; daisies upon
the turf; the hazels in blossom; honeysuckles budding. I saw one solitary strawberry flower under a hedge. The furze gay with blossom. The
moss rubbed from the pailings by the sheep, that leave locks of wool,
and the red marks with which they are spotted, upon the wood.[8]

---

[8] See William's "Ruined Cottage," ll. 330–335.

5th.—Walked to Stowey with Coleridge, returned by Woodlands; a very warm day. In the continued singing of birds distinguished the notes of a blackbird or thrush. The sea overshadowed by a thick dark mist, the land in sunshine. The sheltered oaks and beeches still retaining their brown leaves. Observed some trees putting out red shoots. Query: What trees are they?

6th.—Walked to Stowey over the hills, returned to tea, a cold and clear evening, the roads in some parts frozen hard. The sea hid by mist all the day.

7th.—Turned towards Potsdam, but finding the way dirty, changed our course. Cottage gardens the object of our walk. Went up the smaller Coombe to Woodlands, to the blacksmith's, the baker's, and through the village of Holford. Still misty over the sea. The air very delightful. We saw nothing very new, or interesting.

8th.—Went up the Park, and over the tops of the hills, till we came to a new and very delicious pathway, which conducted us to the Coombe. Sat a considerable time upon the heath. Its surface restless and glittering with the motion of the scattered piles of withered grass, and the waving of the spiders' threads. On our return the mist still hanging over the sea, but the opposite coast clear, and the rocky cliffs distinguishable. In the deep Coombe, as we stood upon the sunless hill, we saw miles of grass, light and glittering, and the insects passing.

9th.—William gathered sticks [. . . .]

10th.—Walked to Woodlands, and to the waterfall. The adder's-tongue and the ferns green in the low damp dell. These plants now in perpetual motion from the current of the air; in summer only moved by the drippings of the rocks. A cloudy day.

11th.—Walked with Coleridge near to Stowey. The day pleasant, but cloudy.

12th.—Walked alone to Stowey. Returned in the evening with Coleridge. A mild, pleasant, cloudy day.

13th.—Walked with Coleridge through the wood. A mild and pleasant morning, the near prospect clear. The ridges of the hills fringed with wood, showing the sea through them like the white sky, and still beyond the dim horizon of the distant hills, hanging as it were in one undetermined line between sea and sky.

14th.—Gathered sticks with William in the wood, he being unwell and not able to go further. The young birch trees of a bright red, through which gleams a shade of purple. Sat down in a thick part of the wood. The near trees still, even to their topmost boughs, but a perpetual motion in those that skirt the wood. The breeze rose gently; its path distinctly marked, till it came to the very spot where we were.

15*th*.—Gathered sticks in the further wood. The dell green with moss and brambles, and the tall and slender pillars of the unbranching oaks. I crossed the water with letters; returned to Wm. and Basil.[9] A shower met us in the wood, and a ruffling breeze.

16*th*.—Went for eggs into the Coombe, and to the baker's; a hail shower; brought home large burthens of sticks, a starlight evening, the sky closed in, and the ground white with snow before we went to bed.

17*th*.—A deep snow upon the ground. Wm. and Coleridge walked to Mr. Bartholemew's, and to Stowey. Wm. returned, and we walked through the wood into the Coombe to fetch some eggs. The sun shone bright and clear. A deep stillness in the thickest part of the wood, undisturbed except by the occasional dropping of the snow from the holly boughs; no other sound but that of the water, and the slender notes of a redbreast, which sang at intervals on the outskirts of the southern side of the wood. There the bright green moss was bare at the roots of the trees, and the little birds were upon it. The whole appearance of the wood was enchanting; and each tree, taken singly, was beautiful. The branches of the hollies pendent with their white burden, but still showing their bright red berries, and their glossy green leaves. The bare branches of the oaks thickened by the snow.

18*th*.—Walked after dinner beyond Woodlands. A sharp and very cold evening; first observed the crescent moon a silvery line, a thready bow, attended by Jupiter and Venus in their palest hues.

19*th*.—I walked to Stowey before dinner; Wm. unable to go all the way. Returned alone; a fine sunny, clear, frosty day. The sea still, and blue, and broad, and smooth.

20*th*.—Walked after dinner towards Woodlands.

21*st*.—Coleridge came in the morning, which prevented our walking. Wm. went through the wood with him towards Stowey; a very stormy night.

22*nd*.—Coleridge came in the morning to dinner. Wm. and I walked after dinner to Woodlands; the moon and two planets; sharp and frosty. Met a razor-grinder with a soldier's jacket on, a knapsack upon his back, and a boy to drag his wheel. The sea very

---

[9] The Wordsworths cared for Basil Montagu, a friend's son, for almost three and a half years.

black, and making a loud noise as we came through the wood, loud as if disturbed, and the wind was silent.

23rd.—William walked with Coleridge in the morning. I did not go out.

24th.—Went to the hill-top. Sat a considerable time overlooking the country towards the sea. The air blew pleasantly round us. The landscape mildly interesting. The Welsh hills capped by a huge range of tumultuous white clouds. The sea, spotted with white, of a bluish grey in general, and streaked with darker lines. The near shores clear; scattered farm houses, half-concealed by green mossy orchards, fresh straw lying at the doors; hay-stacks in the fields. Brown fallows, the springing wheat, like a shade of green over the brown earth, and the choice meadow plots, full of sheep and lambs, of a soft and vivid green; a few wreaths of blue smoke, spreading along the ground; the oaks and beeches in the hedges retaining their yellow leaves; the distant prospect on the land side, islanded with sunshine; the sea, like a basin full to the margin; the dark fresh-ploughed fields; the turnips of a lively rough green. Returned through the wood.

25th.—I lay down in the morning, though the whole day was very pleasant, and the evening fine. We did not walk.

26th.—Coleridge came in the morning, and Mr. and Mrs. Cruikshank[10] walked with Coleridge nearly to Stowey after dinner. A very clear afternoon. We lay sidelong upon the turf, and gazed on the landscape till it melted into more than natural loveliness. The sea very uniform, of a pale greyish blue, only one distant bay, bright and blue as a sky; had there been a vessel sailing up it, a perfect image of delight. Walked to the top of a high hill to see a fortification. Again sat down to feed upon the prospect; a magnificent scene, *curiously* spread out for even minute inspection, though so extensive that the mind is afraid to calculate its bounds. A winter prospect shows every cottage, every farm, and the forms of distant trees, such as in summer have no distinguishing mark. On our return, Jupiter and Venus before us. While the twilight still overpowered the light of the moon, we were reminded that she was shining bright above our heads, by our faint shadows going before us. We had seen her on the tops of the hills, melting into the blue sky. Poole called while we were absent.

27th.—I walked to Stowey in the evening. Wm. and Basil went with me through the wood. The prospect bright, yet *mildly* beautiful. The sea big and white, swelled to the very shores, but round and high

---

[10] Probably John Cruikshank, Lord Egmont's Stowey agent.

in the middle. Coleridge returned with me, as far as the wood. A very bright moonlight night. Venus almost like another moon. Lost to us at Alfoxden long before she goes down the large white sea.

March 1st.—We rose early. A thick fog obscured the distant prospect entirely, but the shapes of the nearer trees and the dome of the wood dimly seen and dilated. It cleared away between ten and eleven. The shapes of the mist, slowly moving along, exquisitely beautiful; passing over the sheep they almost seemed to have more of life than those quiet creatures. The unseen birds singing in the mist.

2nd.—Went a part of the way home with Coleridge in the morning. Gathered fir apples[11] afterwards under the trees.

3rd.—I went to the shoemaker's. William lay under the trees till my return. Afterwards went to the secluded farm house in search of eggs, and returned over the hill. A very mild, cloudy evening. The rose trees in the hedges and the elders budding.

4th.—Walked to Woodlands after dinner, a pleasant evening.

5th.—Gathered fir-apples. A thick fog came on. Walked to the baker's and the shoemaker's, and through the fields towards Woodlands. On our return, found Tom Poole in the parlour. He drank tea with us.

6th.—A pleasant morning, the sea white and bright, and full to the brim. I walked to see Coleridge in the evening. William went with me to the wood. Coleridge very ill. It was a mild, pleasant afternoon, but the evening became very foggy; when I was near Woodlands, the fog overhead became thin, and I saw the shapes of the Central Stars. Again it closed, and the whole sky was the same.

7th.—William and I drank tea at Coleridge's. A cloudy sky. Observed nothing particularly interesting—the distant prospect obscured. One only leaf upon the top of a tree—the sole remaining leaf—danced round and round like a rag blown by the wind.[12]

8th.—Walked in the Park in the morning. I sate under the fir trees. Coleridge came after dinner, so we did not walk again. A foggy morning, but a clear sunny day.

9th.—A clear sunny morning, went to meet Mr. and Mrs. Coleridge. The day very warm.

10th.—Coleridge, Wm., and I walked in the evening to the top of the hill. We all passed the morning in sauntering about the park and gardens, the children playing about, the old man at the top of the hill

[11] Pink and knobbly potatoes.
[12] "The one red leaf, the last of its clan . . ." ("Christabel," ll. 49–52).

gathering furze; interesting groups of human creatures, the young frisking and dancing in the sun, the elder quietly drinking in the life and soul of the sun and air.

11*th*.—A cold day. The children went down towards the sea. William and I walked to the top of the hills above Holford. Met the blacksmith. Pleasant to see the labourer on Sunday jump with the friskiness of a cow upon a sunny day.

12*th*.—Tom Poole returned with Coleridge to dinner, a brisk, cold, sunny day; did not walk.

13*th*.—Poole dined with us. William and I strolled into the wood. Coleridge called us into the house.

15*th*.—I have neglected to set down the occurrences of this week, so I do not recollect how we disposed of ourselves to-day.

16*th*.—William, and Coleridge, and I walked in the Park a short time. I wrote to————. William very ill, better in the evening; and we called round by Potsdam.

17*th*.—I do not remember this day.

18*th*.—The Coleridges left us. A cold, windy morning. Walked with them half way. On our return, sheltered under the hollies, during a hail-shower. The withered leaves danced with the hailstones. William wrote a description of the storm.[13]

19*th*.—Wm. and Basil and I walked to the hill-tops, a very cold bleak day. We were met on our return by a severe hailstorm. William wrote some lines describing a stunted thorn.

20*th*.—Coleridge dined with us. We went more than half way home with him in the evening. A very cold evening, but clear. The spring seemingly very little advanced. No green trees, only the hedges are building and looking very lovely.

21*st*.—We drank tea at Coleridge's. A quiet shower of snow was in the air during more than half our walk. At our return the sky partially shaded with clouds. The horned moon was set. Startled two night birds from the great elm tree.

22*nd*.—I spent the morning in starching and hanging out linen;[14] walked *through* the wood in the evening, very cold.

23*rd*.—Coleridge dined with us. He brought his ballad finished. We walked with him to the Miner's house. A beautiful evening, very starry, the horned moon.

---

[13] Probably "A whirl-blast from behind the hill" (*Lyrical Ballads,* 1800).

[14] Sheets, tablecloths, some clothing such as shirts and underwear made of cotton or linen.

24*th.*—Coleridge, the Chesters,[15] and Ellen Cruikshank called. We walked with them through the wood. Went in the evening into the Coombe to get eggs; returned through the wood, and walked in the park. A duller night than last night: a sort of white shade over the blue sky. The stars dim. The spring continues to advance very slowly,[16] no green trees, the hedges leafless; nothing green but the brambles that still retain their old leaves, the evergreens, and the palms, which indeed are not absolutely green. Some brambles I observed today budding afresh, and those have shed their old leaves. The crooked arm of the old oak tree points upwards to the moon.

25*th.*—Walked to Coleridge's after tea. Arrived at home at one o'clock. The night cloudy but not dark.

26*th.*—Went to meet Wedgwood[17] at Coleridge's after dinner. Reached home at half-past twelve, a fine moonlight night; half moon.

27*th.*—Dined at Poole's. Arrived at home a little after twelve, a partially cloudy, but light night, very cold.

28*th.*—Hung out the linen.

29*th.*—Coleridge dined with us.

30*th.*—Walked I know not where.

31*st.*—Walked.

April 1*st.*—Walked by moonlight.

2*nd.*—A very high wind. Coleridge came to avoid the smoke; stayed all night. We walked in the wood, and sat under the trees. The half of the wood perfectly still, while the wind was making a loud noise behind us. The still trees only gently bowed their heads, as if listening to the wind. The hollies in the thick wood unshaken by the blast; only, when it came with a greater force, shaken by the rain drops falling from the bare oaks above.

3*rd.*—Walked to Crookham, with Coleridge and Wm. to make the appeal.[18] Left Wm. there, and parted with Coleridge at the top of the hill. A very stormy afternoon. . . .

---

[15] John Chester, a friend from Nether Stowey, went to Germany with Coleridge and the Wordsworths in September.

[16] "And the Spring comes slowly up this way" ("Christabel," 1. 22).

[17] Thomas Wedgwood, of the famous family of pottery makers, was Coleridge's friend and benefactor. He experimented in the theory of light.

[18] The Wordsworths may have been protesting a tax or Mrs. St. Albyn's refusal to renew their lease on Alfoxden House.

4*th*.—Walked to the sea-side in the afternoon. A great commotion in the air, but the sea neither grand nor beautiful. A violent shower in returning. Sheltered under some fir trees at Potsdam.

5*th*.—Coleridge came to dinner. William and I walked in the wood in the morning. I fetched eggs from the Coombe.

6*th*.—Went a part of the way home with Coleridge. A pleasant warm morning, but a showery day. Walked a short distance up the lesser Coombe, with an intention of going to the source of the brook, but the evening closing in, cold prevented us. The Spring still advancing very slowly. The horse-chestnuts budding, and the hedgerows beginning to look green, but nothing fully expanded.

7*th*.—Walked before dinner up the Coombe, to the source of the brook, and came home by the tops of the hills; a showery morning, at the hill-tops; the view opened upon us very grand.

8*th*.—Easter Sunday. Walked in the morning in the wood, and half way to Stowey; found the air at first oppressively warm, afterwards very pleasant.

9*th*.—Walked to Stowey, a fine air in going, but very hot in returning. The sloe in blossom, the hawthorns green, the larches in the park changed from black to green in two or three days. Met Coleridge in returning.

10*th*.—I was hanging out linen in the evening. We walked to Holford. I turned off to the baker's, and walked beyond Woodlands, expecting to meet William, met him on the hill; a close warm evening . . . in bloom.

11*th*.—In the wood in the morning, walked to the top of the hill, then I went down into the wood. A pleasant evening, a fine air, the grass in the park becoming green, many trees green in the dell.

12*th*.—Walked in the morning in the wood. In the evening up the Coombe, fine walk. The Spring advances rapidly, multitudes of primroses, dog-violets, periwinkles, stitchwort.

13*th*.—Walked in the wood in the morning. In the evening went to Stowey. I staid with Mr. Coleridge. Wm. went to Poole's. Supped with Mr. Coleridge.

14*th*.—Walked in the wood in the morning. The evening very stormy, so we staid within doors. Mary Wollstonecraft's life, etc., came.[19]

---

[19] William Godwin's soon to be controversial posthumous memoir of Mary Wollstonecraft.

15*th*.—Set forward after breakfast to Crookham, and returned to dinner at three o'clock. A fine cloudy morning. Walked about the squire's grounds. Quaint waterfalls about, about which Nature was very successfully striving to make beautiful what art had deformed—ruins, hermitages, etc. etc. in spite of all these things, the dell romantic and beautiful, though everywhere planted with unnaturalised trees. Happily we cannot shape the huge hills, or carve out the valleys according to our fancy.

16*th*.—New moon. William walked in the wood in the morning, I neglected to follow him. We walked in the park in the evening. . . .

17*th*.—Walked in the wood in the morning. In the evening upon the hill. Cowslips plentiful.

18*th*.—Walked in the wood, a fine sunny morning, met Coleridge returned from his brother's. He dined with us. We drank tea, and then walked with him nearly to Stowey.

20*th*.—Walked in the evening up the hill dividing the Coombes. Came home the Crookham way, by the thorn, and the "little muddy pond." Nine o'clock at our return. William all the morning engaged in wearisome composition. The moon crescent. *Peter Bell* begun.

24*th*.—Walked a considerable time in the wood. Sat under the trees, in the evening walked on the top of the hill, found Coleridge on our return and walked with him towards Stowey.

25*th*.—Coleridge drank tea, walked with him to Stowey.

26*th*.—William went to have his picture taken.[20] I walked with him. Dined at home. Coleridge and he drank tea.

27*th*.—Coleridge breakfasted and drank tea, strolled in the wood in the morning, went with him in the evening through the wood, afterwards walked on the hills: the moon, a many-coloured sea and sky.

28*th, Saturday.*—A very fine morning, warm weather all the week.

May 6th. Sunday.—Expected the painter, and Coleridge. A rainy morning—very pleasant in the evening. Met Coleridge as we were walking out. Went with him to Stowey; heard the nightingale; saw a glow-worm.

---

[20] William Shuter did this earliest known portrait of William at the request of Joseph Cottle, publisher of *Lyrical Ballads*.

7th.—Walked in the wood in the morning. In the evening, to Stowey with Coleridge who called.

8th.—Coleridge dined, went in the afternoon to tea at Stowey, A pleasant walk home.

9th.— . . . Wrote to Coleridge.

Wednesday, 16th May.—Coleridge, William, and myself set forward to the Chedder rocks; slept at Bridgewater.

22nd, Thursday—Walked to Chedder. Slept at Cross.

FROM *JOURNAL OF DAYS SPENT AT HAMBURGH*

*The Wordsworths, Coleridge, and John Chester, a Nether Stowey
acquaintance, traveled to Germany to study the language. Dorothy kept
a notebook from which this excerpt describing their time in Hamburgh is
taken. The text is Knight's, with his styling and punctuation.*

QUITTED London, Friday, 14th September 1798. Arrived at Yarmouth
on Saturday noon, and sailed on Sunday morning at eleven o'clock.
Before we heaved the anchor I was consigned to the cabin, which I
did not quit till we were in still water at the mouth of the Elbe, on
Tuesday morning at ten o'clock. I was surprised to find, when I
came upon deck, that we could not see the shores, though we were
in the river. It was to my eyes a still sea. But oh! the gentle breezes
and the gentle motion! . . . I thought of returning to the cabin in the
evening with a mingled sensation of shuddering and sickness. As we
advanced towards Cuxhaven the shores appeared low and flat, and
thinly peopled; here and there a farm-house, cattle feeding, hay-
stacks, a cottage, a windmill. Some vessels were at anchor at Cuxhaven, an ugly, black-looking place. Dismissed a part of our crew,
and proceeded in the packet-boat up the river.

Cast anchor between six and seven o'clock. The moon shone
upon the waters. The shores were visible rock; here and there a light
from the houses. Ships lying at anchor not far from us. We drank tea
upon deck by the light of the moon. I enjoyed solitude and quietness,
and many a recollected pleasure, hearing still the unintelligible jargon
of the many tongues that gabbled in the cabin. Went to bed between
ten and eleven. The party playing at cards, but they were silent, and
suffered us to go to sleep. At four o'clock in the morning we were
awakened by the heaving of the anchor, and till seven, in the intervals
of sleep, I enjoyed the thought that we were advancing towards
Hamburgh; but what was our mortification on being told that there
was a thick fog, and that we could not sail till it was dispersed. I went
on to the deck. The air was cold and wet, the decks streaming, the
shores invisible, no hope of clear weather. At ten however the sun
appeared, and we saw the green shores. All became clear, and we
set sail. Churches very frequent on the right, with spires red, blue,

sometimes green; houses thatched or tiled, and generally surrounded with low trees. A beautiful low green island, houses, and wood. As we advanced, the left bank of the river became more interesting.

The houses warm and comfortable, sheltered with trees, and neatly painted. Blankenese, a village or town scattered over the sides of three hills, woody where the houses lie and sleep down below, the houses half-concealed by, and half-obtruding themselves from, the low trees. Naked boats with masts lying at the bare feet of the Blankenese hills. Houses more and more frequent as we approach Hamburgh. The banks of the Elbe more steep. Some gentlemen's seats after the English fashion. The spires of Altona and Hamburgh visible a considerable time. At Altona we took a boat, and rowed through the narrow passages of the Elbe, crowded with vessels of all nations. Landed at the Boom House, where we were received by porters, ready to carry our luggage to any part of the town. William went to seek lodgings, and the rest of the party guarded the luggage. Two boats were about to depart. An elegant English carriage was placed in one, and presently a very pretty woman, conducted by a gentleman, seated herself in it, and they rowed off. The other contained a medley crew of all ages. There was an old woman, with a blue cap trimmed with broad silver lace, and tied under her chin. She had a short coloured cloak, etc. While we stood in the street, which was open on one side to the Elbe, I was much amused by the various employments and dresses of the people who passed before us. There were Dutch women with immense straw bonnets, with flat crowns and rims in the shape of oyster shells, without trimming, or with only a plain riband round the crown, and literally as large as a small-sized umbrella. Hamburgher girls with white caps, with broad overhanging borders, crimped and stiff, and long lappets of riband. Hanoverians with round borders, showing all the face, and standing upright, a profusion of riband. . . . Fruit-women, with large straw hats in the shape of an inverted bowl, or white handkerchiefs tied round the head like a bishop's mitre. Jackets the most common, often the petticoat and jacket of different colours. The ladies without hats, in dresses of all fashions. Soldiers with dull-looking red coats, and immense cocked hats. The men little differing from the English, except that they have generally a pipe in their mouths. After waiting about an hour we saw Wm. appear. Two porters carried our luggage upon a sort of wheelbarrow, and we were conducted through dirty, ill-paved streets to an inn, where, with great difficulty, and after long seeking, lodgings had been procured for us.

· · · · · · · · · ·

Breakfasted with Mons. de Loutre. Chester and I went to the promenade. People of all ranks, and in various dresses, walking backwards and forwards. Ladies with small baskets hanging on their arms, long shawls of various colours thrown over their shoulders. The women of the lower order dressed with great modesty. . . . Went to the French theatre in the evening. . . . The piece a mixture of dull declamation and unmeaning rant. The ballet unintelligible to us, as the story was carried on in singing.[1] The body of the house very imperfectly lighted, which has a good effect in bringing out the stage, but the acting was not very amusing.

Sunday.—William went in the boat to Harburgh. In our road to the boat we looked into one of the large churches. Service was just ended. The audience appeared to be simply composed of singing boys dressed in large cocked hats, and a few old women who sat in the aisles. . . . Met many bright-looking girls with white caps, carrying black prayer-books in their hands. Coleridge went to Ratzeberg at five o'clock in the diligence. Chester accompanied me towards Altona. The streets wide and pleasant in that quarter of the town. Immense crowds of people walking for pleasure, and many pleasure-waggons passing and repassing. Passed through a nest of Jews. Were invited to view an exhibition of waxwork. The theatres open, and the billiard-tables attended. The walks very pleasing between Hamburgh and Altona. A large piece of ground planted with trees, and intersected by gravel walks. Music, cakes, fruit, carriages, and foot-passengers of all descriptions. A very good view of the shipping, and of Altona and the town and spires of Hamburgh. I could not but remark how much the prospect would have suffered by one of our English canopies of coal smoke. The ground on the opposite side of the Elbe appears marshy. There are many little canals or lines of water. While the sun was yet shining pleasantly, we were obliged to blink perpetually to turn our eyes to the church clock. The gates are shut at half-past six o'clock, and there is no admittance into the city after that time. This idea deducts much from the pleasure of an evening walk. You are haunted by it long before the time has elapsed. . . .

Wednesday.—Dined with Mr. Klopstock. Had the pleasure of meeting his brother the poet, a venerable old man, retaining the liveliness and alertness of youth, though he evidently cannot be very

---

[1] A combination of art forms—drama, opera, ballet—became standard theater by the nineteenth century.

far from the grave. . . .[2] The party talked with much interest of the French comedy, and seemed fond of music. The poet and his lady were obliged to depart soon after six. He sustained an animated conversation with William during the whole afternoon. Poor old man! I could not look upon him, the benefactor of his country, the father of German poetry, without emotion. . . .

During my residence in Hamburgh I have never seen anything like a quarrel in the streets but once, and that was so trifling that it would scarcely have been noticed in England. . . . In the shops (except the established booksellers and stationers) I have constantly observed a disposition to cheat, and take advantage of our ignorance of the language and money. . . .

Thursday, 28th September.—William and I set forward at twelve o'clock to Altona. . . . The Elbe in the vicinity of Hamburgh is so divided, and spread out, that the country looks more like a plain overflowed by heavy rain than the bed of a great river. We went about a mile and a half beyond Altona: the roads dry and sandy, and a causeway for foot-passengers. The houses on the banks of the Elbe, chiefly of brick, seemed very warm and well built. . . .

The small cottage houses seemed to have little gardens, and all the gentlemen's houses were surrounded by gardens quaintly disposed in beds and curious knots, with ever-twisting gravel walks and bending poplars. The view of the Elbe and the spreading country must be very interesting in a fine sunset. There is a want of some atmospherical irradiation to give a richness to the view. On returning home we were accosted by the first beggar whom we have seen since our arrival at Hamburgh.

Friday, 29th.—Sought Coleridge at the bookseller's, and went to the Promenade. . . . All the Hamburghers full of Admiral Nelson's victory.[3] Called at a baker's shop. Put two shillings into the baker's hands, for which I was to have had four small rolls. He gave me two. I let him understand that I was to have four, and with this view I took one shilling from him, pointed to it and to two loaves, and at the same time offering it to him. Again I took up two others. In a savage manner he half knocked the rolls out of my hand, and when

---

[2] STC had an introduction to this merchant whose brother, Friedrich Gottlieb Klopstock (1724–1803), was a leading poet of the age, influencing Goethe, Schiller, Hölderlin, and eventually WmW.

[3] The Battle of the Nile, August 1789, a victory for Horatio Nelson against Napoleon's fleet.

I asked him for the other shilling he refused to return it, and would neither suffer me to take bread, nor give me back my money, and on these terms I quitted the shop. I am informed that it is the boast and glory of these people to cheat strangers, that when a feat of this kind is successfully performed the man goes from the shop into his house, and triumphantly relates it to his wife and family. The Hamburgher shopkeepers have three sorts of weights, and a great part of their skill, as shopkeepers, consists in calculating upon the knowledge of the buyer, and suiting him with scales accordingly. . . .

Saturday, 30th September.—The grand festival of the Hamburghers, dedicated to Saint Michael, observed with solemnity, but little festivity. Perhaps this might be partly owing to the raininess of the evening. In the morning the churches were opened very early. St. Christopher's was quite full between eight and nine o'clock. It is a large heavy-looking building, immense, without either grandeur or beauty; built of brick, and with few windows. . . . There are some pictures, one of the Saint fording the river with Christ upon his back—a giant figure, which amused me not a little. Walked with Coleridge and Chester upon the promenade. We took places in the morning in the Brunswick coach for Wednesday.

Sunday, 1st October.—Coleridge and Chester went to Ratzeberg at seven o'clock in the morning. . . . William and I set forward at half-past eleven with an intention of going to Blankenese. The buildings all seem solid and warm in themselves, but still they look cold from their nakedness of trees. They are generally newly built, and placed in gardens, which are planted in front with poplars and low shrubs, but the possessors seem to have no prospective view to a shelter for their children. They do not plant behind their houses. All the buildings of this character are near the road which runs at different distances from the edge of the bank which rises from the river. This bank is generally steep, scattered over with trees which are either not of ancient growth, or from some cause do not thrive, but serve very well to shelter and often conceal the more humble dwellings, which are close to the sandy bank of the river. . . . We saw many carriages. In one of them was Klopstock, the poet. There are many inns and eating-houses by the roadside. We went to a pretty village, or nest of houses about a league from Blankenese, and beyond to a large open field, enclosed on one side with oak trees, through which winds a pleasant gravel walk. On the other it is open to the river. When we were within about a mile and a half or two miles of Altona, we turned out of the road to go down to the river, and pursued our way along the path that leads from house to house. These houses are low, never more than two storeys high, built of brick, or a mixture of brick and wood, and thatched or tiled. They have all window-shutters, which are painted frequently a grey light green, but always painted. We were astonished at the excessive neatness which we observed in the arrangement of everything within these houses. They have all window curtains as white as snow; the floors of all that we saw were perfectly clean, and the brass vessels as bright as a mirror. I imagine these houses are chiefly inhabited by sailors, pilots, boat-makers, and others whose business is upon the water.

Monday, October 2nd.—William called at Klopstock's to inquire the road into Saxony. Bought Burgher's poems, the price 6 marks. Sate an hour at Remnant's. Bought Percy's ancient poetry, 14 marks.[4] Walked on the ramparts; a very fine morning. . . .[5]

After leaving Hamburg, they went to Goslar, a trip Dorothy describes in a letter to Mary, taken here from Christopher Wordsworth's *Memoirs of William Wordsworth.*

We quitted Hamburg on Wednesday evening, at five o'clock, reached Luneberg to breakfast on Thursday, and arrived at Brunswick between three and four o'clock on Friday. . . . There we dined. It is an old, silent, dull-looking place; the duke's palace, a large white building, with no elegance in its external appearance. The next morning we set off at eight. You have no idea of the badness of the roads. The diligence arrived at eight at night at the city of Goslar, on Saturday, Oct. 6, the distance being only twenty-five miles.

Coleridge is very happily situated at Ratzeburg for learning the language. We are not fortunately situated here with respect to the attainment of our main object, a knowledge of the language. We have, indeed, gone on improving in that respect, but not so expeditiously as we might have done: for there is no society at Goslar, it is a lifeless town; and it seems that here in Germany a man travelling alone may do very well, but if his sister or wife goes with him, he must give entertainments. So we content ourselves with talking to the people of the house &. and reading German. . . . We have plenty of dry walks; but Goslar is very cold in winter.

---

[4] The Wordsworths had read translations of Gottfried August Burger, famed for his ballads. The other reference is to Percy's *Reliques.*

[5] Knight's edition ends here. De Selincourt's adds Dorothy's account of the Wordsworths' progress to Goslar, where they arrived October 6.

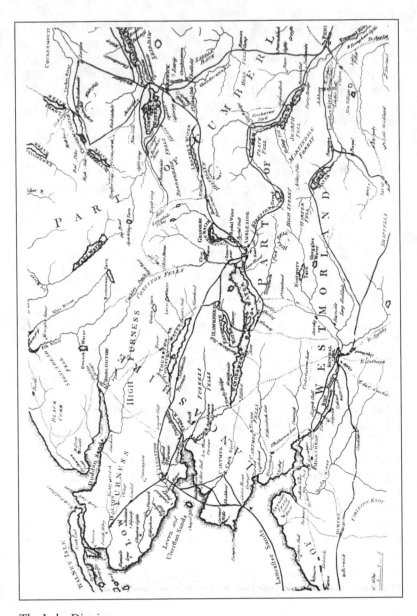

The Lake District

FROM THE GRASMERE JOURNALS

After returning from Germany in 1799, Dorothy and William took up residence at Dove Cottage in Grasmere. In May of 1800, he left to court Mary Hutchinson, and Dorothy began a journal that reflects this triangulation. Like her Alfoxden notebook, this work demonstrates Dorothy's place in a community of writers. Dorothy also describes a fascinating cross section of Grasmere society and catalogues various social and political pressures of British country life.

These journals occupy four notebooks. My text is based primarily on Knight's excerpts to convey how the general public would have first encountered this writing. Ellipses and dotted lines are Knight's; bracketed lines enclose my own ellipses. I also include an example from Christopher Wordsworth's presentation and refer as noted to some of the at least fifteen different editions of the work now in print.

MAY 14–DECEMBER, 1800

May 14th, 1800.—Wm. and John set off into Yorkshire[1] after dinner at half-past two o'clock, cold pork in their pockets. I left them at the turning of the Lowwood bay under the trees. My heart was so full that I could hardly speak to W. when I gave him a farewell kiss. I sate a long time upon a stone at the margin of the lake, and after a flood of tears my heart was easier. The lake looked to me, I knew not why, dull and melancholy, and the weltering on the shores seemed a heavy sound. I walked as long as I could amongst the stones of the shore. The wood rich in flowers; a beautiful yellow (palish yellow) flower, that looked thick, round, and double—the smell very sweet (I supposed it was a ranunculus), crowfoot, the grassy-leaved rabbit-looking white flower, strawberries, geraniums, scentless violets, anemones, two kinds of orchises, primroses, the heck-berry very beautiful, the crab coming out as a low shrub. Met an old man, driving a very large beautiful bull, and a cow. He walked with two sticks. Came home by Clappersgate. The valley very green; many sweet views up to Rydale, when I could juggle away the fine houses; but they disturbed me, even more than when I

---

[1] Mary lived at Gallow Hill, her brother's farm in Yorkshire. The brothers would return on June 7.

have been happier; one beautiful view of the bridge, without Sir Michael's.[2] Sate down very often, though it was cold. I resolved to write a journal of the time till W. and J. return, and I set about keeping my resolve because I will not quarrel with myself, and because I shall give William pleasure by it when he comes home again. At Rydale, a woman of the village, stout and well dressed, begged a half-penny. She had never she said done it before, but these hard times! Arrived at home, set some slips of privet, the evening cold, had a fire, my face now flame-coloured. It is nine o'clock. I shall now go to bed. . . . Oh that I had a letter from William.

Friday Morning 16*th.*—Warm and mild, after a fine night of rain. . . . The woods extremely beautiful with all autumnal variety and softness. I carried a basket for mosses, and gathered some wild plants. Oh! that we had a book of botany. All flowers now are gay and deliciously sweet. The primrose still prominent; the later flowers and the shiny foxgloves very tall, with their heads budding. I went forward around the lake at the foot of Loughrigg Fell. I was much amused with the busyness of a pair of stone-chats; their restless voices as they skimmed along the water, following each other, their shadows under them, and their returning back to the stones on the shore, chirping with the same unwearied voice. Could not cross the water, so I went round by the stepping-stones. . . . Rydale was very beautiful, with spear-shaped streaks of polished steel. . . . Grasmere very solemn in the last glimpse of twilight. It calls home the heart to quietness. I had been very melancholy. In my walk back I had many of my saddest thoughts, and I could not keep the tears within me. But when I came to Grasmere I felt that it did me good. I finished my letter to M. H. . . .

Saturday.—Incessant rain from morning till night. . . . Worked hard, and read *Midsummer Night's Dream,* and ballads. Sauntered a little in the garden. The blackbird sate quietly in its nest, rocked by the wind, and beaten by the rain.

Sunday, 18*th.*—Went to church, slight showers, a cold air. The mountains from this window look much greener, and I think the valley is more green than ever. The corn begins to shew itself. The ashes are still bare. A little girl from Coniston came to beg. She had lain out all night. Her step-mother had turned her out of doors; her father could not stay at home "she flights so."[3] Walked to

---

[2] Rydal Hall, the home of Sir Michael le Fleming. "Without" means "beyond."

[3] His daughter's flightiness drives the father from home. The stepmother turns her out to bring him back.

Ambleside in the evening round the lake, the prospect exceeding beautiful from Loughrigg Fell. It was so green that no eye could weary of reposing upon it. The most beautiful situation for a home is the field next to Mr. Benson's.[4] I was overtaken by two Cumberland people who complimented me upon my walking. They were going to sell cloth, and odd things which they make themselves, in Hawkshead and the neighbourhood. . . . Letters from Coleridge and Cottle. John Fisher[5] overtook me on the other side of Rydale. He talked much about the alteration in the times, and observed that in a short time there would be only two ranks of people, the very rich and the very poor, "for those who have small estates," says he, "are forced to sell, and all the land goes into one hand." Did not reach home till ten o'clock.

Monday.—Sauntered a good deal in the garden, bound carpets, mended old clothes, read *Timon of Athens,* dried linen. . . . Walked up into the Black Quarter.[6] I sauntered a long time among the rocks above the church. The most delightful situation possible, for a cottage, commanding two distinct views of the vale and of the lake, is among those rocks. . . . The quietness and still seclusion of the valley affected me even to producing the deepest melancholy. I forced myself from it. The wind rose before I went to bed.

[. . . . .]

Wednesday.—In the morning walked up to the rocks above Jenny Dockeray's.[7] Sate a long time upon the grass; the prospect divinely beautiful. If I had three hundred pounds, and could afford to have a bad interest for my money, I would buy that estate, and we would build a cottage there to end our days in. I went into her garden and got white and yellow lilies, etc., periwinkle, etc., which I planted. Sate under the trees with my work. Worked between 7 and 8, and then watered the garden. A beautiful evening. The crescent moon hanging above Helm Crag.

Thursday.—In the morning worked in the garden a little. Read *King John.* Miss Simpson, and Miss Falcon, and Mr. S. came very

---

[4] Owners of Dove Cottage, who lived on the west side of Grasmere Lake.

[5] John Fisher, his wife, Aggy, and his sister Molly lived near Dove Cottage and did household work for the Wordsworths.

[6] The Wordsworths' name for Easedale, reflecting the look of the fells.

[7] Dockeray's family owned two farmhouses.

early. Went to Mr. Gill's boat. Before tea we fished upon the lake, amongst us caught 13! . . .[8]

Friday.—In the morning went to Ambleside, forgetting that the post does not come till the evening. How was I grieved when I was so informed. I walked back, resolving to go again in the evening. It rained very mildly and sweetly in the morning as I came home, but came on a wet afternoon and evening, and chilly. I caught Mr. Olliffs[9] lad as he was going for letters. He brought me one from Wm. and 12 papers. I planted London Pride upon the wall, and many things on the borders. John sodded the wall. As I came past Rydale in the morning, I saw a heron swimming with only its neck out of water. It beat and struggled amongst the water, when it flew away, and was long in getting loose.

Saturday.—A sweet mild rainy morning, Grundy the carpet man called. I paid him £1: 10s. Went to the blind man's for plants. I got such a load that I was obliged to leave my basket in the road, and send Molly for it. . . .

Sunday, June 1st.—Rain in the night. A sweet mild morning. Read ballads. Went to church. Singers from Wytheburn. Walked upon the hill above the house till dinner time. Went again to church. After tea, went to Ambleside, round the Lakes. A very fine warm evening. Upon the side of Loughrigg my heart dissolved in what I saw: when I was not startled, but called from my reverie by a noise as of a child paddling without shoes. I looked up, and saw a lamb close to me. It approached nearer and nearer, as if to examine me, and stood a long time. I did not move. At last, it ran past me, and went bleating-along the pathway, seeming to be seeking its mother. I saw a hare on the high road. . . .

Monday.—A cold dry windy morning. I worked in the garden, and planted flowers, etc. Sate under the trees after dinner till tea time. . . . I went to Ambleside after tea, crossed the stepping-stones at the foot of Grasmere, and pursued my way on the other side of Rydale and by Clappersgate. I sate a long time to watch the hurrying waves, and to hear the regularly irregular sound of the dashing waters. The waves round about the little Island seemed like a dance of spirits that rose out of the water, round its small circumference of

---

[8] Rev. Joseph Simpson and his daughter lived on the road to Keswick. William Gell ("Gill" in Knight), an archeologist and one of Queen Caroline's chamberlains, rarely visited his Grasmere cottage and allowed the Wordsworths to use his boat.

[9] The Oliff family lived on the Keswick road.

shore. Inquired about lodgings for Coleridge, and was accompanied by Mrs. Nicholson[10] as far as Rydale. This was very kind, but God be thanked, I want not society by a moonlit lake. It was near eleven when I reached home. I wrote to Coleridge, and went late to bed.

Wednesday.—. . . I walked to the lake-side in the morning, took up plants, and sate upon a stone reading ballads. In the evening I was watering plants, when Mr. and Miss Simpson called, and I accompanied them home, and we went to the waterfall at the head of the valley. It was very interesting in the twilight. I brought Home lemon-thyme, and several other plants, and planted them by moonlight. I lingered out of doors in the hope of hearing my brother's tread.

Thursday.—I sate out of doors great part of the day, and worked in the garden. Had a letter from Mr. Jackson,[11] and wrote an answer to Coleridge. The little birds busy making love, and pecking the blossoms and bits of moss off the trees. They flutter about and about, and beneath the trees as I lie under them. I would not go far from home, expecting my brother. I rambled on the hill above the house, gathered wild-thyme, and took up roots of wild columbine. Just as I was returning with my load, Mr. and Miss Simpson called. We went again upon the hill, got more plants, set them, and then went to the blind man's, for London Pride for Miss Simpson. I went up with them as far as the blacksmith's, a fine lovely moonlight night.

[. . . . .]

Saturday.—A very warm cloudy morning, threatening to rain. I walked up to Mr. Simpson's to gather gooseberries. It was a very fine afternoon. Little Tommy[12] came down with me. We went up the hill, to gather sods and plants; and went down to the lake side, and took up orchises, etc. I watered the garden and weeded. I did not leave home, in the expectation of Wm. and John, and sitting at work till after 11 o'clock I heard a foot at the front of the house, turn round, and open the gate. It was William! After our first joy was over, we got some tea. We did not go to bed till 4 o'clock in the

---

[10] Ambleside's postmistress.

[11] Owner of Greta Hall in Keswick. Dorothy negotiated with him on behalf of Coleridge, who would take up residence there in July.

[12] Mr. Simpson's grandson.

morning, so he had an opportunity of seeing our improvements. The buds were staying; and all looked fresh, though not gay. There was a greyness on earth and sky. We did not rise till near 10 in the morning. We were busy all day in writing to Coleridge, Montagu etc. Mr. and Miss Simpson called in the evening. The little boy carried our letters to Ambleside. We walked with Mr. and Miss S. home, on their return. . . . We met John on our return home.

Monday 9th.—In the morning W. cut down the winter cherry tree. I sowed French beans and weeded. A coronetted landau[13] went by, when we were sitting upon the sodded wall. The ladies (evidently tourists) turned an eye of interest upon our little garden and cottage. Went round to Mr. G[e]ll's boat, and on to the lake to fish. We caught nothing. It was extremely cold. The reeds and bullrushes or bullpipes of a tender soft green, making a plain whose surface moved with the wind. The reeds not yet tall. The lake clear to the bottom, but saw no fish. In the evening I stuck peas, watered the garden, and planted brocoli. Did not walk, for it was very cold. A poor girl called to beg, who had no work, and was going in search of it to Kendal. She slept in Mr. Benson's . . . [lathe, i.e., barn] and went off after breakfast in the morning with 7d. and a letter to the Mayor of Kendal.

Tuesday 10th.—A cold, yet sunshiny morning. John carried letters to Ambleside. Wm. stuck peas. After dinner he lay down. John not at home. I stuck peas alone. Cold showers with hail and rain, but at half-past five, after a heavy rain, the lake became calm and very beautiful. Those parts of the water which were perfectly unruffled lay like green islands of various shapes. William and I walked to Ambleside to seek lodgings for C. No letters. No papers. It was a very cold cheerless evening. John had been fishing in Langdale and was gone to bed.

A very tall woman, tall much beyond the measure of tall women, called at the door.[14] She had on a very long brown cloak and a very white cap, without bonnet. Her face was excessively brown, but it had plainly once been fair. She led a little bare-footed

---

[13] A four-wheeled carriage with facing passenger seats and a roof of two sections that could be raised or lowered separately. "Coronetted" means displaying a coronet or small crown, indicating the vehicle belonged to a member of the peerage, whose group takes note of Dove Cottage.

[14] The basis for William's poem, "Beggars," written in March 1802. That Dorothy wrote about the encounter two weeks after it occurred may have been the result of William's request; he knew a good story.

child about two years old by the hand, and said her husband, who was a tinker, was gone before with the other children. I gave her a piece of bread. Afterwards on my way to Ambleside, beside the bridge at Rydale, I saw her husband sitting by the roadside, his two asses feeding beside him, and the two young children at play upon the grass. The man did not beg. I passed on and about a quarter of a mile further I saw two boys before me, one about 10, the other about 8 years old, at play chasing a butterfly. They were wild figures, not very ragged, but without shoes and stockings. The hat of the elder was wreathed round with yellow flowers, the younger whose hat was only a rimless crown, had stuck it round with laurel leaves. They continued at play till I drew very near, and then they addressed me with the begging cant and the whining voice of sorrow. I said "I served your mother this morning." (The boys were so like the woman who had called at . . . [the door] that I could not be mistaken.) "O" says the elder," you could not serve my mother for she's dead, and my father's on at the next town—he's a potter." I persisted in my assertion, and that I would give them nothing. Says the elder, "Let's away," and away they flew like lightning. They had however sauntered so long in their road that they did not reach Ambleside before me, and I saw them go up to Matthew Harrison's house with their wallet[15] upon the elder's shoulder, and creeping with a beggar's complaining foot. On my return through Ambleside I met in the street the mother driving her asses, in the two panniers of one of which were the two little children, whom she was chiding and threatening with a wand which she used to drive on her asses, while the little things hung in wantonness over the pannier's edge.[16] The woman had told me in the morning that she was of Scotland, which her accent fully proved, but that she had lived (I think at Wigtoun,) that they could not keep a house and so they travelled.

[. . . . .]

Thursday.—A very hot morning. W. and I walked up to Mr. Simpson's. W. and old Mr. S. went to fish in Wytheburn water. I dined with John and lay under the trees. The afternoon changed from clear to cloudy, and to clear again. John and I walked up to

[15] Satchel.

[16] Pannier: a pair of baskets hung across the back of a mule or horse and used to carry produce.

the waterfall, and to Mr. Simpson's, and with Miss Simpson. Met the fishers. W. caught a pike weighing 4 $^3/_4$ lbs. There was a gloom almost terrible over Grasmere water and vale. A few drops fell but not much rain: No Coleridge, whom we fully expected.

Friday.—I worked in the garden in the morning. Wm. prepared pea sticks. Threatening for rain, but yet it comes not. On Wednesday evening a poor man called—a hatter. He had been long ill, but was now recovered. The parish would not help him, because he had implements of trade, etc. etc.[17] We gave him 6d.

Saturday.—Walked up the hill to Rydale lake. Grasmere looked so beautiful that my heart was almost melted away. It was quite calm, only spotted with sparkles of light; the church visible. On our return all distant objects had faded away, all but the hills. The reflection of the light bright sky above Black Quarter was very solemn. . . .

Sunday.—In the evening I planted a honeysuckle round the yew tree. . . . No news of Coleridge. . . .

[. . . . .]

Wednesday.—A very rainy day. I made a shoe. Wm. and John went to fish in Langdale. In the evening I went above the house, and gathered flowers, which I planted, foxgloves, etc. On Sunday Mr. and Mrs. Coleridge and Hartley came. The day was very warm. We sailed to the foot of Loughrigg. They staid with us three weeks, and till the Thursday following, from 1st till the 23rd of July. On the Friday preceding their departure, we drank tea at the island. The weather was delightful, and on the Sunday we made a great fire, and drank tea in Bainriggs with the Simpsons. I accompanied Mrs. C. to Wytheburne, and returned with W. to tea at Mr. Simpson's. It was exceedingly hot, but the day after, Friday 24th July,[18] still hotter. All the morning I was engaged in unpacking our Somersetshire goods. The house was a hot oven. I was so weary I could not walk: so I went out, and sate with Wm. in the orchard. We had a delightful half-hour in the warm still evening.

Saturday, 26th.—Still hotter. I sate with W. in the orchard all the morning, and made my shoe. . . .

[. . . . .]

---

[17] The parish would not aid those deemed able to work, as his tools of trade suggest he was.

[18] [Knight] Friday was the 25th.

Tuesday 5th.—Dried the linen in the morning. The air still cold. I pulled a bag full of peas for Mrs. Simpson. Miss Simpson drank tea with me, and supped, on her return from Ambleside. A very fine evening. I sate on the wall making my shifts till I could see no longer. Walked half-way home with Miss Simpson.

Wednesday, 6th August.—. . . William came home from Keswick at eleven o'clock.

Thursday Morning, 9th August.—. . . William composing in the wood in the morning. In the evening we walked to Mary Point. A very fine sunset.

Friday Morning.—We intended going to Keswick, but were prevented by the excessive heat. Nailed up scarlet beans in the morning. Walked over the mountains by Wattendlath. . . . A most enchanting walk. Wattendlath a heavenly scene. Reached Coleridge's at eleven o'clock.

Saturday Morning.—I walked with Coleridge in the Windy Brow[19] woods.

Sunday.—Very hot. The C.'s went to church. We sailed upon Derwent in the evening.

[. . . . .]

Friday Evening (*29th* August)—We walked to Rydale to inquire for letters. We walked over the hill by the firgrove. I sate upon a rock and observed a flight of swallows gathering together high above my head. They flew towards Rydale. We walked through the wood over the stepping stones. The lake of Rydale very beautiful, partly still. John and I left Wm. to compose an inscription; that about the path.[20] We had a very fine walk by the gloomy lake. There was a curious yellow reflection in the water, as of corn fields. There was no light in the clouds from which it appeared to come.

Saturday Morning, 30th August.—. . . William finished his Inscription of the Pathway, then walked in the wood; and when John returned, he sought him, and they bathed together. I read a little of Boswell's *Life of Johnson*.[21] I went to lie down in the orchard. I was roused by a shout that Anthony Harrison[22] was come. We sate in the

---

[19] Residence of William Calvert, Raisley's brother. The Wordsworths stayed there in 1794.

[20] Probably "When to the attractions of the busy world," first published in *Poems*, 1815.

[21] Boswell's monumental biography of Samuel Johnson was first published in 1791.

[22] A friend from Penrith who would publish *Poetical Recreations* in 1806.

orchard till tea time. Drank tea early, and rowed down the lake which was stirred by breezes. We looked at Rydale, which was soft, cheerful, and beautiful. We then went to peep into Langdale. The Pikes were very grand. We walked back to the view of Rydale, which was now a dark mirror. We rowed home over a lake still as glass, and then went to George Mackareth's to hire a horse for John. A fine moonlight night. The beauty of the moon was startling, as it rose to us over Loughrigg Fell. We returned to supper at 10 o'clock. Thomas Ashburner brought us our 8th cart of coals since May 17th.

Sunday, 31st . . . A great deal of corn is cut in the vale, and the whole prospect, though not tinged with a general autumnal yellow, yet softened down into a mellowness of colouring, which seems to impart softness to the forms of hills and mountains. At 11 o'clock Coleridge came, when I was walking in the still clear moonshine in the garden. He came over Helvellyn. Wm. was gone to bed, and John also, worn out with his ride round Coniston. We sate and chatted till half-past three, Coleridge reading a part of *Christabel*. Talked much about the mountains, etc. etc. . . .

Monday Morning, 1st September.—We walked in the wood by the lake. W. read *Joanna* and the *Firgrove,* to Coleridge. They bathed. The morning was delightful, with somewhat of an autumnal freshness. After dinner, Coleridge discovered a rock-seat in the orchard. Cleared away brambles. Coleridge went to bed after tea. John and I followed Wm. up the hill, and then returned to go to Mr. Simpson's. We borrowed some bottles for bottling rum. The evening somewhat frosty and grey, but very pleasant. I broiled Coleridge a mutton chop, which he ate in bed. Wm. was gone to bed. I chatted with John and Coleridge till near 12.

Tuesday, 2nd.—In the morning they all went to Stickle Tarn.[23] A very fine, warm, sunny, beautiful morning. . . . The fair-day. . . . There seemed very few people and very few stalls, yet I believe there were many cakes and much beer sold. My brothers came home to dinner at 6 o'clock. We drank tea immediately after by candlelight. It was a lovely moonlight night. We talked much about a house on Helvellyn. The moonlight shone only upon the village. It did not eclipse the village lights, and the sound of dancing and merriment came along the still air. I walked with Coleridge and Wm. up the lane and by the church, and then lingered with Coleridge in the garden. John and Wm. were both gone to bed, and all the lights out.

---

[23] Mountain lake.

Wednesday, 3rd September.—Coleridge, Wm., and John went from home, to go upon Helvellyn with Mr. Simpson. They set out after breakfast. I accompanied them up near the blacksmith's.... I then went to a funeral at John Dawson's. About 10 men and 4 women. Bread, cheese, and ale. They talked sensibly and cheerfully about common things. The dead person, 56 years of age, buried by the parish. The coffin was neatly lettered and painted black, and covered with a decent cloth. They set the corpse down at the door; and, while we stood within the threshold, the men, with their hats off, sang, with decent and solemn countenances, a verse of a funeral psalm. The corpse was then borne down the hill, and they sang till they had passed the Town-End. I was affected to tears while we stood in the house, the coffin lying before me. There were no near kindred, no children. When we got out of the dark house the sun was shining, and the prospect looked as divinely beautiful as I ever saw it. It seemed more sacred than I had ever seen it, and yet more allied to human life. The green fields, in the neighbourhood of the churchyard, were as green as possible; and, with the brightness of the sunshine, looked quite gay. I thought she was going to a quiet spot, and I could not help weeping very much. When we came to the bridge, they began to sing again, and stopped during four lines before they entered the churchyard.... Wm. and John came home at 10 o'clock.

[. . . . .]

Sunday, 28th.—We heard of the Abergavenny's[24] arrival....

Monday, 29th.—John left us. Wm. and I parted with him in sight of Ullswater. It was a fine day, showery, but with sunshine and fine clouds. Poor fellow, my heart was right sad. I could not help thinking we should see him again, because he was only going to Penrith.

[. . . . .]

Thursday, 2nd October.—A very rainy morning. We walked after dinner to observe the torrents. I followed Wm. to Rydale. We afterwards went to Butterlip How. The Black Quarter looked marshy, and the general prospect was cold, but the *force*[25] was very grand. The lichens are now coming out afresh. I carried home a collection in the afternoon. We had a pleasant conversation about the manners of the rich; avarice, inordinate desires, and the effeminacy,

[24] John had been named captain of this ship in January 1801. He died at sea.

[25] Waterfall on the stream descending from Easedale Tarn to Grasmere.

unnaturalness, and unworthy objects of education. The moonlight lay upon the hills like snow.

Friday, 3rd October.—Very rainy all the morning. Wm. walked to Ambleside after dinner. I went with him part of the way. He talked much about the object of his essay for the second volume of "L. B." . . . Amos Cottle's[26] death in the *Morning Post.*

N.B.—When William and I returned from accompanying Jones, we met an old man almost double. He had on a coat, thrown over his shoulders, above his waistcoat and coat. Under this he carried a bundle, and had an apron on and a night-cap. His face was interesting. He had dark eyes and a long nose. John, who afterwards met him at Wytheburn, took him for a Jew. He was of Scotch parents, but had been born in the army. He had had a wife, and "she was a good woman, and it pleased God to bless us with ten children." All these were dead but one, of whom he had not heard for many years, a sailor. His trade was to gather leeches, but now leeches were scarce, and he had not strength for it. He lived by begging and was making his way to Carlisle, where he should buy a few godly books to sell. He said leeches were very scarce, partly owing to this dry season, but many years they have been scarce. He supposed it owing to their being much sought after, that they did not breed fast, and were of slow growth. Leeches were formerly 2s. 6d. per 100; they are now 30s. He had been hurt in driving a cart, his leg broken, his body driven over, his skull fractured. He felt no pain till he recovered from his first insensibility. It was then late in the evening, when the light was just going away.[27]

[. . . . .]

Friday, 10th October.—In the morning when I arose the mists were hanging over the opposite hills, and the tops of the highest hills were covered with snow. There was a most lively combination at the head of the vale of the yellow autumnal hills wrapped in sunshine, and overhung with partial mists, the green and yellow trees, and the distant snow-topped mountains. It was a most heavenly morning. The Cockermouth traveller came with thread, hardware, mustard, etc. She is very healthy; has travelled over the mountains these thirty years. She does not mind the storms, if she can keep her goods dry. Her husband will not travel with an ass, because it is the

---

[26] Joseph's older brother.

[27] William uses this description in "Resolution and Independence," initially called "The Leech-Gatherer."

tramper's badge; she would have one to relieve her from the weary load. She was going to Ulverston and was to return to Ambleside Fair. . . . The fern among the rocks exquisitely beautiful . . . Sent off *The Beggars,* etc., by Thomas Ashburner . . . William sat up after me, writing *Point Rash Judgment.*

Saturday, 11*th.*—A fine October morning. Sat in the house working all the morning. William composing. . . . After dinner we walked up Greenhead Gill in search of a sheepfold.[28] We went by Mr. Olliff's, and through his woods. It was a delightful day, and the views looked excessively cheerful and beautiful, chiefly that from Mr. Olliff's field, where our own house is to be built. The colours of the mountains soft, and rich with orange fern; the cattle pasturing upon the hilltops; kites sailing in the sky above our heads; sheep bleating, and feeding in the water courses, scattered over the mountains. They come down and feed, on the little green islands in the beds of the torrents, and so may be swept away. The sheepfold is falling away. It is built nearly in the form of a heart unequally divided. Looked down the brook, and saw the drops rise upwards and sparkle in the air at the little falls. The higher sparkled the tallest. We walked along the turf of the mountain till we came to a track, made by the cattle which come upon the hills.

Sunday, October 12*th.*—Sate in the house writing in the morning while Wm. went into the wood to compose. Wrote to John in the morning; copied poems for the L. B. In the evening wrote to Mrs. Rawson. Mary Jameson[29] and Sally Ashburner dined. We pulled apples after dinner, a large basket full. We walked before tea by Bainriggs to observe the many-coloured foliage. The oaks dark green with yellow leaves, the birches generally still green, some near the water yellowish, the sycamore crimson and crimson-tufted, the mountain ash a deep orange, the common ash lemon-colour, but many ashes still fresh in their peculiar green, those that were discoloured chiefly near the water. Wm. composing in the evening. Went to bed at 12 o'clock.

Monday, October 13*th.*—A grey day. Mists on the hills. We did not walk in the morning. I copied poems on the Naming of Places.[30] A fair at Ambleside. Walked in the Black Quarter at night.

. . . .

[28] William is working on "Michael," which Dorothy calls "The Sheepfold."

[29] A Simpson relative.

[30] Section in volume two of *Lyrical Ballads* (1800).

Wednesday.—A very fine clear morning. After Wm. had composed a little, I persuaded him to go into the orchard. We walked backwards and forwards. The prospect most divinely beautiful from the seat; all colours, all melting into each other. I went in to put bread in the oven, and we both walked within view of Rydale. Wm. again composed at the sheepfold after dinner. I walked with Wm. to Wytheburn, and he went on to Keswick. I drank tea, and supped at Mr. Simpson's. A very cold frosty air in returning. Mr. and Miss S. came with me. Wytheburn looked very wintry, but yet there was a foxglove blossoming by the roadside.

. . . .

Friday, 17th.—A very fine grey morning. The swan hunt . . . I walked round the lake between ¹/₂ past 12, and ¹/₂ past one. . . . In my walk in the morning, I observed Benson's honey-suckles in flower and great beauty. I found Wm. at home, where he had been almost ever since my departure. Coleridge had done nothing for the L. B. Working hard for Stuart.[31] Glow-worms in abundance.

[. . . . .]

Thursday.—We sate in the house all the morning. Rainy weather, played at cards. A poor woman from Hawkshead begged, a widow of Grasmere. A merry African from Longtown . . .

Friday.—Much wind, but a sweet mild morning. I nailed up trees. . . . Two letters from Coleridge, very ill. One from Sara H. . . .[32]

Saturday Morning.—A terrible rain, so prevented William from going to Coleridge's. The afternoon fine. . . . We both set forward at five o'clock. A fine wild night. I walked with W. over the Raise. It was starlight. I parted with him very sad, unwilling not to go on. The hills, and the stars, and the white waters, with their ever varying yet ceaseless sound, were very impressive. I supped at the Simpsons'. Mr. S. walked home with me.

Sunday, 16th November.—A very fine warm sunny morning. A letter from Coleridge, and one from Stoddart. Coleridge better. . . . One beautiful ash tree sheltered, with yellow leaves, one low one quite green. A noise of boys in the rocks hunting some animal. Walked a little in the garden when I came home. Very pleasant now.

---

[31] Daniel Stuart, editor of *The Morning Post.*
[32] Mary Hutchinson's sister.

Rain comes on. Mr. Jackson called in the evening, brought me a letter from C. and W.

Monday Morning.—A fine clear frosty morning with a sharp wind. I walked to Keswick. Set off at 5 minutes past 10, and arrived at ¹/₂ past 2. I found them all well.

On *Tuesday* morning W. and C. set off towards Penrith. Wm. met Sara Hutchinson at Threlkeld. They arrived at Keswick at tea time.

[. . . . .]

OCTOBER 10, 1801–FEBRUARY 14, 1802

The first notebook ends in midsentence with an entry from December 22, 1800. A new notebook begins with a paragraph of phrases, many of which are journal topics. Moorman lists these topics as: Penshurst—Pedlar—Mary H.—Grasmere & Keswick—Sara's waistcoats—Fable of the Dogs—Cows—Lamb's Londoner—Lucy Aikin's poems—Mr Graham—Mrs. Clarkson health—My German—our Riches—Miss Simpson—The poor woman who was drowned—William's health—medicines—The garden—Wm. working there—quietness from company—Letting our house—keeping it—Books that we are to carry—L. degrades himself—narrow minded bigotry—unfortunate quotation—Letter from Sara—Montagu—Dr Dodd—Rubbing tables. Entries prior to 10 October 1801 have not been found.

Saturday, 10th October 1801.—Coleridge went to Keswick, after we had built Sara's seat.[33]

Thursday, 15th . . . Coleridge came in to Mr. Luff's[34] while we were at dinner. William and I walked up Loughrigg Fell, then by the waterside. . . .

Saturday, 24th—Attempted Fairfield, but misty, and we went no further than Green Head Gill to the sheepfold; mild, misty, beautifully soft. Wm. and Tom put out the boat.

Sunday, 25th.—Rode to Legberthwaite with Tom, expecting Mary. . . . Went upon Helvellyn. Glorious sights. The sea at Cartmel. The Scotch mountains beyond sea to the right. Whiteside large,

[33] A stone seat on White Moss Common. Sara Hutchinson also had a gate and a rock named after her.

[34] The Wordsworths met the Luffs through the Clarksons. The Luffs visited Ambleside.

and round, and very soft, and green, behind us. Mists above and below, and close to us, with the sun amongst them. They shot down to the coves. Left John Stanley's at 10 minutes past 12. Returned thither 1/4 past 4, drank tea, ate heartily. Before we went on Helvellyn we got bread and cheese. Paid 4/ for the whole. Reached home at nine o'clock. A soft grey evening; the light of the moon, but she did not shine on us. Mary and I sate in C.'s room a while.

. . . .

Tuesday, 10th [November]—Poor C. left us, and we came home together. We left Keswick at 2 o'clock and did not arrive at Grasmere till 9 o'clock. I burnt myself with Coleridge's aquafortis.[35] C. had a sweet day for his ride. Every sight and every sound reminded me of him—dear, dear fellow, of his many talks to us, by day and by night, of all dear things. I was melancholy, and could not talk, but at last I eased my heart by weeping—nervous blubbering says William. It is not so. O! how many, many reasons have I to be anxious for him.

Wednesday, 11th.—Put aside dearest C.'s letters, and now, at about 7 o'clock, we are all sitting by a nice fire. Wm. with his book and a candle, and Mary writing to Sara.

November 16th.—. . . Wm. is now, at 7 o'clock, reading Spenser. Mary is writing beside me. The little syke[36] murmurs. We are quiet and happy, but poor Peggy Ashburner coughs, as if she would cough her life away. I am going to write to Coleridge and Sara. Poor C.! I hope he was in London yesterday. . . .

[. . . . .]

Tuesday, 24th.—. . . It was very windy, and we heard the wind everywhere about us as we went along the lane, but the walls sheltered us. John Green's house looked pretty under Silver How. As we were going along we were stopped at once, at the distance perhaps of 50 yards from our favourite birch tree. It was yielding to the gusty wind with all its tender twigs. The sun shone upon it, and it glanced in the wind like a flying sunshiny shower. It was a tree in shape, with stem and branches, but it was like a spirit of water. The sun went in, and it resumed its purplish appearance, the twigs still yielding to the wind, but not so visibly to us. The other birch trees that were near it looked bright and cheerful, but it was a creature by its own self

---

[35] Nitric acid, used as solvent.
[36] Syke: stream, often dry in summer.

among them. . . . We went through the wood. It became fair. There was a rainbow which spanned the lake from the island-house to the foot of Bainriggs. The village looked populous and beautiful. Catkins are coming out; palm trees budding; the alder, with its plum-coloured buds. We came home over the stepping stones. The lake was foamy with white waves. I saw a solitary butter flower in the wood . . . Reached home at dinner time. Sent Peggy Ashburner some goose. She sent me some honey with a thousand thanks "Alas! the gratitude of men has," etc.[37] I went in to set her right about this, and sate a while with her. She talked about Thomas's having sold his land. "I," says she, "said many a time he's not come fra London to buy our land, however." Then she told me with what pains and industry they had made up their taxes, interest, etc. etc., how they all got up at 5 o'clock in the morning to spin and Thomas carded, and that they had paid off a hundred pounds of the interest. She said she used to take much pleasure in the cattle and sheep. "O how pleased I used to be when they fetched them down, and when I had been a bit poorly I would gang out upon a hill and look over 't fields and see them, and it used to do me so much good you cannot think." Molly said to me when I came in, "Poor body! she's very ill, but one does not know how long she may last. Many a fair face may gang before her." We sate by the fire without work for some time, then Mary read a poem of Daniel.[38] . . . Wm. read Spenser, now and then, a little aloud to us. We were making his waistcoat. We had a note from Mrs. C, with bad news from poor C.—very ill. William went to John's Grove[39] I went to find him. Moonlight, but it rained. . . . He had been surprised, and terrified, by a sudden rushing of winds, which seemed to bring earth, sky, and lake together, as if the whole were going to enclose him in. He was glad he was in a high road. . . .

In speaking of our walk on Sunday evening, the 22nd November, I forgot to notice one most impressive sight. It was the moon and the moonlight seen through hurrying driving clouds immediately behind the Stone-Man upon the top of the hill, on the forest side. Every tooth and every edge of rock was visible, and the Man stood like a giant watching from the roof of a lofty castle. The hill seemed perpendicular from the darkness below it. It was a sight that I could call to mind at any time, it was so distinct.

[37] "Simon Lee," 95 (*Lyrical Ballads*, 1798).
[38] Historian and poet Samuel Daniel (1562–1619).
[39] Large group of trees, also known as Firgrove.

Wednesday, 25th November.—It was a showery morning and threatened to be a wettish day, but the sun shone once or twice. We were engaged to Mr. Lloyd's and Wm. and Mary were determined to go that it might be over. I accompanied them to the thorn beside Rydale water. I parted from them first at the top of the hill, and they called me back. It rained a little, and rained afterwards all the afternoon. I baked bread, and wrote to Sara Hutchinson and Coleridge. I passed a pleasant evening, but the wind roared so, and it was such a storm that I was afraid for them. They came in at nine o'clock, no worse for their walk, and cheerful, blooming, and happy.

Thursday, 26th.—Mr Olliff called before Wm. was up to say that they would drink tea with us this afternoon. We walked into Easedale, to gather mosses, and to fetch cream. I went for the cream, and they sate under a wall. It was piercing cold.

[. . . . .]

Monday Morning, 7th.—We rose by candlelight. A showery unpleasant morning, after a downright rainy night. We determined, however, to go to Keswick if possible, and we set off a little after 9 o'clock. When we were upon the Raise, it snowed very much; and the whole prospect closed in upon us, like a moorland valley, upon a moor very wild. But when we were at the top of the Raise we saw the mountains before us. The sun shone upon them, here and there; and Wytheburn vale, though wild, looked soft. The day went on cheerfully and pleasantly. Now and then a hail shower attacked us; but we kept up a good heart, for Mary is a famous jockey. . . . We reached Greta Hall at about one o'clock. Met Mrs. C. in the field. Derwent in the cradle asleep. Hartley at his dinner. Derwent the image of his father. Hartley well. We wrote to C. Mrs. C. left us at 1/2 past 2. We drank tea by ourselves, the children playing about us. Mary said to Hartley, "Shall I take Derwent with me?" "No," says H., "I cannot spare my little brother," in the sweetest tone possible, "and he can't do without his mamma." "Well," says Mary, "why can't I be his mamma? Can't he have more mammas than one?" "No," says H. "What for?" "Because they do not love, and mothers do." "What is the difference between mothers and mammas?" Looking at his sleeves, "Mothers wear sleeves like this, pulling his own tight down, and mammas" (pulling them up, and making a bustle about his shoulders) "so." We parted from them at 4 o'clock. It was a little of the dusk when we set off. Cotton mills lighted up. The first star at Nadel Fell, but it was never dark. We rode very briskly. Snow upon the Raise. Reached home at seven o'clock. William at work with Chaucer, The God of Love.[40] Sate latish. I wrote a letter to Coleridge.

[. . . . .]

Tuesday, 22nd.—. . . Wm. composed a few lines of *The Pedlar.*[41] We talked about Lamb's tragedy[42] as we went down the White Moss. We stopped a long time in going to watch a little bird with a salmon-coloured breast, a white cross or T upon its wings, and a brownish back with faint stripes. . . . It began to pick upon the road at the distance of four yards from us, and advanced nearer and nearer till it came within the length of W.'s stick, without any apparent fear of us. As we came up the White Moss, we met an old man, who I saw was a beggar by his two bags hanging over his shoulder; but, from half laziness, half indifference, and wanting to try him, if he would speak, I let him pass. He said nothing, and my heart smote me. I turned back, and said, "You are begging?" "Ay," says he. I gave him [a halfpenny]. William, judging from his appearance, joined in, "I suppose you were a sailor?" "Ay," he replied, "I have been 57 years at sea, 12 of them on board a man-of-war under Sir Hugh Palmer." "Why have you not a pension?" "I have no pension, but I could have got into Greenwich hospital, but all my officers are dead." He was 75 years of age, had a freshish colour in his cheeks, grey hair, a decent hat with a binding round the edge, the hat worn brown and glossy, his shoes were small thin shoes low in the quarters, pretty good. They had belonged to a gentleman. His coat was frock shaped, coming over his thighs. It had been joined up at the seams behind with paler blue, to let it out, and there were three bell-shaped patches of darker blue behind, where the buttons had been. His breeches were either of fustian, or grey cloth, with strings hanging down, whole and tight. He had a checked shirt on, and a small coloured handkerchief tied round his neck. His bags were hung over each shoulder, and lay on each side of him, below his breast. One was brownish and of coarse stuff, the other was white with meal on the outside, and his blue waistcoat was whitened with meal.

. . . .

[40] "The Cuckoo and the Nightingale."

[41] The Pedlar is a frequent presence in this journal. Passages of the poem became part of *The Prelude,* but most find their way into *The Excursion* (1814) in which The Pedlar becomes The Wanderer.

[42] *John Woodvil.*

We overtook old Fleming [43] at Rydale, leading his little Dutchman-like grandchild along the slippery road. The same face seemed to be natural to them both—the old man and the little child—and they went hand in hand, the grandfather cautious, yet looking proud of his charge. He had two patches of new cloth at the shoulder-blades of his faded claret-coloured coat, like eyes at each shoulder, not worn elsewhere. I found Mary at home in her riding-habit, all her clothes being put up. We were very sad about Coleridge. . . . We stopped to look at the stone seat at the top of the hill. There was a white cushion upon it, round at the edge like a cushion, and the rock behind looked soft as velvet, of a vivid green, and so tempting! The snow too looked as soft as a down cushion. A young foxglove, like a star, in the centre. There were a few green lichens about it, and a few withered brackens of fern here and there upon the ground near, all else was a thick snow; no footmark to it, not the foot of a sheep. . . . We sate snugly round the fire. I read to them the Tale of Constance and the Syrian monarch, in the Man of Lawe's Tale, also some of the Prologue. . . .[44]

Wednesday, 23rd.—. . . Mary wrote out the Tales from Chaucer for Coleridge. William worked at The Ruined Cottage[45] and made himself very ill. . . . A broken soldier came to beg in the morning. Afterwards a tall woman, dressed somewhat in a tawdry style, with a long checked muslin apron, a beaver hat, and throughout what are called good clothes. Her daughter had gone before, with a soldier and his wife. She had buried her husband at Whitehaven, and was going back into Cheshire.

Thursday, 24th.—Still a thaw. Wm., Mary, and I sate comfortably round the fire in the evening, and read Chaucer. Thoughts of last year. I took out my old Journal.[46]

Friday, 25th.—Christmas Day. We received a letter from Coleridge. His letter made us uneasy about him. I was glad I was not by myself when I received it.[47]

---

[43] Thomas Fleming, proprietor of the Hare and Hounds Inn at Rydale.

[44] Selections from Chaucer's *Canterbury Tales*.

[45] Tale the Pedlar tells a young poet, incorporated into Book I of *The Excursion*.

[46] Woof speculates that this reference may be to the lost notebook. It could also be to the first part of the Grasmere journal.

[47] Dorothy's thirtieth birthday. The more complete entry, taken here from Mary Moorman's edition is: "*Friday 25th,* Christmas day. A very bad day. We drank tea at John Fisher's—we were unable to walk. I went to bed after dinner. The roads were very slippery. We received a letter from Coleridge while we were at John Fisher's. A terrible night—little John brought the letter. Coleridge poorly but better—his letter made us uneasy about him. I was glad I was not by myself when I received it" (p. 73).

Saturday, 26th.—. . . We walked to Rydale. Grasmere Lake a beautiful image of stillness, clear as glass, reflecting all things. The wind was up, and the waters sounding. The lake of a rich purple, the fields a soft yellow, the island yellowish-green, the copses red-brown, the mountains purple, the church and buildings, how quiet they were! Poor Coleridge, Sara, and dear little Derwent here last year at this time. After tea we sate by the fire comfortably. I read aloud The Miller's Tale.[48] Wrote to Coleridge. . . . Wm. wrote part of the poem to Coleridge.[49]

[. . . . .]

Monday, 28th of December.—William, Mary, and I set off on foot to Keswick. We carried some cold mutton in our pockets, and dined at John Stanley's, where they were making Christmas pies. The sun shone, but it was coldish. We parted from Wm. upon the Raise. He joined us opposite Sara's rock.[50] He was busy in composition, and sate down upon the wall. We did not see him again till we arrived at John Stanley's. There we roasted apples in the room. After we had left John Stanley's, Wm. discovered that he had lost his gloves. He turned back, but they were gone. Wm. rested often. Once he left his Spenser,[51] and Mary turned back for it, and found it upon the bank, where we had last rested. . . . We reached Greta Hall at about ½ past 5 o'clock. The children and Mrs. C. well. After tea message came from Wilkinson,[52] who had passed us on the road, inviting Wm. to sup at the Oak. He went. Met a young man (a predestined Marquis) called Johnston. He spoke to him familiarly of the L. B. He had seen a copy presented by the Queen to Mrs. Harcourt.[53] Said he saw them everywhere, and wondered they did not sell. We all went weary to bed. . . .

Tuesday, 29th.—A fine morning. A thin fog upon the hills which soon disappeared. The sun shone. Wilkinson went with us to the top of the hill. We turned out of the road at the second mile stone, and

---

[48] A bawdy *Canterbury Tale.*

[49] The autobiography later titled *The Prelude.*

[50] Carved on the "Rock of Names" on the roadside about midpoint between Dove Cottage and Keswick are WW, DW, STC, JW, SH. The rock was blasted away during the construction of a dam, but fragments are preserved at the Grasmere Wordsworth Museum.

[51] A short, woolen jacket.

[52] Probably Joshua Lucock Wilkinson, a Cockermouth friend and London solicitor who worked with Richard Wordsworth. He had come north to settle his mother's estate.

[53] The third Earl Harcourt and his wife were part of the royal family's inner circle.

passed a pretty cluster of houses at the foot of St. John's Vale. The houses were among tall trees, partly of Scotch fir, and some naked forest trees. We crossed a bridge just below these houses, and the river winded sweetly along the meadows. Our road soon led us along the sides of dreary bare hills, but we had a glorious prospect to the left of Saddleback, half-way covered with snow, and underneath the comfortable white houses and the village of Threlkeld. These houses and the village want trees about them. Skiddaw was behind us, and dear Coleridge's desert home. As we ascended the hills it grew very cold and slippery. Luckily, the wind was at our backs, and helped us on. A sharp hail shower gathered at the head of Martindale, and the view upwards was very grand—wild cottages, seen through the hurrying hail-shower. The wind drove, and eddied about and about, and the hills looked large and swelling through the storm. We thought of Coleridge. O! the bonny nooks, and windings, and curlings of the beck, down at the bottom of the steep green mossy banks. We dined at the public-house on porridge, with a second course of Christmas pies. We were well received by the landlady, and her little Jewish daughter was glad to see us again. The husband a very handsome man. While we were eating our dinner a traveller came in. He had walked over Kirkstone, that morning. We were much amused by the curiosity of the landlord and landlady to learn who he was, and by his mysterious manner of letting out a little bit of his errand, and yet telling nothing. He had business farther up in the vale. He left them with this piece of information to work upon, and I doubt not they discovered who he was and all his business before the next day at that hour. The woman told us of the riches of a Mr. Walker, formerly of Grasmere. We said, "What, does he do nothing for his relations? He has a sickly sister at Grasmere." "Why," said the man, "I daresay if they had any sons to put forward he would do it for them, but he has children of his own."

(N.B.—His fortune is above £60,000, and he has two children!!)[54]

The landlord went about a mile and a half with us to put us in the right way. The road was often very slippery, the wind high, and it was nearly dark before we got into the right road. I was often obliged to crawl on all fours, and Mary fell many a time. A stout young man whom we met on the hills, and who knew Mr. Clarkson, very kindly set us into the right road, and we inquired again near some houses and were directed, by a miserable, poverty-struck, looking woman,

[54] This gentleman's resources would make him one of the wealthiest men in England.

who had been fetching water, to go down a miry lane. We soon got into the main road and reached Mr. Clarkson's at tea time. Mary H. spent the next day with us, and we walked on Dunmallet before dinner, but it snowed a little. The day following, being New Year's Eve, we accompanied Mary to Howtown Bridge. . . .

[. . . . .]

January 3rd.—Sunday. Mary brought us letters from Sara and Coleridge and we went with her homewards to . . . [Sockbridge]. Parted at the stile on the Pooley side. Thomas Wilkinson[55] dined with us and stayed supper.

I do not recollect how the rest of our time was spent exactly. We had a very sharp frost which broke on Friday the 15th January, or rather the morning of Saturday 16th.

On Sunday the 17th we went to meet Mary. It was a mild gentle thaw. She stayed with us till Friday, 22nd January. On Thursday we dined at Mr. Myers's,[56] and on Friday, 22nd, we parted from Mary. Before our parting we sate under a wall in the sun near a cottage above Stainton Bridge. The field in which we sate sloped downwards to a nearly level meadow, round which the Emont flowed in a small half-circle as at Lochleven. The opposite bank is woody, steep as a wall, but not high, and above that bank the fields slope gently, and irregularly down to it. These fields are surrounded by tall hedges, with trees among them, and there are clumps or grovelets of tall trees here and there. Sheep and cattle were in the fields. Dear Mary! there we parted from her. I daresay as often as she passes that road she will turn in at the gate to look at this sweet prospect. There was a barn and I think two or three cottages to be seen among the trees, and slips of lawn and irregular fields. During our stay at Mr. Clarkson's we walked every day, except that stormy Thursday. We dined at Thomas Wilkinson's on Friday the 5th, and walked to Penrith for Mary. The trees were covered with hoar-frost—grasses, and trees, and hedges beautiful; a glorious sunset; frost keener than ever. Next day thaw. Mrs. Clarkson amused us with many stories of her family and of persons whom she had known. I wish I had set them down as I heard them, when they were fresh in my memory. . . . Mrs. Clarkson knew a clergyman and his wife who brought up ten children upon a curacy, sent two sons to college, and he left £1000 when he died. The wife

---

[55] Quaker friend of Thomas Clarkson and fellow abolitionist.
[56] Reverend Thomas Meyers, an uncle.

was very generous, gave food and drink to all poor people. She had a passion for feeding animals. She killed a pig with feeding it over much. When it was dead she said, "To be sure it's a great loss, but I thank God it did not die *clemmed*" (the Cheshire word for starved). Her husband was very fond of playing backgammon,[57] and used to play whenever he could get anybody to play with him. She had played much in her youth, and was an excellent player; but her husband knew nothing of this, till one day she said to him, "You're fond of backgammon, come play with me." He was surprised. She told him she had kept it to herself, while she had a young family to attend to, but that now she would play with him! So they began to play, and played every night. Mr. C. told us many pleasant stories. His journey from London to Wisbeck on foot when a schoolboy, knife and stick, postboy, etc., the white horse sleeping at the turnpike gate snoring, the turnpike man's clock ticking, the burring story, the story of the mastiff, bull-baiting by men at Wisbeck.

On Saturday, January 23rd, we left Eusemere at 10 o'clock in the morning, I behind Wm. Mr. Clarkson on his Galloway.[58] The morning not very promising, the wind cold. The mountains large and dark, but only thinly streaked with snow; a strong wind. We dined in Grisdale on ham, bread, and milk. We parted from Mr. C. at one o'clock. It rained all the way home. We struggled with the wind, and often rested as we went along. A hail shower met us before we reached the Tarn, and the way often was difficult over the snow; but at the Tarn the view closed in. We saw nothing but mists and snow: and at first the ice on the Tarn below us cracked and split, yet without water, a dull grey white. We lost our path, and could see the Tarn no longer. We made our way out with difficulty, guided by a heap of stones which we well remembered. We were afraid of being bewildered in the mists, till the darkness should overtake us. We were long before we knew that we were in the right track, but thanks to William's skill we knew it long before we could see our way before us. There was no footmark upon the snow either of man or beast. We saw four sheep before we had left the snow region. The vale of Grasmere, when the mists broke away, looked soft and grave, of a yellow hue. It was dark before we reached home. O how happy and comfortable we felt ourselves, sitting by our own fire, when we had

[57] Board game for two played with dice.
[58] Type of pony.

got off our wet clothes. We talked about the Lake of Como, read the description, looked about us, and felt that we were happy. . . .

[. . . . .]

Saturday, January 30th.—A cold dark morning. William chopped wood. I brought it in a basket. . . . He asked me to set down the story of Barbara Wilkinson's turtle dove. Barbara is an old maid. She had two turtle doves. One of them died, the first year I think. The other continued to live alone in its cage for nine years, but for one whole year it had a companion and daily visitor—a little mouse, that used to come and feed with it; and the dove would carry it and cover it over with its wings, and make a loving noise to it. The mouse, though it did not testify equal delight in the dove's company, was yet at perfect ease. The poor mouse disappeared, and the dove was left solitary till its death. It died of a short sickness, and was buried under a tree, with funeral ceremony by Barbara and her maidens, and one or two others.[59]

On *Saturday, 30th,* Wm. worked at The Pedlar all the morning. He kept the dinner waiting till four o'clock. He was much tired. . . .

Sunday, 31st.—Wm. had slept very ill. He was tired. We walked round the two lakes. Grasmere was very soft, and Rydale was extremely beautiful from the western side. Nab Scar was just topped by a cloud which, cutting it off as high as it could be cut off, made the mountain look uncommonly lofty. We sate down a long time with different plans. I always love to walk that way, because it is the way I first came to Rydale and Grasmere, and because our dear Coleridge did also. When I came with Wm., 6 and ¹/₂ years ago, it was just at sunset. There was a rich yellow light on the waters, and the islands were reflected there. Today it was grave and soft, but not perfectly calm. William says it was much such a day as when Coleridge came with him. The sun shone out before we reached Grasmere. We sate by the roadside at the foot of the Lake, close to Mary's dear name, which she had cut herself upon the stone. Wm. cut at it with his knife to make it plainer. We amused ourselves for a long time in watching the breezes, some as if they came from the bottom of the lake, spread in a circle, brushing along the surface of the water, and growing more delicate as it were thinner, and of a paler colour till they died away.

[59] William did not turn this entry into a poem. In 1951, however, Rumer Godden (1907–1998) based her children's story, *The Mousewife,* on it.

Others spread out like a peacock's tail, and some went right forward this way and that in all directions. The lake was still where these breezes were not but they made it all alive. I found a strawberry blossom in a rock. The little slender flower had more courage than the green leaves, for they were but half expanded and half grown, but the blossom was spread full out. I uprooted it rashly, and I felt as if I had been committing an outrage, so I planted it again. It will have but a stormy life of it, but let it live if it can. We found Calvert here. I brought a handkerchief full of mosses, which I placed on the chimneypiece when Calvert was gone. He dined with us, and carried away the encyclopaedias. After they were gone, I spent some time in trying to reconcile myself to the change, and in rummaging out and arranging some other books in their places. One good thing is this— there is a nice elbow place for Wm., and he may sit for the picture of John Bunyan[60] any day. Mr. Simpson drank tea with us. We paid our rent to Benson. . . .

[. . . . .]

Tuesday.—Wm. had slept better. He fell to work, and made himself unwell. We did not walk. A funeral came by of a poor woman who had drowned herself, some say because she was hardly treated by her husband; others that he was a very decent respectable man, and she but an indifferent wife. However this was, she had only been married to him last Whitsuntide and had had very indifferent health ever since. She had got up in the night, and drowned herself in the pond. She had requested to be buried beside her mother, and so she was brought in a hearse. She was followed by some very decent-looking men on horseback, her sister—Thomas Fleming's wife—in a chaise, and some others with her, and a cart full of women. Molly says folks thinks o' their mothers. Poor body, she has been little thought of by any body else. We did a little of Lessing. I attempted a fable, but my head ached; my bones were sore with the cold of the day before, and I was downright stupid. We went to bed, but not till Wm: had tired himself.

[. . . . .]

Friday, 12th.—A very fine, bright, clear, hard frost. Wm. working again. I recopied The Pedlar, but poor Wm. all the time at work. . . . In the afternoon a poor woman came, she said, to beg; . . . but she has

---

[60] In editions of *Pilgrim's Progress,* Bunyan is frequently so pictured in a woodcut.

been used to go a-begging, for she has often come here. Her father lived to the age of 105. She is a woman of strong bones, with a complexion that has been beautiful, and remained very fresh last year, but now she looks broken, and her little boy—a pretty little fellow, and whom I have loved for the sake of Basil—looks thin and pale. I observed this to her. "Aye," says she, "we have all been ill. Our house was nearly unroofed in the storm, and we lived in it so for more than a week." The child wears a ragged drab coat and a fur cap. Poor little fellow, I think he seems scarcely at all grown since the first time I saw him. William was with me when we met him in a lane going to Skelwith Bridge. He looked very pretty. He was walking lazily, in the deep narrow lane, overshadowed with the hedgerows, his meal poke hung over his shoulder. He said he "was going a laiting!" Poor creature! He now wears the same coat he had on at that time. When the woman was gone, I could not help thinking that we are not half thankful enough that we are placed in that condition of life in which we are. We do not so often bless God for this, as we wish for this £50, that £100, etc. etc. We have not, however, to reproach ourselves with ever breathing a murmur. This woman's was but a common case. The snow still lies upon the ground. Just at the closing in of the day, I heard a cart pass the door, and at the same time the dismal sound of a crying infant. I went to the window, and had light enough to see that a man was driving a cart, which seemed not to be very full, and that a woman with an infant in her arms was following close behind and a dog close to her. It was a wild, and melancholy sight. Wm. rubbed his tables after candles were lighted, and we sate a long time with the windows unclosed, and almost finished writing *The Pedlar;* but poor Wm. wore himself out, and me out, with labour. We had an affecting conversation. Went to bed at 12 o'clock.

[. . . . .]

Sunday, 14*th February.*—A fine morning. The sun shines out, but it has been a hard frost in the night. There are some little snowdrops that are afraid to put their white heads quite out, and a few blossoms of hepatica that are half-starved. Wm. left me at work altering some passages of *The Pedlar,* and went into the orchard. The fine day pushed him on to resolve, and as soon as I had read a letter to him, which I had just received from Mrs. Clarkson, he said he would go to Penrith, so Molly was despatched for the horse. I worked hard, got the writing finished, and all quite trim. I wrote to Mrs. Clarkson, and put up some letters for Mary H., and off he went in his blue spencer, and a pair of new pantaloons fresh from London. . . . I then sate over the fire, reading Ben Jonson's *Penshurst*,[61] and other things. Before sunset, I put on my shawl and walked out. The snow-covered mountains were spotted with rich sunlight, a palish buffish colour. . . . I stood at the wishing-gate, and when I came in view of Rydale, I cast a long look upon the mountains beyond. They were very white, but I concluded that Wm. would have a very safe passage over Kirkstone, and I was quite easy about him.[62]

FEBRUARY 15, 1802–MAY 2, 1802

After dinner, a little before sunset, I walked out about 20 yards above Glow–worm Rock. I met a carman, a Highlander I suppose, with four carts, the first three belonging to himself, the last evidently to a man and his family who had joined company with him, and who I guessed to be potters. The carman was cheering his horses, and talking to a little lass about ten years of age who seemed to make him her companion. She ran to the wall, and took up a large stone to support the wheel of one of his carts, and ran on before with it in her arms to be ready for him. She was a beautiful creature, and there was something uncommonly impressive in the lightness and joyousness of her manner. Her business seemed to be all pleasure—pleasure in her own motions, and the man looked at her as if he too was pleased, and spoke to her in the same tone in which he spoke to his horses. There was a wildness in her whole figure, not the wildness of a Mountain lass, but of the Road lass, a traveller from her birth, who had wanted neither food nor clothes. Her mother followed the last cart with a lovely child, perhaps about a year old, at her back, and a good-looking girl, about fifteen years old, walked beside her. All the children were like the mother. She had a very fresh complexion, but she was blown with fagging up the steep hill, and with what she carried. Her husband was helping the horse to drag the cart up by pushing it with his shoulder. I reached home, and read German till about 9 o'clock. I wrote to Coleridge. Went to bed at about 12 o'clock. . . . I slept badly, for my thoughts were full of Wm.

[61] Poem about real and idealized landscape.
[62] The second journal notebook ends here. Dorothy continues the entry in a third notebook. She writes "See the morning former book."

Monday, 15th February.—It snowed a good deal, and was terribly cold. After dinner it was fair, but I was obliged to run all the way to the foot of the White Moss, to get the least bit of warmth into me. I found a letter from C. He was much better, this was very satisfactory, but his letter was not an answer to Wm.'s which I expected. A letter from Annette. I got tea when I reached home, and then set on reading German. I wrote part of a letter to Coleridge, went to bed and slept badly.

Tuesday, 16th.—A fine morning, but I had persuaded myself not to expect Wm., I believe because I was afraid of being disappointed. I ironed all day. He came just at tea time, had only seen Mary H. for a couple of hours between Eamont Bridge and Hartshorn Tree.[63] Mrs. C. better. He had had a difficult journey over Kirkstone, and came home by Threlkeld. We spent a sweet evening. He was better, had altered *The Pedlar*. We went to bed pretty soon.

[64]*Feb. 16*—Mr. Grahame called; said he wished Wm. had been with him the other day. He was riding in a post-chaise; heard a strange cry; called to the chaise driver to stop. It was a little girl that was crying as if her heart would burst. She had got up behind the chaise, and her cloak had been caught by the wheel: she was crying after it. Mr. G. took her into the chaise, and the cloak was released, but it was torn to rags; It had been a miserable cloak before, but she had no other, and it was the greatest sorrow that could befall her. Her name was *Alice Fell*. At the next town, Mr. G. left money to buy her a new cloak.

[. . . . .]

Wednesday.—I was so unlucky as to propose to rewrite The Pedlar. Wm. got to work, and was worn to death. We did not walk. I wrote in the afternoon.

Thursday.—Before we had quite finished breakfast Calvert's man brought the horses for Wm. We had a deal to do, pens to make, poems to put in order for writing, to settle for the press, pack up; and the man came before the pens were made, and he was obliged to leave me with only two. Since he left me at half-past 11 (it is now 2) I have

[63] Local landmark linked to "Hartleap Well" in *Lyrical Ballads*.

[64] This entry is taken from Christopher Wordsworth's *Memoir*. A Glasgow solicitor, Robert Graham[e], was visiting Grasmere when he had this experience that became the basis for William's poem "Alice Fell."

been putting the drawers into order, laid by his clothes which he had thrown here and there and everywhere, filed two months' newspapers and got my dinner, 2 boiled eggs and 2 apple tarts. I have set Molly on to clean the garden a little, and I myself have walked. I transplanted some snowdrops—the Bees are busy. Wm. has a nice bright day. It was hard frost in the night. The Robins are singing sweetly. Now for my walk. I will be busy. I will look well, and be well when he comes back to me. O the Darling! Here is one of his bitten apples. I can hardly find it in my heart to throw it into the fire. . . . I walked round the two Lakes, crossed the stepping-stones at Rydale foot. Sate down where we always sit. I was full of thought about my darling. Blessings on him. I came home at the foot of our own hill under Loughrigg. They are making sad ravages in the woods. Benson's wood is going, and the woods above the River. The wind has blown down a small fir tree on the Rock that terminates John's path. I suppose the wind of Wednesday night. I read German after tea. I worked and read the L. B., enchanted with the *Idiot Boy.*[65] Wrote to Wm. and then went to bed. It snowed when I went to bed.

Friday.—First walked in the garden and orchard, a frosty sunny morning. After dinner I gathered mosses in Easedale. I saw before me sitting in the open field, upon his pack of rags, the old Ragman that I know. His coat is of scarlet in a thousand patches. When I came home Molly had shook the carpet and cleaned everything upstairs. When I see her so happy in her work, and exulting in her own importance, I often think of that affecting expression which she made use of to me one evening lately. Talking of her good luck in being in this house, "Aye, Mistress, them 'at's low laid would have been proud creatures could they but have seen where I is now, fra what they thought wud be my doom." I was tired when I reached home. I sent Molly Ashburner to Rydale. No letters. I was sadly mortified. I expected one fully from Coleridge. Wrote to William, read the L. B, got into sad thoughts, tried at German, but could not go on. Read L. B. Blessings on that brother of mine! Beautiful new moon over Silver How.

Friday Morning.—A very cold sunshiny frost. I wrote *The Pedlar,* and finished it before I went to Mrs. Simpson's to drink tea. Miss S. at Keswick, but she came home. Mrs. Jameson came in and stayed supper. Fletcher's carts went past and I let them go with William's letter. Mr. B. S. came nearly home with me. I found letters from Wm., Mary,

[65] Much ridiculed in the reviews of *Lyrical Ballads.*

and Coleridge. I wrote to C. Sat up late, and could not fall asleep when I went to bed.

. . . .

Sunday Morning.—A very fine, clear frost. I stitched up *The Pedlar;* wrote out *Ruth;* read it with the alterations, then wrote Mary H. Read a little German, . . . and in came William, I did not expect him till to-morrow. How glad I was. After we had talked about an hour, I gave him his dinner. We sate talking and happy. He brought two new stanzas of *Ruth.* . . .

Monday Morning.—A soft rain and mist. We walked to Rydale for letters. The Vale looked very beautiful in excessive simplicity, yet, at the same time, in uncommon obscurity. The Church stood alone—mountains behind. The meadows looked calm and rich, bordering on the still lake. Nothing else to be seen but lake and island. . . .

On Friday evening the moon hung over the northern side of the highest point of Silver How, like a gold ring snapped in two, and shaven off at the ends. Within this ring lay the circle of the round moon, as distinctly to be seen as ever the enlightened moon is. William had observed the same appearance at Keswick, perhaps at the very same moment, hanging over the Newland Fells. Sent off a letter to Mary H., also to Coleridge, and Sara, and rewrote in the evening the alterations of *Ruth,* which we sent off at the same time.

Tuesday Morning.—William was reading in Ben Jonson. He read me a beautiful poem on Love. . . . We sate by the fire in the evening, and read *The Pedlar* over. William worked a little, and altered it in a few places. . . .

Wednesday.—. . . Wm. read in Ben Jonson in the morning. I read a little German. We then walked to Rydale. No letters. They are slashing away in Benson's wood. William has since tea been talking about publishing the Yorkshire Wolds Poem[66] with *The Pedlar.*

Thursday.—A fine morning. William worked at the poem of *The Singing Bird.*[67] Just as we were sitting down to dinner we heard Mr. Clarkson's voice. I ran down, William followed. He was so finely mounted that William was more intent upon the horse than the rider, an offence easily forgiven, for Mr. Clarkson was as proud of it himself as he well could be. . . .

[66] "Peter Bell."

[67] "The Sailor's Mother."

Friday.—A very fine morning. We went to see Mr. Clarkson off. The sun shone while it rained, and the stones of the walls and the pebbles on the road glittered like silver. . . . William finished his poem of *The Singing Bird*. In the meantime I read the remainder of Lessing. In the evening after tea William wrote *Alice Fell*. He went to bed tired, with a wakeful mind and a weary body. . . .

Saturday Morning.—It was as cold as ever it has been all winter, very hard frost. . . . William finished *Alice Fell,* and then wrote the poem of *The Beggar Woman,* taken from a woman whom I had seen in May (now nearly two years ago)[68] when John and he were at Gallow Hill. I sate with him at intervals all the morning, took down his stanzas, etc. . . . After tea I read to William that account of the little boy belonging to the tall woman, and an unlucky thing it was, for he could not escape from those very words, and so he could not write the poem. He left it unfinished, and went tired to bed. In our walk from Rydale he had got warmed with the subject, and had half cast the poem.

Sunday Morning.—William . . . got up at nine o'clock, but before he rose he had finished The Beggar Boy, and while we were at breakfast . . . he wrote the poem To a Butterfly! He ate not a morsel, but sate with his shirt neck unbuttoned, and his waistcoat open while he did it. The thought first came upon him as we were talking about the pleasure we both always felt at the sight of a butterfly. I told him that I used to chase them a little, but that I was afraid of brushing the dust off their wings, and did not catch them. He told me how he used to kill all the white ones when he went to school because they were Frenchmen. . . . I wrote it down and the other poems, and I read them all over to him. . . . William began to try to alter The Butterfly, and tired himself. . . .

Monday Morning.—We sate reading the poems, and I read a little German. . . . During W.'s absence a sailor who was travelling from Liverpool to Whitehaven called, he was faint and pale when he knocked at the door—a young man very well dressed. We[69] sate by the kitchen fire talking with him for two hours. He told us interesting stories of his life. His name was Isaac Chapel. He had been at sea since he was 15 years old. He was by trade a sail-maker. His last

[68] Entry of June 10, 1800, describing encounter of May 27, pp. 30–31.
[69] Probably their Ambleside friend Mr. Luff, who had come to call in the morning before William goes on an errand.

voyage was to the coast of Guinea. He had been on board a slave ship, the captain's name Maxwell, where one man had been killed, a boy put to lodge with the pigs and was half eaten, set to watch in the hot sun till he dropped down dead. He had been away in North America and had travelled thirty days among the Indians, where he had been well treated. He had twice swam from a King's ship in the night and escaped. He said he would rather be in hell than be pressed.[70] He was now going to wait in England to appear against Captain Maxwell. "O he's a Rascal, Sir, he ought to be put in the papers!" The poor man had not been in bed since Friday night. He left Liverpool at 2 o'clock on Saturday morning; he had called at a farm house to beg victuals and had been refused. The woman said she would give him nothing. "Won't you? Then I can't help it." He was excessively like my brother John.

Tuesday.—William went up into the orchard . . . and wrote a part of *The Emigrant Mother.* After dinner I read him to sleep. I read Spenser. . . . We walked to look at Rydale. The moon was a good height above the mountains. She seemed far distant in the sky. There were two stars beside her, that twinkled in and out, and seemed almost like butterflies in motion and lightness. They looked to be far nearer to us than the moon.

Wednesday.—William went up into the orchard and finished the poem. I went and sate with W. and walked backwards and forwards in the orchard till dinner time. He read me his poem. I read to him, and my Beloved slept. A sweet evening as it had been a sweet day, and I walked quietly along the side of Rydale lake with quiet thoughts— the hills and the lake were still—the owls had not begun to hoot, and the little birds had given over singing. I looked before me and saw a red light upon Silver How as if coming out of the vale below,

> There was a light of most strange birth,
> A light that came out of the earth,
> And spread along the dark hill-side.[71]

Thus I was going on when I saw the shape of my Beloved in the road at a little distance. We turned back to see the light but it was

[70] Young men were often impressed or forcibly taken into service.

[71] Darbishire proposes lost lines from "Peter Bell." Woof, noting that the next day Dorothy refers to her attempt to write at poetry, wonders if these are Dorothy's own lines.

fading—almost gone. The owls hooted when we sate on the wall at the foot of White Moss; the sky broke more and more, and we saw the moon now and then. John Gill[72] passed us with his cart; we sate on. When we came in sight of our own dear Grasmere, the vale looked fair and quiet in the moonshine, the Church was there and all the cottages. There were huge slow-travelling clouds in the sky, that threw large masses of shade upon some of the mountains. We walked backwards and forwards, between home and Olliff's, till I was tired. William kindled, and began to write the poem. We carried cloaks into the orchard, and sate a while there. I left him, and he nearly finished the poem. I was tired to death, and went to bed before him. He came down to me, and read the poem to me in bed. A sailor begged here to-day, going to Glasgow. He spoke cheerfully in a sweet tone.

Thursday.—Rydale vale was full of life and motion. The wind blew briskly, and the lake was covered all over with bright silver waves, that were there each the twinkling of an eye, then others rose up and took their place as fast as they went away. The rocks glittered in the sunshine. The crows and the ravens were busy, and the thrushes and little birds sang. I went through the fields, and sate for an hour afraid to pass a cow. The cow looked at me, and I looked at the cow, and whenever I stirred the cow gave over eating. . . . A parcel came in from Birmingham with Lamb's play for us, and for C. . . . As we came along Ambleside vale in the twilight, it was a grave evening. There was something in the air that compelled me to various thoughts—the hills were large, closed in by the sky. . . . Night was come on, and the moon was overcast. But, as I climbed the moss, the moon came out from behind a mountain mass of black clouds. O, the unutterable darkness of the sky, and the earth below the moon, and the glorious brightness of the moon itself! There was a vivid sparkling streak of light at this end of Rydale water, but the rest was very dark, and Loughrigg Fell and Silver How were white and bright, as if they were covered with hoar frost. The moon retired again, and appeared and disappeared several times before I reached home. Once there was no moonlight to be seen but upon the island-house and the promontory of the island where it stands. "That needs must be a holy place," etc. etc.[73] I had many very exquisite feelings, and when I saw this

---

[72] "Gill" in Knight, but probably John Green, the butcher.

[73] Woof suggests the line paraphrases "Home at Grasmere," or, perhaps is again Dorothy's own.

lowly Building in the waters, among the dark and lofty hills, with that bright, soft light upon it, it made me more than half a poet. I was tired when I reached home, and could not sit down to reading. I tried to write verses, but alas! I gave up, expecting William, and went soon to bed.

[. . . . .]

Monday.—A rainy day. William very poorly. 2 letters from Sara, and one from poor Annette. Wrote to my brother Richard. We talked a good deal about C. and other interesting things. We resolved to see Annette, and that Wm. should go to Mary. Wm. wrote to Coleridge not to expect us till Thursday or Friday.

Tuesday.—A mild morning. William worked at *The Cuckoo* poem. I sewed beside him. . . . I read German, and, at the closing-in of day, went to sit in the orchard. William came to me, and walked backwards and forwards. We talked about C. Wm. repeated the poem to me. I left him there, and in 20 minutes he came in, rather tired with attempting to write. He is now reading Ben Jonson. I am going to read German. It is about 10 o'clock, a quiet night. The fire flickers, and the watch ticks. I hear nothing save the breathing of my Beloved as he now and then pushes his book forward, and turns over a leaf . . .

Wednesday.—It was a beautiful spring morning, warm, and quiet with mists. We found a letter from M. H. I made a vow that we would not leave this country for G. Hill. . . . William altered *The Butterfly* as we came from Rydale. . . .

Thursday.—. . . No letter from Coleridge.

Friday.—. . . William wrote to Annette, then worked at *The Cuckoo*. . . . After dinner I sate 2 hours in the orchard. William and I walked together after tea, to the top of White Moss. I left Wm. and while he was absent I wrote out poems. I grew alarmed, and went to seek him. I met him at Mr. Ollif's. He has been trying, without success, to alter a passage—his *Silver How* poem.[74] He had written a conclusion just before he went out. While I was getting into bed, he wrote *The Rainbow*.

Saturday.—A divine morning. At breakfast William wrote part of an ode.[75] . . . We sate all day in the orchard.

[. . . . .]

---

[74] Moorman suggests "The Firgrove."

[75] Probably the first four stanzas of "Ode: Intimations of Immortality."

Monday, 12th.—. . . The ground covered with snow. Walked to T. Wilkinson's and sent for letters. The woman brought me one from William and Mary. It was a sharp, windy night. Thomas Wilkinson came with me to Barton, and questioned me like a catechiser all the way. Every question was like the snapping of a little thread about my heart. I was so full of thought of my half-read letter and other things. I was glad when he left me. Then I had time to look at the moon while I was thinking my own thoughts. The moon travelled through the clouds, tinging them yellow as she passed along, with two stars near her, one larger than the other. These stars grew and diminished as they passed from; or went into, the clouds. At this time William, as I found the next day, was riding by himself between Middleham and Barnard Castle. . . .

Tuesday, 13th April.—. . . Mrs. C. waked me from sleep with a letter from Coleridge. . . . I walked along the lake side. The air was become still, the lake was of a bright slate colour, the hills darkening. The bays shot into the low fading shores. Sheep resting. All things quiet. When I returned William was come. The surprise shot through me. . . .

. . . .

Thursday, 15th—It was a threatening, misty morning, but mild. We set off after dinner from Eusemere. Mrs. Clarkson went a short way with us, but turned back. The wind was furious, and we thought we must have returned. We first rested in the large boathouse, then under a furze bush opposite Mr. Clarkson's. Saw the plough going in the field. The wind seized our breath. The lake was rough. There was a boat by itself floating in the middle of the bay below Water Millock. We rested again in the Water Millock Lane. The hawthorns are black and green, the birches here and there greenish, but there is yet more of purple to be seen on the twigs. We got over into a field to avoid some cows—people working. A few primroses by the roadside— woodsorrel flower, the anemone, scentless violets, strawberries, and that starry, yellow flower which Mrs. C. calls pile wort. When we were in the woods beyond Gowbarrow Park we saw a few daffodils close to the water-side. We fancied that the sea had floated the seeds ashore, and that the little colony had so sprung up. But as we went along there were more and yet more; and at last, under the boughs of the trees, we saw that there was a long belt of them along the shore, about the breadth of a country turnpike road. I never saw daffodils so beautiful. They grew among the mossy stones about and above them; some rested their heads upon these stones, as on a pillow, for weariness; and the rest tossed and reeled and danced, and seemed as if they verily laughed with the wind, that blew upon them over the lake; they looked so gay, ever glancing, ever changing. This wind blew directly over the lake to them. There was here and there a little knot, and a few stragglers higher up; but they were so few as not to disturb the simplicity, unity, and life of that one busy highway. We rested again and again.[76] The bays were stormy, and we heard the waves at different distances, and in the middle of the water, like the sea. . . . All was cheerless and gloomy, so we faced the storm. At Dobson's[77] I was very kindly treated by a young woman. The landlady looked sour, but it is her way. . . . William was sitting by a good fire when I came downstairs. He soon made his way to the library, piled up in a corner of the window. He brought out a volume of Enfield's *Speaker*, another miscellany, and an odd volume of Congreve's plays.[78] We had a glass of warm rum and water. We enjoyed ourselves, and wished for Mary. It rained and blew, when we went to bed.

Friday, 16th April (Good Friday).—When I undrew curtains in the morning, I was much affected by the beauty of the prospect, and the change. The sun shone, the wind had passed away, the hills looked cheerful, the river was very bright as it flowed into the lake. The church rises up behind a little knot of rocks, the steeple not so high as an ordinary three-story house. Trees in a row in the garden under the wall. The valley is at first broken by little woody knolls that make retiring places, fairy valleys in the vale, the river winds along under these hills, travelling, not in a bustle but not slowly, to the lake. We saw a fisherman in the flat meadow on the other side of the water. He came towards us, and threw his line over the two–arched bridge. It is a bridge of a heavy construction, almost bending inwards in the middle, but it is grey, and there is a look of anciency in the architecture of it that pleased me. As we go on the vale opens out more into

[76] See William's "I wandered lonely as a cloud" (1807), popularly called "The Daffodils", pp. 255–56.

[77] A local inn.

[78] In 1774, William Enfield (1741–1797) published a popular book on elocution: *The Speaker: or, Miscellaneous Pieces, selected from the best English Writers, and disposed under proper heads, with a view to facilitate the Improvement of Youth in Reading and Speaking.* It is interesting to note that Mary Wollstonecraft cites Enfield's innovative thinking in the introduction to her *The Female Reader: or Miscellaneous pieces in Prose and Verse: Selected from the Best Writers, and Disposed under Proper Heads: for the Improvement of Young Women,* which she published in 1798 under the name of Mr. Cresswick. William Congreve (1670–1729): Restoration playwright.

one vale, with somewhat of a cradle bed. Cottages, with groups of trees, on the side of the hills. We passed a pair of twin children, two years old. Sate on the next bridge which we crossed—a single arch. We rested again upon the turf, and looked at the same bridge. We observed arches in the water, occasioned by the large stones sending it down in two streams. A sheep came plunging through the river, stumbled up the bank, and passed close to us. It had been frightened by an insignificant little dog on the other side. Its fleece dropped a glittering shower under its belly. Primroses by the road-side, pile wort that shone like stars of gold in the sun, violets, strawberries, retired and half-buried among the grass. When we came to the foot of Brothers Water, I left William sitting on the bridge, and went along the path on the right side of the lake through the wood. I was delighted with what I saw. The water under the boughs of the bare old trees, the simplicity of the mountains, and the exquisite beauty of the path. There was one grey cottage. I repeated *The Glow-worm*,[79] as I walked along. I hung over the gate, and thought I could have stayed for ever. When I returned, I found William writing a poem descriptive of the sights and sounds we saw and heard. There was the gentle flowing of the stream, the glittering, lively lake, green fields without a living creature to be seen on them; behind us, a flat pasture with forty-two cattle feeding; to our left, the road leading to the hamlet. No smoke there, the sun shone on the bare roofs. The people were at work ploughing, harrowing, and sowing; . . . a dog barking now and then, cocks crowing, birds twittering, the snow in patches at the top of the highest hills, yellow palms, purple and green twigs on the birches, ashes with their glittering stems quite bare. The hawthorn a bright green, with black stems under the oak. The moss of the oak glossy. We went on. Passed two sisters at work (they first passed us), one with two pitchforks in her hand, the other had a spade. We had come to talk with them. They laughed long after we were gone, perhaps half in wantonness, half boldness. William finished his poem. Before we got to the foot of Kirkstone, there were hundreds of cattle in the vale. There we ate our dinner. The walk up Kirkstone was very interesting. The becks[80] among the rocks were all alive. William showed me the little mossy streamlet which he had before loved when he saw its bright green track in the snow. The view above Ambleside very beautiful. There we sate and looked down on the green vale. We watched the crows at

---

[79] Poem William wrote for Dorothy after visiting Mary.
[80] Little streams.

a little distance from us become white as silver as they flew in the sunshine, and when they went still further, they looked like shapes of water passing over the green fields. The whitening of Ambleside church is a great deduction from the beauty of it, seen from this point. We called at the Luffs, the Roddingtons there. Did not go in, and went round by the fields. I pulled off my stockings, intending to wade the beck, but I was obliged to put them on, and we climbed over the wall at the bridge. The post passed us. No letters. Rydale Lake was in its own evening brightness: the Island, and Points distinct. Jane Ashburner came up to us when we were sitting upon the wall. The garden looked pretty in the half-moonlight, half-daylight, as we went up the vale. . . .

Saturday 17th.—A mild warm rain. We sate in the garden all the morning. William dug a little. I transplanted a honey-suckle. The lake was still. The sheep on the island, reflected in the water, like the grey-deer we saw in Gowbarrow Park. We walked after tea by moonlight. I had been in bed in the afternoon, and William had slept in his chair. We walked towards Rydale backwards and forwards below Mr. Olliff's. The village was beautiful in the moonlight. Helm Crag we observed very distinct. The dead hedge round Benson's field bound together at the top by an interlacing of ash sticks, which made a chain of silver when we faced the moon. A letter from C. and also one from S. H. I saw a robin chasing a scarlet butterfly this morning.

Sunday, 18th.—Again a mild grey morning, with rising vapours. We sate in the orchard. William wrote the poem on The Robin and the Butterfly.[81] . . . William met me at Rydale . . . with the conclusion of the poem of the Robin. I read it to him in bed. We left out some lines.

. . . .

Tuesday, 20th.—A beautiful morning. The sun shone. William wrote a conclusion to the poem of the Butterfly:—

I've watched you now a full half-hour.

I was quite out of spirits, and went into the orchard. When I came in, he had finished the poem. It was a beautiful afternoon. The sun shone upon the level fields, and they grew greener beneath the eye. Houses, village, all cheerful—people at work. We sate in the orchard

[81] See William's "The Redbreast Chasing the Butterfly." pp. 256–57.

and repeated The Glow-worm and other poems. Just when William came to a well or trough, which there is in Lord Darlington's park, he began to write that poem of The Glow-worm; . . . interrupted in going through the town of Staindrop, finished it about 2 miles and a half beyond Staindrop. He did not feel the jogging of the horse while he was writing; but, when he had done, he felt the effect of it, and his fingers were cold with his gloves. His horse fell with him on the other side of St. Helens, Auckland. So much for *The Glow-worm*. It was written coming from Middleham on Monday, 12th April 1802. . . . On Tuesday 20th, when we were sitting after tea, Coleridge came to the door. I startled him with my voice. C. came up fatigued, but I afterwards found he looked well. William was not well, and I was in low spirits.

[. . . . .]

Thursday, 29th.—. . . After I had written down *The Tinker,* which William finished this morning, Luff called. He was very lame, limped into the kitchen. He came on a little pony. We then went to John's Grove, sate a while at first; afterwards William lay, and I lay in the trench under the fence—he with his eyes shut, and listening to the waterfalls and the birds. There was no one waterfall above another—it was a sound of water in the air—the voice of the air. William heard me breathing, and rustling now and then, but we both lay still, and unseen by one another. He thought that it would be so sweet thus to lie in the grave, to hear the peaceful sounds of the earth, and just to know that our dear friends were near. The lake was still; there was a boat out. Silver How reflected with delicate purple and yellowish hues, as I have seen spar; lambs on the island, and running races together by the half-dozen, in the round field near us. The copses greenish, hawthorns green, . . . cottages smoking. As I lay down on the grass, I observed the glittering silver line on the ridge of the backs of the sheep, owing to their situation respecting the sun, which made them look beautiful, but with something of strangeness, like animals of another kind, as if belonging to a more splendid world. . . . I got mullins[82] and pansies. . . .

Friday, April 30th.—We came into the orchard directly after breakfast, and sate there. The lake was calm, the day cloudy. . . . Two fishermen by the lake side. William began to write the poem of *The Celandine*[83] . . . Walked backwards and forwards with William—he

[82] Probably mulleins: a tall plant with coarse leaves and bright flowers.
[83] "To the Small Celandine," published 1807.

repeated his poem to me, then he got to work again and would not give over. He had not finished his dinner till 5 o'clock. After dinner we took up the fur gown into the Hollins above. We found a sweet seat, and thither we will often go. We spread the gown, put on each a cloak, and there we lay. William fell asleep, he had a bad headache owing to his having been disturbed the night before, with reading C.'s letter. I did not sleep, but lay with half-shut eyes looking at the prospect as on a vision almost, I was so resigned to it. Loughrigg Fell was the most distant hill, then came the lake, slipping in between the copses. Above the copse, the round swelling field; nearer to me, a wild intermixture of rocks, trees, and patches of grassy ground. When we turned the corner of our little shelter, we saw the church and the whole vale. It is a blessed place. The birds were about us on all sides. Skobbies, robins, bull-finches, and crows, now and then flew over our heads, as we were warned by the sound of the beating of the air above. We stayed till the light of day was going, and the little birds had begun to settle their singing. But there was a thrush not far off, that seemed to sing louder and clearer than the thrushes had sung when it was quite day. We came in at 8 o'clock, got tea, wrote to Coleridge, and I wrote to Mrs. Clarkson part of a letter. We went to bed at 20 minutes past 11, with prayers that William might sleep well.

Saturday, May 1st.—Rose not till half-past 8, a heavenly morning. As soon as breakfast was over, we went into the garden, and sowed the scarlet beans about the house. It was a clear sky.

I sowed the flowers, William helped me. We then went and sate in the orchard till dinner time. It was very hot. William wrote *The Celandine*. We planned a shed, for the sun was too much for us. After dinner, we went again to our old resting-place in the Hollins under the rock. We first lay under the Holly, where we saw nothing but the holly tree, and a budding elm tree mossed, with the sky above our heads. But that holly tree had a beauty about it more than its own, knowing as we did when we arose. When the sun had got low enough, we went to the Rock Shade. Oh, the overwhelming beauty of the vale below, greener than green! Two ravens flew high, high in the sky, and the sun shone upon their bellies and their wings, long after there was none of his light to be seen but a little space on the top of Loughrigg Fell. Heard the cuckoo to-day, this first of May. We went down to tea at 8 o'clock, and returned after tea. The landscape was fading: sheep and lambs quiet among the rocks. We walked towards King's, and backwards and forwards.

The sky was perfectly cloudless. *N.B.* it is often so. Three solitary stars in the middle of the blue vault, one or two on the points of the high hills. . . .[84]

MAY 4, 1802–JANUARY 16, 1803

Tuesday, 4th May.—Though William went to bed nervous, and jaded in the extreme, he rose refreshed. I wrote out *The Leech Gatherer* for him, which he had begun the night before, and of which he wrote several stanzas in bed this morning. [They started to walk to Wytheburn.] It was very hot. . . . We rested several times by the way,—read, and repeated *The Leech Gatherer*. . . . We saw Coleridge on the Wytheburn side of the water; he crossed the beck to us. Mr. Simpson was fishing there. William and I ate luncheon, and then went on towards the waterfall. It is a glorious wild solitude under that lofty purple crag. It stood upright by itself; its own self, and its shadow below, one mass; all else was sunshine. We went on further. A bird at the top of the crag was flying round and round, and looked in thinness and transparency, shape and motion like a moth. . . . We climbed the hill, but looked in vain for a shade, except at the foot of the great waterfall. We came down, and rested upon a moss-covered rock rising out of the bed of the river. There we lay, ate our dinner, and stayed there till about four o'clock or later. William and Coleridge repeated and read verses. I drank a little brandy and water, and was in heaven. The stag's horn is very beautiful and fresh, springing upon the fells; mountain ashes, green. We drank tea at a farm house. . . . We parted from Coleridge at Sara's crag, after having looked for the letters which C. carved in the morning. I missed them all. William deepened the X with C.'s pen-knife. We sate afterwards on the wall, seeing the sun go down, and the reflections in the still water. C. looked well, and parted from us cheerfully, hopping upon the side stones. On the Raise we met a woman with two little girls, one in her arms, the other, about four years old, walking by her side, a pretty little thing, but half-starved. . . . Young as she was, she walked carefully with them. Alas, too young for such cares and such travels. The mother, when we accosted her, told us how her husband had left her, and gone off with another woman, and how she "pursued'" them. Then her fury kindled, and her eyes rolled about. She changed again to tears. She was a Cockermouth woman, thirty years

---

[84] A short entry of May 2 is the last in notebook three.

of age—a child at Cockermouth when I was. I was moved, and gave her a shilling. . . . We had the crescent moon with the "auld moon in her arms."[85] We rested often, always upon the bridges. Reached home at about ten o'clock. . . . We went soon to bed. I repeated verses to William while he was in bed; he was soothed, and I left him. "This is the spot"[86] over and over again.

Wednesday, 5th May.—A very fine morning, rather cooler than yesterday. We planted three-fourths of the bower. I made bread. We sate in the orchard. The thrush sang all day, as he always sings. I wrote to the Hutchinsons, and to Coleridge. Packed off *Thalaba*.[87] William had kept off work till near bed-time, when we returned from our walk. Then he began again, and went to bed very nervous. We walked in the twilight, and walked till night came on. The moon had the old moon in her arms, but not so plain to be seen as the night before. When we went to bed it was a boat without the circle. I read *The Lover's Complaint*[88] to William in bed, and left him composed.

Thursday, 6th May.—A sweet morning. We have put the finishing stroke to our bower, and here we are sitting in the orchard. It is one o'clock. We are sitting upon a seat under the wall, which I found my brother building up, when I came to him. . . . He had intended that it should have been done before I came. It is a nice, cool, shady spot. The small birds are singing, lambs bleating, cuckoos calling, the thrush sings by fits, Thomas Ashburner's axe is going quietly (without passion) in the orchard, hens are cackling, flies humming, the women talking together at their doors, plum and pear trees are in blossom—apple trees greenish—the opposite woods green, the crows are cawing, we have heard ravens, the ash trees are in blossom, birds flying all about us, the stitchwort is coming out, there is one budding lychnis, the primroses are passing their prime, celandine, violets, and

---

[85] A portent of disaster in "The Ballad of Sir Patrick Spence"; STC used the full syntax as epigraph to "Dejection: An Ode."

[86] Eleven lines that William never published together, the last six appear in "Ode to Lycoris": This is the spot—how mildly does the sun / Shine in between the fading leaves! The air / In the habitual silence of this wood / Is more than silent; and this bed of heath- / Where shall we find so sweet a resting-place? / Come, let me see thee sink into a dream / Of quiet thoughts, protracted till thine eye / Be calm as water when the winds are gone / And no one can tell whither. My sweet Friend, / We two have had such happy hours together / That my heart melts in me to think of it.

[87] *Thalaba the Destroyer* (1801), a twelve-book epic poem by Robert Southey, ridiculed along with the *Lyrical Ballads* by Francis Jeffrey in the first number of *The Edinburgh Review* (1802).

[88] "A [not The] Lover's Complaint" is a poem by Shakespeare.

wood sorrel for ever more, little geraniums and pansies on the wall. We walked in the evening to Tail End, to inquire about hurdles for the orchard shed. . . . When we came in we found a magazine, and review, and a letter from Coleridge, verses to Hartley, and Sara H. We read the review, etc. The moon was a perfect boat, a silver boat, when we were out in the evening. The birch tree is all over green in small leaf, more light and elegant than when it is full out. It bent to the breezes, as if for the love of its own delightful motions. Sloe-thorns and hawthorns in the hedges.

Friday, 7th May.—William had slept uncommonly well, so, feeling himself strong, he fell to work at *The Leech Gatherer;* he wrote hard at it till dinnertime, then he gave over, tired to death—he had finished the poem. I was making Derwent's frocks.[89] After dinner we sate in the orchard. It was a thick, hazy, dull air. The thrush sang almost continually; the little birds were more than usually busy with their voices. The sparrows are now full fledged. The nest is so full that they lie upon one another; they sit quietly in their nest with closed mouths. I walked to Rydale after tea, which we drank by the kitchen fire. The evening very dull; a terrible kind of threatening brightness at sunset above Easedale. The sloe-thorn beautiful in the hedges, and in the wild spots higher up among the hawthorns. No letters. William met me. He had been digging in my absence, and cleaning the well. We walked up beyond Lewthwaites. A very dull sky; coolish; crescent moon now and then. I had a letter brought me from Mrs. Clarkson while we were walking in the orchard. I observed the sorrel leaves opening at about nine o'clock. William went to bed tired with thinking about a poem.

[. . . . .]

Tuesday, 11th May.—A cool air. William finished the stanzas about C. and himself. He did not go out to-day. Miss Simpson came in to tea, which was lucky enough, for it interrupted his labours. I walked with her to Rydale. The evening cool; the moon only now and then to be seen; the lake purple as we went; primroses still in abundance. William did not meet me. He completely finished his poem, I finished Derwent's frocks. We went to bed at twelve o'clock. . . .

[. . . . .]

---

[89] Young boys wore frocks until about five years of age.

Saturday, 15th.—A very cold and cheerless morning. I sate mending stockings all the morning. I read in Shakespeare. William lay very late because he slept ill last night. It snowed this morning just like Christmas. We had a melancholy letter from Coleridge at bedtime. It distressed me very much, and I resolved upon going to Keswick the next day.

* * * * * [The following is written on the blotting-paper opposite this date:—] * * * *

S. T. Coleridge.

Dorothy Wordsworth. William Wordsworth.

Mary Hutchinson. Sara Hutchinson.

William. Coleridge. Mary.

Dorothy. Sara.

16th May

1802. John Wordsworth.

[. . . . .]

Saturday, 29th.—. . . William finished his poem on going for Mary. I wrote it out. I wrote to Mary H., having received a letter from her in the evening. A sweet day. We nailed up the honeysuckles, and hoed the scarlet beans.

Monday, 31st.—. . . We sat out all the day. . . . I wrote out the poem on "Our Departure," [90] which he seemed to have finished. In the evening Miss Simpson brought us a letter from M. H., and a complimentary and critical letter to W. from John Wilson of Glasgow. [91] . . .

. . . .

---

[90] "A Farewell" (1807).

[91] Seventeen-year old Glasgow undergraduate John Wilson wrote a thoughtful letter to William about *Lyrical Ballads* and eventually became a close family friend. In 1817 he helped found *Blackwood's Magazine,* to which he frequently contributed as Christopher North. Dorothy notes that the letter is "Post Paid." In the entry of Saturday, June 5, she writes that William begins his reply, and that on the next day she helps him with it.

Knight does not include the end of this entry, a comment about her teeth that expresses her ever-growing anxiety about losing William to marriage. "My tooth broke today. They will soon be gone. Let that pass I shall be beloved—I want no more."

Tuesday.—A very sweet day, but a sad want of rain. We went into the orchard after I had written to M. H. Then on to Mr. Olliff's intake. . . . The columbine was growing upon the rocks; here and there a solitary plant, sheltered and shaded by the tufts and bowers of trees. It is a graceful slender creature, a female seeking retirement, and growing freest and most graceful when it is most alone. I observed that the more shaded plants were always the tallest. A short note and gooseberries from Coleridge. We walked upon the turf near John's Grove. It was a lovely night. The clouds of the western sky reflected a saffron light upon the upper end of the lake. All was still. We went to look at Rydale. There was an Alpine, fire-like red upon the tops of the mountains. This was gone when we came in view of the lake. But we saw the lake from a new and most beautiful point of view, between two little rocks, and behind a small ridge that had concealed it from us. This White Moss, a place made for all kinds of beautiful works of art and nature, woods and valleys, fairy valleys and fairy tarns, miniature mountains, alps above alps.

Wednesday, 2nd June.—In the morning we observed that the scarlet beans were drooping in the leaves in great numbers, owing, we guess, to an insect. . . . Yesterday an old man called, a grey-headed man, above seventy years of age. He said he had been a soldier, that his wife and children had died in Jamaica.[92] He had a beggar's wallet over his shoulders; a coat of shreds and patches, altogether of a drab colour; he was tall, and though his body was bent, he had the look of one used to have been upright. I talked a while, and then gave him a piece of cold bacon and some money. Said he, "You're a fine woman!" I could not help smiling; I suppose he meant, "You're a kind woman." Afterwards a woman called, travelling to Glasgow. After dinner we went into Frank's field, crawled up the little glen, and planned a seat. . . . found a beautiful shell-like purple fungus in Frank's field. After tea we walked to Butterlip How, and backwards and forwards there. All the young oak tree leaves are dry as powder. A cold south wind, portending rain. . . .

Thursday, 3rd June 1802.—A very fine rain. I lay in my bed till ten o'clock. William much better than yesterday. We walked into Easedale. . . . The cuckoo sang, and we watched the little birds as we sate at the door of the cow-house. The oak copses are brown, as

---

[92] A soldier there would probably have worked to keep order on plantations and to control the slaves. Many in the army became ill and were shipped home to join the displaced population Dorothy describes. Some married Jamaican women, as perhaps this man had done.

in autumn, with the late frosts. . . . We have been reading the life and some of the writings of poor Logan since dinner. There are many affecting lines and passages in his poem, *e.g.*

And everlasting longings for the lost.[93]

. . . William is now sleeping with the window open, lying on the window seat. The thrush is singing. There are, I do believe, a thousand buds on the honeysuckle tree, all small and far from blowing, save one that is retired behind the twigs close to the wall, and as snug as a bird nest. John's rose tree is very beautiful, blended with the honeysuckle.

Yesterday morning William walked as far as the Swan with Aggy Fisher, who was going to attend upon Goan's dying infant. She said, "There are many heavier crosses than the death of an infant;" and went on, "There was a woman in this vale who buried four grown-up children in one year, and I have heard her say, when many years were gone by, that she had more pleasure in thinking of those four than of her living children, for as children get up and have families of their own, their duty to their parents *wears out and weakens*. She could trip lightly by the graves of those who died when they were young . . . as she went to church on a Sunday."

. . . A very affecting letter came from M. H., while I was sitting in the window reading Milton's *Penserosa* to William. I answered this letter before I went to bed.

. . . .

Wednesday, 16th.—We walked towards Rydale for letters. . . . One from Mary. We went up into Rydale woods and read it there. We sate near the old wall, which fenced a hazel grove, which William said was exactly like the filbert grove at Middleham. It is a beautiful spot, a sloping or rather steep piece of ground, with hazels growing "tall and erect" in clumps at distances, almost seeming regular, as if they had been planted. . . . I wrote to Mary after dinner, while William sate in the orchard. . . . I spoke of the little birds keeping us company, and William told me that that very morning a bird had perched upon his leg. He had been lying very still, and had watched this little creature. It had come under the bench where he

[93] From "Ode: written in a visit to the country in autumn," by John Logan (1748–1788), a poet and preacher subject to bouts of extreme depression.

was sitting. . . . He thoughtlessly stirred himself to look further at it, and it flew on to the apple tree above him. It was a little young creature that had just left its nest, equally unacquainted with man, and unaccustomed to struggle against the storms and winds. While it was upon the apple tree the wind blew about the stiff boughs, and the bird seemed bemazed, and not strong enough to strive with it. The swallows come to the sitting-room window as if wishing to build, but I am afraid they will not have courage for it; but I believe they will build in my room window. They twitter, and make a bustle, and a little cheerful song, hanging against the panes of glass with their soft white bellies close to the glass and their forked fish-like tails. They swim round and round, and again they come.[94] . . . I do not now see the brownness that was in the coppices. The bower hawthorn blossoms passed away. Those on the hills are a faint white. The wild guelder-rose is coming out, and the wild roses. I have seen no honey-suckles yet. . . . Foxgloves are now frequent.

Thursday, 17th.—. . . When I came home I found William at work attempting to alter a stanza in the poem on our going for Mary, which I convinced him did not need altering. We sate in the house after dinner. In the evening walked on our favourite path. A short letter from Coleridge. William added a little to the Ode he is writing.

Friday, 18th June.—When we were sitting after breakfast . . . Luff came in. He had rode over the Fells. He brought news about Lord Lowther's intention to pay all debts, etc.,[95] and a letter from Mr. Clarkson. He saw our garden, was astonished at the scarlet beans, etc. etc. etc. When he was gone, we wrote to Coleridge, M. H., and my brother Richard about the affair. William determined to go to Eusemere on Monday. . . .

Saturday, 19th.—The swallows were very busy under my window this morning. . . . Coleridge, when he was last here, told us that for many years, there being no Quaker meeting at Keswick, a single old Quaker woman used to go regularly alone every Sunday to attend the meeting-house, and there used to sit and perform her worship alone, in that beautiful place among those fir trees, in that spacious vale, under the great mountain Skiddaw!!! . . . On Thursday morning Miss Hudson of Workington called. She said, ". . . I sow flowers

[94] Dorothy's attention to these swallows and their nest reflects her own anxieties about William's marriage and what it may do to her "nest."

[95] When Sir James died, his cousin, who inherited the title, paid his debts including the money he owed John Wordsworth's children.

in the parks several miles from home, and my mother and I visit them, and watch them how they grow." This may show that botanists may be often deceived when they find rare flowers growing far from houses. This was a very ordinary young woman, such as in any town in the North of England one may find a score. I sate up a while after William. He then called me down to him. (I was writing to Mary H.) I read Churchill's *Rosciad*.[96] Returned again to my writing, and did not go to bed till he called to me. The shutters were closed, but I heard the birds singing. There was our own thrush, shouting with an impatient shout; so it sounded to me. The morning was still, the twittering of the little birds was very gloomy. The owls had hooted a quarter of an hour before, now the cocks were crowing, it was near daylight, I put out my candle, and went to bed. . . .

[. . . . .]

Friday, 25th June.—. . . I went, just before tea, into the garden. I looked up at my swallow's nest, and it was gone. It had fallen down. Poor little creatures, they could not themselves be more distressed than I was. I went upstairs to look at the ruins. They lay in a large heap upon the window ledge; these swallows had been ten days employed in building this nest, and it seemed to be almost finished. I had watched them early in the morning, in the day many and many a time, and in the evenings when it was almost dark. I had seen them sitting together side by side in their unfinished nest, both morning and night. When they first came about the window they used to hang against the panes, with their white bellies and their forked tails, looking like fish; but then they fluttered and sang their own little twittering song. As soon as the nest was broad enough, a sort of ledge for them, they sate both mornings and evenings, but they did not pass the night there. I watched them one morning, when William was at Eusemere, for more than an hour. Every now and then there was a motion in their wings, a sort of tremulousness, and they sang a low song to one another.

. . . It is now eight o'clock; I will go and see if my swallows are on their nest. Yes! there they are, side by side, both looking down into the garden. I have been out on purpose to see their faces. I knew by looking at the window that they were there. . . . Coleridge and William came in at about half-past eleven. They talked till after twelve.

[96] Charles Churchill's popular 1761 theatrical satire.

Wednesday, 30th June.—. . . We met an old man between the raise and Lewthwaites. He wore a rusty but untorn hat, an excellent blue coat, waistcoat, and breeches, and good mottled worsted stockings. His beard was very thick and grey, of a fortnight's growth we guessed; it was a regular beard, like grey *plush.* His bundle contained Sheffield ware.[97] William said to him, after we had asked him what his business was, "You are a very old man?" "Aye, I am eighty-three." I joined in, "Have you any children?" "Children? Yes, plenty. I have children and grand-children, and great grand-children. I have a great grand-daughter, a fine lass, thirteen years old." I then said, "Won't they take care of you?" He replied, much offended, "Thank God, I can take care of myself." He said he had been a servant of the Marquis of Granby—"O he was a good man; he's in heaven; I hope he is." He then told us how he shot himself at Bath, that he was with him in Germany, and travelled with him everywhere. "He was a famous boxer, sir." And then he told us a story of his fighting with his farmer. "He used always to call me bland and sharp." Then every now and then he broke out, "He was a good man! When we were travelling he never asked at the public-houses, as it might be there" (pointing to the "Swan"), "what we were to pay, but he would put his hand into his pocket and give them what he liked; and when he came out of the house he would say, Now, they would have charged me a shilling or tenpence. God help them, poor creatures!" I asked him again about his children, how many he had. Says he, "I cannot tell you" (I suppose he confounded children and grand-children together); "I have one daughter that keeps a boarding-school at Skipton, in Craven. She teaches flowering and marking. And another that keeps a boarding-school at Ingleton. I brought up my family under the Marquis." He was familiar with all parts of Yorkshire. He asked us where we lived. At Grasmere. "The bonniest dale in all England!" says the old man. I bought a pair of slippers from him, and we sate together by the road-side. When we parted I tried to lift his bundle, and it was almost more than I could do. . . . After tea I wrote to Coleridge, and closed up my letter to M. H. We went soon to bed. A weight of children a poor man's blessing!

[. . . . .]

Tuesday, 6th July.—. . .We set off towards Rydale for letters. The rain met us at the top of the White Moss, and it came on very

---

[97] Dinnerware, although Dorothy buys slippers from him.

heavily afterwards. It drove past Nab Scar in a substantial shape, as if going to Grasmere was as far as it could go. . . . The swallows have completed their beautiful nest. . . .

Wednesday, 7th.—. . .Walked on the White Moss. Glow-worms. Well for them children are in bed when they shine.

Thursday, 8th.—When I was coming home, a post-chaise passed with a little girl behind in a patched, ragged cloak. In the afternoon, after we had talked a little, William fell asleep. I read the *Winter's Tale;* then I went to bed, but did not sleep. The swallows stole in and out of their nest, and sate there, *whiles* quite still, *whiles* they sung low for two minutes or more, at a time just like a muffled robin. William was looking at *The Pedlar* when I got up. He arranged it, and after tea I wrote it out—280 lines. . . . The moon was behind. William hurried me out in hopes that I should see her. We walked first to the top of the hill to see Rydale. It was dark and dull, but our own vale was very solemn—the shape of Helm Crag was quite distinct, though black. We walked backwards and forwards on the White Moss path; there was a sky-like white brightness on the lake. The Wyke cottage right at the foot of Silver How. Glow-worms out, but not so numerous as last night. O, beautiful place—. Dear Mary, William. The hour is come . . . I must prepare to go. The swallows, I must leave them, the wall, the garden, the roses, all. Dear creatures! they sang last night after I was in bed; seemed to be singing to one another, just before they settled to rest for the night. Well, I must go. Farewell.

ON Friday morning, July 9th, William and I set forward to Keswick on our road to Gallow Hill. We had a pleasant ride, though the day was showery. . . . Coleridge met us at Sara's Rock. . . . We had been told by a handsome man, an inhabitant of Wytheburn, with whom he had been talking (and who seemed, by the bye, much pleased with his companion), that C. was waiting for us. We reached Keswick against tea-time. We called at Calvert's on the Saturday evening. . . . On Monday, 12th July, we went to Eusemere. Coleridge walked with us six or seven miles. He was not well, and we had a melancholy parting after having sate together in silence by the roadside. We turned aside to explore the country near Hutton-John, and had a new and delightful walk. The valley, which is subject to the decaying mansion that stands at its head, seems to join its testimony to that of the house, to the falling away of the family greatness, and the hedges are in bad condition. The land wants draining, and is over-run with brackens; yet there is a something everywhere that tells of its former possessors. The trees are left scattered about as if intended to be like a park, and these are very interesting, standing as they do upon the sides of the steep hills that slope down to the bed of the river, a little stony-bedded stream that spreads out to a considerable breadth at the village of Dacre. A little above Dacre we came into the right road to Mr. Clarkson's, after having walked through woods and fields, never exactly knowing whether we were right or wrong. We learnt, however, that we had saved half-a-mile. We sate down by the river-side to rest, and saw some swallows flying about and under the bridge, and two little schoolboys were loitering among the scars seeking after their nests. We reached Mr. Clarkson's at about eight o'clock after a sauntering walk, having lingered and loitered and sate down together that we might be alone. Mr. and Mrs. C. were just come from Luffs. We spent Tuesday, the 13th of July, at Eusemere; and on Wednesday morning, the 14th, we walked to Emont Bridge, and mounted the coach between Bird's Nest and Hartshorn Tree. . . . At Greta Bridge the sun shone cheerfully, and a glorious ride we had over Gaterly Moor. Every building was bathed in golden light. The trees were more bright than earthly trees, and we saw round us miles beyond miles—Darlington spire, etc. etc. We reached Leeming Lane at about nine o'clock: supped comfortably, and enjoyed our fire. On Thursday morning, at a little before seven, being the 15th July, we got into a post-chaise and went to Thirsk to breakfast. We were well treated, but when the landlady understood that we were going to walk off, and leave our luggage behind, she threw out some saucy words in our hearing. The day was very hot, and we rested often and long before we reached the foot of the Hambledon Hills, and while we were climbing them, still oftener. . . . We were almost overpowered with thirst, when I heard the trickling of a little stream of water. I was before William, and I stopped till he came up to me. We sate a long time by this water, and climbed the hill slowly. I was footsore; the sun shone hot; the little Scotch cattle panted and tossed fretfully about. The view was hazy, and we could see nothing from the top of the hill but an undistinct wide-spreading country, full of trees, but the buildings, towns, and houses were lost. We stopped to examine that curious stone, then walked along the flat common. . . . Arrived very hungry at Rivaux. Nothing to eat at the Millers, as we expected, but at an exquisitely neat farmhouse we got some boiled milk and bread. This strengthened us, and I went down to look at the ruins. Thrushes were singing; cattle feeding among green-grown hillocks about the ruins. The hillocks were scattered over with grovelets of wild roses and other shrubs, and covered with wild flowers. I could have stayed in this solemn quiet spot till evening, without a thought of moving, but William was waiting for me, so in a quarter of an hour I went away. We walked upon Mr. Duncombe's terrace and looked down upon the Abbey. It stands in a larger valley among a brotherhood of valleys, of different length and breadth,—all woody, and running up into the hills in all directions. We reached Helmsly just at dusk. We had a beautiful view of the castle from the top of the hill, and slept at a very nice inn, and were well treated; floors as smooth as ice. On Friday morning, 16th July, we walked to Kirby. Met people coming to Helmsly fair. Were misdirected, and walked a mile out of our way.... A beautiful view above Pickering.... Met Mary and Sara seven miles from G. H. Sheltered from the rain; beautiful glen, spoiled by the large house; sweet church and churchyard. Arrived at Gallow Hill at seven o'clock.

Friday Evening, 16th July.—. . . Sara, Tom, and I rode up Bedale. Wm., Mary, Sara, and I went to Scarborough, and we walked in the Abbey pasture, and to Wykeham; and on Monday, the 26th, we went off with Mary in a post-chaise. We had an interesting ride over the Wolds, though it rained all the way. Single thorn bushes were scattered about on the turf, sheep-sheds here and there, and now and then a little hut. Swelling grounds, and sometimes a single tree or a clump of trees. . . . We passed through one or two little villages, embosomed in tall trees. After we had parted from Mary, there were gleams of sunshine, but with showers. We saw Beverley in a heavy rain, and yet were much pleased with the beauty of the town. Saw the minster—a pretty, clean building, but injured very much with Grecian architecture. The country between Beverley and Hull very rich, but miserably flat—brick windmills, houses again—dull and endless. Hull a frightful, dirty, brickhousey, tradesman-like, rich, vulgar place; yet the river—though the shores are so low that they can hardly be seen—looked beautiful with the evening lights upon it, and boats moving about. We walked a long time, and returned to our dull day-room but quiet evening one, to supper.

Tuesday, 20th.—Market day. Streets dirty, very rainy, did not leave Hull till four o'clock, and left Barton at about six; rained all the way almost. A beautiful village at the foot of a hill with trees. A gentleman's house converted into a lady's boarding-school. . . . We left Lincoln on Wednesday morning, 27th July, at six o'clock. It rained heavily, and we could see nothing but the antientry of some of the buildings as we passed along. The night before, however, we had seen enough to make us regret this. The minster stands at the edge of a hill overlooking an immense plain. The country very flat as we went along; the day mended. We went to see the outside of the minster while the passengers were dining at Peterborough; the west end very grand. . . . On Thursday morning, 29th, we arrived in London. Wm. left me at the Sun. . . . After various troubles and disasters, we left London on Saturday morning at half-past five or six, the 31st of July. We mounted the Dover coach at Charing Cross. It was a beautiful morning. The city, St. Paul's, with the river, and a multitude of little boats, made a most beautiful sight as we crossed Westminster Bridge. The houses were not overhung by their cloud of smoke, and they were spread out endlessly, yet the sun shone so brightly, with such a fierce light, that there was even something like the purity of one of nature's own grand spectacles.[98]

We rode on cheerfully, now with the Paris diligence[99] before us, now behind. We walked up the steep hills, a beautiful prospect everywhere, till we even reached Dover. At first the rich, populous, widespreading, woody country about London, then the River Thames, ships sailing, chalk cliffs, trees, little villages. Afterwards Canterbury, situated on a plain, rich and woody, but the city and cathedral disappointed me. Hop[100] grounds on each side of the road some miles from Canterbury; then we came to a common, the race ground, an elevated plain, villages among trees in the bed of a valley at our right, and, rising above this valley, green hills scattered over with wood, neat gentlemen's houses. One white house, almost hid with green trees, which we longed for, and the parson's house, as neat a place as could be, which would just have suited Coleridge. No doubt we may have found one for Tom Hutchinson and Sara, and a good farm too. We halted at a half-way house—fruit carts under the shade of trees, seats for guests, a tempting place to the weary traveller. Still, as we went along, the country was beautiful and hilly, with cottages lurking under the hills, and their little plots of hop ground like vineyards. It was a bad hop year. A woman on the top of the coach said to me, "It is a sad thing for the poor people, for the hop-gathering is the woman's harvest; there is employment about the hops for women and children."

We saw the castle of Dover, and the sea beyond, four or five miles before we reached it. We looked at it through a long vale, the castle being upon an eminence, as it seemed, at the end of this vale, which

---

[98] William's "Composed upon Westminster Bridge" provides these same details.

[99] Stage coach.

[100] Plant used to flavor beer.

opened to the sea. The country now became less fertile, but near Dover it seemed more rich again. Many buildings stand on the flat fields, sheltered with tall trees. There is one old chapel that might have been there just in the same state in which it now is when this vale was as retired, and as little known to travellers as our own Cumberland mountain wilds thirty years ago. There was also a very old building on the other side of the road, which had a strange effect among the many new ones that are springing up everywhere. It seemed odd that it could have kept itself pure in its ancientry among so many upstarts. It was near dark when we reached Dover. We were told that a packet[101] was about to sail, so we went down to the custom-house in half-an-hour—had our luggage examined, etc. etc., and then we drank tea with the Honourable Mr. Knox[102] and his tutor. We arrived at Calais at four o'clock on Sunday morning, the 31st of July. We stayed in the vessel till half-past seven; then William went for letters at about half-past eight or nine. We found out Annette and C.[103] chez Madame Avril dans la Rue de la Tete d'or. We lodged opposite two ladies, in tolerably decent-sized rooms, but badly furnished. . . . The weather was very hot. We walked by the sea-shore almost every evening with Annette and Caroline, or William and I alone. I had a bad cold, and could not bathe[104] at first, but William did. It was a pretty sight to see as we walked upon the sands when the tide was low, perhaps a hundred people bathing about a quarter of a mile distant from us. And we had delightful walks after the heat of the day was passed—seeing far off in the west the coast of England like a cloud crested with Dover castle, which was but like the summit of the cloud—the evening star and the glory of the sky, the reflections in the water were more beautiful than the sky itself, purple waves brighter than precious stones, for ever melting away upon the sands.[105] The fort, a wooden building, at the entrance of the harbour at Calais, when the evening twilight was coming on, and we could not see anything of the building but its shape, which was far more distinct than in perfect daylight, seemed to be reared upon pillars of ebony, between which pillars the sea was seen in the most beautiful colours that can be conceived. Nothing in romance

---

[101] Boat that travels a regular route carrying mail as well as passengers.

[102] Perhaps Thomas Knox, later Earl of Ranfurly.

[103] The visit to William's former lover, Annette, and their daughter, Caroline, is presumably to settle matters before he marries.

[104] Swim.

[105] William's sonnet "Composed upon Westminster Bridge" and his "Calais" sonnets echo these journal passages.

was ever half so beautiful. Now came in view, as the evening star sunk down, and the colours of the west faded away, the two lights of England, lighted up by Englishmen in our country to warn vessels off rocks or sands. These we used to see from the pier, when we could see no other distant objects but the clouds, the sky, and the sea itself—all was dark behind. The town of Calais seemed deserted of the light of heaven, but there was always light, and life, and joy upon the sea. One night I shall never forget—the day had been very hot, and William and I walked alone together upon the pier. The sea was gloomy, for there was a blackness over all the sky, except when it was overspread with lightning, which often revealed to us a distant vessel near, as the waves roared and broke against the pier, and they were interfused with greenish fiery light. The more distant sea always black and gloomy. It was also beautiful, on the calm hot night, to see the little boats row out of harbour with wings of fire, and the sail boats with the fiery track which they cut as they went along, and which closed up after them with a hundred thousand sparkles, and streams of glow-worm light. Caroline was delighted.

On Sunday, the 29th of August, we left Calais at twelve o'clock in the morning, and landed at Dover at one on Monday the 30th. . . . It was very pleasant to me, when we were in the harbour at Dover, to breathe the fresh air, and to look up, and see the stars among the ropes of the vessel. The next day was very hot. We . . . bathed, and sate upon the Dover Cliffs, and looked upon France with many a melancholy and tender thought. We could see the shores almost as plain as if it were but an English lake. We mounted the coach, and arrived in London at six, the 30th August. It was misty, and we could see nothing. We stayed in London till Wednesday the 22nd of September, and arrived at Gallow Hill on Friday.

September 24th.—Mary first met us in the avenue. She looked so fat and well that we were made very happy by the sight of her; then came Sara, and last of all Joanna. Tom was forking corn, standing upon the corn cart. We dressed ourselves immediately and got tea. The garden looked gay with asters and sweet peas. . .[106] Jack and George came on Friday evening, 1st October. On Saturday, 2nd, we

---

[106] Knight omits several sentences that are erased or inked over in the manuscript. Dorothy herself may have crossed out passages. Or, family members may have wanted to protect her privacy. One omission reports Dorothy ill on Saturday and for the rest of their time at Gallow Hill.

rode to Hackness, William, Jack, George, and Sara single. I behind Tom. On Sunday 3rd, Mary and Sara were busy packing.

On Monday, 4th October 1802, my brother William was married to Mary Hutchinson. I slept a good deal of the night, and rose fresh and well in the morning. At a little after eight o'clock, I saw them go down the avenue towards the church. William had parted from me upstairs[107]. . . When they were absent, my dear little Sara prepared the breakfast. I kept myself as quiet as I could, but when I saw the two men running up the walk, coming to tell us it was over, I could stand it no longer, and threw myself on the bed where I lay in stillness, neither hearing nor seeing anything, till Sara came upstairs to me, and said, "They are coming." This forced me from the bed where I lay, and I moved, I knew not how, straight forward, faster than my strength could carry me, till I met my beloved William, and fell upon his bosom. He and John Hutchinson led me to the house, and there I stayed to welcome my dear Mary. As soon as we had breakfasted, we departed. It rained when we set off. Poor Mary was much agitated, when she parted from her brothers and sisters, and her home. Nothing particular occurred till we reached Kirby. We had sunshine and showers, pleasant talk, love and cheerfulness. We were obliged to stay two hours at K. while the horses were feeding. We wrote a few lines to Sara, and then walked out; the sun shone, and we went to the churchyard after we had put a letter into the post-office for the *York Herald*. We sauntered about, and read the grave-stones. There was one to the memory of five children, who had all died within five years, and the longest lived had only lived four years. . . .

We left Kirby at about half-past two. There is not much variety of prospect from K. to Helmsley, but the country is very pleasant, being rich and woody, and Helmsley itself stands very sweetly at the foot of the rising grounds of Duncombe Park, which is scattered over with tall woods; and, lifting itself above the common buildings of the town, stands Helmsley Castle, now a ruin, formerly inhabited by the gay Duke of Buckingham. Every foot of the road was of itself interesting to us, for we had travelled along it on foot, William and I, when we went to fetch our dear Mary, and had sate upon the

---

[107] Another omission—The recovered text, published in later twentieth-century editions, describes William's leave-taking of Dorothy to go to his wedding, which she did not attend. "I gave him the wedding ring—with how deep a blessing! I took it from my forefinger where I had worn it the night before—he slipped it again onto my finger and blessed me fervently."

turf by the roadside more than once. Before we reached Helmsley, our driver told us that he could not take us any further, so we stopped at the same inn where we had slept before. My heart danced at the sight of its cleanly outside, bright yellow walls, casements overshadowed with jasmine, and its low, double gavel-ended front. . . . Mary and I warmed ourselves at the kitchen fire. We then walked into the garden, and looked over a gate, up to the old ruin which stands at the top of the mount, and round about it the moats are grown up into soft green cradles, hollows surrounded with green grassy hillocks, and these are overshadowed by old trees, chiefly ashes. I prevailed upon William to go up with me to the ruins. The sun shone, it was warm and very pleasant. One part of the castle seems to be inhabited. There was a man mowing nettles in the open space which had most likely once been the castle-court. There is one gateway exceedingly beautiful. Children were playing upon the sloping ground. We came home by the street. After about an hour's delay, we set forward again; had an excellent driver, who opened the gates so dexterously that the horses never stopped. Mary was very much delighted with the view of the castle from the point where we had seen it before. I was pleased to see again the little path which we had walked upon, the gate I had climbed over, and the road down which we had seen the two little boys drag a log of wood, and a team of horses struggle under the weight of a great load of timber. We had felt compassion for the poor horses that were under the governance of oppression and ill-judging drivers, and for the poor boys, who seemed of an age to have been able to have dragged the log of wood merely out of the love of their own activity, but from poverty and bad food they panted for weakness, and were obliged to fetch their father from the town to help them. Duncombe house looks well from the road—a large building, though I believe only two-thirds of the original design are completed. We rode down a very steep hill to Rivaux valley, with woods all round us. We stopped upon the bridge to look at the Abbey, and again when we had crossed it. Dear Mary had never seen a ruined abbey before except Whitby. We recognised the cottages, houses, and the little valleys as we went along. We walked up a long hill, the road carrying us up the cleft or valley with woody hills on each side of us. When we went to G. H. I had walked down the valley alone. William followed me.

Before we had crossed the Hambledon Hill, and reached the point overlooking Yorkshire, it was quite dark. We had not wanted, however, fair prospects before us, as we drove along the flat plain of the high hill. Far far off from us, in the western sky, we saw shapes of castles, ruins among groves, a great spreading wood, rocks, and single trees, a minster with its tower unusually distinct, minarets in another quarter, and a round Grecian Temple also; the colours of the sky of a bright grey, and the forms of a sober grey, with a dome. As we descended the hill there was no distinct view, but of a great space; only near us we saw the wild (and as the people say) bottom-less tarn in the hollow at the side of the hill. It seemed to be made visible to us only by its own light, for all the hill about us was dark. Before we reached Thirsk we saw a light before us, which we at first thought was the moon, then lime-kilns;[108] but when we drove into the market-place it proved a large bonfire, with lads dancing round it, which is a sight I dearly love. The inn was like an illuminated house—every room full. We asked the cause, and were told by the girl that it was "Mr. John Bell's birthday, that he had heired his estate." The landlady was very civil. She did not recognise the despised foot-travellers. We rode on in the dark, and reached Leeming Lane at eleven o'clock. . . .

The next morning we set off at about half-past eight o'clock. It was a cheerful, sunny morning. . . . We had a few showers, but when we came to the green fields of Wensley, the sun shone upon them all, and the Ure in its many windings glittered as it flowed along under the green slopes of Middleham Castle. Mary looked about for her friend Mr. Place, and thought she had him sure on the contrary side of the vale from that on which we afterwards found he lived. We went to a new built house at Leyburn, the same village where William and I had dined on our road to Grasmere two years and three-quarters ago, but not the same house. The landlady was very civil, giving us cake and wine, but the horses being out we were detained at least two hours, and did not set off till two o'clock. We paid for thirty-five miles, i.e. to Sedbergh, but the landlady did not encourage us to hope to get beyond Hawes. . . . When we passed through the village of Wensley my heart melted away, with dear recollections—the bridge, the little water-spout, the steep hill, the church. They are among the most vivid of my own inner visions, for they were the first objects that I saw after we were left to ourselves, and had turned our whole hearts to Grasmere as a home in which we were to rest. The vale looked most beautiful each way. To the left the bright silver stream inlaid the flat and very green

---

[108] Tall furnace for converting lime to quicklime, used for agriculture and building.

meadows, winding like a serpent. To the right, we did not see it so far, it was lost among trees and little hills. I could not help observing, as we went along, how much more varied the prospects of Wensley Dale are in the summer time than I could have thought possible in the winter. This seemed to be in great measure owing to the trees being in leaf, and forming groves and screens, and thence little openings upon recesses and concealed retreats, which in winter only made a part of the one great vale. The beauty of the summer time here as much excels that of the winter, as the variety (owing to the excessive greenness) of the fields, and the trees in leaf half concealing, and—where they do not conceal—softening the hard bareness of the limey white roofs. One of our horses seemed to grow a little restive as we went through the first village, a long village on the side of a hill. It grew worse and worse, and at last we durst not go on any longer. We walked a while, and then the post boy was obliged to take the horse out, and go back for another. We seated ourselves again snugly in the post-chaise. The wind struggled about us and rattled the window, and gave a gentle motion to the chaise, but we were warm and at our ease within. Our station was at the top of a hill, opposite Bolton Castle, the Ure flowing beneath. William has since written a sonnet on this our imprisonment. "Hard was thy durance, poor Queen Mary! compared with ours.". . .[109]

We had a sweet ride till we came to a public-house on the side of a hill, where we alighted and walked down to see the waterfalls. The sun was not set, and the woods and fields were spread over with the yellow light of evening, which made their greenness a thousand times more green. There was too much water in the river for the beauty of the falls, and even the banks were less interesting than in winter. Nature had entirely got the better in her struggles against the giants who first cast the mould of these works; for, indeed, it is a place that did not in winter remind one of God, but one could not help feeling as if there had been the agency of some "mortal instruments," which Nature had been struggling against without making a perfect conquest. There was something so wild and new in this feeling, knowing, as we did in the inner man, that God alone had laid his hand upon it, that I could not help regretting the want of it; besides, it is a pleasure to a real lover of Nature to give winter all the glory he can, for summer will make its own way, and speak its own praises. We saw the pathway which William and I took at the close of evening, the path leading to the rabbit warren

---

[109] This sonnet probably concerns the arrest and execution of Mary, Queen of Scots.

where we lost ourselves. Sloe farm, with its holly hedges, was lost among the green hills and hedgerows in general, but we found it out, and were glad to look at it again. William left us to seek the waterfalls. . . .

At our return to the inn, we found new horses and a new driver, and we went on nicely to Hawes, where we arrived before it was quite dark. . . . We rose at six o'clock—a rainy morning. . . . There was a very fine view about a mile from Hawes, where we crossed a bridge; bare and very green fields with cattle, a glittering stream, cottages, a few ill-grown trees, and high hills. The sun shone now. Before we got upon the bare hills, there was a hunting lodge on our right, exactly like Greta Hill, with fir plantations about it. We were very fortunate in the day, gleams of sunshine, passing clouds, that travelled with their shadows below them. Mary was much pleased with Garsdale. It was a dear place to William and me. We noted well the public-house (Garsdale Hall) where we had baited. . . . and afterwards the mountain which had been adorned by Jupiter in his glory when we were here before. It was midday when we reached Sedbergh, and market day. We were in the same room where we had spent the evening together in our road to Grasmere. We had a pleasant ride to Kendal, where we arrived at two o'clock. The day favoured us, M. and I went to see the house where dear Sara had lived. . . . I am always glad to see Staveley; it is a place I dearly love to think of—the first mountain village that I came to with William when we first began our pilgrimage together. . . . Nothing particular occurred till we reached Ings chapel. The door was open, and we went in. It is a neat little place, with a marble floor and marble communion table with a painting over it of the last supper, and Moses and Aaron on each side. The woman told us that "they had painted them as near as they could by the dresses as they are described in the Bible," and gay enough they are. The marble had been sent by Richard Bateman from Leghorn.[110] The woman told us that a man had been at her house a few days before, who told her he had helped to bring it down the Red Sea, and she believed him gladly! We . . . arrived at Grasmere at about six o'clock on Wednesday evening, the 6th of October 1802. . . . I cannot describe what I felt. . . . We went by candle light into the garden, and were astonished at the growth of the brooms, Portugal laurels, etc. etc. etc. The next day, Thursday, we unpacked the boxes. On Friday, 8th, . . . Mary and I

[110] The story of Bateman, who became rich and sent stone from Italy to rebuild his childhood chapel, is told in "Michael," ll. 258–270.

walked first upon the hill-side, and then in John's Grove, then in view of Rydale, the first walk that I had taken with my sister.

[. . . . .]

Sunday, 17th.—We had thirteen of our neighbours to tea. William came in just as we began tea.

[. . . . .]

24th December.—Christmas Eve. William is now sitting by me, at half-past ten o'clock. I have been repeating some of his sonnets to him, listening to his own repeating, reading some of Milton's, and the *Allegro* and *Penseroso.* It is a quick, keen frost. . . . Coleridge came this morning with Wedgwood. We all turned out . . . one by one, to meet him. He looked well. We had to tell him of the birth of his little girl, born yesterday morning at six o'clock. William went with them to Wytheburn in the chaise, and M. and I met W. on the Raise. It was not an unpleasant morning. . . . The sun shone now and then, and there was no wind, but all things looked cheerless and distinct; no meltings of sky into mountains, the mountains like stone work wrought up with huge hammers. Last Sunday was as mild a day as I ever remember. . . . Mary and I went round the lakes. There were flowers of various kinds—the topmost bell of a foxglove, geraniums, daisies, a buttercup in the water (but this I saw two or three days before), small yellow flowers (I do not know their name) in the turf. A large bunch of strawberry blossoms. . . . It is Christmas Day, Saturday, 25th December 1802. I am thirty-one years of age. It is a dull, frosty day.

. . . On Thursday, 30th December, I went to Keswick. William rode before me to the foot of the hill nearest K. There we parted close to a little watercourse, which was then noisy with water, but on my return a dry channel. . . . We stopped our horse close to the ledge, opposite a tuft of primroses, three flowers in full blossom and a bud. They reared themselves up among the green moss. We debated long whether we should pluck them, and at last left them to live out their day, which I was right glad of at my return the Sunday following; for there they remained, uninjured either by cold or wet. I stayed at Keswick over New Year's Day, and returned on Sunday, the 2nd January. . . . William was alarmed at my long delay, and came to within three miles of Keswick. . . . Coleridge stayed with us till Tuesday, January 4th. W. and I . . . walked with him to Ambleside. We parted with him at the turning of the lane, he going on horseback to the top of Kirkstone. On Thursday 6th, C. returned, and on Friday, the 7th, he and Sara went to Keswick. W. accompanied them to the foot of Wytheburn. . . . It was a gentle day, and when William and I returned home just before sunset, it was a heavenly evening. A soft sky was among the hills, and a summer sunshine above, and blending with this sky, for it was more like sky than clouds; the turf looked warm and soft.

. . . .

Monday, January 10*th* 1803.—I lay in bed to have a drench of sleep till one o'clock. Worked all day. . . . Ominously cold.

Tuesday, January 11*th.*—A very cold day, . . . but the blackness of the cold made us slow to put forward, and we did not walk at all. Mary read the Prologue to Chaucer's tales to me in the morning. William was working at his poem to C. Letter from Keswick and from Taylor[111] on William's marriage. C. poorly, in bad spirits. . . . Read part of *The Knight's Tale* with exquisite delight. Since tea Mary has been down stairs copying out Italian poems for Stuart. William has been working beside me, and here ends this imperfect summary.[112]

[111] Probably John Taylor, a drama critic.

[112] But the journal does not end here. In the next sentence, Dorothy resolves to "take a nice Calais book" and write "regularly" and "legibly" in the future. For two more entries, one of January 12, the other January 16, that describe the extreme cold and purchasing gingerbread, see the *Longman Anthology of British Literature*, 2A, p. 557.

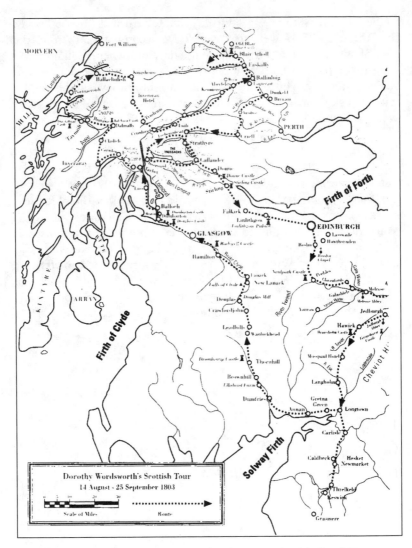

Recollections of a Tour Made in Scotland A.D. *1803.* (Ed. Carol Kyros Walker © Yale University Press, 1997.)

FROM *RECOLLECTIONS OF A TOUR MADE IN SCOTLAND* A.D. *1803*

In mid-August, 1803, William and Dorothy joined Samuel Taylor Coleridge for a six-week tour of Scotland. On the 14th, the day before their departure, Coleridge wrote to Southey: "We have bought a stout Horse, aged but stout and spirited, and an open vehicle called a Jaunting Car. There is room in it for three. . . ."

Dorothy's Recollections, *which describe their time of walking, talking, and writing, are not a day-by-day journal, but were written after her return. Unlike so many authors of travel narratives, she did not write for immediate publication. She tells Catherine Clarkson in January 1806: "I wrote my journal, or rather* recollections *for the sake of my Friends who it seemed ought to have been with us, but were confined at home by other duties." But her friends so loved these recollections that they urged her to publish her work. The project was delayed until William's concerns for his sister's health put a stop to her labors, a process I have discussed in the introduction to this book.*

In 1874, Principal Shairp published the Recollections. *Dorothy's first, full-length conventionally published work almost immediately went into a second edition, my source here. Bracketed ellipses are mine.*

TOUR SUMMARY

First Week

Day

1. Left Keswick—Mosedale—Hisket—Newmarket—Falls
2. Rose Castle—Hatfield—Longtown
3. Solway Moss—Enter Scotland—Gretna Green—Dumfries
4. Burns's Grave—Elisland—Vale of Brownhill—Poem to Burns's Sons
5. Thornhill—River Nith—Turnpike House—Sportsman—Vale of Menock—Wanlockhead—Leadhills—Miners—Honetoun mansion—Hostess
6. Road to Crawfordjohn—Douglas Mill—Clyde—Lanerk—Boniton Linn

Second Week

7. Falls of the Clyde—Cartland Crags—Fall of Stonebyres of the Clyde—Hamilton
8. Hamilton House—Baroncleugh—Bothwell Castle—Glasgow
9. Bleaching ground (Glasgow Green)—Road to Dumbarton
10. Rock and Castle of Dumbarton—Vale of Leven—Smollett's Monument—Loch Lomond—Luss
11. Islands of Loch Lomond—Road to Tarbet—The Cobbler—Tarbet
12. Left Tarbet for the Trossachs—Rob Roy's Caves—Inversneyde Ferryhouse and Waterfall—Singular building—Loch Ketterine—Glengyle—Mr. Mcfarlane's
13. Breakfast at Glengyle—Lairds of Glengyle—Rob Roy—Burying-ground—Ferryman's hut—Trossachs—Loch Achray—Return to Ferryman's hut

Third Week

14. Left Loch Ketterine—Garrison House—Highland Girls—Ferryhouse at Inversneyd—Poem to the Highland Girl—Return to Tarbet
15. Coleridge resolves to go home—Arrochar—Loch Long—Parted with Coleridge—Glen Croe—The Cobbler—Glen Kinglas—Cairndow
16. Road to Inverary—Inverary
17. Vale of Arey—Loch Awe—Kilchurn Castle—Dalmally
18. Loch Awe—Taynuilt—Bunawe—Loch Etive—Tinkers
19. Road by Loch Etive downwards—Dunstaffnage Castle—Loch Crerar—Strath of Apple—Portnacroish—Islands of Loch Linnhe—Morven—Lord Tweeddale—Strath of Duror—Ballachulish
20. Road to Glen Cove up Loch Leven—Blacksmith's House—Glen Coe—Whiskey hovel—King's House

Fourth Week

21. Road to Inveroran—Inveroran—Public-House—Road to Tyndrum—Tyndrum—Loch Dochart
22. Killin—Loch Tay—Kenmore

23. Lord Breadalbane's grounds—Vale of Tay—Alberfeldy—Falls of Moness—River Tummel—Vale of Tummel—Fascally—Blair
24. Duke of Athol's gardens—Falls of Bruar—Mountain road to Lake Tummel—Loch Tummel—Rivers Tummel and Garry Fascally
25. Pass of Killicrankie—Sonnet—Fall of Tummel—Dunkeld—Fall of the Bran
26. Duke of Althols gardens—Glen of the Bran—Rumbling Brig—Narrow Glen—Poem—Crieff
27. Strath Erne—Loch Lubnaig—Bruce the Traveller—Pass of Leny—Callander

Fifth Week

28. Road to the Trossachs—Vennachar—Loch Achray—Trossachs—Road up Loch Ketterine—Poem "Stepping Westward"—Boatman's Hut
29. Road to Loch Lomond—Ferryhouse at Inversneyde—Walk up Loch Lomond—Glenfalloch—Glengyle—Rob Roy's Grave—Poem—Boatman's Hut
30. Mountain road to Loch Voil—Poem: "The Solitary Reaper"—Strath Eyer
31. Loch Lubnaig—Callander—Stirling—Falkirk
32. Linlithgow—Road to Edinburgh
33. Edinburgh—Roslin
34. Roslin—Hawthornden—Road to Peeble

Sixth Week

35. Peebles—Neidpath Castle—Sonnet—Tweed—Clovenford—Poem on Yarrow
36. Melrose—Melrose Abbey
37. Dryburgh—Jedburgh—Old Woman—Poem
38. Vale of Jed—Ferniehurst
39. Jedburch—The Assizes—Vale of Teviot—Hawick
40. Vale of Teviot—Branxholm—Moss Paul—Langholm
41. Road to Longtown—River Esk—Carlisle
42. Arrived at Home

[DEPARTURE—DAY 1]

WILLIAM and I parted from Mary on Sunday afternoon, 14th, 1803; and William, Coleridge, and I left Keswick on Monday morning, the 15th at twenty minutes after eleven o'clock. The day was very hot; we walked up the hills, and along all the rough road, which made our walking half the day's journey. Travelled under the foot of Atnock, a mountain covered with stones on the lower part; above, it is very rocky, but sheep pasture there; we saw several where there seemed to be no grass to tempt them. Passed the foot of Grisdale and Mosedale, both pastoral valleys, narrow, and soon terminating in the mountains—green, with scattered trees and houses, and each a beautiful stream. At Grisdale our horse backed upon a steep bunk where the road was not fenced, just above a pretty mill at the foot of the valley; and we had a second threatening of a disaster in crossing a narrow bridge between the two dales; but this was not the fault of either man or horse. [. . .]

[DAYS 3–4]

Tuesday, August 16th.—Passed Rose Castle upon the Caldew, an ancient building of red stone with sloping gardens, an ivied gateway, velvet lawns, old garden walls, trim flower-borders with stately and luxuriant flowers. We walked up to the house and stood some minutes watching the swallows that flew about restlessly, and flung their shadows upon the sun bright walls of the old building; the shadows glanced and twinkled, interchanged and crossed each other, expanded and shrunk up, appeared and disappeared every instant: as I observed to William and Coleridge, seeming more like living things than the birds themselves. Dined at Carlisle; the town in a bustle with the assizes;[1] so many strange faces known in former times and recognised, that it half seemed as if I ought to know them all, and, together with the noise, the fine ladies, etc., they put me into confusion. This day Hatfield[2] was condemned. I stood at the door of the gaoler's house, where he was; William entered the house, and Coleridge saw him. I fell into conversation with a debtor, who told me in a dry way that he was "far over-learned," and another man observed to

---

[1] Periodic sessions of country courts.
[2] Under the name Honorable A. A. Hope, M.P., John Hatfield forged a number of documents and cheated many local people. He was also a bigamist. In Book VII of the 1805 *Prelude*, William tells the story of Hatfield and Mary, the Maid of Buttermere.

William that we might learn from Hatfield's fate "not to meddle with pen and ink." We gave a shilling to my companion, whom we found out to be a friend of the family, a fellow-sailor with my brother John "in Captain Wordsworth's ship." Walked upon the city walls, which are broken down in places and crumbling away, and most disgusting from filth. The city and neighbourhood of Carlisle disappointed me; the banks of the river quite flat, and, though the holms are rich, there is not much beauty in the vale from the want of trees—at least to the eye of a person coming from England, and, I scarcely know how, but to me the holms had not a *natural* look; there was something townish in their appearance, a dulness in their strong deep green. To Longtown—not very interesting, except from the long views over the flat country; the road rough, chiefly newly mended. Reached Longtown after sunset, a town of brick houses belonging chiefly to the Graham family. Being in the form of a cross and not long, it had been better called Crosstown. There are several shops, and it is not a very small place; but I could not meet with a silver thimble, and bought a halfpenny brass one. Slept at the Graham's Arms, a large inn. Here, as everywhere else, the people seemed utterly insensible of the enormity of Hatfield's offences; the ostler[3] told William that he was quite a gentleman, paid every one genteelly, etc. etc. He and Mary had walked together to Gretna Green; a heavy rain came on when they were there; a returned chaise happened to pass, and the driver would have taken them up; but Mr. Hope's carriage was to be sent for; he did not choose to accept the chaise-driver's offer.

Wednesday August 17th.—Left Longtown after breakfast. About half a mile from the town a guide-post and two roads, to Edinburgh and Glasgow; we took the left-hand road to Glasgow. Here saw a specimen of the luxuriance of the heath-plant, as it grows in Scotland; it was in the enclosed plantations—perhaps sheltered by them. These plantations appeared to be not well grown for their age; the trees were stunted. Afterwards the road, treeless, over a peat-moss common—the Solway Moss; here and there an earth-built hut with its peat stack, a scanty growing willow hedge round the kail-garth, perhaps the cow pasturing near,—a little lass watching it,—the dreary waste cheered by the endless singing of larks.

We enter Scotland by crossing the river Sark; on the Scotch side of the bridge the ground is unenclosed pasturage; it was very green, and scattered over with that yellow flowered plant which we call

[3] Stableman.

grunsel; the hills heave and swell prettily enough; cattle feeding; a few corn fields near the river. At the top of the hill opposite is Springfield, a village built by Sir William Maxwell[4]—a dull uniformity in the houses, as is usual when all built at one time, or belonging to one individual, each just big enough for two people to live in, and in which a family, large or small as it may happen, is crammed. There the marriages are performed. Further on, though almost contiguous, is Gretna Green,[5] upon a hill and among trees. This sounds well, but it is a dreary place; the stone houses dirty and miserable, with broken windows. There is a pleasant view from the churchyard over Solway Firth[6] to the Cumberland mountains. Dined at Annan. On our left as we travelled along appeared the Solway Firth and the mountains beyond, but the near country dreary. Those houses by the roadside which are built of stone are comfortless and dirty; but we peeped into a clay 'biggin' that was very 'canny,' and I daresay will be as warm as a swallow's nest in winter. The town of Annan made me think of France and Germany; many of the houses large and gloomy, the size of them outrunning the comforts. One thing which was like Germany pleased me: the shopkeepers express their calling by some device or painting; bread-bakers have biscuits, loaves, cakes, painted on their window-shutters; blacksmiths horses' shoes, iron tools, etc. etc. and so on through all trades.

Reached Dumfries at about nine o'clock—market-day; met crowds of people on the road, and every one had a smile for us and our car. . . . The inn was a large house, and tolerably comfortable; Mr. Rogers and his sister,[7] whom we had seen at our own cottage at Grasmere a few days before, had arrived there that same afternoon on their way to the Highlands; but we did not see them till the next morning, and only for about a quarter of an hour.

Thursday, August 18th.—Went to the churchyard where Burns[8] is buried. A bookseller accompanied us. He showed us the outside of Burns's house, where he had lived the last three years of his life

---

[4] Maxwell built several planned villages organized around different trades. Springfield was founded in 1791 as a center for weaving.

[5] First town over the border and a destination for elopers, owing to the Scottish church's lax marriage laws.

[6] Narrow sea inlet.

[7] See Rogers's description of this encounter (p. 254).

[8] Robert Burns (1759–1796), celebrated Scottish poet interested in Scottish folklore and poetry written in Scots.

and where he died. It has a mean appearance, and is in a bye situation whitewashed; dirty about the doors, as almost all Scotch houses are; flowering plants in the windows.

Went on to visit his grave. He lies at a corner of the churchyard and his second son, Francis Wallace, beside him. There is no stone to mark the spot; but a hundred guineas have been collected, to be expended on some sort of monument. "There," said the book-seller, pointing to a pompous monument, "there lies Mr. Such-a-one"—I have forgotten his name,—"a remarkably clever man; he was an attorney, and hardly ever lost a cause he undertook. Burns made many a lampoon upon him, and there they rest, as you see." We looked at the grave with melancholy and painful reflections, repeating to each other his own verses:—

> 'Is there a man whose judgment clear
> Can others teach the course to steer,
> Yet runs himself life's mad career
>   Wild as the wave?—
> Here let him pause, and through a tear
>   Survey this grave.
> The poor Inhabitant below
> Was quick to learn, and wise to know
> And keenly felt the friendly glow
>   And softer flame;
> But thoughtless follies laid him low,
>   And stain'd his name.'[9]

The churchyard is full of grave-stones and expensive monuments in all sorts of fantastic shapes—obelisk-wise, pillar-wise, etc. In speaking of Gretna Green, I forgot to mention that we visited the churchyard. The church is like a huge house; indeed, so are all the churches, with a steeple, not a square tower or spire,—a sort of thing more like a glass–house chimney than a Church of England steeple; grave–stones in abundance, few verses, yet there were some—no texts. Over the graves of married women the maiden name instead of that of the husband, "spouse" instead of "wife," and the place of abode preceded by "in" instead of "of."[...]

[9] Burns's "A Bard's Epitaph," stanzas II and IV.

[ROAD TO CRAWFORD JOHN—DAY 6]

. . . The air was keen and cold; we might have supposed it to be three months later in the season and two hours earlier in the day. The landlady had not lighted us a fire; so I was obliged to get myself toasted in the kitchen, and when we set off I put on both grey cloak and spencer.

Our road carried us down the valley, and we soon lost sight of Leadhills for the valley made a turn almost immediately, and we saw two miles, perhaps, before us; the glen sloped somewhat rapidly— heathy, bare, no hut or house. Passed by a shepherd, who was sitting upon the ground, reading, with the book on his knee, screened from the wind by his plaid, while a flock of sheep were feeding near him among the rushes and coarse grass—for, as we descended we came among lands where grass grew with the heather. Travelled through several reaches of the glen, which somewhat resembled the valley of Menock on the other side of Wanlockhead; but it was not near so beautiful; the forms of the mountains did not melt so exquisitely into each other, and there was a coldness, and, if I may so speak, a want of simplicity in the surface of the earth; the heather was poor, not covering a whole hill-side; not in luxuriant streams and beds inter-veined with rich verdure; but patchy and stunted, with here and there coarse grass and rushes. But we soon came in sight of a spot that impressed us very much. At the lower end of this new reach of the vale was a decayed tree, beside a decayed cottage, the vale spreading out into a level area which was one large field, without fence and without division, of a dull yellow colour; the vale seemed to partake of the desolation of the cottage, and to participate in its decay; and yet the spot was in its nature so dreary that one would rather have wondered how it ever came to be tenanted by man, than lament that it was left to waste and solitude. Yet the encircling hills were so exquisitely formed that is was impossible to conceive any-thing more lovely than this place would have been if the valley and hill-sides had been interspersed with trees, cottages, green fields, and hedgerows. But all was desolate; the one large field which filled up the area of the valley appeared, as I have said, in decay, and seemed to retain the memory of its connexion with man in some way analogous to the ruined building; for it was as much of a field as Mr. King's best pasture scattered over with his fattest cattle.

We went on, looking before us, the place losing nothing of its hold upon our minds, when we discovered a woman sitting right in the middle of the field, alone, wrapped up in a grey cloak or plaid. She sat motionless all the time we looked at her, which might be nearly half an hour. We could not conceive why she sat there, for there were neither sheep nor cattle in the field; her appearance was very melancholy. In the meantime our road carried us nearer to the cottage, though we were crossing over the hill to the left, leaving the valley below us, and we perceived that a part of the building was inhabited, and that what we had supposed to be *one* blasted tree was eight trees, four of which were entirely blasted; the others partly so, and round about the place was a little potato and cabbage garth, fenced with earth. No doubt, that woman had been an inhabitant of the cottage. However this might be, there was so much obscurity and uncertainty about her, and her figure agreed so well with the desolation of the place, that we were indebted to the chance of her being there for some of the most interesting feelings that we had ever had from natural objects connected with man in dreary solitariness.

We had been advised to go along the *new* road, which would have carried us down the vale; but we met some travellers who recommended us to climb the hill, and go by the village of Crawfordjohn as being much nearer. We had a long hill, and after having reached the top, steep and bad roads, so we continued to walk for a considerable way. The air was cold and clear—the sky blue. We walked cheerfully along in the sunshine, each of us alone, only William had the charge of the horse and car, so he sometimes took a ride, which did but poorly recompense him for the trouble of driving. I never travelled with more cheerful spirits than this day. Our road was along the side of a high moor. I can always walk over a moor with a light foot; I seem to be drawn more closely to nature in such places than anywhere else; or rather I feel more strongly the power of nature over me, and am better satisfied with myself for being able to find enjoyment in what unfortunately to many persons is either dismal or insipid. This moor, however, was more than commonly interesting; we could see a long way, and on every side of us were larger or smaller tracts of cultivated land. Some were extensive farms, yet in so large a waste they did but look small, with farmhouses, barns, etc., others like little cottages, with enough to feed a cow, and supply the family with vegetables. In looking at these farms we had always one feeling. Why did the plough stop there? Why might not they as well have carried it twice as far? There were no hedgerows near the farms, and very few trees. As we were passing along, we saw an old man, the first we had seen in a Highland bonnet, walking with a staff at a very slow pace by the edge of one of the moorland corn-fields; he wore a grey plaid, and a dog was by his side. There was a scriptural solemnity in this man's figure, a sober simplicity which was most impressive. Scotland is the country above all others that I have seen, in which a man of imagination may carve out his own pleasures. There are so many *inhabited* solitudes, and the employments of the people are so immediately connected with the places where you find them, and their dresses so simple, so much alike, yet, from their being folding garments, admitting of an endless variety, and falling often so gracefully.

After some time we descended towards a broad vale, passed one farm-house, sheltered by fir trees, with a burn close to it; children playing, linen bleaching. The vale was open pastures and corn-fields unfenced, the land poor. The village of Crawfordjohn on the slope of a hill a long way before us to the left. Asked about our road of a man who was driving a cart; he told us to go through the village, then along some fields, and we should come to a "herd's house by the burn side." The highway was right through the vale, unfenced on either side; the people of the village, who were making hay, all stared at us and our carriage. We inquired the road of a middle-aged man, dressed in a shabby black coat, at work in one of the hay fields; he looked like the minister of the place, and when he spoke we felt assured that he was so, for he was not sparing of hard words, which, however, he used with great propriety, and he spoke like one who had been accustomed to dictate. Our car[10] wanted mending in the wheel, and we asked him if there was a blacksmith in the village. "Yes," he replied, but when we showed him the wheel he told William that he might mend it himself without a blacksmith, and he would put him in the way; so he fetched hammer and nails and gave his directions, which William obeyed, and repaired the damage entirely to his own satisfaction and the priest's, who did not offer to lend any assistance himself; not as if he would not have been willing in case of need; but as if it were more natural for him to dictate, and because he thought it more fit that William should do it himself. He spoke much about the propriety of every man's lending all the assistance in his power to travellers and with some

---

[10] The jaunting car.

ostentation of self-praise. Here I observed a honeysuckle and some flowers growing in a garden, the first I had seen in Scotland. It is a pretty cheerful-looking village, but must be very cold in winter; it stands on a hillside, and the vale itself is very high ground, unsheltered by trees.

Left the village behind us, and our road led through arable ground for a considerable way, on which were growing very good crops of corn and potatoes. Our friend accompanied us to show us the way, and Coleridge and he had a scientific conversation concerning the uses and properties of lime and other manures. He seemed to be a well–informed man; somewhat pedantic in his manners; but this might be only the difference between Scotch and English. [. . .]

[SECOND WEEK—GLASGOW AND THE BLEACHING FIELDS—DAYS 8–9]

. . . Saw nothing remarkable after leaving Bothwell, except the first view of Glasgow, at some miles distance, terminated by the mountains of Loch Lomond. The suburbs of Glasgow extend very far, houses on each side of the highway,—all ugly, and the inhabitants dirty. The roads are very wide; and everything seems to tell of the neighbourhood of a large town. We were annoyed by carts and dirt, and the road was full of people, who all noticed our car in one way or other; the children often sent a hooting after us.

Wearied completely, we at last reached the town, and were glad to walk, leading the car to the first decent inn, which was luckily not far from the end of the town. William, who gained most of his road-knowledge from ostlers, had been informed of this house by the ostler at Hamilton; it proved quiet and tolerably cheap, a new building—the Saracen's Head. I shall never forget how glad I was to be landed in a little quiet back-parlour, for my head was beating with the noise of carts which we had left, and the wearisomeness of the disagreeable objects near the highway; but with my first pleasant sensations also came the feeling that we were not in an English inn—partly from its half-unfurnished appearance, which is common in Scotland, for in general the deal wainscots and doors are unpainted, and partly from the dirtiness of the floors. Having dined, William and I walked to the post–office, and after much seeking found out a quiet timber-yard wherein to sit down and read our letter. We then walked a considerable time in the streets, which are perhaps as handsome as streets can be, which derive no particular effect from their situation in connexion with natural advantages, such as rivers, sea, or hills. The Trongate, an old street, is very picturesque—high houses, with an intermixture of gable fronts towards the street. The New Town is built of fine stone, in the best style of the very best London streets at the west end of the town, but, not being of brick, they are greatly superior. One thing must strike every stranger in his first walk through Glasgow—an appearance of business and bustle, but no coaches or gentlemen's carriages; during all the time we walked in the streets I only saw three carriages, and these were travelling chaises. I also could not but observe a want of cleanliness in the appearance of the lower orders of the people, and a dulness in the dress and outside of the whole mass, as they moved along. We returned to the inn before it was dark. I had a bad headache, and was tired, and we all went to bed soon.

Tuesday, August 23rd.—A cold morning. Walked to the bleaching-ground, a large field bordering on the Clyde, the banks of which are perfectly flat, and the general face of the country is nearly so in the neighbourhood of Glasgow. This field, the whole summer through, is covered with women of all ages, children, and young girls spreading out their linen, and watching it while it bleaches. The scene must be very cheerful on a fine day, but it rained when we were there, and though there was linen spread out in all parts, and great numbers of women and girls were at work, yet there would have been many more on a fine day, and they would have appeared happy, instead of stupid and cheerless. In the middle of the field is a wash-house, whither the inhabitants of this large town, rich and poor, send or carry their linen to be washed. There are two very large rooms, with each a cistern in the middle for hot water; and all round the rooms are benches for the women to set their tubs upon. Both the rooms were crowded with washers; there might be a hundred, or two, or even three; for it is not easy to form an accurate notion of so great a number; however, the rooms were large, and they were both full. It was amusing to see so many women, arms, head, and face all in motion, all busy in an ordinary household employment, in which, we are accustomed to see, at the most, only three or four women employed in one place. The women were very civil. I learnt from them the regulations of the house; but I have forgotten the particulars. The substance of them is that "so much" is to be paid for each tub of water, "so much" for a tub and the privilege of washing for a day, and, "so much" to the general over-lookers of the linen, when it is left to be bleached. An old man and woman have this office, who were walking about, two melancholy figures.

The shops at Glasgow are large, and like London shops, and we passed by the largest coffee-room[11] I ever saw. You look across the piazza of the Exchange, and see to the end of the coffee-room, where there is a circular window, the width of the room. Perhaps there might be thirty gentlemen sitting on the circular bench of the window, each reading a newspaper. They had the appearance of fig-ures in a fantoccine,[12] or men seen at the extremity of the opera-house, diminished into puppets.

I am sorry I did not see the High Church: both William and I were tired, and it rained very hard after we had left the bleaching-ground; besides, I am less eager to walk in a large town than any-where else; so we put it off, and I have since repented of my irresolution.

Dined, and left Glasgow at about three o'clock, in a heavy rain. We were obliged to ride through the streets to keep our feet dry, and, in spite of the rain, every person as we went along stayed his steps to look at us; indeed, we had the pleasure of spreading smiles from one end of Glasgow to the other—for we travelled the whole length of the town. A set of schoolboys, perhaps there might be eight, with satchels over their shoulders, and, except one or two, without shoes and stockings, yet very well dressed in jackets and trousers, like gentle-men's children, followed us in great delight, admiring the car and longing to jump up. At last, though we were seated, they made sev-eral attempts to get on behind; and they looked so pretty and wild, and at the same time so modest, that we wished to give them a ride, and there being a little hill near the end of the town, we got off, and four of them who still remained, the rest having dropped into their homes by the way, took our places and indeed I would have walked two miles, willingly, to have had the pleasure of seeing them so happy. When they were to ride no longer, they scampered away, laughing and rejoicing. New houses are rising up in great numbers round Glasgow, citizen-like houses, and new plantations, chiefly of fir; the fields are frequently enclosed by hedgerows, but there is no richness, nor any particular beauty for some miles.

[11] Coffee rooms were local gathering places for news and conversation.
[12] Puppet show in which the wires of the puppets are obscured.

The first object that interested us was a gentleman's house upon a green plain or holm, almost close to the Clyde, sheltered by tall trees, a quiet modest mansion, and, though white-washed, being an old building, and no other house near it, or in connexion with it, and standing upon the level field, which belonged to it, its own domain, the whole scene together brought to our minds an image of the retiredness and sober elegance of a nunnery; but this might be owing to the greyness of the afternoon, and our having come immediately from Glasgow, and through a country which, till now, had either had a townish taint, or at best little of rural beauty. While we were looking at the house we overtook a foot-traveller, who, like many others, began to talk about our car. We alighted to walk up a hill, and, continuing the conversation, the man told us, with something like a national pride, that it belonged to a Scotch Lord, Lord Semple; he added, that a little further on we should see a much finer prospect, as fine a one as ever we had seen in our lives. Accordingly, when we came to the top of the hill, it opened upon us most magnificently. We saw the Clyde, now a stately sea-river, winding away mile after mile, spotted with boats and ships, each side of the river hilly, the right populous with single houses and villages—Dunglass Castle upon a promontory, the whole view terminated by the rock of Dumbarton, at five or six miles' distance, which stands by itself, without any hills near it, like a sea-rock.

We travelled for some time near the river, passing through clusters of houses which seemed to owe their existence rather to the wealth of the river than the land, for the banks were mostly bare, and the soil appeared poor, even near the water. The left side of the river was generally uninhabited and moorish, yet there are some beautiful spots: for instance, a nobleman's house, where the fields and trees were rich, and, in combination with the river, looked very lovely. As we went along William and I were reminded of the views upon the Thames in Kent, which, though greatly superior in richness and softness, are much inferior in grandeur. Not far from Dumbarton, we passed under some rocky, copse-covered hills, which were so like some of the hills near Grasmere that we could have half believed they were the same. Arrived at Dumbarton before it was dark, having pushed on briskly that we might have start of a traveller at the inn, who was following us as fast as he could in a gig. Every front room was full, and we were afraid we should not have been admitted. They put us into a little parlour, dirty, and smelling of liquors, the table uncleaned, and not a chair in its place; we were glad, however, of our sorry accommodations.

While tea was preparing we lolled at our ease, and though the room-window overlooked the stable-yard, and at our entrance there appeared to be nothing but gloom and unloveliness, yet while I lay stretched upon the carriage cushions on three chairs, I discovered a little side peep[13] which was enough to set the mind at work. It was no more than a smoky vessel lying at anchor, with its bare masts, a clay hut and the shelving bank of the river, with a green pasture above. Perhaps you will think that there is not much in this, as I describe it: it is true; but the effect produced by these simple objects, as they happened to be combined, together with the gloom of the evening, was exceedingly wild. Our room was parted by a slender partition from a large dining-room, in which were a number of officers and their wives, who, after the first hour, never ceased singing, dancing, laughing, or loud talking. The ladies sang some pretty songs, a great relief to us. We went early to bed; but poor Coleridge could not sleep for the noise at the street door; he lay in the parlour below stairs. It is no uncommon thing in the best inns of Scotland to have shutting-up beds in the sitting-rooms.

[THE HIGHLANDS—DAY 12]

[. . .] Our road was rough, and not easy to be kept. It was between five and six o'clock when we reached the brook side, where Coleridge and I stopped, and William went up towards the house, which was in a field, where about half a dozen people were at work. He addressed himself to one who appeared like the master, and all drew near him, staring at William as nobody could have stared but out of sheer rudeness, except in such a lonely place. He told his tale, and inquired about boats; there were no boats, and no lodging nearer than Callander, ten miles beyond the foot of the lake. A laugh was on every face when William said we were come to see the Trossachs;[14] no doubt they thought we had better have stayed at our own homes. William endeavoured to make it appear not so very foolish, by informing them that it was a place much celebrated in England, though perhaps little thought of by them, and that we

[13] Small opening.

[14] Area of woodlands and lakes east of Ben Lomond popularized by Walter Scott's description, especially in *The Lady of the Lake.*

only differed from many of our countrymen in having come the wrong way in consequence of an erroneous direction.

After a little time the gentleman said we should be accommodated with such beds as they had, and should be welcome to rest in their house if we pleased. William came back for Coleridge and me; the men all stood at the door to receive us, and now their behaviour was perfectly courteous. We were conducted into the house by the same man who had directed us hither on the other side of the lake, and afterwards we learned that he was the father of our hostess. He showed us into a room up-stairs, begged we would sit at our ease, walk out, or do just as we pleased. It was a large square deal wainscoted[15] room, the wainscot black with age, yet had never been painted: it did not look like an English room, and yet I do not know in what it differed, except that in England it is not common to see so large and well–built a room so ill-furnished there were two or three large tables, and a few old chairs of different sorts, as if they had been picked up one did not know how, at sales, or had belonged to different rooms of the house ever since it was built. We sat perhaps three-quarters of an hour, and I was about to carry down our wet coffee and sugar and ask leave to boil it, when the mistress of the house entered, a tall fine-looking woman, neatly dressed in a dark-coloured gown, with a white handkerchief tied round her head; she spoke to us in a very-pleasing manner, begging permission to make tea for us, an offer which we thankfully accepted. Encouraged by the sweetness of her manners, I went down-stairs to dry my feet by the kitchen fire; she lent me a pair of stockings, and behaved to me with the utmost attention and kindness. She carried the tea-things into the room herself, leaving me to make tea, and set before us cheese and butter and barley cakes. These cakes are as thin as our oat-bread, but, instead of being crisp, are soft and leathery, yet we, being hungry, and the butter delicious, ate them with great pleasure, but when the same bread was set before us afterwards we did not like it.

After tea William and I walked out; we amused ourselves with watching the Highlanders at work: they went leisurely about everything, and whatever was to be done, all followed, old men, and young, and little children. We were driven into the house by a shower, which came on with the evening darkness, and the people leaving their work paused at the same time. I was pleased to see them a

---

[15] Wainscot[t]ed: wood paneling applied to the lower half of a wall.

while after sitting round a blazing fire in the kitchen, father and son-in-law, master and man, and the mother with her little child on her knee. When I had been there before tea I had observed what a contrast there was between the mistress and her kitchen; she did not differ in appearance from an English country lady; but her kitchen, roof, walls, and floor of mud, was all black alike; yet now, with the light of a bright fire upon so many happy countenances, the whole room made a pretty sight.

We heard the company laughing and talking long after we were in bed; indeed, I believe they never work till they are tired. The children could not speak a word of English: they were very shy at first; but after I had caressed the eldest, and given her a red leather purse, with which she was delighted, she took hold of my hand and hung about me, changing her side-long looks for pretty smiles. Her mother lamented they were so far from school, they should be obliged to send the children down into the Lowlands to be taught reading and English. Callander, the nearest town, was twenty miles from them, and it was only a small place: they had their groceries from Glasgow. She said that at Callander was their nearest church, but sometimes "got a preaching at the Garrison." In explaining herself she informed us that the large building which had puzzled us in the morning had been built by Government, at the request of one of the Dukes of Montrose, for the defence of his domains against the attacks of Rob Roy.[16] I will not answer for the truth of this; perhaps it might have been built for this purpose, and as a check on the Highlands in general; certain it is, however, that it was a garrison; soldiers used to be constantly stationed there, and have only been withdrawn within the last thirteen or fourteen years. Mrs. Macfarlane attended me to my room; she said she hoped I should be able to sleep upon blankets, and said they were "fresh from the fauld."

[RETURN FROM THE TROSSACHS — DAY 13]

[. . .] We returned, of course, by the same road. Our guide repeated over and over again his lamentations that the day was so bad, though we had often told him—not indeed with much hope that he would believe us—that we were glad of it. As we walked along he pulled a leafy twig from a birch-tree, and, after smelling it, gave it to me, saying, how "sweet and halesome" it was, and that it

---

[16] Seventeenth-century leader of the MacGregor clan whose life became legend in Walter Scott's *Rob Roy*.

was pleasant and very halesome on a fine summer's morning to sail under the banks where the birks[17] are growing. This reminded me of the old Scotch songs, in which you continually hear of the "pu'ing the birks." Common as birches are in the north of England, I believe their sweet smell is a thing unnoticed among the peasants. We returned again to the huts to take a farewell look. We had shared our food with the ferryman and a traveller whom we had met here, who was going up the lake, and wished to lodge at the ferry-house, so we offered him a place in the boat. Coleridge chose to walk. We took the same side of the lake as before, and had much delight in visiting the bays over again; but the evening began to darken, and it rained so heavily before we had gone two miles that we were completely wet. It was dark when we landed, and on entering the house I was sick with cold.

The good woman had provided, according to her promise, a better fire than we had found in the morning; and indeed when I sate down in the chimney-corner of her smoky biggin' I thought I had never been more comfortable in my life. Coleridge had been there long enough to have a pan of coffee boiling for us, and having put our clothes in the way of drying, we all sate down, thankful for a shelter. We could not prevail upon the man of the house to draw near the fire though he was cold and wet, or to suffer his wife to get him dry clothes till she had served us, which she did, though most willingly, not very expeditiously. A Cumberland man of the same rank would not have had such a notion of what was fit and right in his own house, or if he had, one would have accused him of servility; but in the Highlander it only seemed like politeness, however erroneous and painful to us, naturally growing out of the dependence of the inferiors of the clan upon their laird; he did not, however, refuse to let his wife bring out the whisky-bottle at our request: 'She keeps a dram.' as the phrase is; indeed, I believe there is scarcely a lonely house by the wayside in Scotland where travellers may not be accommodated with a dram.[18] We asked for sugar, butter, barley-bread, and milk, and with a smile and a stare more of kindness than wonder, she replied, "Ye'll get that," bringing each article separately.

We caroused our cups of coffee, laughing like children at the strange atmosphere in which we were: the smoke came in gusts, and spread along the walls and above our heads in the chimney, where

---

[17] Birches.

[18] Alcoholic drink measuring one-eighth ounce.

the hens were roosting like light clouds in the sky. We laughed and laughed again, in spite of the smarting of our eyes, yet had a quieter pleasure in observing the beauty of the beams and rafters gleaming between the clouds of smoke. They had been crusted over and varnished by many winters, till, where the firelight fell upon them, they were as glossy as black rocks on a sunny day cased in ice. When we had eaten our supper we sate about half an hour, and I think I had never felt so deeply the blessing of a hospitable welcome and a warm fire. The man of the house repeated from time to time that we should often tell of this night when we got to our homes, and interposed praises of this, his own lake, which he had more than once, when we were returning in the boat, ventured to say was "bonnier than Loch Lomond."

Our companion from the Trossachs, who it appeared was an Edinburgh drawing–master going during the vacation on a pedestrian tour to John o' Groat's House,[19] was to sleep in the barn with William and Coleridge, where the man said he had plenty of dry hay. I do not believe that the hay of the Highlands is often very dry, but this year it had a better chance than usual, wet or dry, however, the next morning they said they had slept comfortably. When I went to bed, the mistress, desiring me to 'go ben,' attended me with a candle, and assured me that the bed was dry, though not 'sic as I had been used to.' It was of chaff; there were two others in the room, a cupboard and two chests, on one of which stood the milk in wooden vessels covered over; I should have thought that milk so kept could not have been sweet, but the cheese and butter were good. The walls of the whole house were of stone unplastered. It consisted of three apartments,—the cow-house at one end, the kitchen or house in the middle, and the spence[20] at the other end. The rooms were divided, not up to the rigging, but only to the beginning of the roof, so that there was a free passage for light and smoke from one end, of the house to the other.

I went to bed some time before the family. The door was shut between us, and they had a bright fire, which I could not see; but the light it sent up among the varnished rafters and beams, which crossed each other in almost as intricate and fantastic a manner as I have seen

[19] John o' Groats, Britain's northernmost village, is named for Dutchman Jan de Groot, who in the fifteenth century began ferry service from there to the Orkney Islands. The phrase "Land's End to John o' Groats" denotes the entire length of Great Britain or a great distance.

[20] Larder or pantry.

the under-boughs of a large beech-tree withered by the depth of the shade above, produced the most beautiful effect that can be conceived. It was like what I should suppose an underground cave or temple to be, with a dripping or moist roof, and the moonlight entering in upon it by some means or other, and yet the colours were more like melted gems. I lay looking up till the light of the fire faded away, and the man and his wife and child had crept into their bed at the other end of the room. I did not sleep much, but passed a comfortable night, for my bed, though hard, was warm and clean: the unusualness of my situation prevented me from sleeping. I could hear the waves beat against the shore of the lake; a little syke close to the door made a much louder noise; and when I sate up in my bed I could see the lake through an open window-place at the bed's head. Add to this, it rained all night. I was less occupied by remembrance of the Trossachs, beautiful as they were, than the vision of the Highland hut, which I could not get out of my head. I thought of the Fairyland of Spenser, and what I had read in romance at other times, and then, what a feast would it be for a London pantomime-maker, could he but transplant it to Drury Lane,[21] with all its beautiful colours!

[THIRD WEEK — RETURN TO TARBET, SEPARATION FROM COLERIDGE — DAYS 14–15]

[. . .] We were rowed over speedily by the assistance of two youths, who went backwards and forwards for their own amusement, helping at the oars, and pulled as if they had strength and spirits to spare for a year to come. We noticed that they had uncommonly fine teeth, and that they and the boatman were very handsome people. Another merry crew took our place in the boat.

We had three miles to walk to Tarbet. It rained, but not heavily; the mountains were not concealed from us by the mists, but appeared larger and more grand; twilight was coming on, and the obscurity under which we saw the objects, with the sounding of the torrents, kept our minds alive and wakeful; all was solitary and huge—sky, water, and mountains mingled together. While we were walking forward, the road leading us over the top of a brow, we stopped suddenly at the sound of a half-articulate Gaelic[22] hooting

---

[21] One of London's principal theaters.

[22] Ancient language of Scotland and Ireland; Celtic.

from the field close to us. It came from a little boy, whom we could see on the hill between us and the lake, wrapped up in a grey plaid. He was probably calling home the cattle for the night. His appearance was in the highest degree moving to the imagination: mists were on the hillsides, darkness shutting in upon the huge avenue of mountains, torrents roaring, no house in sight to which the child might belong; his dress, cry, and appearance all different from anything we had been accustomed to. It was a text, as William has since observed to me, containing in itself the whole history of the Highlander's life—his melancholy, his simplicity, his poverty, his superstition, and above all, that visionariness which results from a communion with the unworldliness of nature.

When we reached Tarbet the people of the house were anxious to know how we had fared, particularly the girl who had waited upon us. Our praises of Loch Ketterine made her exceedingly happy, and she ventured to say, of which we had heard not a word before, that it was "bonnier to *her* fancy than Loch Lomond." The landlord, who was not at home when we had set off, told us that if he had known of our going he would have recommended us to Mr. Macfarlane's or the other farmhouse, adding that they were hospitable people in that vale. Coleridge and I got tea, and William and the drawing-master chose supper; they asked to have a broiled fowl, a dish very common in Scotland, to which the mistress replied, "Would not a 'boiled' one do as well?" They consented, supposing that it would be more easily cooked; but when the fowl made its appearance, to their great disappointment it proved a cold one that had been stewed in the broth at dinner.

Monday, August 29th.—It rained heavily this morning, and, having heard so much of the long rains since we came into Scotland, as well as before, we had no hope that it would be over in less than three weeks at the least, so poor Coleridge, being very unwell, determined to send his clothes to Edinburgh and make the best of his way thither, being afraid to face much wet weather in an open carriage. William and I were unwilling to be confined at Tarbet, so we resolved to go to Arrochar, a mile and a half on the road to Inverary, where there is an inn celebrated as a place of good accommodation for travellers. Coleridge and I set off on foot, and William was to follow with the car, but a heavy shower coming on, Coleridge left me to shelter in a hut and wait for William, while he went on before. . . .

Left Arrochar at about four o'clock in the afternoon. Coleridge accompanied us a little way; we portioned out the contents of our purse before our parting; and, after we had lost sight of him, drove heavily along. Crossed the bridge, and looked to the right, up the vale, which is soon terminated by mountains: it was of a yellow green, with but few trees and few houses; sea-gulls were flying above it. Our road—the same along which the carriages had come—was directly under the mountains on our right hand, and the lake was close to us on our left, the waves breaking among stones overgrown with yellow sea-weed; fishermen's boats, and other larger vessels than are seen on fresh-water lakes were lying at anchor near the opposite shore; sea-birds flying overhead; the noise of torrents mingled with the beating of the waves, and misty mountains enclosed the vale;—a melancholy but not a dreary scene. Often have I, in looking over a map of Scotland, followed the intricate windings of one of these sea-lochs, till, pleasing myself with my own imaginations, I have felt a longing, almost painful, to travel among them by land or by water.

This was the first sea-loch we had seen. We came prepared for a new and great delight, and the first impression which William and I received, as we drove rapidly through the rain down the lawn of Arrochar, the objects dancing before us, was even more delightful than we had expected. But, as I have said, when we looked through the window, as the mists disappeared and the objects were seen more distinctly, there was less of sheltered valley–comfort than we had fancied to ourselves, and the mountains were not so grand; and now that we were near to the shore of the lake, and could see that it was not of fresh water, the wreck, the broken sea-shells, and scattered sea-weed gave somewhat of a dull and uncleanly look to the whole lake, and yet the water was clear, and might have appeared as beautiful as that of Loch Lomond, if with the same pure pebbly shore. Perhaps, had we been in a more cheerful mood of mind we might have seen everything with a different eye. The stillness of the mountains, the motion of the waves, the Streaming torrents, the sea-birds, the fishing-boats were all melancholy; yet still, occupied as my mind was with other things, I thought of the long windings through which the waters of the sea had come to this inland retreat, visiting the inner solitudes of the mountains, and I could have wished to have mused out a summer's day on the shores of the lake. From the foot of these mountains whither might not a little barque carry one away? Though so far inland, it is but a slip of the great ocean: seamen, fishermen, and shepherds here find a natural home. We did not travel far down the lake, but, turning to the right through an opening of the mountains, entered a glen called Glen Croe.

Our thoughts were full of Coleridge, and when we were enclosed in the narrow dale, with a length of winding road before us, a road that seemed to have insinuated itself into the very heart of the mountains—the brook, the road, bare hills, floating mists, scattered stones, rocks, and herds of black cattle being all that we could see,—I shivered at the thought of his being sickly and alone, travelling from place to place.

The Cobbler, on our right, was pre-eminent above the other hills; the singular rocks on its summit, seen so near, were like ruins—castles or watch-towers. After we had passed one reach of the glen, another opened out, long, narrow, deep, and houseless, with herds of cattle and large stones; but the third reach was softer and more beautiful, as if the mountains had there made a warmer shelter, and there were a more gentle climate. The rocks by the river-side had dwindled away, the mountains were smooth and green, and towards the end, where the glen sloped upwards, it was a cradle-like hollow, and at that point where the slope became a hill, at the very bottom of the curve of the cradle, stood one cottage, with a few fields and beds of potatoes. There was also another house near the roadside, which appeared to be a herdsman's hut. The dwelling in the middle of the vale was a very pleasing object. I said within myself, How quietly might a family live in this pensive solitude, cultivating and loving their own fields! but the herdsman's hut, being the only one in the vale, had a melancholy face; not being attached to any particular plot of land, one could not help considering it as just kept alive and above ground by some dreary connexion with the long barren tract we had traveled through.

The afternoon had been exceedingly pleasant after we had left the vale of Arrochar; the sky was often threatening, but the rain blew off, and the evening was uncommonly fine. The sun had set a short time before we had dismounted from the car to walk up the steep hill at the end of the glen. Clouds were moving all over the sky—some of a brilliant yellow hue, which shed a light like bright moonlight upon the mountains. We could not have seen the head of the valley under more favourable circumstances.

The passing away of a storm is always a time of life and cheerfulness, especially in a mountainous country; but that afternoon and evening the sky was in an extraordinary degree vivid and beautiful.

We often stopped in ascending the hill to look down the long reach of the glen. The road, following the course of the river as far as we could see, the farm and cottage hills, smooth towards the base and rocky higher up, were the sole objects before us. This part of Glen Croe reminded us of some of the dales of the north of England— Grisdale above Ulswater, for instance; but the length of it, and the broad highway, which is always to be seen at a great distance, a sort of centre of the vale, a point of reference, gives to the whole of the glen, and each division of it, a very different character.

At the top of the hill we came to a seat with the well-known inscription, "Rest and be thankful." On the same stone it was recorded that the road had been made by Col. Wade's regiment.[23][. . .]

[FERRY RIDE—DAY 19]

[. . .] The shores of Loch Etive, in their moorish, rocky wildness, their earthly bareness, as they lay in length before us, produced a contrast which, with the pure sea, the brilliant sunshine, the long distance, contributed to the aerial and romantic power with which the mountain island was invested.

Soon after, we came to the ferry. The boat being on the other shore, we had to wait a considerable time, though the water was not wide, and our call was heard immediately. The boatmen moved with surly tardiness, as if glad to make us know that they were our masters. At this point the lake was narrowed to the breadth of not a very wide river by a round ear or promontory on the side on which we were, and a low ridge of peat-mossy ground on the other. It was a dreary place, shut out from the beautiful prospect of the Isle of Mull, and Dunstaffnage Castle—so the fortress was called. Four or five men came over with the boat; the horse was unyoked, and being harshly driven over rough stones, which were as slippery as ice, with slimy seaweed, he was in terror before he reached the boat, and they completed the work by beating and pushing him by main force over the ridge of the boat, for there was no open end, or plank, or any other convenience for shipping either horse or carriage. I was very uneasy when we were launched on the water. A blackguard-looking fellow, blind of one eye, which I could not but think had

---

[23] Part of 250 miles of road built under the supervision of George Wade (1673–1748), the British military commander in Scotland; the section from Glencoe is called Rest-and-be-Thankful.

been put out in some strife or other, held him by force like a horse-breaker, while the poor creature fretted, and stamped with his feet against the bare boards, frightening himself more and more with every stroke; and when we were in the middle of the water I would have given a thousand pounds to have been sure that we should reach the other side in safety. The tide was rushing violently in, making a strong eddy with the stream of the loch, so that the motion of the boat and the noise and foam of the waves terrified him still more, and we thought it would be impossible to keep him in the boat, and when we were just far enough from the shore to have been all drowned he became furious, and, plunging desperately, his hind-legs were in the water, then, recovering himself, he beat with such force against the boat-side that we were afraid he should send his feet through. All the while the men were swearing terrible oaths, and cursing the poor beast, redoubling their curses when we reached the landing-place, and whipping him ashore in brutal triumph.

We had only room for half a heartful of joy when we set foot on dry land, for another ferry was to be crossed five miles further. We had intended breakfasting at this house if it had been a decent place; but after this affair we were glad to pay the men off and depart, though I was not well and needed refreshment. The people made us more easy by assuring us that we might easily swim the horse over the next ferry. The first mile or two of our road was over a peat-moss; we then came near to the sea-shore, and had beautiful views backwards towards the Island of Mull and Dunstaffnage Castle, and forward where the sea ran up between the hills. In this part, on the opposite side of the small bay or elbow of the sea, was a gentleman's house on a hillside, and a building on the hill-top which we took for a lighthouse, but were told that it belonged to the mansion, and was only lighted up on rejoicing days—the laird's birthday, for instance.

Before we had left the peat-moss to travel close to the sea-shore we delighted ourselves with looking on a range of green hills, in shape like those bordering immediately upon the sea, abrupt but not high; they were, in fact, a continuation of the same; but retiring backwards, and rising from the black peat-moss. These hills were of a delicate green, uncommon in Scotland; a foaming rivulet ran down one part, and near it lay two herdsmen full in the sun, with their dogs, among a troop of black cattle which were feeding near, and sprinkled over the whole range of hills—a pastoral scene, to our eyes the more beautiful from knowing what a delightful prospect it must overlook. We now came under the steeps by the sea-side, which were bold rocks, mouldering scars, or fresh with green grass. Under the brow of one of these rocks was a burying-ground, with many upright grave-stones and hay–cocks between, and fenced round by a wall neatly sodded. Near it were one or two houses, with out-houses under a group of trees, but no chapel. The neatness of the burying-ground would in itself have been noticeable in any part of Scotland where we have been; but it was more interesting from its situation than for its own sake—within the sound of the gentlest waves of the sea, and near so many quiet and beautiful objects. There was a range of hills opposite, which we were here first told were the hills of Morven, so much sung of by Ossian.[24] We consulted with some men respecting the ferry, who advised us by all means to send our horse round the loch, and go ourselves over in the boat: they were very civil, and seemed to be intelligent men, yet all disagreed about the length of the loch, though we were not two miles from it: one said it was only six miles long, another ten or fifteen, and afterwards a man whom we met told us it was twenty.

We lost sight of the sea for some time, crossing a half-cultivated space, then reached Loch Creran, a large irregular sea loch, with low sloping banks, coppice woods, and uncultivated grounds, with a scattering of corn fields; as it appeared to us, very thinly inhabited: mountains at a distance. We found only women at home at the ferry-house. I was faint and cold, and went to sit by the fire, but, though very much needing refreshment, I had not heart to eat any-thing there—the house was so dirty, and there were so many wretchedly dirty women and children; yet perhaps I might have got over the dirt, though I believe there are few ladies who would not have been turned sick by it, if there had not been a most disgusting combination of laziness and coarseness in the countenances and manners of the women, though two of them were very handsome. It was a small hut, and four women were living in it: one, the mother of the children and mistress of the house; the others I supposed to be lodgers, or perhaps servants; but there was no work amongst them. They had just taken from the fire a great pan full of potatoes,

---

[24] Ossian, son of Fingal, was a construction of the poet James Macpherson (1736–1796). In *The Works of Ossian* (1765), he claimed the poems were Gaelic equivalents of classical epics such as the *Iliad* and *Odyssey*.

which they mixed up with milk, all helping themselves out of the same vessel, and the little children put in their dirty hands to dig out of the mess at their pleasure. I thought to myself, How light the labour of such a house as this! Little sweeping, no washing of floors, and as to scouring the table, I believe it was a thing never thought of. [. . .]

[BALLACHULLISH TO GLEN COE—DAYS 19–20]

[. . .] The road grew very bad, and we had an anxious journey till we saw a light before us, which with great joy we assured ourselves was from the inn; but what was our distress when, on going a few steps further, we came to a bridge half broken down, with bushes laid across to prevent travellers from going over. After some perplexity we determined that I should walk on to the house before us—for we could see that the bridge was safe for foot-passengers— and ask for assistance. By great good luck, at this very moment four or five men came along the road towards us and offered to help William in driving the car through the water, which was not very deep at that time, though, only a few days before, the damage had been done to the bridge by a flood.

I walked on to the inn, ordered tea, and was conducted into a lodging-room. I desired to have a fire, and was answered with the old scruple about "giving fire"[25]—with, at the same time, an excuse "that it was so late"—the girl, however, would ask the landlady, who was lying-in; the fire was brought immediately, and from that time the girl was very civil. I was not, however, quite at ease, for William stayed long, and I was going to leave my fire to seek after him, when I heard him at the door with the horse and car. The horse had taken fright with the roughness of the river-bed and the rattling of the wheels—the second fright in consequence of the ferry—and the men had been obliged to unyoke him and drag the car through, a troublesome affair for William; but he talked less of the trouble and alarm than of the pleasure he had felt in having met with such true goodwill and ready kindness in the Highlanders. They drank their glass of whisky at the door, wishing William twenty good wishes, and asking him twice as many questions,—if he was married,

[25] The local folklore involves many superstitions concerning beliefs about fires and spirits.

if he had an estate, where he lived, etc. etc. This inn is the ferry-house on the main road up into the Highlands by Fort-William, and here Coleridge, though unknown to us, had slept three nights before.

Saturday, September 3rd.—When we have arrived at an unknown place by moonlight, it is never a moment of indifference when I quit it again with the morning light, especially if the objects have appeared beautiful, or in any other way impressive or interesting. I have kept back, unwilling to go to the window, that I might not lose the picture taken to my pillow at night. So it was at Ballachulish: and instantly I felt that the passing away of my own fancies was a loss. The place had appeared exceedingly wild by moonlight; I had mistaken corn-fields for naked rocks, and the lake had appeared narrower and the hills more steep and lofty than they really were.

We rose at six o'clock, and took a basin of milk before we set forward on our journey to Glen Coe. It was a delightful morning, the road excellent, and we were in good spirits, happy that we had no more ferries to cross, and pleased with the thought that we were going among the grand mountains which we saw before us at the head of the loch. We travelled close to the water's edge, and were rolling along a smooth road, when the horse suddenly backed, frightened by the upright shafts of a roller rising from behind the wall of a field adjoining the road. William pulled, whipped, and struggled in vain; we both leapt upon the ground, and the horse dragged the car after him, he going backwards down the bank of the loch, and it was turned over, half in the water, the horse lying on his back, struggling in the harness, a frightful sight! I gave up everything; thought that the horse would be lamed, and the car broken to pieces. Luckily a man came up in the same moment, and assisted William in extricating the horse, and, after an hour's delay, with the help of strings and pocket-handkerchiefs, we mended the harness and set forward again, William leading the poor animal all the way, for the regular beating of the waves frightened him, and any little gushing stream that crossed the road would have sent him off. The village where the blacksmith lived was before us—a few huts under the mountains, and, as it seemed, at the head of the loch; but it runs further up to the left, being narrowed by a hill above the village, near which, at the edge of the water, was a slate quarry, and many large boats with masts, on the water below, high mountains shutting in the prospect, which stood in single, distinguishable shapes, yet clustered together—simple and bold in their forms, and their surfaces of all characters and all colours—some that looked as if scarified by fire, others green; and there was one that might have been blasted by an eternal frost, its summit and sides for a considerable way down being as white as hoar-frost at eight o'clock on a winter's morning. No clouds were on the hills; the sun shone bright, but the wind blew fresh and cold.

When we reached the blacksmith's shop, I left William to help to take care of the horse, and went into the house. The mistress, with a child in her arms and two or three running about, received me very kindly, making many apologies for the dirty house, which she partly attributed to its being Saturday; but I could plainly see that it was dirt of all days. I sate in the midst of it with great delight, for the woman's benevolent, happy countenance almost converted her slovenly and lazy way of leaving all things to take care of themselves into a comfort and a blessing.

It was not a Highland hut, but a slated house built by the master of the quarry for the accommodation of his blacksmith,—the shell of an English cottage, as if left unfinished by the workmen, without plaster, and with floor of mud. Two beds, with not over-clean bed-clothes, were in the room. Luckily for me there was a good fire and a boiling kettle. The woman was very sorry she had no butter; none was to be had in the village: she gave me oaten and barley bread. We talked over the fire; I answered her hundred questions, and in my turn put some to her. She asked me, as usual, if I was married, how many brothers I had, etc. etc. I told her that William was married, and had a fine boy; to which she replied, "And the man's a decent man too." Her next-door neighbour came in with a baby on her arm, to request that I would accept of some fish, which I broiled in the ashes. She joined in our conversation, but with more shyness than her neighbour, being a very young woman. She happened to say that she was a stranger in that place, and had been bred and born a long way off. On my asking her where, she replied, "At Leadhills"; and when I told her that I had been there, a joy lighted up her countenance which I shall never forget, and when she heard that it was only a fortnight before, her eyes filled with tears. I was exceedingly affected with the simplicity of her manners; her tongue was now let loose, and she would have talked forever of Leadhills, of her mother, of the quietness of the people in general, and the goodness of Mrs. Otto, who, she told me, was a "varra discreet woman." She was sure we should be "well put up" at Mrs. Otto's, and praised her house and furniture; indeed, it seemed she thought all earthly comforts were gathered together under the bleak heights that surround the villages of Wanlockhead and Leadhills: and afterwards, when I said it was a wild country thereabouts, she even seemed surprised, and said it was not half so wild as where she lived now. One circumstance which she mentioned of Mrs. Otto I must record, both in proof of her "discretion" and the sobriety of the people at Leadhills, namely that no liquor was ever drunk in her house after a certain hour of the night—I have forgotten what hour; but it was an early one, I am sure not later than 10. [. . .]

[RETURN HOME—DAYS 41–42]

[. . .] *Saturday, September 24th.*—Rose very early and travelled about nine miles to Longtown, before breakfast, along the banks of the Esk. About half a mile from Langholm crossed a bridge. At this part of the vale, which is narrow, the steeps are covered with old oaks and every variety of trees. Our road for some time through the wood, then came to a more open country, exceedingly rich and populous; the banks of the river frequently rocky, and hung with wood; many gentlemen's houses. There was the same rich variety while the river continued to flow through Scottish grounds; but not long after we had passed through the last turnpike gate in Scotland and the first in England—but a few yards asunder—the vale widens, and its aspect was cold, and even dreary, though Sir James Graham's plantations are very extensive. His house, a large building, stands in this open part of the vale. Longtown was before us, and ere long we saw the well-remembered guide-post, where the circuit of our six weeks' travels had begun, and now was ended.

We did not look along the white line of the road to Solway Moss without some melancholy emotion, though we had the fair prospect of the Cumberland mountains full in view, with the certainty, barring accidents, of reaching our own dear home the next day. Breakfasted at the Graham's Arms. The weather had been very fine from the time of our arrival at Jedburgh, and this was a very pleasant day. The sun "shone fair on Carlisle's walls"[26] when we first saw them

[26] A variation of "The sun shines fair on Carlisle wall," the second line of the stanzas in Scott's "It was an English Ladye Bright," from *Lay of the Last Minstrel,* Canto 6, XI–XII: "She leaned her back against a thorn / The sun shines fair on Carlisle's walls./ And there she has her young lord born, / And the lyon shall be lord of a'." At the end of the tour the Wordsworths made Scott's acquaintance, and he shared some work in progress (John Gibson Lockhart, *Memoirs of the Life of Sir Walter Scott,* 2, 160–161). The line is adapted from an old Scots ballad.

from the top of the opposite hill. Stopped to look at the place on the sand near the bridge where Hatfield had been executed. Put up at the same inn as before, and were recognised by the woman who had waited on us. Everybody spoke of Hatfield as an injured man. After dinner went to a village six miles further, where we slept.

Sunday, September 25th, 1803.—A beautiful autumnal day. Breakfasted at a public-house by the road-side; dined at Threlkeld; arrived at home between eight and nine o'clock, where we found Mary in perfect health, Joanna Hutchinson with her, and little John asleep in the clothes-basket by the fire. [. . .]

MARY JONES AND HER PET-LAMB

Designed for her niece and nephew, this tale is perhaps the piece
mentioned to Lady Beaumont in Dorothy's letter of April 20, 1806.[1]
Like so much of her work, it ponders the vulnerability of the family
circle and a natural world that preserves and destroys.

MARY JONES AND HER PET-LAMB. A TALE WRITTEN TO
AMUSE JOHN & DOROTHY

William Jones and Margaret his Wife lived at the farthest house in
one of the Cumberland Dales, just at the foot of the mountains. It
was a pretty place; William's Father & Grandfather were born &
had dwelt there all their lives; & they had planted trees round their
cottage to keep off the cold winds that blew from the Mountains:
and now the trees were grown tall and spreading, and made a pleasant shade in summer, and though the wind roared among their
branches on boisterous winter nights, telling of the storm, they fenced
the Cottage and kept it warm, and, while William & Margaret sate
by their fire of peat and sticks with their little Daughter on her
three–legged stool beside them they blessed God for their comfortable lot; and often talked with thankful and chearful hearts of the
innocent lives their Forefathers had spent.

I have told you that William Jones's little Daughter used to sit
by her Father & Mother on her stool in the winter's evenings: she
had her own place in the chimney–corner; and every evening she
read to them a chapter in the Bible, or often a story out of one of
her little books; for when her Father went to the market town he
seldom came home without a new book for Mary, because she took
care of them, and though she had never been at school was a good
scholar, and noticed so well what she read that she could tell over
again many of the histories which she found in the Bible or in other
books. Her Parents had no child but her; and they loved her dearly.
She was her Mother's companion when her Husband was out in the
fields; and often too she followed her Father; and sometimes went

---

[1] Telling of how she cannot write verse, she continues: "Descriptions, Sentiments, or
little stories for children was all I could be ambitious of doing, and I did try one
story, but failed so sadly that I was completely discouraged."

with him a long way up the mountains when he, with help of his Dog, gathered the sheep together; and he would call her his little Shepherdess. Their house was far from any other Dwelling, so that Mary Jones (having no Brothers or Sisters) had not any Companions like herself; yet she had playfellows; the great Sheep-dog fondled, & jumped about her; & she fed the Chickens & the Ducks, & they would flock round her whenever she went into the yard; and nobody had such sleek beautiful cats as little Mary. It was a pretty sight to see her by the blazing fire; often with one cat on her knee, another at her feet, and a pair of kittens playing beside her; she had pigeons, too, & they would peck out of her hand, and she loved to sit and watch the bees carry their burthens to the hive: she was not afraid of them, for, as she did not tieze them, they never stung her. One snowy morning in February her Father brought a young Lamb home in his arms. Its Mother had died, and the helpless creature was nearly perishing with cold. It could not stand; so a basket was brought to the fire, and it was put into it, and covered up with wool, and Mary watched over it the whole day, and fed it with warm milk. She dreamt about it at night; and pleased she was, the next morning, to see it stand upon the hearth; but its limbs tottered, and it bleated piteously. The Child continued to nurse it till it grew strong; and then it was truly her favorite Playmate: it followed her all about in house and field, so that you hardly ever saw Mary without her Lamb, except when she went to Church, and as the Church was at the foot of the Valley above three miles off, Mary and her Mother could only go thither when the weather was fine. One Sunday after noon, towards the end of the month of June, when she had been at Church she straightway ran to seek her Lamb: she had her hands full of flowers which she had gathered by the way to make a garland for its neck: she was used to play with such fancies, & the Lamb would stand still and patient while she was busied with her work; and, when the work was done, she in pride and love, would praise its beauty, and strength, and lusty size, burying her hands in its white warm fleece. As I have said, as soon as she came from Church she went to seek for the Lamb; she called to it by its name, but it did not run to her as usual, & it was nowhere to be found. That evening both she and all the household went about searching every nook in the fields, but all in vain; and poor Mary, long after she was in bed, cried bitterly. The next morning she waked in sorrow, I believe for the first time in her life, for though she had had her little griefs as all Children will have, she never before felt a grief that a night's sleep did not wear away. She began to weep again upon her pillow; but soon, looking about, she saw the pleasant sunshine upon the hills, and, drying her tears, she dressed herself with a lighter heart, hoping now that the lost one would be found, or would come home.

Again she searched, and in vain; and, at noon she sate down very sad, and all that afternoon she was grave and silent, and did not stir from her seat. At supper-time, however, she bethought her that the Lamb had been brought from the mountains, & perhaps was gone thither again; so, without telling any body what was in her mind, she left her porringer of milk upon the table, put her piece of bread into her pocket, and, slipping out of doors, began to climb the mountain, and she had got to the very top without observing that the sun had long been sunk behind the hills on the other side of the Valley. She then sate down quite tired; but she looked about for her Pet lamb, and fancied she saw it jump down a Rock at a little distance: she shouted; & presently the Creature ran to her, & leaping up, put its paws round her waist. I know not whether the Child or her Lamb was more glad. Mary sate down to rest again, and took out her bread, & they feasted together: for she had eaten no supper till now. When this was done she began to think of going home again, and how pleased her Mother would be that the Lamb was found; but when she looked for her way down she was quite at a loss. It was not dark, but the day light was faded, and she could not see her Father's house, or the trees, or the fields; she wandered about & about, often stumbling over the rocks: little did it serve her now that she had been a stout climber by her Father's side. At last she sate down with the Lamb beside her, & if she was in trouble the night before, what must she have felt now! She could not go a step further for weariness & fear, and, almost broken-hearted at the thought that she should never more see her Father & Mother, she laid herself on the ground & wept aloud. The poor Lamb lay down close to her, as if it wanted to keep her warm, and after a long time the Child fell asleep.

Mary had not been gone many minutes from the house before her Parents missed her but they thought little of it at first because she was accustomed to stray by herself in the fields; however at 1/2 past nine o'clock when the Family were preparing to go to bed, the Mother said, "but where is little Mary?" & called for her at the door, and as Mary did not answer she went out into the fields to seek her, shouting all the while, and, when she had gone all over their own grounds and did not find her Child her heart misgave her: she returned to the house to fetch her Husband, & they passed a miserable night, wandering about, & scarcely knowing whither. Towards morning, without any hope of finding her alive, they went up the mountain, and just after the sun had risen they came to the spot where she had fallen asleep, & still lay with her arms clasped round the Lamb's neck, as the Babes in the Wood were lying when Robin Red-breast covered them with leaves. William & Margaret, almost out of their senses with fear to find her dead & cold, went to her, & touched her: and Oh! what comfort and joy they had to feel that that part of her body which was close to the Lamb was warm, and to hear her breathe sweetly!—one moment, they wept in thankfulness over their Child; but stayed not; The Father took her up in his arms without waking her, wrapped her in his coat and bore her homeward, the Mother by their side, & the Lamb following.

By happy chance (poor thing! she had been too wretched to *think* about what she was doing) Mary had lain in the midst of a large plot of hether (perhaps the toil of wading through it had caused her to drop down there!) and the hether was so thick and dry that the damp from the ground could hardly reach her; and surely the Heavens looked graciously upon her helpless state; for it had been the mildest night of all the year; and now the morning was serene and beautiful. When they had reached the house the Mother softly undressed her; and Mary did not awake till nine o'clock the next morning. At her first waking she knew not where she had been, and hardly knew where she then was; for all that had passed was like a dream; but soon she cried for joy to find herself in her Mother's arms.

The Father & Mother fervently thanked God for having preserved their Child, and she, from that day, never strayed from home unknown to them & was a very dutiful and good Girl, and continued to be a comfort to her Parents, and after she was grown up to be a Woman, took care of them when they were infirm and old.

The Pet-lamb became a fine Ewe and brought forth many Lambs, and the Father said that, in memory of that night, it should never be killed by knife, so it lived on many years, and died of old age in the field close to the house, and was buried under a rose tree beside the bee-hives.

A NARRATIVE CONCERNING GEORGE
AND SARAH GREEN

After attending a Langdale farm sale in March of 1808, George and Sarah Green perished in a snowstorm while trying to return over the hills to their home in Easedale. The people of Grasmere organized to care for the orphans, eight children under the age of sixteen. Dorothy wrote this account as a fund-raising document. The narrative, "Addressed to a Friend," probably Joanna Hutchinson, is presented as a kind of particular discourse that life at Grasmere generates: "fireside talk in our cottages." The text here is my transcription of the copy Dorothy sent to Catherine Clarkson.

A NARRATIVE CONCERNING GEORGE AND SARAH
GREEN OF THE PARISH OF GRASMERE ADDRESSED
TO A FRIEND

You remember a single Cottage at the foot of Blentern Gill:—it is the only dwelling on the western Side of the upper reaches of the Valley of Easedale, and close under the mountain; a little stream runs over rocks and stones beside the garden wall, after tumbling down the crags above. I am sure you recollect the spot: if not, you remember George and Sarah Green who dwelt there. They left their home to go into Langdale the afternoon of Saturday the 19th of March last: it was a very cold day with snow showers. They fixed upon that time for going because there was to be a Sale there; not that they wanted to make purchases; but for the sake of mingling a little amusement with the main object of the woman's journey which was to see her Daughter who was in service[1] there, and to settle with her Mistress about her continuing in her place. Accordingly, after having spent a few hours at the Sale, they went to the house where the young Woman lived, drank tea, and set off homewards at about five o'clock, intending to crossover right over the Fells, and drop down just upon their own Cottage; and they were seen nearly at the top of the hill in their direct course, by some persons in Langdale, and were never more seen alive. It is supposed that soon

---

[1] Typically commencing at age eight, "service" involved domestic labor in exchange for room and board and perhaps a small salary.

afterwards they must have been bewildered by a mist, otherwise they might almost have reached their own Cottage at the bottom of the hill on the opposite side before daylight was entirely gone. They had left a Daughter at home, eleven years of age, with the care of five other Children younger than herself, the youngest an Infant at the breast; and they, poor Things! sate up till eleven o'clock expecting their Parents: they then went to bed thinking they stayed all night in Langdale because of the weather. All next day they continued to expect them, and again went to bed as before; and at noon on Monday one of the Boys went to the nearest house to borrow a Cloak, and, on being asked for what purpose, he replied that his Sister was going to Langdale, as he expressed it, "to lait their Folk," meaning to seek their Father and Mother, who had not come home again, as they expected them, on Saturday. The Man of the house started up immediately, saying that "they were lost!"—he spread the alarm through the neighbourhood; and many Men went out upon the hills to search; but in vain; no traces of them could be found; nor any tidings heard, except what I have mentioned, and that Shepherd who had been upon the Mountains on Sunday morning had observed indistinct foot-marks of two Persons who had walked close together. Those foot-marks were now covered with fresh snow: the spot where they had been seen was at the top of Blea Crag above Easedale Tarn, that very spot where I myself had sate down six years ago, unable to see a yard before me, or to go a step further over the Crags. I had left my brother at Stickell Tarn. A mist came on after I had parted with him, and I wandered long, not knowing whither. When at last the mist cleared away I found myself at the edge of the Precipice, and trembled at the Gulph below, which appeared immeasurable. Happily I had some hours of daylight before me; and after a laborious walk I arrived at home in the evening. The neighbourhood of this Precipice had been searched above and below, wherever foot could come; yet, recollecting my own dreadful situation, I could not help believing that George and Sarah Green were lying somewhere thereabouts. On Tuesday as long as daylight lasted the search was continued. It was like a sabbath in the Vale: for all the Men who were able to climb the heights had left their usual work, nor returned to it till the Bodies of the unfortunate Pair were found, which was on Wednesday afternoon. The Woman was first discovered upon some rough ground just above the mountain enclosures beside Mill Beck, in Langdale, which is the next stream or torrent to that which forms Dungeon Gill Waterfall.

Several Persons, the day before, had been within a few yards of the spot where she lay; but her body had then been covered with snow, which was now melted. Her Husband was found at no great distance: he had fallen down a Precipice; and must have perished instantly, for his skull was much fractured. It is supposed that his Wife had been by his side when he fell, as one of her shoes was left midway on the Bank above the Precipice; afterwards (probably having stumbled over a crag) she had rolled many yards down the breast of the hill. Her body was, terribly bruised. It is believed that they must have perished before midnight, their cries or shrieks having been distinctly heard by two Persons in Langdale at about ten o'clock; but they paid little attention to the sounds, thinking they came from some drunken People who had been at the Sale. At that time the wretched Pair had no doubt resigned all hope of reaching their own home, and were attempting to find a shelter any where; and, at the spot where they perished they might have seen lights from the windows of that same house where their cries were actually heard.

Soon after the alarm had been spread on Monday afternoon (and from that moment all were convinced of the truth; for it was well known that if the Mother had been alive she would have returned to her sucking Babe) two or three Women, Friends of the Family (Neighbours they call themselves; but they live at the opposite side of the dale) went to take care of the poor Children, and they found them in a wretched state—all crying together. They had passed two whole days (from Saturday noon till Monday noon) without seeing anybody, waiting patiently and without fear; and when the word came that their Father and Mother must have died upon the hills it was like a thunderstroke. In a little time, however, they were somewhat pacified; and food was brought into the house; for their stock was almost exhausted, their Parents being the poorest People in the Vale, though they had a small estate of their own, and a Cow. This morsel of Land, now deeply mortgaged, had been in the possession of the Family for many generations, and they were loth to part with it: consequently they had never had any assistance from the Parish. George Green had been twice married. By his former Wife he has left one Son and three Daughters; and by her who died with him four Sons and four Daughters, all under sixteen years of age. They must very soon have parted with their Land if they had lived; for their means were reduced by little and little till scarcely anything but the Land was left. The Cow was grown old; and they had not money to buy another; they had sold their Horse; and were in the habit of carrying any trifles they could spare out of house or stable to barter for potatoes or oat-meal. Luxuries they had none. They never made tea; and when the Neighbours went to look after the Children they found nothing in the house but two boilings of potatoes, a very little meal, a little bread, and three or four legs of lean dried mutton. The Cow at that time did not give a quart of milk in the day.—You will wonder how they lived at all; and indeed I can scarcely tell you. They used to sell a few peats in the summer, which they dug out of their own hearts' heart, their Land; and the old Man (he was sixty-five years of age) might earn a little money by doing jobs for his neighbours; but it was not known till now (at least *by us*) how much distressed they must have been: for they were never heard to murmur or complain. See them when you would, both were chearful; and when they went to visit a Friend or to a Sale they were decently dressed. Alas! a love of Sales had always been their failing, being perhaps the only publick meetings in this neighbourhood where social pleasure is to be had without the necessity of expending money, except, indeed, our annual Fair, and on that day I can recollect having more than once seen Sarah Green among the rest with her chearful Countenance—two or three little-ones about her; and their youngest Brother or Sister, an Infant, in her arms. These things are now remembered; and the awful event checks all disposition to harsh comments; perhaps formerly it might be said, and with truth, the Woman had better been at home; but who shall assert that this same spirit which led her to come among her Neighbours as an equal, like them seeking society and pleasure, that this spirit did not assist greatly in preserving her in cheerful independance of mind through the many hardships and privations of extreme poverty? Her Children, though very ragged, were always cleanly, and are as pure and innocent, and in every respect as promising Children as any I ever saw. The three or four latest born, it is true, look as if they had been checked in their growth for want of full nourishment; yet none appear unhealthy except the youngest, a fair and beautiful Infant. It looks sickly, but not suffering: there is a heavenly patience in its countenance; and, while it lay asleep in its cradle three days after its Mother's death, one could not look upon it without fanciful thoughts that it had been sent into this world but to be her Companion, and was ready to follow her in tranquil peace. It would not be easy to give you an idea of the suspense and trouble in every face before the bodies were found: it seemed as if nothing could be done, nothing else thought of, till the unhappy Pair were brought again to their own house:—the first question was, "Have you heard anything from the Fells?" On the second evening I asked a young Man, a next-door Neighbour of ours, what he should do tomorrow? "Why, to be sure, go out again," he replied, and I believe that though he left a profitable employment (he is by trade a Shoemaker), he would have persevered daily, though the search had continued many days longer, even weeks.

Mary and I went to visit the Orphans on the Wednesday: we found all calm and quiet—two little boys were playing about on the floor—the Infant was asleep; and two of the old Man's up-grown Daughters wept silently while they pursued the business of the House: but several times one of them went out to listen at the door—"Oh!" said they, "the worst for us is yet to come! we shall never be at rest till they are brought home, and that will be a dreadful moment."— Their grief then broke out afresh; and they spoke of a miserable time, above twenty years ago, when their own Mother and Brother died of a malignant fever:—nobody would come near them; and their Father was forced himself to lay his Wife in her coffin. "Surely," they often repeated, "this is an afflicted House!"—and indeed, in like manner have I since frequently heard it spoken of by Persons less nearly concerned; but who still retain a vivid remembrance of the former affliction. It is, when any unusual event happens, affecting to listen to the fireside talk in our Cottages; you then find how faithfully the inner histories of Families, their lesser and greater cares, their peculiar habits, and ways of life are recorded in the breasts of their Fellow-inhabitants of the Vale; much more faithfully than it is possible that the lives of those, who have moved in higher stations and had numerous Friends in the busy world, can be preserved in remembrance, even when their doings and sufferings have been watched for the express purpose of recording them in written narratives. I heard a Woman, a week ago, describe in as lively a manner the sufferings of George Green's Family, when the former two Funerals went out of the house, as if that trouble had been the present trouble. Among other things she related how Friends and Acquaintances, as is the custom here when any one is sick, used to carry presents; but, instead of going to comfort the Family with their company and conversation, laid their gifts upon a Wall near the house, and watched till they were taken away.

It was, as I have said, upon the Wednesday that we went to visit the Orphans. A few hours after we had left them John Fisher came to tell us that the men were come home with the bodies. A great shout had been uttered when they were found; but we could not hear it as it was on the Langdale side of the Mountains.

The pair were buried in one grave on the Friday afternoon—My Sister[2] and I attended the funeral. A great number of people of decent and respectable appearance were gathered together at the house. I went into the parlour where the two Coffins were placed, the elder of the Mourners sitting beside them: the younger Girls gathered about the kitchen fire, partly amused, perhaps, by the unusual sight of so many persons in their house: the Baby and its Sister Jane (she who had been left by the Mother with the care of the Family) sate on a little stool in the chimney-corner, and, as our Molly[3] said, after having seen them on the Tuesday, "they looked such an innocent Pair!" The young Nurse appeared to have touches of pride in her important office; for every one praised her for her notable management of the Infant, while they cast tender looks of sorrow on them both. The Child would go to none but her; and while on her knee its countenance was perfectly calm—more than that: it seemed to express thoughtful resignation.

Mary and I went out of doors, and were much moved by the rude and simple objects before us—the noisy stream, the craggy mountain down which the old Man and his Wife had hoped to make their way on that unhappy night—the little garden, untilled—with its box-tree and a few peeping flowers . . . The furniture of the house was decayed and scanty; but there was one oaken cupboard which was so bright with rubbing that it was plain it had been prized as an ornament and a treasure by the poor Woman then lying in her Coffin.

Before the Bodies were taken up a threepenny loaf of bread was dealt out to each of the Guests: My sister was unwilling to take hers, thinking that the Orphans were in no condition to give away anything; she immediately, however, perceived that she ought to accept of it, and a Woman, who was near us observed that it was an ancient custom now much disused; but probably, as the Family had lived long in the Vale, and had done the like at funerals formerly, they thought it proper not to drop the custom. There was something very solemn in the Funeral procession passing through the solitary valley of Easedale, and, altogether, I never witnessed a more moving scene. As

---

[2] Mary Wordsworth.

[3] Molly Fisher, who worked for the Wordsworths.

is customary here, there was a pause before the Bodies were borne through the Church-yard Gate, while part of a psalm was sung, the Men standing with their hats off. In the Church the two Coffins were placed near the Altar, and the whole Family knelt on the floor on each side of the Father's Coffin, leaning over it. The eldest Daughter had been unable to follow with the rest of the Mourners, and we had led her back to the house before she got through the first field; the second fainted by the Grave-side; and their Brother stood like a Statue of Despair, silent and motionless; the younger Girls sobbed aloud. Many tears were shed by persons who had known little of the Deceased; and all the people who were gathered together appeared to be united in one general feeling of sympathy for the helpless condition of the Orphans. After the Funeral the Family returned to their melancholy home. There was a Sale of the furniture on the Thursday following; and the next day the house was left empty and silent.

A Lady from Ambleside had fetched the four little Boys on the day of the Funeral, to keep them till it should be settled how they were to be disposed of. I saw them go past our door; they walked up the hill beside the Car in which they had been riding, and were chattering to their new Friend, no doubt well pleased with the fine carriage. We had been told that she was going to take them and bring them up entirely herself; and my Sister came downstairs with tears of joy in her Eyes. "Aye," said our Neighbour, Peggy Ashburner, "that woman will win Heaven for protecting the Fatherless and Motherless;" and she too wept. Afterwards, however, we were undeceived, and were afraid that the Lady's kindness was ill-judged, that it might unsettle them when they should be taken away from the grand house to a more humble dwelling.

There are eight Children left under sixteen years of age. The eldest, a Girl, is in service; the second has lived with us more than half a year, and we had intended parting with her at Whitsuntide;[4] but when we heard of the loss of her Parents, we determined to keep her till she also is fit for service. The eldest, and only remaining Son of George Green by his first Wife, will maintain one of the Boys and bring him up to his own trade; so that there remain five to be provided for by the Parish; for, after the Father's estate is sold and the Mortgage paid off, little or nothing will remain for his Family.

It is the custom at Grasmere, and I believe in many other places, to let, as they call it, those Children who depend wholly upon the

---

[4] Week beginning with the seventh Sunday after Easter.

Parish, to the lowest bidder, that is, to board them out with those Persons who will take them at the cheapest rate; and such as are the least able to provide for them properly are often the readiest bidders, for the sake of having a little money coming in, though in fact the profit can be but very small: but they feel that they get something when the money comes, and do not feel exactly what they expend for the Children because they are fed out of the common stock. At ten years of age they are removed from their boarding-houses, and generally put out as Parish Apprentices, at best a slavish condition; but sometimes they are hardly used, and sometimes all moral and religious instruction is utterly neglected. I speak from observation: for I am sorry to say that we have daily before our eyes an example of such neglect, in the Apprentice of one of our near Neighbours. From the age of seven or eight till he was eleven or twelve years old the poor Boy was employed in nursing his Mistress's numerous Children, and following them up and down the lanes. Sunday was no holiday for him:—he was not, like others, dressed on that day, and he never went to Church. I recollect, when I first came to live in this Country, a little more than eight years ago, observing his vacant way of roaming about. I remarked that there was an appearance of natural quickness with much good nature in his countenance; but he looked wild and untutored. It was the face of a Child who had none to love him, and knew not in his heart what love was. He is now sixteen years old and a strong handsome-featured Boy but, though still the same traces of natural sense and good-temper appear, his countenance expresses almost savage ignorance with bold vice. To this day he does not know a letter in a book, nor can he say his prayers: (as Peggy Ashburner expressed it strongly in speaking of him to Sara) "That poor Lad, if aught were to happen to him, cannot bid God bless him!" His master has a couple of crazy horses; and he now employs him in carrying slates to the next market–town, and, young as he is, he has often come home intoxicated. Sometimes no doubt the liquor is given to him, but he has more than once been detected in dishonest practices, probably having been tempted to them by his desire of obtaining liquor. I hope and believe that it does not often happen in this neighbourhood that Parish Apprentices are so grossly neglected as this Boy has been; and I need not give you my reasons for thinking that there is not another Family in Grasmere who would have done the like: nor could it have been so bad even in this instance if the Boy had not come from a distant place, and consequently the Parish

Officers are not in the way of seeing how he goes on; and I am afraid that in such cases they seldom take the trouble of making inquiries.

You will not wonder, after what I have said, that we have been anxious to preserve these Orphans whom we saw so uncorrupted from the possibility of being brought up in such a manner, especially as there is no likelihood that they would all have been quartered in their native Vale. From the moment we heard that their Parents were lost we anxiously framed plans for raising a sum of money for the purpose of assisting the Parish in placing them with respectable Families; and to give them a little School-learning; and I am happy to tell you that others, at the same time, were employing their thoughts in like manner; and our united efforts have been even more successful than we had dared to hope.

It was a month yesterday since the sad event happened; and the Children are all settled in their several homes, and all are in the Vale of Grasmere except the eldest Boy, George, who is with his Brother at Ambleside. A Subscription has been made for the purpose of adding a little to the weekly allowance of the Parish, to send them to School, to apprentice the Boys, and to fit the Girls out for service; and if there be any surplus, it is to be dealt out among them as they shall prove deserving, or according to their several needs to set them forward in Life. It was very pleasing to observe how much all, both rich and poor, from the very first appeared to be interested for the Orphans; and the Subscription-book, which we have seen this evening, is equally creditable to all ranks. With five guineas, ten guineas, three guineas, is intermingled a long list of shillings and sixpences, and even one threepence—many of these from labouring people and Servants. A Committee of six of the neighbouring Ladies has been appointed to overlook the Children and manage the funds. They had a meeting, and it was agreed that Mrs. Wordsworth and Mrs. King should engage with two Families who were willing to take three of the Orphans, less for the sake of profit than from a liking to Children in general, and from a wish to see these children well taken care of, who had been left in circumstances of such peculiar distress. Another Lady had commission to conclude an engagement with a third Person who was willing to have the charge of the Infant and her Sister Jane. That lady, who, I am sorry to say, cannot do a charitable action without the pleasure of being busy, was galled that the whole concern had not been entrusted to her guidance; and had before (without any authority) herself (though only recently come into the country and having no connection with Grasmere) engaged to place all the Children with an old Woman in indigent circumstances, who was totally incapable of the charge.— I will not blemish a Narrative of events so moving, which have brought forward so many kind and good feelings, by entering into the cabals and heart-burnings of Mrs. North.[5] It is enough to say that Miss Knott, the Lady who has had the four boys under her protection since the day of their Parents' Funeral, came to conduct the three youngest and their two Sisters to their new homes, attended by Mrs. North. George, the eldest, had been left at his brother's house at Ambleside where he is to remain. The Ladies called at our door in their way; and I was deputed to attend them, John being very poorly his Mother could not leave him.—. I had the satisfaction of seeing all the five children hospitably welcomed. It had been declared with one voice by the people of the Parish, men and women, that the Infant and her Sister Jane should not be parted. The Woman, who was to have the care of these two, was from home, and had requested a Neighbour to be in the way to receive them when they should come. She has engaged to instruct Jane in sewing and reading, being, according to the phrase of this country "a fine Scholar." Her Husband is living; but she has never had any Children of her own. They are in good circumstances, and her Husband, a Blacksmith, is a remarkably ingenious and clever Man; and she appears to be a kind-hearted Woman, which is shewn by her motives for taking these poor Children. She said to my Sister with great simplicity and earnestness, "I should not have done it if we had not been such near relations; for my Uncle George's (namely the late George Green's) first Wife and my Husband's Mother were own Sisters," from which odd instance of near relationship you may judge how closely the bonds of family connection are held together in these retired vallies. Jane and her Sister took possession of their new abode with the most perfect composure: Jane went directly to the fireside, and seated herself with the Babe on her knee: it continues to call out "Dad!" and "Mam!" but seems not to fret for the loss of either: she has transferred all her affections to her Sister, and will not leave her for a moment to go to anyone else. This same little Girl, Jane, had been noticed by William and Mary some months ago, when they chanced to meet her in Easedale, first

---

[5] Although Mrs. North and her husband had purchased Rydal Mount in 1803, Dorothy regards her as a newcomer.

not knowing who she was. They were struck, at a distance, with her beautiful figure and her dress, as she was tripping over the wooden Bridge at the entrance of the Valley; and, when she drew nearer, the sweetness of her countenance, her blooming cheeks, her modest, wild, and artless appearance quite enchanted them. My Brother could talk of nothing else for a long time after he came home, and he minutely described her dress—a pink petticoat peeping under a long dark blue Cloak (which was on one side gracefully elbowed out, or distended as with a blast of wind by her carrying a Basket on her arm) and a pink bonnet tyed with a blue ribband, the lively colours harmonizing most happily with her blooming complexion. Part of this dress had probably been made up of her elder Sister's cast–off cloaths: for they were accustomed to give to their Father's Family whatever they could spare; often, I believe, more than they could well afford. Little did William at that time think that she was so soon to be called to such important duties; and as little that such a creature was capable of so much: for this was the Child who was left by her Parents at the head of the helpless Family, and was as a Mother to her Brothers and Sisters when they were fatherless and motherless, not knowing of their loss. Her conduct at that time was the admiration of every body. She had nursed the Baby, and, without confusion or trouble, provided for the other Children who could run about: all were kept quiet—even the Infant that was robbed of its Mother's breast. She had conducted other matters with perfect regularity, had milked the cow at night and morning, wound up the clock, and taken care that the fire should not go out, a matter of importance in that house so far from any other, a tinder-box[6] being a convenience which they did not possess. This little Girl I saw, as I have told you, take her place in her new home with entire composure: I know not indeed how to find a word sufficiently strong to express what I mean, it was a calmness amounting to dignity, which gave to every motion a perfect grace.

We next went with two Boys in petticoats[7] to a neat Farm house: the Man and his Wife came down the lane a hundred yards to meet us, and would have taken the Children by the hand with almost parental kindness; but they clung to Miss Knott, the Lady who had fetched them from their Father's Cottage on the day of the

---

[6] Metal box containing materials for a fire: tinder, flint, and steel.

[7] Boys did not wear breeches until age 5 or so.

Funeral, and had treated them tenderly ever since. The younger sate upon her lap while we remained in the house, and his Brother leaned against me: they continued silent; but I felt some minutes before our departure, by the workings of his breast, that the elder Boy was struggling with grief at the thought of parting with his old Friend. I looked at him and perceived that his eyes were full of tears: the younger Child, with less foresight, continued calm till the last moment, when both burst into an agony of grief. We have since heard that a slice of bread and butter soon quieted their distress: no doubt, the good Woman's kind looks, though she gave to the bread and butter the whole merit of consoling them, had far more effect.—She is by nature loving to Children, mild and tender— inclining to melancholy, which has grown upon her since the sudden Death of a Son, twenty years of age, who was not only the pride of his Father's House, but of the whole Vale. She has other Children, but they are scattered abroad, except one Daughter, who is only occasionally with her, so that she has of late spent many hours of the day in solitude, and the Husband yielded to her desire of taking these poor Orphans, thinking that they might divert her brooding thoughts. She has begun to teach them to read; and they have already won the hearts of the rest of the family by their docility, and quiet affectionate dispositions; and my Sister thought, when she was at the house the other day that she perceived a greater chearfulness in the kind Woman's manners than she had observed in her for a long time. They, poor Things! are perfectly contented; one of them was overheard saying to the other, "My Daddy and Mammy are dead, but we will never go away frae this house!"

We next went with the last remaining one of our charge, a Boy seven years old; his sorrow gathered while we were in the Chaise at the apprehension of parting from his Friend: he repeated more than once, however, that he was glad to go to the house whither we were taking him; and Miss Knott, turning to me, said he told her that he should like to live with John Fleming (that is the Man's name) for he had been kind to his Father and Mother, and had given them two sheep last year. She also related what seemed to me a remarkable proof of the Child's sensibility. There had been some intention of fixing him at another place, and he was uneasy at the thought of going thither, because, as he said, the Master of the House had had a quarrel with his Father. It appears that John Fleming and George Green had a particular regard for each other; he was the Godfather of his Friend's Daughter Jane, to whom he says, he will give a fleece of wool every year to spin for her own stockings, and, from the day that the death of their Parents was known, he expressed a wish to have the care of little John. The manner in which he greeted the Boy, who could not utter a word for weeping, corresponded with this; he took hold of him and patted his head as lovingly as if he had been his Grandfather, saying, "Never fear, mun! thou shalt go upon the hills after the sheep!" then (addressing himself to us) "This Lad and his Brothers and Sisters used always to come to our Clippings, and they were the quietest Bairns that ever I saw, we never had any disturbance among them." Meanwhile poor John did not cease crying, and continued to weep as long as we remained in the house; but we have since seen him as happy and contented as plenty of food and kindness could make any Child. His Master is feeble and paralytic, but he spends most of his time out of doors, looking over his own fields or following the sheep. In these walks he had formerly no Companion but his Dog and his Staff: now, morning and night, before and after school hours, the Boy goes with him—I saw them yester-evening on their return homeward: little John was running here and there, as sportive as a mountain lamb; for the Child may wander at will after his own fancies, and yet be a faithful attendant upon his Master's course; for he creeps at a slow pace with tottering steps. Much as the old Man delights in his new charge, his Housekeeper appears to take little less pleasure in him: I found her last night knitting stockings for him with yarn spun from the Master's fleeces, which is a gratuitous kindness, their allowance being half a crown weekly for board and lodging. I said to her that I hoped the boy was dutiful to her; and she replied that there was "no need to give him any correction for he did nothing amiss, and was always peaceable,—and happy too"; and she related some little circumstances which seemed to prove that she had watched him feelingly; among the rest, that on Saturday, his weekly holiday, he had gone with her and her Master to a mountain enclosure near Blentern Gill, where they had some Sheep; they passed by his Father's door, and the Child said to her (looking about, I suppose, in one of the fields which had belonged to his Parents) "My Mother's Ewe has got a fine Lamb!" The Woman watched his countenance and could not perceive that he had any painful thoughts; but was pleased to see the newborn Lamb and his Mother's Ewe.

The Ladies returned to Ambleside after we left John Fleming's house. Mrs. North (it hurts me to say it) in her way to our door where we parted, appeared sullen and dissatisfied that she had not had the sole management of the concern; but Miss Knott who has a true interest in the Children's well-doing, expressed great pleasure in what she had observed of the people who had taken charge of them, adding that she trusted the Family would prosper; for she had never seen nor even heard of any set of Children who were so amiable as the four who had been under her roof: they were playful but not quarrelsome; and, though with hundreds of objects around them that were perfectly new and strange, they never had done any mischief, hardly had need of a caution! The contentedness with which they have taken to their new homes proves that no wayward desires had been raised in them by the luxuries among which they had lived for the last three weeks: and we have been truly happy to perceive that our fears that this might happen were ill-grounded.

Not only the Ladies of the Committee (except the one I have mentioned) but all the People of Grasmere with whom I have conversed, approve entirely of the several situations in which the Orphans have been placed. Perhaps the irregular interference of Mrs. North may have called forth a few unbecoming expressions of resentment from some of the Inhabitants of the Vale; but I must say that the general feelings have been purely kind and benevolent, arising from compassion for the forlorn condition of the Orphans and from a respectful regard for the memory of their Parents who have left in them a living example of their own virtuous conduct.

I am almost afraid that you may have thought that my account of the characters of these Children was but a Romance, a dream of fanciful feeling, proceeding in great measure from pity, pity producing love; but I hope that the few facts which I have mentioned concerning them will partly illustrate what I have said. You will conclude with me that if the Parents had not shewn an example of honesty, good temper, and good manners, these happy effects could not have followed; but I believe that the operation of their example was greatly aided by the peculiar situation of themselves and their Children. They lived in a lonely house where they seldom saw either Strangers or neighbors. These Children had no Playfellows but their own Brothers and Sisters; and wayward inclinations or uneasy longings, where there was no choice of food or toys, no luxuries to contend for, could scarcely exist, they seeing nothing of such feelings in their Parents. There was no irregular variety in the earlier part of their infancy and childhood, and when they were old enough to be trusted from home they rarely went further than their own fields, except to go on errands; so that even then they would be governed by the sense of having a duty to perform. No doubt many Families are brought up in equal solitude and under the same privations, and we see no such consequences; and I am well aware that these causes have often a baneful effect if the Parents themselves be vicious; but such very poor People as in their situation most resemble these are generally in a state of dependance; and the chain which holds them back from dishonesty or any disgraceful conduct is by no means so strong. While George and Sarah Green held possession of the little estate inherited from their Forefathers they were in a superior station; and thus elevated in their own esteem they were kept secure from any temptation to unworthiness. The love of their few fields and their ancient home was a salutary passion, and no doubt something of this must have spread itself to the Children. The Parents' cares and their chief employments were centred there; and as soon as the Children could run about even the youngest could take part in them, while the elder would do this with a depth of interest which cannot be felt, even in rural life, where people are only transitory occupants of the soil on which they live.

I need not remind you how much more such a situation as I have described is favourable to innocent and virtuous habits and feelings than that of those Cottagers who live in solitude and poverty without any out-of-doors employment. It is pleasant to me here to recollect how I have seen these very Children (with no Overlooker except when it was necessary for the elder to overlook the younger) busied in turning the peats which their Father had dug out of the field, and bearing away those which were dry in burthens of three or four upon their shoulders. In this way the Family were bound together by the same cares and exertions; and already one of them has proved that she maintained this spirit after she had quitted her Father's Roof. The eldest, Mary, when only fourteen years of age, spared a portion of her year's wages to assist them in paying the expenses of the Funeral of her Grandfather. She is a Girl of strong sense, and there is a thoughtfulness and propriety in her manners which I have seldom seen in one so young; this with great appearance of sensibility which shewed itself at the time of her Parents' death, and since, in her love and anxiety for her Brothers and Sisters. Much, indeed, as I have said of the moral causes tending to produce that submissive, gentle, affectionate, and I may add useful character in these Children, I have omitted to speak of the foundation of all, their own natural dispositions, or rather their constitutional temperament of mind and body. I am convinced from observation that there is in the whole Family a peculiar tenderness of Nature, perhaps inherited from their Father, whom I have several times heard speak of his own Family in a manner that shewed an uncommonly feeling heart; once especially, two or three years ago, when his Boy George had scalded himself and was lying dangerously ill, we met him in Easedale, and he detained us a full quarter of an hour while he talked of the Child's sufferings and his surpassing patience. I well remember the poor Father's words—"He never utters a groan— never so much as says 'Oh dear!' but when he sees us grieved for him encourages us and often says: "Never fear, I warrant you I shall get better again." These circumstances and many more which I do not so distinctly recollect the old Man repeated with tears streaming down his cheeks; yet we often saw a smile of pride in his face while he spoke of the Boy's fortitude and undaunted courage.

I have said that George Green had been twice married, and that his Son and Daughters by the first Wife are in a respectable condition of life; but he had not only brought up thus far his own large Family; but also two Children, a Son and a Daughter, whom his wife had borne before marriage. He received eighteen pence weekly towards the maintenance of each, and brought them up as his own Children. I do not know what Sarah Green's general conduct before marriage may have been further than that she was a young Woman when these Children were born. She had been a Parish Apprentice, and therefore, probably, a neglected Child, and, having had the merit of conquering her failings, she for that cause may perhaps be entitled to a higher praise than would have been her due if she had never fallen. Her conduct as a Wife and a Mother were irreproachable. Though she could not read herself, she had taught all her Children, even to the Youngest but one, to say their prayers; and had encouraged in them a love and respect for learning; the elder could read a little, though none of them had been at school except Sally, whose schooling was paid for by a Lady in whose house she had been a short time. Since their Parents' death two of the boys have gone regularly to school; and George, the eldest, takes particular delight in his Book. The little fellow used to lie down upon the carpet in Miss Knott's parlour poring over the "Reading-made-Easy" by firelight, and would try to spell words out of his own head.

The Neighbours say that George and Sarah Green had only one fault; they were rather "too stiff", unwilling to receive favours, but the "keenest payers"—always in a hurry to pay when they had money, and for this reason those who knew them best were willing to lend them a little money to help them out of a difficulty; yet very lately they had sent to the shop for a loaf of bread; and because the Child went without ready money the Shopkeeper refused to let them have the bread. We in our connection with them have had one opportunity of remarking (Alas! we gained our knowledge since their death) how chearfully they submitted to a harsh necessity, and how faithful they were to their word. Our little Sally wanted two shifts: we sent to desire her Mother to procure them; the Father went the very next day to Ambleside to buy the cloth and promised to pay for it in three weeks. The shifts were sent to Sally without a word of the difficulty of procuring them, or anything like a complaint. After her Parents' death we were very sorry (knowing now so much of their extreme poverty) that we had required this of them, and on enquiring whether the cloth was paid for (intending to discharge that debt) we were told by one of the Daughters that she had been to the shop purposely to make the inquiry, and found that, two or three days before the time promised, her Father had himself gone to pay the money. Probably if they had lived a week longer they must have carried some article of furniture out to barter for that week's provisions. I have mentioned how very little food there was in the house at that time—there was no money—not even a single half-penny! The pair had each threepence in their pockets when they were found upon the mountains. With this eagerness to discharge their debts their unwillingness to receive favours was so great that the neighbours called it "pride" or as I have said "stiffness". Without this pride what could have supported them? Their chearful hearts would probably have sunk, and even their honesty might have slipped from them. (The other day I was with Mary Cowperthwaite, the Widow of one of our Statesmen; she began to talk of George and Sarah Green who, she said, "had made a hard struggle; but they might have done better if they had not had quite so high a spirit." She then told me that she had called at their house last Summer to look after some cattle that she had put upon George Green's Land. Sarah brought out a phial with a little gin in it, poured out a glass, and insisted that her visitor should drink, saying, "I should not have had it to offer you if it had not been for that little thing," pointing to the cradle, "it has been badly in its bowels, and they told me that a little common gin would mend it." Mrs. Cowperthwaite took the gin much against her mind, on condition that Sarah Green should drink tea with her the next Sunday, which she promised to do, and

Mary Cowperthwaite told her that she would have a bundle of cloaths ready for her to take home: however, she did not go on the Sunday afternoon; and Mrs. C. says that she believes that the fear of receiving this gift had prevented her: for she had never seen her at her house afterwards, though the promise was made several months before her Death. It is plain that the poor Woman had no secret cause of offence against her intended benefactress, for on the day on which she died she followed Mrs. Cowperthwaite's Son all up and down at the Sale, urging him to request his Mother to take her Daughter Mary as a Servant, she being then in service at a publick House, a situation which she did not altogether approve of.)

Within the last few days of her life her thoughts had been very much occupied with her Children. On the day before she died she went to Ambleside with butter to sell, and talked with our neighbour, John Fisher, about her Daughter Sally, who is with us, and said she should "think of him," that is, be grateful to him as long as she lived for having been the means of placing Sally at our house, regretted that we could not keep her longer; but, in her chearful way, ended with "we must do as well as we can." On her road home she fell into company with another Person, and talked fondly of her Infant who, she said, was "the quietest creature in the world." You will remember that the object of her last fatal journey was to look after her Daughter who was a Servant at a house in Langdale; and that while she was at the Sale she took unwearied pains about another (namely her eldest by her husband)—Poor Woman! she is now at rest. I have seen one of her Sons playing beside her grave; and all her Children have taken to their new homes, and are chearful and happy. In the night of her anguish, if she could but have had a foresight of the kindness that would be shewn to her Children, what a consolation would it have been to her! With her many cares and fears for her helpless Family, she must at that time have mingled some bitter self-reproaches for her boldness in venturing over the Mountains: for they had asked two of the Inhabitants of the Vale to accompany them, who refused to go by that way on account of the bad weather, and she laughed at them for being cowardly. It is now said that her Husband was always fond of doing things that nobody else liked to venture upon, though he was not strong and had lost one eye by an accident. She was healthy and active, one of the freshest Women of her years that I ever noticed, and she walked with an uncommonly vigorous step. She was forty-five years of age at her Death.

Her Husband's Daughters speak of their Mother-in-law[8] with great respect; she always, whenever they went to their Father's house, strove to make it as comfortable to them as she could, and never suffered her own Children to treat them unbecomingly. One of the young Women, who has long been a Servant in respectable Families in the neighbourhood, told us with tears in her eyes, that once, not very long ago, she went to Blentern Gill not intending to stay all night, and when she took up her cloak to go away her Mother said to her "What, you cannot stop in such a poor house!" The Daughter after this had not the heart to go away and laid aside her Cloak. Another time when the chearful Creature was pressing her to stay longer she said to her "What, Aggy, to be sure we have no tea, but we have very good tea-leaves." By the bye, those tea leaves came from our house: one of the little Girls, our own Sally, or another, used to come three times in the week to fetch them—two long miles!—I well recollect (it is now four or five years ago) how we were then struck with the pretty simple manners of these little-ones. I have spoken much of the interest we take in the younger Children of George Green; and I may add that the same constitutional tenderness appears even in a much more marked degree in the elder part of his Family: we have observed in them many proofs of tender, and even delicate sensibility, as well as of strong and deep feeling—so much respect for every thing that had belonged to the Deceased—the few cloaths, the furniture and the old Family Dwelling. In no situation of life did I ever witness marks of more profound distress than appeared in them immediately after the death of their Father and Mother; for they called her Mother. The eldest Son, on returning to his own house at Ambleside, after having been at Grasmere on the day when it was first known that they were lost, was unable to lift the latch of his own door, and fainted on the threshold, and might have perished also, if his Wife had not happened to hear him; for it was a bitter cold night.

I may say with the Pedlar in the "Recluse,"

> "I feel
> The story linger in my heart," my memory
> Clings to this poor Woman and her Family

---

[8] Stepmother.

and I fear I have spun out my narrative to a tedious length.[9] I cannot give *you* the same feelings that *I* have for them as Neighbors and Fellow-inhabitants of this Vale; therefore what is in my mind a full and living picture will be to you but a feeble sketch. You cannot, however, but take part in my earnest prayer that the Children may grow up, as they have begun, in innocence and virtue; and that the awful end of their Parents may hereafter be remembered by them in such a manner as to implant in their hearts a reverence and sorrow for them which may purify their thoughts and make them wiser and better. There is, at least, this consolation, that the Father and Mother have been preserved by their untimely end from that dependance which they dreaded. The Children are likely to be better instructed in reading and writing, and may acquire knowledge which their Parents' poverty would have kept them out of the way of attaining: and perhaps, after the Land had been sold, the happy chearfulness of George and Sarah Green might have forsaken them, and their latter days have been tedious and melancholy.

DOROTHY WORDSWORTH GRASMERE, MAY 4TH, 1808.

Notes [by DW]

"Blentern Gill"—Probably *Blind Tarn* Gill, as there is upon the Mountain a swamp out of which the little stream runs. This swamp is shaped like a Tarn and might (if it werc worth while) with very little trouble be formed into a small Lake or Tarn.

"She went to Ambleside with butter."

I myself met her and desired that she would leave one pound (of the four which she had in her basket) at our house. Those four Pounds of Butter must have been the produce of at least a fortnight's careful savings as the Cow gave very little milk at that time. She had not left a morsel at home for their own use, a striking proof of her resolute self-denial. I have said that they never had any luxuries. My account of the stock of provisions in the House at the time

---

[9] From Wm Wordsworth's manuscript lines of the Pedlar speaking of Margaret, whose deranged husband has left her. In *The Excursion* (1814), the lines will read: "Sir, I feel / The story linger in my heart; I fear / 'T is long and tedious; but my spirit clings / To that poor Woman" (I, 777–780).

of her Death is literally true. If I were to enumerate all the things that were wanting even to the ordinary supply of a very poor house what a long list it would be. There was no sugar in the house—no salt. . . .

I ought to have mentioned that George Green's debts, save the Mortgage on his Estate, were very small and few in number. The household goods sold for their full worth, perhaps more. The cupboard which I have mentioned was bought for fourteen shillings and sixpence, an oaken chest for twenty-four shillings, and their only Feather Bed for three pounds. The Cow sold for but twenty-four shillings, and I believe that was its full value. These articles which I have mentioned were the most valuable of their moveable possessions. We purchased the poor Woman's Churn and milking Can, for which we gave eight shillings and sixpence.

An affecting circumstance is related of Sarah Green's natural Daughter with whom she parted on the Saturday evening after having drunk tea with her Mistress. The Girl did not hear of the melancholy event till Monday evening, and she was with difficulty kept from going herself over the Mountains, though night was coming on. In her distraction she thought that she surely could find them. I do not speak of this as denoting any extraordinary sensibility, for I believe most young persons in the like dreadful situation would have felt in the same manner—and perhaps old ones too, for the circumstance reminds me of Mary Watson, then 73 years of age, who when her Son was drowned in the Lake six years ago, walked up and down upon the shore entreating that she might be suffered to go in one of the Boats, for though others could not find him, she said "Do let *me* go I am sure I can spy him!" I never shall forget the agony of her face—without a tear—She looked eagerly towards the Island near the shore of which her Son had been lost, and wringing her hands, said, while I was standing close to her, "I was fifty years old when I bore him, and he never gave me any sorrow till now." The Death of this young Man, William Watson, caused universal regret in the Vale of Grasmere. He was drowned on a fine summer's Sunday afternoon, having gone out in a Boat with some companions to bathe. His Body was not found till the following morning, though the spot where he had sunk was exactly known. All night, boats were on the water with lights; and it was a very dismal sight from our windows. He could not swim, and had got into one of the wellsprings of the lake which are always very deep.

FROM *TOUR ON THE CONTINENT,* 1820

In July 1820, Dorothy, William, and Mary, accompanied by Mary's cousin Thomas Monkhouse and his new wife, toured Belgium, Germany, Switzerland, Italy, and France. Henry Crabb Robinson joined them in Lucerne. Developing her account from an extensive diary, Dorothy records her delight and stamina in traveling. She also writes to William's journey of 1790 and to their French trip together in 1802 just before his marriage, memorializing their shared past and placing her present experiences alongside his youthful adventures. Again, Dorothy works as part of a writing community. Robinson and Mary Wordsworth wrote journals of the trip ("Viewing the World" pp. 296–313). William's Memorials of a Tour on the Continent appeared in 1822.

Dorothy writes to Catherine Clarkson on May 31, 1821, of copying her "tedious" journal and, at William's request, of "amplifying" and "arranging" her observations. The excerpts here, with two noted exceptions, are taken from Knight's published text of about 100 pages and are set off with bracketed dividing lines; ellipses are from Knight.

Monday, July 10*th,* 1820.—We—William, Mary, and Dorothy Wordsworth—left the Rectory House, Lambeth, at a quarter to eight o'clock. Had the "Union" coach to ourselves, till within two stages of Canterbury, when two young ladies demanded inside places. . . . The Cathedral of Canterbury, described by Erasmus as lifting itself up in "such majesty towards heaven, that it strikes religion into the beholders from a distance,"[1] looks stately on the plain, when first seen from the gently descending road, and appeared to me a much finer building than in former times; and I felt, as I had often done during my last abode in London, that, whatever change, tending to melancholy, twenty years might have produced, they had called forth the capacity of enjoying the sight of ancient buildings to which my youth was, comparatively, a stranger. Between London and Canterbury the scenes are varied and cheerful; first Blackheath, and its bordering villas, and shady trees; goats, asses, sheep, etc., pasturing at large near the houses. The Thames glorious; ships like castles, cutting their way as through green

---

[1] Dutch philosopher Desiderius Erasmus (1466–1536) made the comment when he visited the cathedral in 1512.

meadows, the river being concealed from view; then it spreads out like a wide lake, scattered over with vessels.

Dover, Tuesday, July 11*th.*—We walked to the Castle[2] before breakfast. The building, when you are close to it, appears even *sublime,*[3] from its immense height and bulk; but it is not rich or beautiful in architecture. The old warder stood in waiting upon the hill to lead us forward. After ascending above a hundred stone steps, we were greeted by the slender tinkling of a bell, a delicately wild sound in that place. It is fixed at the top of a pillar, on which is inscribed a poetical petition in behalf of the prisoners confined above in the Castle.

Calais, Tuesday, July 11*th.*—Landed on the shores of France at half-past one. What shall I say of Calais? I looked about for what I remembered, and looked for new things, and in both quests was gratified. . . . With[4] one consent we stopped to gaze at a group— rather a *line* of women and girls, seated beside dirty fish baskets under the old gate-way and ramparts—their white night caps, brown and puckered faces, bright eyes &c., &c., very striking. The arrangements—how unlike those of a fish-market in the South of England!

On my bedroom door is inscribed "Sterne's Room,"[5] and a print of him hangs over the fireplace. The walls painted in panels, handsome carpets, chimney-piece marble-coloured, hearth red, bed-curtains white, sheets coarse, coverlet a mixture of cotton and woollen, beautifully white; but how clumsy all contrivances of braziers and smiths![6] The bell hangs on the outside of the wall, and gives a single, loud, dull stroke when pulled by the string, so that you must stand and pull four or five times, as if you were calling the people to prayers.

Calais, Wednesday, July 12*th.*—We rose at five; sunshine and clear, but rather cold air. The Cathedral, a large edifice, not finely wrought; but the first effect is striking, from the size of the numerous

[2] Built from 1066 to 1170, Dover Castle had served as a school, a poorhouse, and when Dorothy visited, a prison.

[3] For the aesthetics of the sublime see pp. 281–285.

[4] The rest of this paragraph is from Knight, *Poetical Works,* 6: 198.

[5] Novelist Laurence Sterne (1713–1768) wrote about the hotel and its proprietor, Mons. Dessein, in the opening sections of *A Sentimental Journey through France and Italy* (1768).

[6] The room seems in bad taste, the mantel (chimney-piece) and other decorations being the contrivances of workers in brass (braziers) and metal (smiths).

pillars and arches, though they are paltry in the finishing, merely white-washed and stuck over with bad pictures and tawdry images; yet the whole view at the entrance was affecting. Old men and women—young women and girls kneeling at their silent prayers, and some we espied, in obscure recesses, before a concealed crucifix, image, or altar. One grey-haired man I cannot forget, whose countenance bore the impression of worldly cares subdued, and peace in heavenly aspiration. . . . Another figure I must not leave unnoticed, a squalid, ragged woman. She sate alone upon some steps at the side of the entrance to the quire. There she sate, with a white dog beside her; no one was near, and the dog and she evidently belonged to each other, probably her only friend, for never was there a more wretchedly forlorn and miserable-looking human being. She did not notice us; but her rags and her sickly aspect drew a penny from me, and the change in the woman's skinny, doleful face is not to be imagined: it was brightened by a light and gracious smile—the effect was almost as of something supernatural—she bowed her body, waved her hand, and, with a politeness of gesture unknown in England in almost any station of life, beckoned that we might enter the church, where the people were kneeling upon chairs, of which there might be a thousand—two thousand—I cannot say how many—piled up in different parts of the Cathedral. . . .

9 o'clock, Inn-yard, Calais.—Off we drove, preceded by our friends, each postilion smacking his whip along the street with a dexterity truly astonishing. Never before did I know the power of a clumsy whip, in concert with the rattling of wheels upon rough pavement![7] The effect was certainly not less upon the spectators, and we jolted away as merry as children—showed our passports— passed the gateways, drawbridges, and shabby soldiers, and, fresh to the feeling of being in a foreign land, drove briskly forward, watchful and gay. The country for many miles populous; this makes it amusing, though sandy and flat; no trees worth looking at singly *as* trees. . . .

Half-past 10.—The party gone to bed. This *salle,* where I sit, how unlike a parlour in an English inn! Yet the history of a sea-fight, or a siege, painted on the walls, with the costumes of Philip the Second, or even of our own time, would have better suited my associations, with the names of Gravelines and Dunkirk, than the story of Cupid and Psyche now before my eyes, as large as life, on

[7] The Wordsworths purchased two carriages for their group.

French paper!⁸ The paper is in panels, with big mirrors between, in gilt frames. With all this taste and finery, and wax candles, and Brussels carpets, what a mixture of troublesome awkwardness! They brought us a ponderous teapot that would not pour out the tea; the latches (with metal enough to fasten up a dungeon) can hardly, by unpractised hands, be made to open and shut the doors. I have seen the diligence come into the yard and unload—heavy, dirty, dusty—a lap-dog walking about the top, like a panther in its cage, and viewing the gulf below. A monkey was an outside passenger when it departed.

Fumes, July 13th Thursday, 5 o'clock.—I will describe this Square. Houses yellow, grey, white, and there is a green one! Yet the effect is not gaudy—a half Grecian church, with Gothic spire; storks have built their nests, and are sitting upon the venerable tower of another church, a sight that pleasingly reminds us of our neighbourhood to Holland. The interior of that which outwardly mimics the Grecian is Gothic, and rather handsome in form, but whitewashed, and bedaubed with tinsel, and dolls, and tortured images. . . . Bells continually tinkling. There goes a woman to her prayers, in a long black cloak, and bright blue stockings; here comes a nicely-dressed old woman, leaning on her staff! Surely it is a blessing to the aged in Roman Catholic countries to have the churches always open for them, if it were only that it makes a variety in the course of a long day! How soothing, how natural to the aged, thus to withdraw from the stir of household cares, and occupations in which they can no longer take a part! and I must say (little as I have yet seen of this mode of worshipping God) I never beheld more of the expression of piety and earnest feeling than in some of the very old people in these churches. Every avenue of the square of this town presents some picturesque continuation of buildings. All is old, and old-fashioned; nothing to complain of but a want of Dutch cleanliness, yet it does not obtrude on the eye, out of doors, and the exterior is grave, decent, and quiet. . . .

The priests in their gaudy attire, with their young white-robed attendants, made a solemn appearance, while clouds of incense were ascending over their heads to the large crucifix above the altar; and the "pealing organ" sounded to the "full-voiced quire."⁹ There

---

⁸ The parlor (*salle*) is decorated with the story of Cupid and Psyche. Gravelines and Dunkirk are battles between the British navy and the Spanish Armada, sent in 1588 by Philip II to conquer England.

⁹ John Milton, *Il Penseroso*, 161–162.

was a beautiful nun in a grey garment with a long black scarf, white forehead band, belt, and rosary. Intent upon her devotions, she did not cast an eye towards us, and we stood to look at her. The faces of many of the women are handsome, but the steady grace, the chastened motions of their persons, and the mild seriousness of their countenances, are *most* remarkable. . . .

[. . . . .]

Monday, July 17*th.—Brussels.*—Brussels exhibits in its different quarters the stateliness of the ancient and the princely splendour of modern times, mixed with an uncouth irregularity, resembling that of the lofty tiers of houses at Edinburgh; but the general style of building in the old streets is by no means so striking as in those of Ghent or Bruges. . . .

Waterloo.—Waterloo[10] is a mean village; straggling on each side of the broad highway, children and poor people of all ages stood on the watch to conduct us to the church. Within the circle of its interior are found several mural monuments of our brave soldiers—long lists of naked names inscribed on marble slabs—not less moving than laboured epitaphs displaying the sorrow of surviving friends. . . . Here we took up the very man who was Southey's guide (Lacoste), whose name will make a figure in history. He bowed to us with French ceremony and liveliness, seeming proud withal to show himself as a sharer in the terrors of that time when Buonaparte's confusion and overthrow released him from unwilling service. He had been tied upon a horse as Buonaparte's guide through the country previous to the battle, and was compelled to stay by his side till the moment of flight. . . .

Monday, July 17*th.—Brussels.*—The sky had been overshadowed by clouds during most of our journey, and now a storm threatened us, which helped our own melancholy thoughts to cast a gloom over the open country, where few trees were to be seen except forests on the distant heights. The ruins of the severely contested chateau of Hougomont had been ridded away since the battle, and the injuries done to the farm-house repaired. Even these circumstances, natural and trivial as they were, suggested melancholy thoughts, by furnishing grounds for a charge of ingratitude against the course of things, that was thus hastily removing from the spot

---

[10] After Napoleon's defeat at Waterloo in 1815, the battlefield became a major tourist attraction.

all vestiges of so momentous an event. Feeble barriers against this tendency are the few frail memorials erected in different parts of the field of battle! and we could not but anticipate the time, when through the flux and reflux of war, to which this part of the Continent has always been subject, or through some turn of popular passion, *these* also should fall; and "Nature's universal robe of green, humanity's appointed shroud, enwrap them"[11]—and the very names of those whose valour they record be cast into shade, if not obliterated even in their own country, by the exploits of recent favourites in future ages.

[. . . . .]

Thursday, July 20th.—Aix-la-Chapelle.—I went to the Cathedral, a curious building, where are to be seen the chair of Charlemagne, on which the Emperors were formerly crowned, some marble pillars much older than *his* time, and many pictures; but I could not stay to examine any of these curiosities, and gladly made my way alone back to the inn to rest there. The marketplace is a fine old square; but at Aix-la-Chapelle there is always a mighty preponderance of poverty and dulness, except in a few of the showiest of the streets, and even there, a flashy meanness, a slight patchery of things falling to pieces, is everywhere visible. . . .

Road to Cologne.—At the distance of ten miles we saw before us, over an expanse of open country, the Towers of Cologne. Even at this distance they appeared very tall and bulky; and Mary pointed out that one of them was a ruin, which no other eyes could discover. To the left was a range of distant hills; and, to the right, in front of us, another range—rather a *cluster*—which we looked at with peculiar interest, as guardians and companions of the famous river Rhine, whither we were tending, and (sick and weary though I was) I felt as much of the glad eagerness of hope as when I first visited the Wye, and all the world was fresh and new. Having travelled over the intermediate not interesting country, the massy ramparts of Cologne, guarded by grotesque turrets, the bridges, and heavy arched gateways, the central towers and spires, rising above the concealed mass of houses in the city, excited something of gloomy yet romantic expectation.

Friday, July 21st.—Cologne.—I busied myself repairing garments already tattered in the journey, at the same time observing the traffic

[11] Version of *The Excursion* (7: 996–997).

and business of the river, here very wide, and the banks low. I was a prisoner; but really the heat this morning being oppressive, I felt not even a wish to stir abroad, and could, I believe, have been amused more days than one by the lading and unlading of a ferry-boat, which came to and started from the shore close under my window. Steadily it floats on the lively yet smooth water, a square platform, not unlike a section cut out of a thronged market-place, and the busy crowd removed with it to the plain of water. The square is enclosed by a white railing. Two slender pillars rise from the platform, to which the ropes are attached, forming between them an inverted arch, elegant enough. When the boat draws up to her mooring-place, a bell, hung aloft, is rung as a signal for a fresh freight. All walk from the shore, without having an inch to rise or to descend. Carts with their horses wheel away—rustic, yet not without parade of stateliness—the foreheads of the meanest being adorned with scarlet fringes. In the neighbourhood of Brussels (and indeed all through the *Low Countries*), we remarked the large size and good condition of the horses, and their studied decorations, but near Brussels those decorations were the *most* splendid. A scarlet net frequently half-covered each of the six in procession. The frock of the driver, who paces beside the train, is often handsomely embroidered, and its rich colour (Prussian blue) enlivens the scarlet ornaments of his steeds. But I am straying from my ferry-boat. The first debarkation which we saw early in the morning was the most amusing. Peasants, male and female, sheep, and calves; the women hurrying away, with their cargoes of fruit and vegetables, as if eager to be beforehand with the market. But I will transcribe verbatim from my journal, "written at mid-day," the glittering Rhine spread out before me, in width that helped me to image forth an American lake. . . . "It has gone out with a fresh load, and returned every hour; the comers have again disappeared as soon as landed; and now, the goers are gathering together. Two young ladies trip forward, their dark hair *basketed* round the crown of the head, green bags on their arms, two gentlemen of their party; next a lady with smooth black hair stretched upward from the forehead, and a skull-cap at the top, like a small dish. The gentry passengers seem to arrange themselves on one side, the peasants on the other;—how much more picturesque the peasants. *There* is a woman in a sober dark-coloured dress; she wears no cap. Next, one with red petticoat, blue jacket, and cap as white as snow. Next, one with a red handkerchief over her head, and a long brown cloak. There a smart female of the bourgeoise—dark shawl, white cap, blue dress. Two women (now seated side by side) make a pretty picture: their attire is scarlet, a pure white handkerchief falling from the head of each over the shoulders. They keep watch beside a curiously constructed basket, large enough to contain the marketing of a whole village. A girl crosses the platform with a handsome brazen ewer[12] hanging on her arm. Soldiers—a dozen at least—are coming in. They take the centre. Again two women in scarlet garb, with a great fruit basket. A white cap next; the same with a green shawl. *There* is a sunburnt daughter of toil, her olive skin whitens her white head-dress, and she is decked in lively colours. One beside her, who, I see, counts herself of higher station, is distinguished by a smart French mob. I am brought round to the gentry side, which is filled up, as you may easily fancy, with much less variety than the other. A cart is in the centre, its peasant driver, not to be unnoticed, with a polished tobacco-pipe hung over his cleanly blue frock. Now they float away!"

[. . . . .]

Road to Schaffhausen.—A part of the way through the uncleared forest was pleasingly wild; juniper bushes, broom, and other woodland plants, among the moss and flowery turf. Before we had finished our last ascent, the postilion told us what a glorious sight we *might* have seen, in a few moments, had we been here early in the morning or on a fine evening; but, as it was midday, nothing was to be expected. That glorious sight which *should* have been was no less than the glittering prospect of the mountains of Switzerland. We did burst upon an extensive view; but the mountains were hidden; and of the Lake of Constance we saw no more than a vapoury substance where it lay among apparently low hills. This first sight of that country, so dear to the imagination, though then of no peculiar grandeur, affected me with various emotions. I remembered the shapeless wishes of my youth—wishes without hope—my brother's wanderings thirty years ago, and the tales brought to me the following Christmas holidays at Forncett, and often repeated while we paced together on the gravel walk in the parsonage garden, by moon or star light. . . . The towers of Schaffhausen appear under the shelter of woody and vine-clad hills, but no greetings from the river Rhine, which is not visible from this approach, yet flowing

[12] Pitcher.

close to the town. . . . But at the entrance of the old city gates you cannot but be roused, and say to yourself, "Here is something which I have not seen before, yet I hardly know what!" The houses are grey, irregular, dull, overhanging, and clumsy; streets narrow and crooked—the walls of houses often half-covered with rudely-painted representations of the famous deeds of the defenders of this land of liberty. . . . In place of the splendour of faded aristocracy, so often traceable in the German towns, there is a character of ruggedness over all that we see. . . . Never shall I forget the first view of the stream of the Rhine from the bank, and between the side openings of the bridge—rapid in motion, bright, and green as liquid emeralds! and wherever the water dashed against tree, stone, or pillar of the bridge, the sparkling and the whiteness of the foam, melting into and blended with the green, can hardly be imagined by any one who has not seen the Rhine, or some other of the great rivers of the Continent, before they are sullied in their course. . . .

The first visible indication of our approach to the cataracts was the sublime tossing of vapour above them, at the termination of a curved reach of the river. Upon the woody hill, above that tossing vapour and foam, we saw the old chateau, familiar to us in prints, though there represented in connection with the falls themselves; and now seen by us at the end of the rapid, yet majestic, sweep of the river; where the ever-springing tossing clouds are all that the eye beholds of the wonderful commotion. But an awful sound ascends from the concealed abyss; and it would almost seem like irreverent intrusion if a stranger, at his first approach to this spot, should not pause and listen before he pushes forward to seek the revelation of the mystery. . . . We were gloriously wetted and stunned and deafened by the waters of the Rhine. It is impossible even to remember (therefore, how should I enable any one to imagine?) the power of the dashing, and of the sounds, the breezes, the dancing dizzy sensations, and the exquisite beauty of the colours! The whole stream falls like liquid emeralds—a solid mass of translucent green hue; or, in some parts, the green appears through a thin covering of snow-like foam. Below, in the ferment and hurly-burly, drifting snow and masses resembling collected snow mixed with sparkling green billows. We walked upon the platform, as dizzy as if we had been on the deck of a ship in a storm. Mary returned with Mrs. Monkhouse to Schaffhausen, and William recrossed in a boat with Mr. Monkhouse and me, near the extremity of the river's first sweep, after its fall, where its bed (as is usual at the foot of all cataracts) is exceedingly widened, and larger in proportion to the weight of waters. The boat is trusted to the current, and the passage, though long, is rapid. At first, when seated in that small unresisting vessel, a sensation of helplessness and awe (it was not fear) overcame me, but that was soon over. From the centre of the stream the view of the cataract in its majesty of breadth is wonderfully sublime. Being landed, we found commodious seats, from which we could look round at leisure, and we remained till the evening darkness revealed two intermitting columns of fire, which ascended from a forge close to the cataract.

[. . . . .]

Sarnen, Monday, August 14*th.*—The road to the monastery is marked by small pillars of grey stone, not more than a quarter of a mile asunder. At the top of each pillar is a square cupboard, as I may call it, or it more resembles the head of a clock, where, secure from the rain, are placed paintings of the history of our Saviour from His birth to His ascension. Some of the designs are very pretty (taken, no doubt, from better pictures) and they generally tell their tale intelligibly. The pillars are in themselves pleasing objects in connection with the background of a crag or overhanging tree—a streamlet, or a bridge—and how touchingly must their pictured language have spoken to the heart of many a weary devotee! The ascent through the forest was interesting on every account. It led us sometimes along the brink of precipices, and always far above the boisterous river. We frequently met, or were overtaken, by peasants (mostly bearing heavy burthens). We spoke to each other; but here I could not understand three words of their language, nor they of mine.

Engelberg, Mount Titlis, Tuesday, August 15*th.*—We breakfasted in view of the flashing, silver-topped Mount Titlis, and its grey crags, a sight that roused William's youthful desires; and in spite of weak eyes, and the weight of fifty winters, he could not repress a longing to ascend that mountain. . . . But my brother had had his own visions of glory, and, had he been twenty years younger, sure I am that he would have trod the summit of the Titlis. Soon after breakfast we were warned to expect the procession, and saw it issuing from the church. Priests in their white robes, choristers, monks chanting the service, banners uplifted, and a full-dressed image of the Virgin carried aloft. The people were divided into several classes; the men, bareheaded; and maidens, taking precedence of the married women, I suppose, because it was the festival of the Virgin. The procession formed a beautiful stream upon the green level, winding round the church and convent. Thirteen hundred people were assembled at Engelberg, and joined in this service. The unmarried women wore straw hats, ornamented with flowers, white bodices, and crimson petticoats. The dresses of the elder people were curious. What a display of neck-chains and earrings! of silver and brocaded stomachers! Some old men had coats after the mode of the time of *The Spectator,*[13] with worked seams. Boys, and even young men, wore flowers in their straw hats. We entered the convent; but were only suffered to go up a number of staircases, and through long whitewashed galleries, hung with portraits of saints, and prints of remarkable places in Switzerland, and particularly of the vale and convent of Engelberg, with plans and charts of the mountains, etc. There are now only eighteen monks; and the abbot no longer exists: his office, I suppose, became extinct with his temporal princedom. . . . I strolled to the chapel, near the inn, a pretty white edifice, entered by a long flight of steps. No priest, but several young peasants, in shepherdess attire of jackets, and showy petticoats, and flowery hats, were paying their vows to the Virgin. A colony of swallows had built their nests within the cupola, in the centre of the circular roof. They were flying overhead; and their voices seemed to me an harmonious accompaniment to the silent devotions of those rustics.

[. . . . .]

*Wednesday, August 22nd.—Amsteg.—*After Wasen our road at times very steep—rocky on both sides of the glen; and fewer houses than before. We had left the forest, but smaller fir-trees were thinly sprinkled on the hills. Looking northward, the church tower on its eminence most elegant in the centre of the glen backed by the bare pyramid of Meisen. Images by the wayside though not frequent, I recollect a poor idiot hereabouts, who with smiles and uncouth gestures placed himself under the Virgin and Child, pleading so earnestly that there was no resisting him. Soon after, when I was lingering behind upon a stone, beside a little streamlet of clear water, a procession of mules approached, laden with wine-casks—forty at least—which I had long seen winding like a creeping serpent along the side of the bare hill before me, and heard the stream of sound

---

[13] A fashion-determining, influential periodical in print from 1711 to 1714.

from their bells. Two neatly-dressed Italian women, who headed the cavalcade, spoke to me in their own sweet language; and one of them had the kindness to turn back to bring me a glove, which I had left on the stone where I had been sitting. I cannot forget her pretty romantic appearance—a perfect contrast to that of the poor inhabitants of her own sex in this district, no less than her soft speech! She was rather tall, and slender, and wore a small straw hat tied with coloured riband, different in shape from those worn in Switzerland. It was the first company of muleteers we had seen, though afterwards we met many. Recrossed the Reuss, and, ascending a very long and abrupt hill covered with impending and shattered crags, had again that river on our left, but the hill carried us out of sight of it. I was alone—the first in the ascent. A cluster of mountain masses, till then unseen, appeared suddenly before me, black—rugged—or covered with snow. I was indeed awe-struck; and, while I sate for some minutes, thought within myself, now indeed we are going among the terrors of the Alps; for the course of the Reuss being hidden, I imagined we should be led towards those mountains. Little expecting to discover traces of human habitations, I had gone but a little way before I beheld, stretching from the foot of the savage mountains, an oblong valley thickly strewn over with rocks, or, more accurately speaking, huge stones; and among them huts of the same hue, hardly to be distinguished, except by their shape. At the foot of the valley appeared a village beside a tall slender church tower;—every object of the same hue except the foaming glacier stream and the grassy ground, exquisitely green among the crags. The hills that flanked the dismal valley told its history:—their precipitous sides were covered with crags, mostly in detached masses, that seemed ready to be hurled down by avalanches. Descending about half a mile we were at the village,[14] and turning into the churchyard to the left, sate there, overlooking the pass of the torrent. Beside it lay many huge fragments of rock fallen from above, resembling one of still more enormous size, called the Devil's stone, which we had passed by on the right-hand side of the road near the entrance of the village. How lavishly does nature in these desolate places dispense *beautiful* gifts! The craggy pass of the stream coming out of that valley of stones was decorated with a profusion of gorgeous bushes of the mountain ash, with delicate flowers, and

---

[14] Named Goschenen. It is 2100 feet above the lake of Waldstellen and 3282 above the level of the Vierwaldstadtersee.—D.W.

with the richest mosses. And, even while looking upon the valley itself, it was impossible, amid all its images of desolation, not to have a mild pleasure in noticing the harmonious beauty of its form and proportions. Two or three women came to us to beg; and all the inhabitants seemed to be miserably poor. No wonder! for they are not merely *summer* tenants of the village:—and who, that could find another hold in the land, would dwell there the year through? Near the church is a picturesque stone bridge, at the further end spanned by the arch of a ruined gateway (no gate is *there* now), and its stone pillars are crested with flowers and grass. We cross the bridge; and, winding back again, come in sight of the Reuss far below, to our left, and were in that part of the pass especially called by Ebel the valley of Schollenen,[15] so well known for its dangers at the time of the dissolving of the snow, when the muleteers muffle their bells and do not venture to speak a word, lest they should stir some loose masses overhead by agitating the air. Here we passed two muleteers stretched at ease upon a plot of verdant turf, under a gigantic crag, their mules feeding beside them. The road is now, almost continuously very steep—the hills rugged—often ruinous— yet straggling pine-trees are seen even to their summits; and goats fearlessly browsing upon the overhanging rocks. The distance from Ghestinen to the vale of Ursern is nearly two leagues. After we had been long ascending, I perceived on the crags on the opposite side of the glen two human figures. They were at about the same elevation as ourselves; yet looked no bigger than a boy and girl of five years' growth, a proof that, narrow as the glen appears to be, its width is considerable:—and this shows how high and steep must be the mountains. Those people carried each a large burthen, which we supposed to be of hay; but where was hay to be procured on these precipices? A little further—and the mystery was solved, when we discovered a solitary mower among slips of grass on the almost per- pendicular side of the mountain. The man and woman must have been bearing their load to the desolate valley. Such are the summer labours of its poor inhabitants. In winter, their sole employment out of their houses and cattle-sheds must be the clearing away of snow, which would otherwise keep the doors barred up. But even at that season, I believe, seldom a week passes over their heads without

---

[15] Ramond gives this name to the whole valley from Amsteg to the entrance of Ursern. Ebel gives to it, altogether, the name of the Haute-Reuss; and says that it is called by the inhabitants the Graccenthal—Goschenen.—D. W.

tidings from the top of St. Gothard or the valley of Altorf, winter being the season when merchandise is constantly passing upon sledges between Italy and Switzerland:—and Ghestinen is one of the halting-places. The most dangerous time of travelling is the spring. For *us* there were no dangers. The excellent paved road of granite masters all difficulties even up the steepest ascents; and from safe bridges crossing the torrents we looked without trepidation into their gulfs, or pondered over their hasty course to the Reuss. Yet in the Gorge of Schoellenen it is not easy to forget the terrors which visit that houseless valley. Frequent memorials of deaths on the spot are discovered by the way-side,—small wooden crosses placed generally under the shelter of an overhanging stone. They might easily be passed unnoticed; and are so slightly put together that a child might break them to pieces:—yet they lie from year to year, as safe as in a sanctuary.

[. . . . .]

Sunday, September 9th.—Domo d'Ossola.—Soon after, we perceive a large and very striking building terminating a narrow reach of the valley. A square tower at the further end of the roof; and, towards us, a lofty gable front, step-like on each steeply-sloping side, in the style of some of our old roofs in the north of England. The building is eight stories high, and long and broad in proportion. We perceived at once that it must be a Spittal[16] of the old times; and W., who had been lingering behind, when he came up to us, pronounced it to be the very same where he and his companion had passed an awful night. Unable to sleep from other causes, their ears were stunned by a tremendous torrent (then swollen by rainy weather) that came thundering down a chasm of the mountain on the opposite side of the glen. That torrent, still keeping the same channel, was now, upon this sunny clear day, a brisk rivulet, that cheerfully bounded down to the Vedro. A lowly Church stands within the shade of the huge Spittal, beside a single dwelling-house: small, yet larger than the Church. We entered that modest place of worship; and were charmed with its rustic splendours and humble neatness. Here were two very pretty well-executed pictures in the Italian style, so much superior to anything of the kind in the country churches of Switzerland. Rested some while beside the Church and cottage, looking towards the Spittal on the opposite side of the

---

[16] Roadside shelter for travelers.

road, the wildest of all harbours, yet even stately in its form, and seemingly fitted to war with the fiercest tempests. I now regret not having the courage to pass the threshold alone. I had a strong desire to see what was going on within doors for the sake of tales of thirty years gone by: but could not persuade W. to accompany me. Several foot or mule travellers were collected near the door, I bought some *poor* peaches (very refreshing at that time) from a man who was carrying them and other things, to the village of Simplon—three sous the pound. Soon after leaving the Spittal, our path was between precipices still more gloomy and awful than before (what must they have been in the time of rain and vapour when my brother was here before—on the narrow track instead of our broad road that smooths every difficulty!) Skeletons of tall pine-trees beneath us in the dell, and above our heads,—their stems and shattered branches as grey as the stream of the Vedro or the crags strewn at their feet. The scene was truly sublime when we came in view of the finest of the galleries. We sate upon the summit of a huge precipice of stone to the left of the road—the river raging below after having tumbled in a tremendous cataract down the crags in front of our station. On entering the Gallery we cross a clear torrent pent up by crags. While pausing here, a step or two before we entered, a carriage full of gentlemen drove through: they just looked aside at the torrent; but stopped not; I could not but congratulate myself on our being on foot; for a hundred reasons the pleasantest mode of travelling in a mountainous country. After we had gone through the last, and least interesting, though the longest but one of the galleries, the vale (now grassy among scattered rocks, and wider—more of a hollow) bends to the left; and we see on the hill, in front of us, a long doubling of the road, necessary, from the steepness of the hill, to accomplish an easy ascent. At the angle, where, at the foot of the hill, this doubling begins, M. and I, being before W., sate and pondered. A foot-path leads directly upwards, cutting off at least a mile, and we perceived one of our young fellow-travellers climbing up it, but could not summon the courage to follow him, and took the circuit of Buonaparte's road. The bed of the river, far below to our left (wide and broken up by torrents), is crossed by a long wooden bridge from which a foot-path, almost perpendicular, ascends to a hamlet at a great height upon the side of the steep. A female crossing the bridge gave life and spirit to a scene characterised, in comparison with other scenes, more by wildness than grandeur; and though presided over by a glacier mountain and craggy and snowy pikes (seemingly at the head of the hollow vale) less impressive, and less interesting to the imagination than the narrow passes through which we had been travelling. After some time the curve of the road carries us again backward on the mountain-side, from the valley of the Tusa. Our eyes often turned towards the bridge and the upright path, little thinking that it was the same we had so often heard of, which misled my brother and Robert Jones in their way from Switzerland to Italy. They were pushing right upwards, when a peasant, having questioned them as to their object, told them they had no further ascent to make;—"The Alps were crossed!" The ambition of youth was disappointed at these tidings; and they remeasured their steps with sadness. At the point where our fellow-travellers had rejoined the road, W. was waiting to show us the track, on the green precipice. It was impossible for me to say how much it had moved him, when he discovered it was the very same which had tempted him in his youth. The feelings of that time came back with the freshness of yesterday, accompanied with a dim vision of thirty years of life between. We traced the path together, with our eyes, till hidden among the cottages, where they had first been warned of their mistake.[17]

[17] William's account in 6: 500–524 of *The Prelude*, 1805, reads:

Our noon's repast, from which the Travellers rose,	500
Leaving us at the Board. Erelong we follow'd,	
Descending by the beaten road that led	
Right to a rivulet's edge, and there broke off,	
The only track now visible was one	
Upon the further side, right opposite,	505
And up a lofty mountain. This we took,	
After a little scruple, and short pause,	
And climb'd with eagerness, though not, at length,	
Without surprize and some anxiety	
On finding that we did not overtake	510
Our Comrades gone before. By fortunate chance,	
While every moment now encreas'd our doubts,	
A Peasant met us and from him we learn'd	
That to the place which had perplex'd us first	
We must descend, and there should find the road,	515
Which in the stony channel of the Stream	
Lay a few steps, and then along its Banks;	
And, further, that thenceforward all our course,	
Was downwards, with the current of that Stream.	
Hard of belief we questioned him again,	520
And all the anwers which the Man return'd	
To our inquiries, in their sense and substance,	
Translated by the feelings which we had,	
Ended in this, that we had cross'd the Alps.	

Hereabouts, a few peasants were on the hills with cattle and goats. In the narrow passage of the glen we had, for several miles together, seen no moving objects, except chance travellers, the streams, the clouds, and trees stirred sometimes by gentle breezes. At this spot we watched a boy and girl with bare feet running as if for sport, among the sharp stones, fearless as young kids. The round hat of the Valais tied with a coloured riband, looked shepherdess-like on the head of another, a peasant girl roaming on craggy pasture-ground, to whom I spoke, and was agreeably surprised at being answered in German (probably a barbarous dialect), but we contrived to understand one another. The valley of the Vedro now left behind, we ascend gradually (indeed the whole ascent is gradual) along the side of steeps covered with poor grass—an undulating hollow to the right—no trees—the prospect, in front, terminated by snow mountains and dark pikes. The air very cold when we reached the village of Simplon. There is no particular grandeur in the situation, except through the accompanying feeling of removal from the world and the near neighbourhood of summits so lofty, and of form and appearance only seen among the Alps. We were surprised to find a considerable village. The houses, which are of stone, are large, and strong built, and gathered together as if for shelter. The air, nipping even at this season, must be dreadfully cold in winter; yet the inhabitants weather all seasons. The Inn was filled with guests of different nations and of various degrees, from the muleteer and foot-traveller to those who loll at ease, whirling away as rapidly as their companion, the torrent of the Vedro. Our party of eleven made merry over as good a supper in this naked region (five or six thousand feet above the level of the sea) as we could have desired in the most fertile of the valleys, with a dessert of fruit and cakes. We were summoned out of doors to look at a living chamois,[18] kept in the stable, more of a treat than the roasted flesh of one of its kind which we had tasted at Lucerne. Walked with some of the gentlemen about half a mile, after W. and M. were retired to rest. The stars were appearing above the black pikes, while the snow on others looked as bright as if a full moon were shining upon it. Our beds were comfortable. I was not at all fatigued, and had nothing to complain of but the cold, which did not hinder me from falling asleep and sleeping soundly. The distance from Duomo d'Ossola six leagues.

[18] Mountain antelope.

Monday, September 10—*Simplon.*—Rose at five o'clock, as cold as a frosty morning in December. The eleven breakfasted together, and were ready—all but the lame one,—to depart on foot to Brieg in the Haut Valais (seven leagues). The distance from the village of Simplon to the highest point of the Pass is nearly two leagues. We set forward together, forming different companies—or sometimes solitary—the peculiar charm of pedestrian travelling, especially when the party is large—fresh society always ready—and solitude to be taken at will. In the latter part of the Pass of St. Gothard, on the Swiss side, the grandeur diminishes—and it is the same on the Italian side of the Pass of Simplon; yet when (after the gradual ascent from the village, the last inhabited spot) a turning of the road first presents to view in a clear atmosphere, beneath a bright blue sky (so we were favoured), the ancient Spittal with its ornamented Tower standing at the further end of a wide oblong hollow, surrounded by granite pikes, snow pikes—masses of granite—cool, black, motionless shadows, and sparkling sunshine, it is not possible for the dullest imagination to be unmoved. When we found ourselves within that elevated enclosure, the eye and the ear were satisfied with perfect stillness. We might have supposed ourselves to be the only visible moving creatures; but ere long espied some cows and troops of goats which at first we could not distinguish from the scattered rocks! but by degrees tracked their motions, and perceived them in great numbers creeping over the yellow grass that grows among crags on the declivities above the Spittal and in the hollow below it; and we then began to discover a few brown *chalets* or cattle-sheds in that quarter. The Spittal, that dismal, yet secure sheltering-place (inhabited the winter through), is approached by a side track from the present road; out of the way of storms as it could have been. Carts and carriages of different kinds (standing within and near the door of a shed, close to the road) called to mind the stir and traffic of the world in a place which might have been destined for perpetual solitude—where the thunder of heaven, the rattling of avalanches, and the roaring of winds and torrents seemed to be the only *turbulent* sound, that had a right to take place of the calm and silence which surrounded us.

Wednesday, September 12*th.*—*Baths of Leuk.*—Rose at 5 o'clock. From my window looked towards the crags of the Gemmi, then covered with clouds. Twilight seemed scarcely to have left the valley; the air was sharp, and the smoking channel of hot water a comfortable sight in the cold gloom of the village. But soon, with promise of a fine day, the vapours on the crescent of crags began to break, and its yellow towers, touched by the sunshine, gleamed through the edges of the floating masses; or appeared in full splendour for a moment, and were again hidden.

After six o'clock, accompanied by a guide (who was by trade a shoemaker, and possessed a small stock of mountain cattle), we set forward on our walk of eight leagues, the turreted barrier facing us. Passed along a lane fenced by curiously crossed rails,—thence (still gently ascending) through rough ground scattered over with small pine-trees, and stones fallen from the mountains. No wilder object can be imagined than a shattered guidepost at the junction of one road with another, which had been placed there because travellers, intending to cross the Gemmi, had often been misled, and some had perished, taking the right-hand road toward the snow mountain, instead of that to the left. Even till we reached the base of that rocky rampart which we were to climb, the track of ascent, in front of us, had been wholly invisible. Sometimes it led us slanting along the bare side of the crags:—sometimes it was scooped out of them, and over-roofed, like an outside staircase of a castle or fortification: sometimes we came to a level gallery—then to a twisting ascent—or the path would take a double course—backwards and forwards,— the dizzy height of the precipices above our heads more awful even than the gulfs beneath us! Sometimes we might have imagined our-selves looking from a parapet into the inner space of a gigantic castle—a castle a thousand times larger than was ever built by human hands; while above our heads the turrets appeared as majes-tic as if we had not climbed a step nearer to their summits. A small plot or two of turf, never to be cropped by goat or heifer, on the ledge of a precipice; a bunch of slender flowers hanging from a chink—and one luxuriant plot of the bright blue monkshood, lodged like a little garden amid the stone-work of an Italian villa— were the sole marks of vegetation that met our eyes in the ascent, except a few distorted pine trees on one of the summits, which reminded us of watchmen, on the look-out. A weather-beaten, com-plex, wooden frame, something like a large sentry-box, hanging on the side of one of the crags, helped out this idea, especially as we were told it had been placed there in troublesome times to give warning of approaching danger. It was a very wild object, that could not but be noticed; and when noticed the question must follow—how came it there? and for what purpose? We were preceded by some travellers on mules, who often shouted as if for their own pleasure; and the shouts were echoed through the circuit of the rocks. Their guide afterwards sang a hymn, or pensive song: there was an aerial sweetness in the wild notes which descended to our ears. When *we* had attained the same height, *our* guide sang the same air, which made me think it might be a customary rite, or practice, in that part of the ascent. The Gemmi Pass is in the direct road from Berne to the Baths of Leuk. Invalids, unable to walk, are borne on litters by men, and frequently have their eyes blinded that they may not look down; and the most hardy travellers never venture to descend on their horses or mules. Those careful creatures make their way safely, though it is often like descending a steep and rugged staircase: and there is nothing to fear for foot-travellers if their heads be not apt to turn giddy. The path is seldom traceable, either up or down, further than along one of its zig-zags; and it will happen, when you are within a yard or two of the line which is before you, that you cannot guess what turning it shall make. The labour and ingenuity with which this road has been constructed are truly astonishing. The canton of Berne,[19] eighty years ago, furnished gunpowder for blasting the rocks, and labourers were supplied by the district of the Valais. The former track (right up an apparently almost perpendicular precipice between overhanging crags) must have been utterly impassable for travellers such as we, if any such had travelled in those days, yet it was, even now, used in winter. The peasants ascend by it with pikes and snowshoes, and on their return to the valley slide down, an appalling thought when the precipice was before our eyes; and I almost shudder at the remembrance of it! . . .

A glacier mountain appears on our left, the haunt of chamois, as our guide told us; he said they might often be seen on the brow of the Gemmi barrier in the early morning. We felt some pride in treading on the out-skirts of the chamois' play-ground—and what a boast for us, could we have espied one of those light-footed creatures bounding over the crags! But it is not for them who have been laggards in the vale till 6 o'clock to see such a sight.

The total absence of all *sound* of living *creature* was very striking: silent moths in abundance flew about in the sunshine, and the muddy Lake weltered below us; the only sound when we checked our

---

[19] Swiss territorial division; a state.

voices to listen. Hence we continued to journey over rocky and barren ground till we suddenly looked down into a warm, green nook, into which we must descend. Twelve cattle were there enclosed by the crags, as in a field of their own choosing. We passed among them, giving no disturbance, and again came upon a tract as barren as before. After about two leagues from the top of the Gemmi crags, the summer chalet, our promised resting-place, was seen facing us, reared against the stony mountain, and overlooking a desolate round hollow. Winding along the side of the hill (that deep hollow beneath us to the right) a long half-mile brought us to the platform before the door of the hut. It was a scene of wild gaiety. Half-a-score of youthful travellers (military students from the College of Thune) were there regaling themselves. Mr. Robinson became sociable; and we, while the party stood round us talking with him, had our repast spread upon the same table where they had finished theirs. They departed; and we saw them winding away towards the Gemmi on the side of the precipice above the dreary hollow— a long procession, not less interesting than the group at our approach. But every object connected with animated nature (and human life especially) is interesting on such a road as this; we meet no one with a stranger's heart! I cannot forget with what pleasure, soon after leaving the hut, we greeted two young matrons, one with a child in her arms, the other with hers, a lusty babe, ruddy with mountain air, asleep in its wicker cradle on her back. Thus laden they were to descend the Gemmi Rocks, and seemed to think it no hardship, returning us cheerful looks while we noticed the happy burthens which they carried. Those peasant travellers out of sight, we go on over the same rocky ground, snowy pikes and craggy eminences still bounding the prospect. But ere long we approach the neighbourhood of trees, and overlooking a long smooth level covered with poor yellowish grass, saw at a distance, in the centre of the level, a group of travellers of a different kind—a party of gentry, male and female, on mules. On meeting I spoke to the two ladies in English, by way of trying their nation, and was pleased at being answered in the same tongue. The lawn here was prettily embayed, like a lake, among little eminences covered with dwarf trees, aged or blighted; thence, onward to another open space, where was an encampment of cattle sheds, the large plain spotted with heaps of stones at irregular distances, as we see lime, or manure, or hay-cocks in our cultivated fields. Those heaps had been gathered together by the industrious peasants to make room for a scanty herbage for their cattle. The turf was very poor, yet so lavishly overspread with close-growing flowers it reminded us of a Persian carpet. The *silver* thistle, as we then named it, had a singularly beautiful effect; a glistering star lying on the ground, as if enwrought upon it. An avalanche had covered the surface with stones many years ago, and many more will it require for nature, aided by the mountaineers' industry, to restore the soil to its former fertility. On approaching the destined termination of our descent, we were led among thickets of Alpine Shrubs, a rich covering of berry-bearing plants overspreading the ground. We followed the ridge of this wildly beautiful tract, and it brought us to the brink of a precipice. On our right, when we looked into the savage valley of Gastron—upwards toward its head, and downwards to the point where the Gastron joins the Kandor, their united streams thence continuing a tumultuous course to the Lake of Thun. The Lead of the *Kandor Thal* was concealed from us, to our left, by the ridge of the hill on which we stood. By going about a mile further along the ridge to the brow of its northern extremity, we might have seen the junction of the two rivers, but were fearful of being overtaken by darkness in descending the *Gemmi,* and were, indeed, satisfied with the prospect already gained. The river Gastron winds in tumult over a stony channel, through the apparently level area of a grassless vale, buried beneath stupendous mountains—not a house or hut to be seen. A roaring sound ascended to us on the eminence so high above the vale. How *awful* the tumult when the river carries along with it the spring tide of melted snow! We had long viewed in our journey a snow-covered pike, in stateliness and height surpassing all the other eminences. The whole mass of the mountain now appeared before us, on the same side of the Gastron vale on which we were. It seemed very near to us, and as if a part of its base rose from that vale. We could hardly believe our guide when he told us that pike was one of the summits of the Jungfrau, took out maps and books, and found it could be no other mountain. I never before had a conception of the space covered by the bases of these enormous piles. After lingering as long as time would allow, we began to remeasure our steps, thankful for the privilege of again feeling ourselves in the neighbourhood of the Jungfrau, and of looking upon those heights that border the Lake of Thun, at the feet of which we had first entered among the inner windings of Switzerland. Our journey back to the chalet was not less pleasant than in the earlier part of the day. The guide, hurrying on before us, roused the large house-dog to give us a welcoming bark, which echoed round the mountains like the tunable voices of a full pack of hounds—a heart-stirring concert in that silent place where no waters were heard at that time—no tinkling of cattle bells; indeed the barren soil offers small temptation for wandering cattle to linger there. In a few weeks our rugged path would be closed up with snow, the hut untenanted for the winter, and not a living creature left to rouse the echoes—echoes which our Bard would not suffer to die with us.

    Friday, September 14*th.—Martigny.*—Oh! that I could describe,— nay, that I could *remember* the sublime spectacle of the pinnacles and towers of Mont Blanc[20] while we were travelling through the vale, long deserted of the sunshine that still lingered on those summits! A large body of moving clouds covered a portion of the side of the mountain. The pinnacles and towers above them seemed as if they stood in the sky;—of no soft aerial substance, but appearing, even at that great distance, as they really are, huge masses of solid stone, raised by Almighty Power, and never, but by the same Power, to be destroyed. The village of Chamouny is on the opposite (the north-western) side of the vale; in this part considerably widened. Having left the lanes and thickets, we slanted across a broad unfenced level, narrowing into a sort of village green, with its may-pole, as in England, but of giant stature, a pine of the Alps. The col-lected village of Chamouny and large white Church appeared before us, above the river, on a gentle elevation of pasture ground, sloping from woody steeps behind. Our walk beside the suburban cottages was altogether new, and very interesting:—a busy scene of preparation for the night! Women driving home their goats and cows,—labourers returning with their tools,—sledges (an unusual sight in Alpine valleys) dragged by lusty men, the old looking on,— young women knitting; and ruddy children at play,—(a race how different from the languishing youth of the hot plains of the Valais!)— Cattle bells continually tinkling—no silence, no stillness here,—yet the bustle and the various sounds leading to thoughts of quiet, rest, and silence. All the while the call to the cattle is heard from different

[20] An icon for tourists and writers, at nearly 16,000 feet Mont Blanc is the highest peak in Europe. By 1820, its summit had been reached only a few times. Dorothy's description here recalls Percy Bysshe Shelley's poem "Mont Blanc" and Coleridge's "Hymn before Sunrise in the Vale of Chamounix," a place he himself never visited; Mary Shelley explores the mountain in *Frankenstein*.

quarters; and the rapid Arve roars through the vale, among rocks and stones (its mountain spoils)—at one time split into divers branches—at another collected into one rough channel.

Passing the turn of the ascent, we come to another cross (placed there to face the traveller ascending from the other side) and, from the brow of the eminence, behold! to our left, the huge Form of Mont Blanc—pikes, towers, needles, and wide wastes of everlasting snow in dazzling brightness. Below, is the river Arve, a grey-white line, winding to the village of Chamouny, dimly seen in the distance. Our station, though on a height so commanding, was on the lowest point of the eminence; and such as I have sketched (but how imperfectly!) was the scene uplifted and outspread before us. The higher parts of the mountain in our neighbourhood are sprinkled with brown chalets. So they were thirty years ago, as my brother well remembered; and he pointed out to us the very quarter from which a boy greeted him and his companion with an Alpine cry.—

The Stranger seen below, the Boy
Shouts from the echoing hills with savage joy.[21]

Sunday, September 16*th.*—*Chamouny.*—There is no carriage road further than to Argentiere.—When, having parted with our car and guide, we were slowly pursuing our way to the foot-path, between the mountains, which was to lead us to the Valorsine, and thence, by the Tete-noire, to Trient, we heard from the churchyard of Argentiere, on the opposite side of the river, a sound of voices chanting a hymn, or prayer, and, turning round, saw in the green enclosure a lengthening procession—the priest in his robes, the host, and banners uplifted, and men following, two and two;—and, last of all, a great number of females, in like order; the head and body of each covered with a white garment. The stream continued to flow on for a long time, till all had paced slowly round the church, the men gathering close together, to leave unencumbered space for the women, the chanting continuing, while the voice of the Arve joined in accordant solemnity.[22] The procession was grave and simple, agreeing with the simple decorations of a village chinch:—the banners made no glittering show:—the females composed a

---

[21] From William's *Descriptive Sketches 1793,* (440–441).

[22] William's poem "Processions Suggested on a Sabbath Morning in the Vale of Chamouny" describes this monthly ceremony.

moving girdle round the church; their figures, from head to foot, covered with one piece of white cloth, resembled the small pyramids of the Glacier, which were before our eyes; and it was impossible to look at one and the other without fancifully connecting them together. Imagine the moving figures, like a stream of pyramids—the white Church, the half-concealed Village, and the Glacier close behind among pine-trees,—a pure sun shining over all! and remember that these objects were seen at the base of those enormous mountains, and you may have some faint notion of the effect produced on us by that beautiful spectacle. It was a farewell to the Vale of Chamouny that can scarcely be less vividly remembered twenty years hence than when (that wondrous vale being just out of sight) after ascending a little way between the mountains, through a grassy hollow, we came to a small hamlet under shade of trees in summer foliage. A very narrow clear rivulet, beside the cottages, was hastening with its tribute to the Arve. This simple scene transported us instantly to our vallies of Westmoreland. A few quiet children were near the doors, and we discovered a young woman in the darkest, coolest nook of shade between two of the houses, seated on the ground, intent upon her prayer-book. The rest of the inhabitants were gone to join in the devotions at Argentine. The top of the ascent (not a long one) being gained, we had a second cheering companion in our downward way, another Westmoreland brook of larger size, as clear as crystal; open to the sun, and (bustling but not angry) it coursed by our side through a tract of craggy pastoral ground. I do not speak of the needles of Montanvert, behind; nor of other pikes up-rising before us. Such sights belong not to Westmoreland; and I could fancy that I then paid them little regard, it being for the sake of Westmoreland alone that I like to dwell on this short passage of our journey, which brought us in view of one of the most interesting of the vallies of the Alps. We descended with our little stream, and saw its brief life in a moment cut off, when it reached the Berard, the River of Black Water, which is seen falling, not in black but grey cataracts within the cove of a mountain that well deserves the former epithet, though a bed of snow and glacier ice is seen among its piky and jagged ridges. Below those bare summits, pine forests and crags are piled together, with lawns and cottages between.

We enter at the side of the valley, crossing a wooden bridge—then, turning our backs on the scene just described, we bend our course downward with the river, that is hurrying away, fresh from its glacier fountains; how different a fellow-traveller from that little rivulet we had just parted from, which we had seen still bright as silver—drop into the grey stream! The descending vale before us beautiful—the high enclosing hills interspersed with woods, green pasturage, and cottages. The delight we had in journeying through the Valorsine is not to be imagined—sunshine and shade were alike cheering; while the very numerousness of the brown wood cottages (descried among trees, or outspread on the steep lawns), and the people enjoying their Sabbath leisure out of doors, seemed to make a quiet spot more quiet.

Wednesday, September 19*th.—Lausanne.*—We met with some pleasant Englishmen, from whom we heard particulars concerning the melancholy fate of our young friend, the American, seen by us for the last time on the top of the Righi. The tidings of his death had been first communicated, but a few hours before, by Mr. Mulloch. We had the comfort of hearing that his friend had saved himself by swimming, and had paid the last duties to the stranger, so far from home and kindred, who lies quietly in the churchyard of Kusnacht on the shores of Zurich.[23]

[The Wordsworths went to Paris, where Mary met Annette Vallon and William's daughter, Caroline, for the first time. Dorothy writes: "Mr. Eustace Baudonin[24] met us at the door of our lodgings:—and here ends my Journal." She does, however, make further entries, excerpted below, about the voyage home.]

Monday, October 29*th,—Boulogne.*—We walked to Buonaparte's Pillar, which, on the day when he harangued his soldiers (pointing to the shores of England whither he should lead them to conquest), he decreed should be erected in commemoration of the Legion of Honour.[25] The pillar is seen far and wide, *unfinished,* as the intricate casing of *scaffolding, loftier than itself, shows at whatever distance* it is seen. It is said the Bourbons[26] intend to complete the work, and give it a new name; but I think it more probable that the scaffolding may be left to fall away, and the pile of marble remain strewn round, as it is, with unfinished blocks, an undisputed

[23] See H. C. Robinson's account, pp. 299–302.

[24] William's friend, whose elder brother married Caroline.

[25] Then established—[D.W.] Founded in 1802 by Napoleon, when he was First Consul, the *Ordre national de la Légion d'honneur* recognizes French men and women for bravery and merit.

[26] Royal dynasty that preceded and replaced Napoleon.

monument of the Founder's vanity and arrogance; and *so* it may stand as long as the brick towers of Caligula have done, a remnant of which yet appears on the cliffs.[27] We walked on the ground which had been covered by the army that dreamt of conquering England, and were shown the very spot where their Leader made his boastful speech.

On the day fixed for our departure from Boulogne, the weather being boisterous and wind contrary, the *Packet*[28] could not sail, and we trusted ourselves to a small vessel, with only one effective sailor on board. Even *Mary* was daunted by the breakers outside the Harbour, and *I* descended into the vessel as unwillingly as a criminal might go to execution, and hid myself in bed. Presently our little ship moved; and before ten minutes were gone she struck upon the sands. I felt that something disastrous had happened; but knew not what till poor Mary appeared in the cabin, having been thrown down from the top of the steps. There was again a frightful beating and grating of the bottom of the vessel—water rushing in very fast. A young man, an Italian, who had risen from a bed beside mine, as pale as ashes, groaned in agony, kneeling at his prayers. My condition was not much better than his; but I was more quiet. Never shall I forget the kindness of a little Irish woman who, though she herself, as she afterwards said, was much frightened, assured me even cheerfully that there was no danger. I cannot say that her words, as assurances of safety, had much effect upon me; but the example of her courage made me become more collected; and I felt her human kindness even at the moment when I believed that we might be all going to the bottom of the sea together; and the agonising thoughts of the distress at home were rushing on my mind.[29]

[. . . . .]

---

[27] Emperor of Rome from 37 to 41 A.D.; Caligula's campaign to invade Britain and his mental stability have been much debated.

[28] A substantial boat, often a steamer that carries mail, freight, and passengers.

[29] De Selincourt's edition continues: My brother, thinking it would be impossible to save his wife and me, had stripped off his coat to be ready to swim; but what was our joy and thankfulness when he came into the cabin to tell us that the retreating tide would soon leave the ship bare; and all was safe. No more water came in: and in the course of half an hour, carts were seen on the shore in preparation to come and take us away. A little more time and we were summoned on deck; and very soon the Irish woman and we were seated with our luggage. How pleasant was the jolting and the noise of the cart wheels over the rocky bed of the sea now dry! Thus we drove through the streets of Boulogne.

[FROM KNIGHT, *Poems*, 6: 287]

It was, I think, 10 o'clock when we left Dover. The day was pleasant, and every English sight delightful, the fields sprinkled with cattle, the hedgerows, the snug small cottages, the pretty country-houses. Many a time we said to each other, "What a pleasant country this must appear to the eyes of a Frenchman!"

JOURNALS, 1824–1835

In fifteen journal notebooks from 1824 to 1835, Dorothy writes of—among other things—her own and her family's coming and goings, of walking from Grasmere to Rydal, of visiting Jane Pollard and Maria Jane Jewsbury, of sitting for a portrait, of vacationing at Gwerndovennant, of a walking tour on the Isle of Man, of her failing health, and of problems with the servants at Rydal mount. Carl Ketcham's study of these later journals remains the best introduction to them; the short excerpts here are, unless otherwise noted, taken from his work: Carl Ketcham. "Dorothy Wordsworth's Journals, 1824–1836." The Wordsworth Circle 9: 1 (1978): 3–16.

Wednesday December 1st, 1824.—Ground thinly covered with snow—snow showers—rain—hail—walk before dinner with M & W After to Mr Carr's—still hail-showers—freely moon light returning with Mr & Mrs Carr—Fine clouds day and night.

July 7, 1825.—A little way from Liddle [Lindale] discover well on side of road. Entrance arched—rather lintelled over with old ash stem—roof arched with stone—green with moss—hung with Adder's Tongue, fern, and Geraniums. Descend by steps—8—broken with age—3 niches. What Saint has this been dedicated [to]? Inquire of woman—"Never noticed it." Of Boys—"Oh yes!" "What do they call it—what name has it?" "Oh! It's Dicky Grayson Well." "Why so?" "Perhaps he made it." "Does he live there now?" "Nay, he's sellt up." "It must be very auld." "Ay," says Boy, "I remember it a long time" (he not more than 16). Companion rolling in Dust like an ass of the desart.

May 5, 1826.—Walk ... after dinner to Old John's Cottage on the hill—He is 87—"His wife works out of doors with him."[1] We found them in one of their several orchards planting potatoes and working with rake and hoe to break the lumps in the clayey soil—Again and again they struck at the same Lump—Yet that little square was almost finished—very neat—their plot of Wheat half-eaten by the Squire's Men and horses are always busy—and his ploughing done by other means.

[1] Until 1837, "Simon Lee" included the line, "Old Ruth works out of doors with him" [Ketcham].

July, 1828[2] *Thursday, July 3rd.*—A fine morning, but still misty on hills. On Douglas heights, the sea-rocks tremendous; wind high; a waterfowl sporting on the roughest part of the sea; flocks of jackdaws, very small; a few gulls; two men reclined at the top of a precipice with their dogs; small boats tossing in the eddy, and a pleasure-boat out with ladies; misery it would have been for me; guns fired from the ship, a fine echo in the harbour; saw the flash long before the report. Sir Win. Hilary saved a boy's life to-day in the harbour. He raised a regiment for Government, and chose his own reward—a Baronetcy!

Friday, 4th July.—Walked with Henry to the Harbour of Peace, and up the valley; very pretty overarched bridge; neat houses, and hanging gardens, and blooming fences—the same that are so ugly seen from a distance: the wind sweeping those fences, they glance and intermingle colours as bright as gems.

Saturday.—Very bright morning. Went to the Duke's gardens, which are beautiful. I thought of Italian villas, and Italian bays, looking down on a long green lawn adorned with flower-beds, such as ours, at one end; a perfect level, with grand walks at the ends, woods rising from it up the steeps; and the dashing sea, boats, and ships, and ladies struggling with the wind; veils and gay shawls and waving flounces. The gardens beautifully managed,—wild, yet neat enough for plentiful produce; shrubbery, forest trees, vegetables, flowers, and hot-houses, all connected, yet divided by the form of the ground. Nature and art hand in hand, tall shrubs, and Spanish chestnut in great luxuriance. Lord Fitzallan's children keeping their mother's birthday in the strawberry beds. Loveliest of evenings. Isle perfectly clear, but no Cumberland; the sea alive with all colours, the eastern sky as bright as the west after sunset.

October 10, 1830.—I alone to afternoon Church and on Western Terrace—Lake as steady as a mirror—cattle motionless in field—as the few sheaves of corn still remaining—Birds and streamlets silent—no moving thing but the breath of smoke from Nab Chimney reflected in Lake—at intervals the Bull bellows in field beyond and above Boat-house—the echo from the bowels of Nab Scar exquisitely musical—all else silent to eye and ear—perfect stillness—perfect steadiness.

---

[2] From June 26 to July 23, 1828, Dorothy made a tour of the Isle of Man in the company of Henry and Joanna Hutchinson. Knight prints her journal entries as *Tour in the Isle of Man,* from which the July 1828 entries are taken.

February 19, 1834.—I was very ill after dinner, why or where-fore I know not—pain—sickness—head-ache—perspiration—heat and Cold.

Tuesday Evening Decr. 30, 1834.—William came to me rejoiced to hear thickly falling rain after so long a pause—I could not but feel a touch of sympathy with him in memory of many a moist tramp.

November 4, 1835.—I take up the pen once again,—After a try-ing illness I have risen to dinner, without pain at present. Wm. is at Workington—John has been in Radorshire—Dora not unwell.

[A final entry of disconnected words scrawled irregularly on the page, some of which I decipher as:]

No dark thick [wels?] enough it [———d]
And [———] hopes [g——] [-r——] sonnet
Torments brother private room
No metal hinges
sight is hers to tell [———] [———]
dismal doom

1833 Crosthwaite Portrait of Dorothy at 62 (Wordsworth Family, Rydal Mount.)

COLLECTED POEMS

Despite insisting that she could not write poetry, Dorothy Wordsworth wrote at least twenty-seven poems. William published three in his collection of 1815 and more in 1836 and 1842. Knight printed some in volume eight of his 1896 Poetical Works of William Wordsworth. *Late in the nineteenth century, several poems found their way into such periodicals as* The Monthly Packet. *In 1987, I collected all the poems I could find and published them, with scholarly critical apparatus as an appendix to* Dorothy Wordsworth and Romanticism, *my source here.*

Because Dorothy wrote, rewrote, copied again and again, many poems have numerous versions. For each poem here I give a base text, and indicate locations of various versions using these abbreviations:

BL—British Library
CB—Commonplace Book preserved at Dove Cottage
CCB—Coleortan Commonplace Book
CCVL—Coleridge Collection, Victoria University Library, Toronto
CR—Clarkson Recollections
1815—William's Poems of 1815
MBA—Mary Barker Album
MJA—Mary Jones Album
RN—Rydal Notebook
TA—Trevenan Album (Wordsworth Collection, Cornell University)

One exemplary set of variants is provided: (pp. 210–211).

Like many people, Dorothy kept "commonplace books": scrapbooks that included recipes, newspaper clippings, medical remedies, and other items she found interesting. These books and the albums that are primarily autograph or souvenir books are main sources of her poetry. That Dorothy worked with lines, sometimes for years, before placing them in a poem, makes dating difficult. I present the poems in rough chronology:

(1805)	To my Niece Dorothy, a sleepless Baby.
(1806)	An address to a Child in a high wind
(1807)	The Mother's Return
(18??)	a Sketch
(18??)	Grasmere—A Fragment
(1826)	Lines Addressed to Joanna H. from Gwerndovennant June 1826
(1826)	A Holiday at Gwerndovennant

Three poems, probably Dorothy's, follow:

> *Fragment Christmas day*
> *"This flower, the garden's proudest boast"*
> *To E.C.*

To my Niece Dorothy, a Sleepless Baby.[1]

The days are cold; the nights are long
The north wind sings a doleful song
Then hush again upon my breast;
All *merry* things are now at rest
    Save thee my pretty love!   5

The kitten sleeps upon the hearth;
The crickets long have ceased their mirth
There's nothing stirring in the house
Save one wee hungry nibbling mouse
    Then why so busy thou?   10

---

[1] Dorothy (1804–1847), soon called Dora to avoid confusion.

Nay, start not at that sparkling light
'Tis but the moon that shines so bright
On the window-pane bedropp'd with rain
Then, little Darling, sleep again
    And wake when it is Day.   15
            By Miss Wordsworth

In the RN Dorothy crosses out the following two stanzas and the title, The address to my Niece/Altered by my Brother

Ah! If I were a Lady gay
I should not grieve with thee to play
Right gladly would I lie awake
Thy lively spirits to partake
    And ask no better cheer.

But Babe! there's none to work for me.
And I must rise to industry:
Soon as the Cock begins to crow
Thy Mother to the fold must go
    To tend the sheep & kine.

Catherine Clarkson observes: "N.B. The third and fourth stanza's are by W. W." They were published with the poem in 1896.
Versions: (1) DW's fair copy, CCB (2) fair copy MBA (3) WmW's version in *Poems* 1815 (4) fair copy in CR (5) DW's fair copy in RN

An Address to a Child in a High Wind

What way does the wind come? what way does he go?
He rides over the water and over the snow,
Through the valley, and over the hill
And roars as loud as a thundering Mill.
He tosses about in every bare tree,   5
As, if you look up you plainly may see
But how he will come, and whither he goes
There's never a Scholar in England knows.

He will suddenly stop in a cunning nook
And rings a sharp larum:—but if you should look   10
There's nothing to see but a cushion of snow,
Round as a pillow and whiter than milk
And softer than if it were cover'd with silk.

Sometimes he'll hide in the cave of a rock;
Then whistle as shrill as a buzzard cock;   15
—But seek him and what shall you find in his place
Nothing but silence and empty space
Save in a corner a heap of dry leaves
That he's left for a bed for beggars or thieves.

As soon as 'tis daylight tomorrow with me   20
You shall go to the orchard & there you will see
That he has been there, & made a great rout,
And cracked the branches, & strew'd them about:
Heaven grant that he spare but that one upright twig
That look'd up at the sky so proud & so big   25
All last summer, as well you know
Studded with apples, a beautiful shew!

Hark! over the roof he makes a pause
And growls as if he would fix his claws
Right in the slates, and with a great rattle   30
Drive them down like men in a battle.
—But let him range round; he does us no harm
We build up the fire; we're snug and warm,
Old Madam has brought us plenty of coals
And the Glazier has closed up all the holes   35
In every window that Johnny broke
And the walls are tighter than Molly's new cloak.

Come, now we'll to bed, and when we are there
He may work his own will, & what shall we care.
He may knock at the door—we'll not let him in   40
May drive at the windows—we'll laugh at his din
Let him seek his own home wherever it be
Here's a canny warm house for Johnny and me.

Versions: (1) DW's fair copy, CCB (2) fair copy MBA initialed
DW at end (3) 1815 (4) CR (5) DW's copy in RN

The Mother's Return

Sweet Babes a month is past and gone
Since your dear Mother went away,
And she is coming home again;
Tomorrow is the happy day.

O blessed tidings! thought of joy!   5
John heard me speak with steady glee;
He silent stood; then laugh'd amain,
And shouted, "Mother, come to me!"

Louder & louder did he shout
With childish hope to bring her near   10
"Nay, patience! patience! little Boy
Your tender Mother cannot hear."

I told of hills, and far-off Towns,
And long, long Vales to travel through
He listens, puzzled, sore perplex'd,   15
But he submits; what can he do?

No strife disturbs his sister's breast;
She wars not with the mystery
Of time and distance, night, and day,
The bonds of our humanity.   20

Her joy is like an instinct, joy
Of Kitten, bird, or summer's fly;
She dances; runs, without an aim
She chatters in her ecstacy.

Now John takes up the giddy note,   25
And echoes back his sister's glee;
They hug the infant in my arms,
As if to force his sympathy

Then settling into fond discourse,
We rested in the garden Bower;   30
While sweetly shone the evening Sun
In his departing hour.

We told o'er all that we had done—
Our rambles by the running stream
'Mong pebbles fair, through beds of flowers,   35
Sights fresher than the brightest dream.

We talk'd of change, of winter gone
Of green leaves on the hawthorne spray,
Of birds that build their nests & sing;
And all since Mother went away!   40

To her these tales they will repeat,
To her our new-born tribes will shew,
The goslings green, the ass's colt,
The lambs that in the meadow go.

—Now strikes the clock that gives the Law   45
To bed the children must depart;
A moments heaviness they feel,
A sadness at the heart.

'Tis gone—and in a merry fit
They run up stairs in gamesome race,   50
I, too, infected by their mood,
I could have joined the wanton chace.

Five minutes passed—and Oh the change!
Asleep upon their beds they lie,
Their busy limbs in perfect rest,   55
    And closed the sparkling eye.

Note: In his published version, WmW dates the poem 1807. In
April of that year, William and Mary visited London for a month,
leaving Dorothy at Coleorton in charge of John, almost 4; Dorothy,
2½; and Thomas, 10 months.

Versions: (1) DW's fair copy CCB (2) DW's signed fair copy, inscribed on the last page by Lady Monteagle, to whom DW gave the manuscript "Lines written by Dorothy Wordsworth when her brothers Children had been left in her care—on their parents' expected return" BL (3) fair copy initialed DW in MBA (4) 1815 (5) fair copy CR (6) working copy RN

A SKETCH[2]

There is one Cottage in our Dale,
In naught distinguish'd from the rest
Save by a tuft of flourishing trees,
The shelter of that little nest

The publick road through Grasmere Vale   5
Winds close beside that Cottage small;
And there 'tis hidden by the trees
That overhang the orchard wall.

You lose it there—its serpent line
Is lost in that close household grove—   10
—A moment lost—and then it mounts
The craggy hills above.

Versions: (1) DW's fair copy CB (2) DW's fair copy MJA (3) DW's fair copy CCB (4) fair copy CR (5) DW's fair copy RN

GRASMERE—A FRAGMENT

Peaceful our valley, fair and green,
And beautiful her cottages,
Each in its nook, its sheltered hold,
Or underneath its tuft of trees

Many and beautiful they are;   5
But there is *one* that I love best,

---

[2] This sketch, worked into "Grasmere—A Fragment," has its own integrity.

A lowly shed, in truth, it is,
A brother of the rest.

Yet when I sit on rock or hill,
Down looking on the valley fair,   10
That Cottage with its clustering trees
Summons my heart; it settles there.

Others there are whose small domain
Of fertile fields and hedgerows green
Might more seduce a wanderer's mind   15
To wish that *there* his home had been.

Such wish be his! I blame him not,
My fancies they perchance are wild
—I love that house because it is
The very Mountains' child.   20

Fields hath it of its own, green fields,
But they are rocky steep and bare;
Their fence is of the mountain stone,
And moss and lichen flourish there.

And when the storm comes from the North   25
It lingers near that pastoral spot,
And, piping through the mossy walls,
It seems delighted with its lot.

And let it take its own delight;
And let it range the pastures bare;   30
Until it reach that group of trees,
—It may not enter there!

A green unfading grove it is,
Skirted with many a lesser tree,
Hazel & holly, beech and oak,   35
A bright and flourishing company.

Precious the shelter of those trees;
They screen the cottage that I love;

The sunshine pierces to the roof,
And the tall pine-trees tower above.   40

When first I saw that dear abode,
It was a lovely winter's day:
After a night of perilous storm
The west wind ruled with gentle sway;

A day so mild, it might have been   45
The first day of the gladsome spring;
The robins warbled, and I heard
One solitary throstle sing.

A Stranger, Grasmere, in thy Vale,
All faces then to me unknown,   50
I left my sole companion-friend
To wander out alone.

Lured by a little winding path,
I quitted soon the public road,
A smooth and tempting path it was,   55
By sheep and shepherds trod.

Eastward, toward the lofty hills,
This pathway led me on
Until I reached a stately Rock,
With velvet moss o'ergrown.   60

With russet oak and tufts of fern
Its top was richly garlanded;
Its sides adorned with eglantine
Bedropp'd with hips of glossy red.

There, too, in many a sheltered chink   65
The foxglove's broad leaves flourished fair,
And silver birch whose purple twigs
Bend to the softest breathing air.

Beneath that Rock my course I stayed,
And, looking to its summit high,   70

"Thou wear'st," said I, "a splendid garb,
Here winter keeps his revelry."

"Full long a dweller on the Plains,
I griev'd when summer days were gone;
No more I'll grieve; for Winter here   75
Hath pleasure gardens of his own.

What need of flowers? The splendid moss
Is gayer than an April mead;
More rich its hues of various green,
Orange, and gold, & glittering red."   80

—Beside that gay and lovely Rock
There came with merry voice
A foaming streamlet glancing by;
It seemed to say "Rejoice!"

My youthful wishes all fulfill'd,   85
Wishes matured by thoughtful choice,
I stood an Inmate of this vale
How *could* I but rejoice?

D Wordsworth Senr Rydal Mount Sept. 26th 1829

Versions: (1) DW's fair copy signed and dated September 26,
1829 TA (2) DW's fair copy 10 stanzas CB (3) DW's fair copy
2 stanzas CB (4) DW's fair copy different 10 stanzas from 2 CB
(5) DW's fair copy MJA (6) DW's fair copy MBA (7) DW's fair copy
CCB (8) fair copy CR (9) DW's fair copy RN

A twofold harmony is here,
I listen with the bodily ear
But dull and cheerless is the sound
Contrasted with the heart's rebound.

Lines Addressed to Joanna H. From Gwerndovennant[3] June 1826

Now at the close of fervid June   5
Upon this breathless hazy noon
I seek the deepest, darkest shade
Within the covert of that glade

Which you and I first named our own
When primroses were fully blown,   10
Oaks just were budding, and the grove
Rang with the gladdest songs of love.

Then did the Leader of the Band,
A gallant Thrush, maintain his stand
Unshrouded from the eye of day   15
Upon yon beech's topmost spray.

Within the self-same lofty Tree
A Thrush sings *now*—perchance tis He—
The lusty, joyous, gallant Bird,
Which on that April morn we heard.   20

Yet Oh! how different that voice,
Which bade the very hills rejoice!
—Through languid air, through leafy boughs
It falls, and can no echo rouze.

But in the workings of my heart   25
Doth memory act a busy part;
That jocund April morn lives there,
Its cheering sounds, its hues so fair.

[3] Thomas Hutchinson owned a small farm in Gwerndyffnant (or Gwerndovennant or Werndunvan—DW spells variously). She visited in May 1826.

Why mixes with remembrance blithe
Which nothing but the restless scythe   30
Of death can utterly destroy,
A heaviness a dull alloy?

Ah Friend! thy heart can answer why,
—Even then I heav'd a bitter sigh,
No word of sorrow didst thou speak   35
But tears stole down thy tremulous cheek.

The wish'd-for hour at length was come,
And thou hadst hous'd me in thy home
On fair Werndunvan's billowy hill,
Hadst led me to its crystal rill,   40

And led me through the dingle deep
Up to the highest grassy steep,
The sheep-walk where the snow-white lambs
Sported beside their quiet dams.

But thou wert destin'd to remove   45
From all these objects of thy love,
In this thy later day to roam
Far off, and seek another home.

Now thou art gone—belike 'tis best—
And I remain, a passing guest,   50
Yet, for thy sake, beloved Friend,
When from this spot my way shall tend,

Mournfully shall I say farewell
To this deep verdant, woody Dell.
And to that neighboring sunny Cot   55
Where thou so oft hast bless'd thy lot.

And, if my timid soul might dare
To shape the future in its prayer,
Then fervently would I entreat
Our gracious God to guide thy feet   60
Back to the peaceful sunny cot

Where thou so oft hast bless'd thy lot
Where lonely Nature led thy soul
To brood on Heaven—where no controul
Of fashion check'd thy steadfast aim   65

To satisfy whatever claim
A tender conscience might suggest
Of faithful cares leading to pious rest.

Versions: (1) DW's fair copy journal 25 Sept.–1 Nov. 1826 (2) DW's fair copy CB (3) DW working copy journal 29 June–24 Sept. 1826

A HOLIDAY AT GWERNDOVENNANT
IRREGULAR STANZAS[4]

You're here for one long vernal day,
We'll give it all to social play,
Though forty years have roll'd away
    Since we were young as you.

Then welcome to our spacious Hall!   5
Tom, Bessy, Mary, welcome all!
Though remov'd from busy men,
Yea lonesome as the fox's den
'Tis a place for joyance fit,
For frolic games & inborn wit.   10

'Twas Nature built this Hall of ours,
She shap'd the banks, she framed the bowers
    That close it all around;
From her we hold our precious right;
And here through live-long day & night,   15
    She rules with mildest sway.

Our carpet is her verdant sod;
A richer one was never trod
In prince's proud saloon;
Purple & gold & spotless white,   20

---

[4] Verse without regular metrical pattern.

And quivering shade, & sunny light,
   Blend with the emerald green.

She open'd for the mountain brook
A gently-winding, pebbly way
Into this placid, secret nook—   25
It's bell-like tinkling—list! you hear—
   —'Tis never loud, yet always clear
     As linnet's song in May.

And we have other music here,
A thousand songsters through the year   30
   Dwell in these happy groves;
And in this season of their loves
They join their voices with the doves'
To raise a perfect harmony.

Thus spake I, while with sober pace   35
We slipp'd into that chosen place,
And from the centre of our Hall
The young ones gaz'd around;
Then like a flock of vigorous lambs
That quit their grave & slow-paced dams   40
   To gambol o'er the mead,

That innocent, fraternal Troop,
(Erewhile a steady listening groupe)
Off-starting—Girl & Boy—
In gamesome race, with agile bound   45
Beat o'er & o'er the grassy ground
As if in motion perfect joy.

So vanishes my idle scheme
That we through this long vernal day,
Associates in their youthful play   50
With them might travel in one stream.
Ah! how should we whose heads are grey?
   —Light was my heart, my spirits gay,
    And fondly did I dream.

But now, recall'd to consciousness   55
With weight of years of changed estate,

Thought is not needed to repress
Those shapeless fancies of delight
That flash'd before my dazzled sight
   Upon this joy-devoted morn.   60

Gladly we seek the stillest nook
Whence we may read as in a book
A history of years gone by,
Recall'd to faded memory's eye
By bright reflexion from the mirth   65
Of youthful hearts, a transient second birth
    Of our own childish days.

Pleasure unbidden is their Guide—
Their Leader,—faithful to their side—
Prompting each wayward feat of strength,   70
The ambitious leap, the emulous race,
The startling shout, the mimic chace
The simple half-disguisèd wile
Detected through the fluttering smile.

A truce to this unbridled course   75
Doth intervene—no need of force—
We spread upon the flowery grass
The noon-tide meal—each Lad & Lass
Obeys the call; we form a Round
And all are seated on the ground.   80

The sun's meridian hour is pass'd:
—Again begins the emulous race,
Again succeeds the sportive chace,
And thus was spent that vernal day
Till twilight check'd the noisy play;   85
Then did they feel a languor spread
Over their limbs—the beating head
Was still'd, the busy throbbing heart,
    And silently we all depart.

The shelter of our rustic Cot   90
Receives us, & we envy not
The palace or the stately dome,

But wish that *all* had such a home.
Each Child repeats his nightly prayer
That God may bless their parents' care   95
To guide them in the way of truth
Through helpless childhood, giddy youth.

The closing hymn of chearful praise
Doth yet again their spirits raise,
And 'tis not now a *thoughtless* joy;   100
For tender parents, loving friends,
And all the gifts God's bounty sends,
Feelingly do they bless his name

That homage paid, the Young retire
With no unsatisfied desire;   105
Theirs is one long, one steady sleep,
Till the sun, tip toe on the Steep
In front of our beloved Cot
Casts on the walls his brightest beams.
Within a startling lustre streams;   110
They all awaken suddenly
As at the touch of magic spell,
Or as the pilgrim at the bell
That summons him to matin prayer.

And is it sorrow that they feel?   115
(Nay—call it not by such a name)
The stroke of sadness that doth steal
With rapid motion through their hearts
When comes the thought that yesterday
With all its joys is pass'd away   120
The long-expected happy day!

An instant—and all sadness goes,
Nor brighter looks the half-blown rose
Than does the countenance of each Child
Whether of ardent soul or mild;   125
The hour was fix'd—they are prepared,
And homeward now they must depart,
And, after many a brisk adieu,

On ponies trim, & fleet of limb
Their bustling journey they pursue.   130

The fair-hair'd, gentle, quiet Maid,
And She who is of daring mood,
The valiant, & the timid Boy
Alike are rouz'd to hardihood
And where so e'er the Troop appear   135
They scatter smiles, a hearty cheer
Comes from both Old & Young,
And blessings fall from many a tongue.

They reach the dear paternal roof,
Nor dread a cold or stern reproof   140
While they pour forth the history
Of three days' mirth and revelry.
Ah Children! happy is your lot,
Still bound together in one knot
Beneath your tender Mother's eye!   145
—Too soon these blessed days shall fly
And Brothers shall from Sisters part.

And trust me, whatsoe'er your doom,
Whate'er betide through years to come,
The punctual pleasures of your home   150
Shall linger in your thoughts—
Dearer than any future hope,
Though Fancy take her freest scope.
For Oh! too soon your hearts shall own
The past is all that is your own.   155

And every day of *Festival*
Gratefully shall ye then recal,
Less for their own sakes than for this
That each shall be a resting-place
For memory, & divide the race   160
Of childhood's smooth & happy years,
Thus lengthening out that term of life
Which, govern'd by your Parents' care
Is free from sorrow & from strife.

Versions: (1) DW's fair copy pasted into CB with this postscript: "*Finis*—and again I say tune up your musical pipes & put on your accommodating ears—be in good humour & forgive—bad metre, bad rhymes—no rhymes—identical rhymes & all that is lawless— As to dullness I leave that to take care of itself" (2) DW's fair copy CB (3) DW's fair copy, journal of 25 Sept.–1 Nov. 1826 (4) DW's part fair, part repetitive copy, journal of June–Sept. 1826, pages cut out of the back thereby cutting off the first 34 lines (5) DW's copy part ink, part illegible scrawl, journal June–Sept. 1826 (6) parts of poem in DW's pencil, journal 10 Feb.–22 June 1826 (7) DW's fair copy of last 5 stanzas, journal 25 Sept.–1 Nov. 1826

Irregular Verses

Ah Julia![5] ask a Christmas rhyme
Of *me* who in the golden time
Of careless, hopeful, happy youth
Ne'er strove to decorate the truth,
Contented to lay bare my heart
To one dear Friend, who had her part
In all the love and all the care
And every joy that harboured there.
—To her I told in simple prose
Each girlish vision, as it rose   10
Before an active busy brain
That needed neither spur nor rein;
That still enjoyed the present hour
Yet for the *future* raised a tower
Of bliss more exquisite and pure
Bliss that (so deemed we) should endure
Maxims of caution, prudent fears
Vexed not the projects of those years
Simplicity our steadfast theme,
No works of Art adorned our scheme,—   20
A cottage in a verdant dell

A foaming stream, a crystall Well,
A garden stored with fruit and flowers

[5] DW's goddaughter, Julia Marshall, daughter of Jane Pollard Marshall.

And sunny seats and shady bowers,
A file of hives for humming bees   25
Under a row of stately trees
And, sheltering all this faery ground,
A belt of hills must wrap it round,
Not stern or mountainous, or bare,
Nor lacking herbs to scent the air;   30
Nor antient trees, nor scattered rocks,
And pastured by the blameless flocks
That print their green tracks to invite
Our wanderings to the topmost height.

    Such was the spot I fondly framed   35
When life was new, and hope untamed:
There with my one dear Friend would dwell,
Nor wish for aught beyond the dell.
    Alas! the cottage fled in air,
The streamlet never flowed: 40
—Yet did those visions pass away
So gently that they seemed to stay,
Though in our riper years we each pursued a different way.

—We parted, sorrowful; by duty led;
My Friend, ere long a happy Wife   45
Was seen with dignity to tread
The paths of usefulness, in active life;
And such her course through later days;
The same her honour and her praise;
As thou canst witness, thou dear Maid,   50
One of the Darlings of her care;
Thy *Mother* was that Friend who still repaid
Frank confidence with unshaken truth:
This was the glory of her youth,
A brighter gem than shines in prince's diadem.   55

    You ask why in that jocund time
Why did I not in jingling rhyme
Display those pleasant guileless dreams
That furnished still exhaustless themes?
—I *reverenced* the Poet's skill,   60

And *might have* nursed a mounting Will
To imitate the tender Lays
Of them who sang in Nature's praise;
But bashfulness, a struggling shame
A fear that elder heads might blame   65
—Or something worse—a lurking pride
Whispering my playmates would deride
Stifled ambition, checked the aim
If e'er by chance "the numbers came"
—Nay even the mild maternal smile,   70
That oft-times would repress, beguile
The over-confidence of youth,
Even that dear smile, to own the truth,
Was dreaded by a fond self-love;
" 'Twill glance on me—and to reprove   75
Or," (sorest wrong in childhood's school)
"Will *point* the sting of ridicule."

    And now, dear Girl, I hear you ask
Is this your lightsome, chearful task?
You tell us tales of forty years,   80
Of hopes extinct, of childish fears,
Why cast among us thoughts of sadness
When we are seeking mirth and gladness?
    Nay, ill those words befit the Maid
Who pleaded for my Christmas rhyme   85
Mirthful she is; but placid—staid—
Her heart beats to no giddy chime
Though it with Chearfulness keep time
For Chearfulness, a willing guest,
Finds ever in her tranquil breast   90
A fostering home, a welcome rest.
And well she knows that, casting *thought* away,
We lose the best part of our day;
That joys of youth remembered when our youth is past
Are joys that to the end of life will last;   95

    And if this poor memorial strain,
Breathed from the depth of years gone by,

Should touch her Mother's heart with tender pain,
Or call a tear into her loving eye,
She will not check the tear or still the rising sigh.   100
—The happiest heart is given to sadness;
The saddest heart feels deepest gladness.

Thou dost not ask, thou dost not need
A verse from me; nor wilt thou heed
A greeting masked in laboured rhyme   105
From one whose heart has still kept time
With every pulse of thine

Versions: (1) DW's fair copy CB (2) DW's crossed-out fair copy CB (3) DW's fair copy, MJA

[Innocent Were the Lives They Led]

Innocent were the lives they led
Those gentle spirits that are fled
    To God who reigns above
Two duteous Daughters they & kind
Sisters they were in heart & mind   5
    For they were full of love

Too weak afflictions rod to bear
By accident & by sorrow were
    In early noon of life

Removèd from this world of care   10
In heavenly blessings sweet to share
    From trouble free & strife

Versions: DW's working copy, journal 11 Nov. 1827– 24 June 1828. DW worked on this stanza in the journal, but rejected it.

Too weak afflictions to bear
Sickness & sorrow—not despair
Blighted them in the noon of life
Composed they left this world of care
In heavenly happiness to share
Too pure for earthly strife

[No More the Pastor with His Flock]

No more the Pastor with his flock
    Assemble here in prayer
No more the chapel bell or chimes
    Sound sweetly thro' the air

Deserted are these sacred walls   5
    Deep silence here does reign
That still small voice in spirit calls
    And whispers Hope to gain

A blessed Mansion in the skies
    That Land of promise fair   10
Thither by love inspired rise
    Above this world of care.

How pensive is this autumn day
    With quiet pleasure fraught
Here slowly I pursue my way   15
    And soothed in every thought

To break the Calm here is no sound
    All nature is at rest
Hence pious feelings, clear profound
    Settle within my breast.   20

Version: DW's working copy at the end of her journal for 11 Nov. 1827–24 June 1828

To D.[6]

A thousand delicate fibres link
My heart in love to thee dear Maid
Though thine be youth's rejoicing prime
My lively vigour long decayed

Thou art a native of these hills   5
And their prized nursling still hast been
And thou repay'st their fostering love
As testify thy happy looks, thy graceful joyous mien.

---

[6] "D" must be Dora Wordsworth.

This mountain land delights us both
We love each rocky hill;   10
I hither came in age mature
With thoughtful choice and placid Will.

And I have found the peace I sought
Which thou *un*sought hast found

Version: DW's fair copy CB

FLOATING ISLAND AT HAWKSHEAD, AN INCIDENT IN THE SCHEMES OF NATURE

Harmonious Powers with Nature work
On sky, earth, river, lake, and sea:
Sunshine and storm, whirlwind and breeze
All in one duteous task agree.

Once did I see a slip of earth,   5
By throbbing waves long undermined,
Loosed from its hold;—*how* no one knew
But all might see it float, obedient to the wind.

Might see it, from the verdant shore
Dissevered float upon the Lake,   10
Float, with its crest of trees adorned
On which the warbling birds their pastime take.

Food, shelter, safety there they find
There berries ripen, flowerets bloom;
There insects live their lives—and die: 15
A peopled *world* it is;—in size a tiny room.

And thus through many seasons' space
This little Island may survive
But Nature, though we mark her not,
Will take away—may cease to give.   20

Perchance when you are wandering forth
Upon some vacant sunny day

Without an object, hope, or fear,
Thither your eyes may turn—the Isle is passed away.

Buried beneath the glittering Lake!   25
Its place no longer to be found,
Yet the lost fragments shall remain,
To fertilize some other ground.

M. D Wordsworth

Versions: (1) DW's fair copy CB (2) version initialed D.W. in WmW's poems 1842, with the headnote "These lines are by the Author of the Address to the Wind & c. published heretofore along with my Poems."

Lines Intended for my Niece's Album

Dear Maiden did thy youthful mind
Dally with emblems sad? or gay?
When thou gavest the word—and it was done,—
"My Book shall appear in green array."

Well didst thou speak, and well devise;   5
'Tis Nature's choice, her favored hue,
The badge she carries on her front,
And Nature faithful is, and true.

She, careful Warder, duly guards
The works of God's Almighty power,   10
Sustains with her diffusive breath
All moving things & tree & herb & flower

Like office hath this tiny Book;
Memorials of the Good and Wise,
Kind counsels, mild reproofs that bind   15
The Dead to the Living by holy ties,

Parental blessings, Friendship's vows,
Hope, love, and Brother's truth
Here, all preserved with duteous care,
Retain their dower of endless youth.   20

Perennial green enfolds these leaves;
They lie enclosed in glossy sheath
As spotless as the lily flower,
Till touched by a quickening breath

And it *has* touched them: Yes dear Girl,   25
In reverence of thy "gifted Sire"
A wreath for thee is here entwined
By his true Brothers of the Lyre

The Farewell of the laurelled Knight
Traced by a brave but tremulous hand,   30
Pledge of his truth and loyalty,
Through changeful years unchanged shall stand.

Confiding hopes of youthful hearts
And each bright visionary scheme
Shall here remain in vivid hues,   35
The hues of a celestial dream.

But why should *I* inscribe my name,
No poet I—no longer young?
The ambition of a loving heart
Makes garrulous the tongue.   40

Memorials of thy aged Friend,
Dora! thou dost not need,
And when the cold earth covers her
No praises shall she heed.

Yet still a lurking wish prevails   45
That, when from Life we all have passed
The Friends who love thy Parents' name
On her's a thought may cast.

Rydal—May—1832

Versions: (1) DW's fair copy CB, with a line drawn down the right of the page marking off the first 6 stanzas and in the right-hand margin, in DW's hand: "not to be put in the album." (2) fair copy pasted into CB, transcribed by L.H., dated June 1832, the version in Dora's album.

LOVING & LIKING[7]

You may not love a roasted fowl
But you may love a screaming owl
Or even a spotted slimy toad
That crawls from his secure abode,
His mossy nook in your garden wall,   5
When evening dews begin to fall
You may not love a dainty frog,
Scared by the Frenchman from his bog
When in a fricassee or Stew
He floats, or delicate ragout.
But you may love him in his pool   10
Where tho' he ne'er was put to school,
He swims by perfect law of Nature
A model for a human creature

Version: DW's fair copy CB

LOVING & LIKING. IRREGULAR VERSES ADDRESSED TO A CHILD. —

There's more in words than I can teach,
But listen Child!—I would not preach;
Yet would I give some plain directions,
To guide your speech and your affections.

Say not you *love* a roasted fowl;   5
But you may love a screaming owl,
Or even a black unwieldy toad
That crawls from his secure abode
Within your mossy garden wall,
When evening dews begin to fall.   10

You may not love a dainty frog
Drawn as in France from fen or bog,
When in a fricassee or stew
Served up, or delicate ragout;

---

[7] Incorporated in the poem that follows, this selection merits separate publication as a quasi sonnet.

—But you may love him in his pool   15
Where, though he ne'er was put to school
He swims by perfect law of Nature,
A model for a human creature,
Glancing amid the water bright,
And sending upward sparkling light.   20

And when the Bird with scarlet breast
Hops round the carpet, a bold guest
Though Susan[8] make an angry stir
To scare him as a trespasser
Do you step forth and take his part   25
Encouraged by a loving heart.

Nor blush if o'er that heart be stealing
A love for things that have no feeling
Nor can repay, by loving you,
Aught that your care for them may do: 30
The peeping rose, that first *you* spied
May fill your breast with joyful pride
And you may love the strawberry flower
And love the strawberry in its bower
But when the fruit on which you gazed   35
With pleasure to your lip is raised
Say not you *love* the delicate treat;
But *like* it, enjoy it, and thankfully eat.

Long may you love your pensioner mouse,
Though one of a tribe that torment the house,   40
Nor dislike, for her cruel sport, the cat,
That deadly foe of mouse and rat:
Remember she follows the law of her Kind;
And Instinct is neither wayward nor blind.
Then think of her beautiful gliding form,   45
Her tread that would not crush a worm,
And her soothing song by the winter fire,
Soft as the dying throb of the lyre.

---

[8] Standard epithet for a maid.

I would not circumscribe your love;
It may soar with the eagle and brood with the dove 50
May pierce the earth with the patient mole,
Or track the hedgehog to his hole
Loving & liking are the solace of life
They foster all joy, & extinguish all strife.

You love your Father and your Mother, 55
Your grown-up, and your baby Brother,
You love your Sisters and your Friends,
And countless blessings which God sends.
And while these right affections play
You *live* each moment of your day; 60
They lead you on to full content
And Likings fresh and innocent.

That store the mind, the memory feed,
And prompt to many a gentle deed.
But *Likings* come, and pass away; 65
'Tis *Love* that remains 'till our latest day.
Our heavenward guide is holy love
And it will be our bliss with Saints above.

Versions: (1) DW's working copy CB (2) WmW's 1836 *Poems*

LINES INTENDED FOR EDITH SOUTHEY'S ALBUM.[9]

Composed in June 1832 in recollection of a request made by her
some years ago, & of my own promise till now unfulfilled.

Fair Edith of the Classic Hill
Pleads for a tributary Lay
In memory of her long-known Friend,
And I with willing heart obey.

The "Laureate's Child" though Edith be, 5
Queen regent of that honoured Mount,
Yet will she not disdain the verse
That issues from a lowly Fount.

[9] Edith Southey (b. 1804), Robert Southey's daughter, married the Reverend John
Wood Warner.

For truth is all that she requires,
Truth steadfast, unadorned;   10
The studied phrase of flattery
She from her infant days has scorned.

And though the truth might rouze the *Bard*
To sound her praise in transport high,
Tell of her goodness and her grace   15
I would not wound her modesty.

Indeed it were a needless task
Is not the Maid by all approved
—Enough to say why she's *obeyed*—
Because she ever is beloved.   20

But let this page a record stand
Of tender love which may not die,
Friendship betwixt the Old and Young,
The growth of faithful sympathy.

. . . .

A strong cord draws me to the Maid,   25
And face to face I speak to *her,*
Uttering the pensive word, farewell,
While no unruly pangs my bosom stir.

. . . .

Edith, farewell: and trust me, friend,
All anxious hopes are now at rest;   30
The evening sun shines on my bed;
As bright the Calm within my breast.

Sickness and sorrow, grief and pain
Are precious to the humbled soul
For Mercy wounds with pitying love,   35
That can all wayward thoughts control.

"'Tis *God* that maketh soft the heart,
The Almighty that doth trouble me,"
Loosening my bon'dage to this earth
By pain, by joy—an awful mystery!   40

And when with agony worn down,
So gently doth it pass away,
My shattered frame sinks into rest
As soothing as the light of day.

Thus God afflicts; thus heals the wound: 45
—And workings of benignant Power,
Gentle or terrible, we trace—
Through every passing hour.

Order prevails: and can there be
A soul so impious, so forlorn   50
As slight these witnesses of grace—
And more—the Word of Promise scorn?

If such there be, how blest the day
Of sickness, pain, or pining grief
If it inform the torpid sense,   55
And to far worse than sorrow bring relief!

The Warnings long vouchsafed to me
Prompted that tender thought; farewell;
And if blithe Health should e'er return
Oh, may I not in thanklessness rebel!   60

—Forgetful of the feverish strife
That wraps me up in stillest peace,
Or of the fearful rush of pain
That, if it last, the pulse of life must cease.

Forgetful of wise Nature's skill   65
To soothe, or rouze and elevate,
While she her daily task pursues,
And we submissive wait!

The Great, the Rich, in dazzling pomp;
And their next Followers in degree;   70
And such as, far removed from these,
With cold and hunger pine in misery;

Each lifts the veil that overspreads
Our wishes, objects, restless cares;
—How different the voice of each!   75
The *same* the meaning it declares,

That all our labours, our desires
Are senseless as a maniac's strife
Save such as lead the enduring soul
To one blest end, eternal life.   80

And he whose heart is truly wise
Must inwardly perceive
That when we part from kindred—Friends—
It is in weakness that we grieve.

Weakness, God pities and will heal;   85
Yet the poor Mortal here would stay,
"The wonders of this beauteous world,
How leave them?"—They, too pass away.

Oh, that *my* aim might still be fix'd
On objects that shall still endure!   90
But we are weak,—and health brings joy
That dazzles us—bedims the pure.

Feelings our holiest, and our best
Insure for what we *see* a fond regard;
And the *un*seen, the permanent,   95
Offers in vain the unknown reward.

We stifle memory's warning voice.
Heaven grant me power to hear it, & beware!
Would that I never might forget
What now still prompts my daily prayer.   100

Then pray with me that in the hour
When here on earth I must no longer dwell,
Must part from Friends, & this fair world,
I may in calmness speak the *last* farewell!

Versions: (1) DW's working copy CB (2) DW's fair copy in Edith Southey's Album, preserved in the Bristol Central Library, between leaves 104 and 105 (3) DW's fair copy in the same. The first six stanzas appear on leaf 78. The rest are in a letter placed between 105 and 106 that states: "I enclose a 'Continuation' of the lines addressed to you—or rather I should say the lines written at your request. . . . I do not send these verses for their merit's sake, (if any they have except *truth* of feeling) but, being addressed to you, they are by right yours; and for my sake you will keep them in your Desk; and perhaps many a year hence they may, when they chance to meet your eye, call forth pleasing & tender recollections of one who has known and loved you from infancy."

Thoughts on my Sick-Bed[10]

And has the remnant of my life
Been pilfered of this sunny Spring?
And have its own prelusive sounds
Touched in my heart no echoing string?

Ah! say not so—the hidden life   5
Couchant within this feeble frame
Hath been enriched by kindred gifts,
That, undesired, unsought-for, came

With joyful heart in youthful days
When fresh each season in its Round   10
I welcomed the earliest Celandine
Glittering upon the mossy ground;

With busy eyes I pierced the lane
In quest of known and *un*known things,
—The primrose a lamp on its fortress rock,   15
The silent butterfly spreading its wings,

[10] In a letter of May 25, 1832, Dora Wordsworth writes that this poem expresses DW's happiness at receiving the first flowers of spring while she lay ill. Variants given here provide one example of how she worked on her poems.

The flowers and places of this poem reflect her own journal entries and William's poetry: the violet of "She dwelt among th' untrodden ways," "The Small Celandine," "To a Butterfly." His "Intimations Ode," "Lines Written in Early Spring," "Tintern Abbey," and "A slumber did my spirit seal" are also engaged.

The violet betrayed by its noiseless breath,
The daffodil dancing in the breeze,
The carolling thrush, on his naked perch,
Towering above the budding trees.   20

Our cottage-hearth no longer our home,
Companions of Nature were we,
The Stirring, the Still, the Loquacious, the Mute—
To all we gave our sympathy.

Yet never in those careless days   25
When spring-time in rock, field, or bower
Was but a fountain of earthly hope
A promise of fruits & the *splendid* flower.

No! then I never felt a bliss
That might with *that* compare   30
Which, piercing to my couch of rest,
Came on the vernal air.

When loving Friends an offering brought,
The first flowers of the year,
Culled from the precincts of our home,   35
From nooks to Memory dear.

With some sad thoughts the work was done,
Unprompted and unbidden,
But joy it brought to my *hidden* life,
To consciousness no longer hidden.   40

I felt a Power unfelt before,
Controlling weakness, languor, pain;
It bore me to the Terrace walk
I trod the Hills again;—

No prisoner in this lonely room,   45
I *saw* the green Banks of the Wye,
Recalling thy prophetic words,
Bard, Brother, Friend from infancy!

No need of motion, or of strength,
Or even the breathing air: 50
—I thought of Nature's loveliest scenes;
And with Memory I was there.

Versions: (1) DW's fair copy CB (2) fair copy written under entries of journal 12 Feb. 1831– 7 Sept. 1833, plus fragments.

title	*omitted* (2)
7	kindred] precious (2)
9	How joyfully in my day of strength (2)
10	When each season was fresh in its punctual round (2)
11	earliest] new-born (2)
16	spreading] trying (2)
21	Our] The (2)
24	Each claimant could hold our sympathy (2)
25	Yet] But (2)
26	rock, field] field, rock (2)
28	*splendid*] perfect (2)
29	No] Ah (2)
30	*that*] this (2)
35–52	*omitted* (2)

FRAGMENTS:

DW's fair copy CB

A Prisoner in this quiet Room,
Nature's best gifts are mine—
Friends, books & rural sights & sounds,
Why should I then repine?

Journal, 1831–33

A prisoner in this quiet room
Nature's best gifts are mine
Friends—books—& rural sights & sounds
Why should I then repine

1833, Written Sideways down the Page

A prisoner in this lonely room
No bondage do I feel

No prisoner am I
[?] [?] & gifts are mine
Nature's best gifts are mine
Tho friends look [?] at sights & sounds
Why should I then repine
And if perchance my feet shall come
Thoughts images of early youth

Continued Sideways down Next Page

Thoughts images of early youth
To this poor [?] Grace
Imprisoned in this lonely room
Ye gave a power I know not nor care [?]

No need of motion or of strength
Or even the breathing air
I thought of nature's lovliest haunts
And with Memory I was there

And gratefully I remembered oer
The years that are for ever gone
With greatful heart I numbered o'er
And all the blessings that remain
Friends kindred—[?] [?] of immortality growing
Strengthening as the Body decays—feelings kept down &
repressed by exuberant health & thoughts

Underwritten at Various Angles on Page

That fluttered in this feeble frame
To this hidden life
No need of motion or of strength

Sideways in Pencil and Ink down Last Page of Journal

With some sad thoughts the work was done
Unprompted & unbidden
But joy it brought to my hidden life
My *hidden* life
To my inner self no longer hidden
To my consciousness no longer hidden

Lines Written (Rather Say *Begun*) on the Morning of Sunday April 6th, the Third Approach of Spring-Time since my Illness Began. It was a Morning of Surpassing Beauty.

The worship of this sabbath morn,
How sweetly it begins!
With the full choral hymn of birds
Mingles no sad lament for sins.

The air is clear, the sunshine bright.   5
The dew-drops glitter on the trees;
My eye beholds a perfect Rest,
I hardly hear a stirring breeze.

A robe of quiet overspreads
The living lake and verdant field;   10
The very earth seems sanctified,
Protected by a holy shield.

The steed, now vagrant on the hill,
Rejoices in this sacred day,
Forgetful of the plough—the goad—   15
And, though subdued, is happy as the gay.

A chastened call of bleating lambs
Drops steadily from that lofty Steep;
—I could believe this sabbath peace
Was felt even by the mother sheep.   20

Conscious that they are safe from man
On this glad day of punctual rest,
By God himself—his work being done—
Pronounced the holiest and the best

'Tis but a fancy, a fond thought,   25
To which a waking dream gave birth,
Yet heavenly, in this brilliant Calm,
—Yea *heavenly* is the spirit of earth—

Nature attunes the pious heart
To gratitude and fervent love   30
By visible stillne[?ss] the chearful voice
Of living things in budding trees & in the air above.

Fit prelude are these lingering hours
To man's appointed, holy task
Of prayer and social gratitude: 35
They prompt our hearts in faith to ask,

Ask humbly for the precious boon
Of pious hope and fixed content
And pardon, sought through trust in Him
Who died to save the Penitent.   40

And now the chapel bell invites
The Old, the Middle-aged, and Young
To meet beneath those sacred walls,
And give to pious thought a tongue

That simple bell of jingling tone   45
To careless ears unmusical,
Speaks to the Serious in a strain
That might their wisest hours recal.

Alas! my feet no more may join
The chearful sabbath train;   50
But if I inwardly lament
Soon may a will subdued all grief restrain.

No prisoner am I on this couch
My mind is free to roam,
And leisure, peace, and loving Friends   55
Are the best treasures of an earthly home.

Such gifts are mine: then why deplore
The body's gentle slow decay,
A warning mercifully sent
To fix my hopes upon a surer stay?   60

Versions: (1) DW's fair copy CB, where the stanza at the end is lined through vertically (2) DW's fair copy of stanzas 1–5 CB (3) DW's fair copy of four stanzas on notepaper pasted into CB; signed "Rydal Mount, August 20th 1849. Addressed To Mr. Graham." (4) DW's fair copy on the flyleaf of *The River Duddon a Series of Sonnets* (London, 1820), "For Mr. Monkhouse" and signed Dorothy Wordsworth, Rydal Mount, August 5, 1845 (6) fair copy of 4 stanzas in Lilly Library, Indiana University (7) 4 stanzas in DW's hand and signed CCVL.

To Thomas Carr, my Medical Attendant[11]

Five years of sickness & of pain
This weary frame has travell'd o'er
But God is good—& once again
I rest upon a tranquil shore

I rest in quietness of mind   5
Oh! may I thank my God
With heart that never shall forget
The perilous path I've trod!

They tell me of one fearful night
When thou, my faithful Friend,   10
Didst part from me in holy trust
That soon my earthly cares must end.

Versions: (1) DW's fair copy, letter to Edward Ferguson, "Rydal Mount 8 October, 1837," Wordsworth Collection, Cornell Univ. (2) DW fair copy, letter to James Greenwood "Rydal Mount October 1835" with note: "Copied by DW for Mr. Greenwood," Brown Univ. Library (3) DW's fair copy, letter to Hannah Hoare, September 1837 preserved at Dove Cottage (4) facsimile of DW's fair copy signed D Wordsworth Senr and dated Nov. 7th, 1837, Wordsworth Collection, Cornell Univ. (5) DW's fair copy CCVL.

---

[11] Ambleside surgeon Thomas Carr attended the Wordsworth family. In the letter to Hannah Hoare containing version 3, Dorothy wrote, "On that night Mr. Carr left me because he could do no more for me, & my poor Brother went to lie down on his bed thinking he could not bear to see me die."

To Rotha Quillinan[12]

Ah! Rotha, many a long long day
And many a night has worn away
Since last I saw thy chearful face
But God is kind; & I am blest
By his prevailing grace.   5
Though helpless, feeble are my limbs
My heart is firm, my head is clear,
And I can look upon the past without a pang,
   without a fear.
The past that to thy heart recals   10
Bright days of mirth & innocent glee,
And let this token of good-will,
The Rosebud drawn by James's skill
Upon this paper here to bloom
As in a never-fading prime.   15
My youthful Friend be unto thee
A record of that happy time.

           DW Sr.

Version : DW's fair copy CCVL.

Lines to Dora H.[13]

No fairy pen wherewith to write
No fairy prompter to indite
Waits Dora upon me
Yet on thy tiny spotless book
With playful fancy I can look   5
And with a spark of childlike glee
My tremulous fingers feeble hands

---

[12] Probably composed in the mid-1830s. A note on the ms. reads: "Poor Miss Ws Poem written after her melancholy illness." Rotha's father, Edward Quillinan, married Dora after the death of his first wife, who suffered a mental collapse and catastrophic burns. Dorothy nursed her until the end. As William's godchild, Rotha spent a great deal of time at Rydal Mount. The "James" may be James Dixon, Rydal Mount's gardener for almost 30 years.

[13] Probably Dora Hutchinson, Mary's niece. Eliz. Hutchinson, the copier, is another niece who visited Rydal Mount through 1835 and Dorothy's goddaughter.

Refuse to labour with the mind
And that full oft is misty dul & blind
How venture then to draw a line   10
Over this delicate book of thine
The gorgeous insects gauzy wing
The butterfly's resplendent ring
Would fitliest deck its spotless leaves
Or violet nursed in April dew   15
A half blown rose of vermeil hue
Or humming bird from India's land
Portrayed by youthful lady's hand
Such cunning skill was never mine
Nor in my early years the line   20
Eer flowed in fancy's theme
Nor aim held I but simple truth
The wild growth of a happy youth
Now age my eyesight oft bedims
My failing strength my tottering limbs   25
Into a prison change this room
Though it is not a cheerless spot
A cell of sorrow or of gloom
No damp cold walls enclose it round
No heavy hinges grating sound   30
Disturb the silence & the calm
To the weak body health & balm
Free entrance finds the summer breeze
Mine eyes behold the leafy trees
The sky the clouds the gleaming showers   35
Craggs lakes & odoriferous flowers
And fond affections nestle hear
With faithful recollections dear
Children whose parents I on buoyant knee
Carressed & fondled in their infancy   40
With visions of a pure delight
Not needing aim from bodily sight
Thou Dora then among the first
Dost nurture joy & pious trust
I call to mind thy Mother's girlish grace   45
And the mild gladness of her face

The prayer I then breathed forth for her
Doth now again my bosom stir
I prayed that innocence might guide her youth
Along the paths of sacred truth.

Miss Wordsworth
June 1835—Eliz. Hutchinson

Version: Elizabeth Hutchinson's fair copy taped into CB plus many fragments near end of journal of 4 Oct. 1834–4 Nov. 1835.

[WHEN SHALL I TREAD YOUR GARDEN PATH?]

When shall I tread your garden path?
Or climb your sheltering hill?
When shall I wander, free as air,
And track the foaming rill?

A prisoner on my pillowed couch   5
Five years in feebleness I've lain,
Oh! shall I e'er with vigorous step
Travel the hills again?

To Mr Carter[14] DW
Novr. 11—1835

Versions: (1) DW's fair copy CB (2) DW's fair copy CCVL

MISS B. SOUTHEY[15]

Fit person is she for a Queen
To head those ancient Amazonian Files
Or ruling Bandit's wife
Among the Grecian Isles

---

[14] Hired by William to help with the stamp distributorship, John Carter was also the Wordsworths' handyman for over 40 years. In a letter of 1855, Mary Wordsworth told Mary Hutchinson that he was one of those "present at the *Close.*"

[15] Robert Southey's daughter Bertha (b. 1809) visited Rydal Mount in 1836, the probable time of the poem's composition. Version 2 contains this penciled note: "The occasion of this was Bertha going into her room in a [?shewofy] dress, & Miss W. immediately quoted this stanza & afterward threw off the next—all she writes are done in like prompt manner."

Or is she from far India's shore?   5
From Afric's golden Coast?
Nay she is fair as lily flower,
And might be British London's boast

> D Wordsworth Old Poetess
> October 7th 1836—

Versions: (1) DW's fair copy in Southey Album owned by the family of the late Jonathan Wordsworth. (2) DW's fair copy CCVL

To Sarah Foxcroft's Infant

I will not seek to fathom God's decrees
Nor look beyond the present happy time,
Trusting that, careless as the summer breeze
A hand divine will lead thee through thy prime.

> DW
> Copied Novr 17—1836

Versions: (1) DW's fair copy CB (2) DW's fair copy CCVL entitled To Sarah Heming's Baby

To Christopher Rennison (Her Maid's Father) Ravenstonedale[16]

Long may'st thou roam the heathy hills
Round bonny Rusendale,
And to thy loving Children bring
Full many a sports man's tale!

And when at length thy race is run,   5
Thy daily task of duty done
Oh! mayst thou peacefully resign
The life which here is but *begun!*

Versions: (1) DW's fair copy CCVL (2) DW's fair copy signed and dated "Rydal Mount Sept. 3rd 1836," housed in the Swarthmore

---

[16] Wordsworth family members occasionally hunted at Ravenstonedale.

College Library. Written on card from Dobell's Antiquarian Bookstore, evidently where the Swarthmore manuscript was purchased, is: "Dear Miss Margaret, To make amends for my carelessness I will copy for you another poem which I think you will like better than either the one you *have* already, or the other which I intended to send."

CHRISTMAS DAY[17]

This is the day when kindred meet
Round one accustomed social fire:
If still survive the hoary Sire
In patriarchal age, beside his honour'd feet
His Children's Children claim the appropriate seat;　　　　5
And if the Partner of his youthful days,
His dear supporter through the uncertain ways
Of busy life—if *she* be spared,
She who all joy, all grief has shared
Now is their happiness complete:　　　　10
Their Children & their Children's Children meet
Beneath the Grandsire's reverenced roof,
Where faithful love through trying years has stood all proof.

Dorothy Wordsworth
January 5th 1837

Versions: (1) DW's fair copy Wordsworth Collection, Cornell Univ. (2) DW's fair copy CB plus fragments

A TRIBUTE TO THE MEMORY OF THE REV[D] JOHN CURWEN[18]

Yes! let the poor afflicted weep
The widow & the orphan mourn!
This stedfast friend, in death asleep
Can soothe no more the heart forlorn

---

[17] DW's birthday, perhaps her fifty-sixth.

[18] Dorothy's nephew John married Isabella Curwen, from a prominent Lake District family.

His was the candid generous soul—   5
The liberal hand, the kinder heart;
And never did a death-bell toll
For one more free from worldly art.

And never was the cry of grief,
Disease, or poverty, or pain   10
Or supplication for relief
Addressed to his kind heart in vain.

But ready still, by night or day
Was he the poor man's prayer to hear,
The sufferer's anguish to allay   15
The desolate orphan's heart to chear.

The cherished Friends who knew his work
By firm esteem to him were bound
And gaiety & harmless mirth
In him a kind promoter found.   20

His long descent—his ancient line—
Too oft in men the cause of pride—
He counted naught!—his great design
Was to far nobler thoughts allied.

It was the spread of Christian love   25
And charity 'mongst small & great;
His lifelong aim was to remove
Dissension, enmity, & hate.

Although a carping few there be
Who slightingly his merits hold,   30
Yet hundreds more will say with me
A warmer heart death ne'er made cold.

D Wordsworth. March 3rd 1840

Version: DW's fair copy CB

Probably by Dorothy, the following three poems cannot definitely be attributed to her.

FRAGMENT CHRISTMAS DAY

Not calmer was that glorious night
When on the Syrian plain
The Shepherds saw the heavenly light
And heard the angelic strain
Glory to God and peace on earth   5
Good-will to Man—the promised Birth
The Expectancy fulfilled

Version: DW's fair copy in CB opposite the poem "Christmas day"

[THIS FLOWER, THE GARDEN'S PROUDEST BOAST]

This flower, the garden's proudest boast
Is destined, dearest Maid, for thee—
When Love & joy attend thee most
Ah! then thou wilt remember me.

Oh thank these pretty harmless doves   5
Such be your joys & such your loves
Oh! never yield to feverish strife
Then shall you lead a happy life!

Version: DW's fair copy in CB on same page as "Fragment Christmas Day," although the handwriting indicates a much later date of writing.

To E.C.[19]

I've marked thee from a little Child:
—Thy ways unfettered, yet not wild,
Obedient to the silent law
Of filial love, with placid awe,
Promised a vigorous active life   5

Version: DW's fair copy CB

---

[19] Probably Elizabeth Cookson (b. 1797). A frequent visitor in the household, she helped copy William's verse.

LETTERS

Dorothy's correspondence is voluminous. She writes to friends and relatives, conducting business and describing her writing and familial life. The letters here show the teenager sharing confidences with a school friend becoming the woman who arranges her life in the Wordsworth household.

[To Jane Pollard]

Penrith [1787][1]

My Dear Jane
[. . .] I do not now pass half my time alone. I can bear the ill nature of all my relations, for the affection of my brothers consoles me in all my Griefs, but how soon shall I be deprived of this consolation! They [. . .] are so affectionate and so kind to me as makes me love them more and more every day. Wm and Christopher are very clever boys . . . John, (who is to be the sailor,) has a most excellent heart, he is not so bright as either Wm or Christopher but he has very good common sense and is very well calculated for the profession he has chosen. Richard (the oldest) is equally affectionate and good, but is far from being as clever as William. I have no doubt of his succeeding in his business for he is very diligent and far from being dull. Many a time have Wm, J, C, and myself shed tears together, tears of the bitterest sorrow, we all of us, each day, feel more sensibly the loss we sustained when we were deprived of our parents. . . . I was for a whole week kept in expectation of my Brothers, who staid at school all that time after the vacation begun owing to the ill-nature of my Uncle, who would not send horses for them, because when they wrote they did not happen to mention them, and only said when they should break up. At last they were sent for, but not till my Brother Wm had hired a horse for himself and came over. . . . Our fortunes will I fear be very small as Lord Lonsdale will most likely only pay a very small part of his debt,

---

[1] DW is unhappily living with her Cookson grandparents, but then moves into her uncle's household.

which is 4700 pound. My uncle Kit (who is our Guardian) having said many disrespectful things of him, and having always espoused the Cause of the Duke of Norfolk, has incensed him so much that I fear we shall feel through life the effects of his imprudence. We shall however have sufficient to educate my Brothers. John, poor fellow! says that he shall have occasion for very little, £200 will be enough to fit him out, and he should wish Wm to have the rest for his education; as he has a wish to be a Lawyer, if his health will permit, and it will be very expensive. We shall have I believe about £600s a piece if Lord L. does not pay. It will be very little, but it will be quite enough for my Brothers' education; and, after they are put forward in the world there is little doubt of their succeeding, and for me, while they live I shall never want a friend. . . .

Yours affectionately,
D. Wordsworth

[To Jane Pollard]

Friday, December 7th, [1787]

. . . Oh! that I could but see you! how happy we should be! I really think that for an hour after our meeting there could nothing pass betwixt us but tears of joy, fits of laughter, and unconnected exclamations. . . . It is now seven months since we parted. We have never been separated so long for these nine years. I shall soon have been here a year; and in two years more I am determined I will come to Halifax, if I cannot sooner; but I hope my uncle is now on the road to preferment. . . . I assure you I am a very skillful architect. I have so many different plans of building our castle, so many contrivances! Do you ever build castles?[2]

When I last wrote I forgot to thank you for those verses you were so kind as to transcribe for me. My brother William was here at the time I got your letter. I told him you had recommended the book to me. He had read it, and admired many of the pieces very much, and promised to get it for me at the book-club, which he did. I was very much pleased with them indeed. The one which you mentioned to me is, I think, very comical. I mean the address to a

[2] See poems, p. 194.

Louse.[3] There is one to a Mountain Daisy which is very pretty. . . . It is a very fine morning, most likely you are taking a walk up the bank, or in Mr. Cargill's walk. As for me, I never go out but on a Sunday.

[To Jane Pollard]

[Penrith, no date]

. . . One would imagine that a grandmother would feel for her grandchild all the tenderness of a mother, particularly when that grandchild had no other parent, but there is so little of tenderness in her manner, or of anything affectionate, that while I am in her house I cannot at all consider myself as at home. I feel like a stranger. I was never remarkable for taciturnity, but now I sit for whole hours without saying anything except that I have a shirt to mend &c. Our only conversation is about *work,* or what sort of a servant such a one's is! What can be more uninteresting than such conversation as this. . . . I often go to the Cowpers, and like Miss D. C. better than ever. I wish my uncle and she would marry. As long as my grandmother lives I must stay with her. . . . I am now writing beside that uncle I so much love.[4] He is a friend to whom next to my aunt I owe the greatest obligations. Every day gives me new proofs of his affection, and every day I like him better than I did before. I am now with him two hours every morning, from nine till eleven. I then read and write French, and learn arithmetic. When I am a good arithmetician I am to learn geography. I sit in his room when we have a fire. He knows I am often pinched for time when I write, so he told me I might do that instead of my French. . . . I had my brother William with me for three weeks. I was very busy during his stay, preparing him for Cambridge. . . .

I have heard from my brother William since his arrival at Cambridge. He spent three or four days at York upon the road. They have sent me word from Whitehaven that they shall fully expect me at Christmas. John and Kit will be there, but I must not go. Poor lads! I shall not see them till next summer, and John will very likely be going off to India in spring. If so, to be sure he will spend a little time here, before his going. . . .

[3] Robert Burns, *Poems,* 1786.
[4] D. C., Dorothy Cowper, does become Mrs. Cookson, wife of this uncle.

[To Jane Pollard — Seeing the Royals]

Windsor, October 16, [1792]

. . . We left Forncett on the last day of July, and arrived at London the following morning. . . . I did not like London at all, and was heartily glad to quit it for Windsor, exactly a week after I had found myself there. . . . I was at the top of Saint Paul's, from whence on a clear day you have a view of the whole city which is most magnificent. I reached Windsor on the 9th of August, and I was charmed with it. When I first set foot upon the terrace I could scarcely persuade myself of the reality of the scene. I fancied myself treading upon fairy ground, and that the country around was brought there by enchantment. The royal family were there. . . . The king stopped to talk with my uncle and aunt, and to play with the children, who—though not acquainted with the new-fangled doctrine of liberty and equality—thought a king's stick as fair game as any other man's, and that princesses were not better than mere cousin Dollys! I think it is impossible to see the king and his family at Windsor, without loving them; even if you eye them with impartiality, and consider them merely as man and woman, not king and princesses. But I am too much of an aristocrat, or what you please to call me, not to reverence him because he is a monarch more than I should were he a private gentleman, and not to see his daughters treated with more respect than ordinary people. I say it is impossible to see them at Windsor without loving them, because at Windsor they are seen unattended by pomp or state, and they are so desirous to please that nothing but ill nature or envy can help [people.] being pleased. The king's good temper shews itself in no instance so much as in his affection for children. He was quite delighted with Christopher and Mary. Mary he considers a great beauty, and desired the Duke of York to come to see her. The first time she appeared before him, she had an unbecoming and rather a shabby hat on. We had got her a new one. "Ah" says he, "Mary that's a pretty hat." . . . Do not imagine that I am dazzled by royalty when I say that I do not think I ever saw so handsome a family. The Princess Royal and Princess Mary are certainly the most beautiful; the former has all the dignity becoming her high rank, with a great deal of grace; the latter has perhaps equal grace, but of a different kind. Hers are the winning graces of sixteen. Perhaps at five and twenty she will not be so fine a woman as her sister. . . .

[To Catherine Clarkson—Life at Allan Bank]

December 8, Thursday Evening   [Postmark, Keswick, 1808?]

MY DEAR FRIEND.

. . . I will not attempt to detail the height and depth and number of our sorrows in connection with the smoky chimneys. They are so very bad that if they cannot be mended we must leave the house,[5] beautiful as everything will soon be out of doors, dear as is the vale where we have so long lived. The labour of the house is literally doubled. Dishes are washed, and no sooner set into the pantry than they are covered with smoke. Chairs, carpets, the painted ledges of the rooms, all are ready for the reception of soot and smoke, requiring endless cleaning, and are never clean. . . . In fact we have seldom an hour's leisure (either Mary or I) till after 7 o'clock (when the children go to bed), for all the time that we have for sitting still in the course of the day we are obliged to employ in scouring (and many of our evenings also). We are regularly thirteen in the family, and on Saturdays and Sundays 15 (for when Saturday morning is not very stormy Hartley and Derwent come). I include the servants in the number, but as you may judge, in the most convenient house there would be work enough for two maids and a little Girl. In ours there is far too much. We keep a cow—the stable is two short field lengths from the house, and the cook has both to fodder, and clean after the cow. We have also two pigs, bake all our bread at home and though we do not wash all our clothes, yet we wash a part every week, and mangle or iron the whole. . . . William and Mary (alas! all involved in smoke) in William's study, where she is writing for him (he dictating). He is engaged in a work which occupies all his thoughts. It will be a pamphlet of considerable length, entitled *The Convention of Cintra brought to the Test of Principles and the People of England justified from the Charge of Prejudging,* or something to that effect.[6] I believe it will first appear in the *Courier* in different sections. Mr. De Quincey, whom you would love dearly, as I am sure I do, is beside me, quietly turning over the leaves of a Greek book—and God be praised *we* are breathing a clear air, for

[5] Allan Bank, where the chimneys smoke, but now favored by the Wordsworths since Mr. Crump has consulted them in the rebuilding of the "ruinous mansion," especially in redoing the gardens.

[6] William's pamphlet protests the 1808 agreement giving safe passage home to Napoleon's army after its defeat by the British and Spanish.

the night is calm, and this room (the Dining-room) only smokes very much in a high wind. Mr. De Q. will stay with us, we hope, at least till the Spring. We feel often as if he were one of the Family—he is loving, gentle, and happy—a very good scholar, and an acute logician—so much for his mind and manners. His person is *unfortunately* diminutive, but there is a sweetness in his looks, especially about the eyes, which soon overcomes the oddness of your first feeling at the sight of so very little a Man. John sleeps with him and is passionately fond of him. . . .

[TO JANE MARSHALL ON MOVING TO RYDAL MOUNT]

Rydal Mount, Thursday Morning, 1813.

Arrived yesterday. The weather is delightful, and the place a paradise; but my inner thoughts will go back to Grasmere. I was the last person who left the house yesterday evening. It seemed as quiet as the grave; and the very church-yard, where out darlings lie, when I gave it a last look, seemed to cheer my thoughts. There I could think of life and immortality. The house only reminded me of desolate gloom, emptiness, and cheerless silence. But why do I now turn to these things? The morning is bright, and I am more cheerful.

[TO MRS. POLLARD, SISTER-IN-LAW OF JANE POLLARD MARSHALL—ON RECOVERING]

April 12, [1834.]

. . . You will forgive me, for a solitary bed-chamber does not furnish a variety of incidents. Solitary I call it, but my friends are very kind, and sit with me as much and as often as leisure will allow, except when the fear of fatiguing me keeps them away. Sometimes of late I have chid myself for impatience, for the sun shines so bright and the birds sing so sweetly that I have an almost painful longing to go out of doors, and am half tempted to break my bonds and sally forth into the garden; but I must be content to wait till the wind changes its quarters, and before that happens rain will surely come (which may still keep me confined), for damp is almost as dangerous a foe as the east wind. . . . Strange to say it, this poor scrawl has been the work of four days. Yesterday with a thankful heart I revisited the garden and green terrace in my little carriage. I cannot express the joy I felt, and though much fatigued I did not suffer in any other way. No one but an invalid can imagine the pleasure (after long

Dorothy Wordsworth in a Wheelchair, 1842 (ink on paper) by John Harden (1772–1847) (© Abbot Hall Art Gallery, Kendal, Cumbria, UK/The Bridgeman Art Library.)

confinement) of being surrounded again by sunshine and fresh air, budding trees, flowers and birds. I looked about for young lambs, but discovered not one. Do not think, however, that my confinement has been irksome to me: quite the contrary; for within this little square I have a collection of treasures, and on the outside of my window I have had a garden of ever-blooming flowers, and you know how beautiful a prospect. Never have my flower pots been seen unadorned, in addition to the bright berries of winter holly etc. I have plenty of good old books and most of the news are supplied by friends or neighbors. . . . I never want anything that I can desire or wish for.

Rydal Mount, Sunday, October 8th 1837.

My Dear Cousin Edward,[7]
A Madman might as well attempt to relate the history of his doings, and those of his fellows in confinement, as I to tell you one hundredth part of what I have felt, suffered and done.

Through God's Mercy I am now calm and easy . . .

---

[7] Writing this letter to Edward Ferguson, Dorothy seems to have recovered her faculties.

I have not seen dear Charles Lamb's Book.[8] His Sister still survives—a solitary twig, patiently enduring the storm of life. In losing her Brother she lost her all—all but the remembrance of him—which cheers her the day through.

Give my best Love to your Sister, and Aunt if she can understand it—

May god bless you.

Yours ever truly
Dorothy Wordsworth

[Dorothy places her poem "To Thomas Carr, My Medical Attendant" at the end of this letter.]

October 22nd 1853[9]

MY DEAREST SISTER,
I have had a good night so I think I will write. The weather was rough. I was in bed all day. I am well today. My love to Miss Fenwick and Miss Jane—love to Hanna.

Dorothy Wordsworth.

Mrs Pearson is very poorly and the Doctors say she cannot live. We have got a cow and very good milk she gives. I only wish you were here to have some of it.

Thomas Flick is a little better and we are all quite fit. Mary Fisher's Sister is just dead.

---

[8] *The Letters of Charles Lamb with a Sketch of His Life* was published by Thomas Noon Talfourd in 1837.

[9] Hill, *Letters*, 8: 918. DW's last known letter, written to Mary, who was visiting London.

CONTEXTS

Money and Distance

Dorothy's writing reveals a persistent concern with money spent and distances traveled. The following helps illuminate these references:

MONEY[1]

During the eighteenth century, the Bank of England issued 10-and 20-pound notes. A 20-pound note would have purchased about $1,000 of goods today. To expand the money supply needed for the Napoleonic wars, especially the cash needed to pay soldiers, the bank began issuing one-pound notes. Most people used coins for daily transactions:

farthing—¼ of a penny
pence or penny—¹/₂₀ of a pound
shilling—12 pence
crown—5 shillings
1 pound gold coin—20 shillings, or 240 pence
Guinea—a gold coin last minted in 1813 worth 21 shillings

Also in circulation were sixpence and threepenny bits.

Money symbols included: "£" for pound, "s" for shilling, and "d" for pence (from the Latin *denarius*, "containing 10"). The leech-gatherer tells William and Dorothy that the price of leeches is two shillings six pence per hundred, a sum that could be written as 2s. 6d. or as 2/6-. One pound, four shillings, the weekly sum that the essayist William Cobbett finds necessary to support a family of five, could be written as: £ 1. 4s. or £1/4/-.

The sale of the Greens's possessions gives some idea of nineteenth-century purchasing power: "The cupboard which I have mentioned

---

[1] Information taken from: Jack Weatherford, *The History of Money* (Crown, 1997).

was bought for fourteen shillings and sixpence, an oaken chest for twenty-four shillings, and their only Feather Bed for three pounds. The Cow sold for but twenty-four shillings, and I believe that was its full value." William's annual income, in 1798, included the Calvert legacy along with £50 a year for taking care of and educating Basil Montague and was about £175. It was sufficient for him and Dorothy to live independently. When William married, DW asked Richard for an annual stipend of £60 for her independent use. Agricultural workers made £15–£22 per year in 1800, working six days a week, fifty weeks a year. Per year, governesses earned £12–£20, skilled laborers about £55.

DISTANCES

Dorothy often uses the "league," which equals about 2.6 miles, as a measure of distance. Thus the distance from Alfoxden House to Nether Stowey is about three miles. The walk from Grasmere to Keswick is about sixteen miles. Dorothy routinely walked at least three miles a day and often covered twenty miles or more a day.

Descriptions of
Dorothy Wordsworth

The following descriptions reflect the particular energy, talent, intelligence and sympathy that her contemporaries saw in Dorothy Wordsworth as well as the anxiety her life involved. From Virginia Woolf to Amy Clampitt[1] twentieth-century observers have also recorded the power as well as the self-conflict that she experienced.

✤ Samuel Taylor Coleridge
From Letter to Joseph Cottle, Notebook, October, 1802

Writing in July, 1797,[2] to Joseph Cottle, his patron and publisher, Samuel Taylor Coleridge renders an image of Dorothy, paraphrasing his lines about Joan of Arc, first published that year in The Morning Post *and then incorporated into his poem "Destiny of Nations." An entry a few years later in his notebooks shows Dorothy's presence in both his waking and sleeping thoughts.*

Wordsworth & his exquisite Sister are with me—She is a woman indeed!—in mind, I mean, & heart—for her person is such, that if you expected to see a pretty woman, you would think her

---

[1] Virginia Woolf. "Dorothy Wordsworth," *The Second Common Reader*, (Harcourt, 1986), 164–173. Describing Dorothy's frequent headaches—"packed ganglion's black blood clot"—Amy Clampitt writes: "so dense a node the ache still bleeds / still binds, but cannot speak." "Grasmere" in *Archaic Figure* (Knopf, 1987), 52.

[2] *Collected Letters of Samuel Taylor Coleridge*, ed. Leslie Griggs (Oxford: Clarendon, 1956), I, 330–331.

ordinary—if you expected to find an ordinary woman, you would think her pretty!—But her manners are simple, ardent, impressive—.

> In every motion her most innocent soul
> Outbeams so brightly, that who saw would say,
> Guilt was a thing impossible in her

Her information various—her eye watchful in minutest observation of nature—and her taste a perfect electrometer[3]—it bends, protrudes, and draws in, at subtlest beauties & most recondite faults.

She with her Brother desire their kindest respects to you—

. . . .

FROM COLERIDGE'S NOTEBOOKS[4]:

[October 1802] October 3—Night—My Dreams uncommonly illustrative of the non-existence of Surprize in sleep—I dreamt that I was asleep in the Cloyster at Christs Hospital & had awoken with a pain in my hand from some corrosion/boys & nurses daughters peeping at me/On their implying that I was not in the School, I answered yes I am/I am only twenty—I then recollected that I was thirty, & of course could not be in the School—& was perplexed—but not the least surprize that I could fall into such an error/So I dreamt of Dorothy, William & Mary—& that Dorothy was altered in every feature, a fat, thick-limbed & rather red-haired—in short, no resemblance to her at all—and I said, if I did not know you to be Dorothy, I never should suppose it/Why, says she—I have not a feature the same/& yet I was not surprized—

I was followed up & down by a frightful pale woman who, I thought, wanted to kiss me, & had the property of giving a shameful Disease by breathing in the face/ & again I dreamt that a figure of a woman of a gigantic Height, dim & indefinite & smokelike appeared—& that I was forced to run up toward it—& then it changed to a stool—& then appeared again in another place—& again I went up in great fright—& it changed to some other common thing—yet I felt no surprize.

[3] Instrument for measuring electric potential or voltage.

[4] *Samuel Taylor Coleridge, Oxford Authors,* ed. H. J. Jackson (Oxford: Oxford UP), 543.

✤ Thomas De Quincey
From *Recollections of the Lake Poets*

Thomas De Quincey went to Grasmere in 1807 to meet the poet he so admired and began his intense relationship with the Wordsworth family. In this excerpt from Recollections of the Lake Poets, *published in* Tait's Edinburgh Magazine *in 1839, he describes seeing Dorothy for the first time.*

Immediately behind her [Mary] moved a lady, shorter, slighter, and perhaps, in all other respects, as different from her in personal characteristics as could have been wished for the most effective contrast. "Her face was of Egyptian brown";[5] rarely, in a woman of English birth, had I seen a more determinate gipsy tan. Her eyes were not soft, as Mrs. Wordsworth's, nor were they fierce or bold; but they were wild and startling[6] and hurried in their motion. Her manner was warm and even ardent; her sensibility seemed constitutionally deep; and some subtle fire of impassioned intellect apparently burned within her, which, being alternately pushed forward into a conspicuous expression by the irrepressible instincts of her temperament, and then immediately checked, in obedience to the decorum of her sex and age, and her maidenly condition (for she had rejected all offers of marriage, out of pure sisterly regard to her brother and his children), gave to her whole demeanour, and to her conversation, an air of embarrassment, and even of self–conflict, that was almost distressing to witness. Even her very utterance and enunciation often suffered, in point of clearness and steadiness, from the agitation of her excessive organic sensibility. At times, the self-counteraction and self-baffling of her feelings caused her even to stammer, and so determinately to stammer that a stranger who should have seen her and quitted her in that state of feeling would have certainly set her down for one plagued with that infirmity of speech as distressingly as Charles Lamb himself. This was Miss Wordsworth, the only sister of the poet—his "Dorothy"; who naturally owed so much to the lifelong intercourse with her great brother in his most solitary and sequestered years; but, on the other hand, to whom he has acknowledged obligations of the profoundest nature; and, in particular, this

---

[5] De Quincey here rewrites line 7 of William's poem "Beggars": "Her skin was of Egyptian brown."

[6] William describes Dorothy's eyes in "Tintern Abbey": ". . . in the shooting lights/ Of thy wild eyes" (119–120).

mighty one, through which we also, the admirers and the worshippers of this great poet, are become equally her debtors—that, whereas the intellect of Wordsworth was, by its original tendency, too stern, too austere, too much enamoured of an ascetic harsh sublimity, she it was—the lady who paced by his side continually through sylvan and mountain tracks, in Highland glens, and in the dim recesses of German charcoal-burners—that first couched his eye to the sense of beauty, humanized him by the gentler charities, and engrafted with her delicate female touch, those graces upon the ruder growths of his nature which have since clothed the forest of his genius with a foliage corresponding in loveliness and beauty to the strength of its boughs and the massiness of its trunks. The greatest deductions from Miss Wordsworth's attractions, and from the exceeding interest which surrounded her in right of her character, of her history, and of the relation which she fulfilled towards her brother, were the glancing quickness of her motions, and other circumstances in her deportment (such as her stooping attitude when walking), which gave an ungraceful, and even an unsexual character to her appearance when out-of-doors. She did not cultivate the graces which preside over the person and its carriage. But, on the other hand, she was a person of very remarkable endowments intellectually; and, in addition to the other great services which she rendered to her brother, this I may mention, as greater than all the rest, and it was one which equally operated to the benefit of every casual companion in a walk—viz. the exceeding sympathy, always ready and always profound, by which she made all that one could tell her, all that one could describe, all that one could quote from a foreign author, reverberate, as it were, à plusieurs reprises [in several returns], to one's own feelings, by the manifest impression it made upon hers. The pulses of light are not more quick or more inevitable in their flow and undulation, than were the answering and echoing movements of her sympathizing attention. Her knowledge of literature was irregular, and thoroughly unsystematic. She was content to be ignorant of many things; but what she knew and had really mastered lay where it could not be disturbed—in the temple of her own most fervid heart.

A much larger number of voices would proclaim her to have been unfortunate in life because she made no marriage connexion; and certainly, the insipid as well as unfeeling ridicule which descends so plentifully upon those women who, perhaps from strength of character, have refused to make such a connexion where it promised little of elevated happiness, does make the state of singleness somewhat of a trial to the patience of many; and to many the vexation of this trial has proved a snare for beguiling them of their honourable resolutions. Meantime, as the opportunities are rare in which all the conditions concur for happy marriage connexions, how important it is that the dignity of high-minded women should be upheld by society in the honourable election they make of a self-dependent virgin seclusion, by preference to a heartless marriage! Such women, as Mrs Trollope[7] justly remarks, fill a place in society which in their default would *not* be filled, and are available for duties requiring a tenderness and a punctuality that could not be looked for from women preoccupied with household or maternal claims. If there were no regular fund (so to speak) of women free from conjugal and maternal duties, upon what body could we draw for our "sisters of mercy," &c? In another point Mrs Trollope is probably right: few women live unmarried from necessity. Miss Wordsworth had several offers; amongst them, to my knowledge, one from Hazlitt; all of them she rejected decisively. And she did right. A happier life, by far, was hers in youth.

Miss Wordsworth was too ardent and fiery a creature to maintain the reserve essential to dignity; and dignity was the last thing one thought of in the presence of one so natural, so fervent in her feelings, and so embarrassed in their utterance—sometimes, also, in the attempt to check them. It must not, however, be supposed that there was any silliness or weakness of enthusiasm about her. She was under the continual restraint of severe good sense, though liberated from that false shame which, in so many persons, accompanies all expressions of natural emotion; and she had too long enjoyed the ennobling conversation of her brother, and his admirable comments on the poets, which they read in common, to fail in any essential point of logic or propriety of thought. Accordingly, her letters, though the most careless and unelaborate—nay, the most hurried that can be imagined—are models of good sense and just feeling. In short, beyond any person I have known in this world, Miss Wordsworth was the creature of impulse; but, as a woman most thoroughly virtuous and well-principled, as one who could not fail to be kept right by her own excellent heart, and as an intellectual

---

[7] Woman of letters Frances Trollope (1780–1863), mother of novelist Anthony Trollope.

creature from her cradle, with much of her illustrious brother's pecu-
liarity of mind—finally, as one who had been, in effect, educated and
trained by that very brother—she won the sympathy and the
respectful regard of every man worthy to approach her. ∗ ∗ ∗ Properly, and in a spirit of prophecy, was she named *Dorothy;* in its
Greek meaning, gift of God, well did this name prefigure the relation
in which she stood to Wordsworth, the mission with which she was
charged—to wait upon him as the tenderest and most faithful of
domestics; to love him as a sister; to sympathize with him as a confi-
dante; to counsel him; to cheer him and sustain him by the natural
expression of her feelings—so quick, so ardent, so unaffected—upon
the probable effect of whatever thoughts or images he might conceive; finally, and above all other ministrations, to in graft, by her
sexual[8] sense of beauty, upon his masculine austerity that delicacy
and those graces which else (according to the grateful acknowledg-
ments of his own maturest retrospect) it never could have. ∗ ∗ ∗ I
may sum up in one brief abstract the amount of Miss Wordsworth's
character, as a companion, by saying, that she was the very wildest
(in the sense of the most natural) person I have ever known; and also
the truest, most inevitable, and at the same time the quickest and
readiest in her sympathy with either joy or sorrow, with laughter or
with tears, with the realities of life or the larger realities of the poets!

Meantime, amidst all this fascinating furniture of her mind,
won from nature, from solitude, from enlightened companionship,
Miss Wordsworth was as thoroughly deficient (some would say
painfully deficient—I say charmingly deficient) in ordinary female
accomplishments.[9] But the case in which the irregularity of Miss
Wordsworth's education did astonish one was in that part, which
respected her literary knowledge. In whatever she read, or neglected
to read, she had obeyed the single impulse of her own heart; where
that led her, there she followed: where that was mute or indifferent,
not a thought had she to bestow upon a writer's high reputation, or
the call for some acquaintance with his works to meet the demands
of society. And thus the strange anomaly arose, of a woman deeply
acquainted with some great authors, whose works lie pretty much
out of the fashionable beat; able, moreover, in her own person, to
produce brilliant effects; able on some subjects to write delightfully,

---

[8] Female.

[9] Activities that were considered essential to proper young ladies: singing, dancing,
drawing. Dorothy's letters to Jane Pollard suggest that she possessed such skills.

and with the impress of originality upon all she uttered; and yet ignorant of great classical works in her own mother tongue, and careless of literary history in a degree which at once exiled her from the rank and privileges of *bluestockingism*.[10] * * *

But the point in which Miss Wordsworth made the most ample amends for all that she wanted of more customary accomplishments, was this very originality and native freshness of intellect, which settled with so bewitching an effect upon some of her writings, and upon many a sudden remark or ejaculation, extorted by something or other that struck her eye, in the clouds, or in colouring, or in accidents of light and expression, or at least far beyond any pretensions that she ever made for herself. Of poetry she has written little indeed; and that little not, in my opinion, of much merit. The verses published by her brother, and beginning, "Which way does the wind come?"[11] meant only as nursery lines, are certainly wild and pretty; but the other specimen is likely to strike most readers as feeble and trivial in the sentiment. Meantime, the book which is in very deed a monument to her power of catching and expressing all the hidden beauties of natural scenery, with a felicity of diction, a truth and strength, that far transcend Gilpin,[12] or professional writers on those subjects, is her record of a first tour in Scotland, made about the year 1802. * * * I here notice a defect in Miss Wordsworth's self-education of something that might have mitigated the sort of suffering which, more or less, ever since the period of her too genial, too radiant youth, I suppose her to have struggled with. I have mentioned the narrow basis on which her literary interests had been made to rest—the exclusive character of her reading, and the utter want of pretension, and of all that looks like *bluestockingism,* in the style of her habitual conversation and mode of dealing with literature. Now, to me it appears, upon reflection, that it would have been far better had Miss Wordsworth condescended a little to the ordinary mode of pursuing literature; better for her own happiness if she *had* been a bluestocking; or, at least, if

---

[10] A term first applied to lady intellectuals for whom university education was banned and who therefore met to discuss literature on their own; by the nineteenth century, used disparagingly. According to Boswell in his *Life of Johnson,* Benjamin Stillingfleet, who in the 1750s was invited to one of the first literary salons, could not afford formal black silk hosiery and wore his everyday blue stockings. In solidarity, many of the women also wore blue stockings.

[11] See p. 179.

[12] See pp. 281–285.

she had been, in good earnest, a writer for the press with the pleasant cares and solicitudes of one who has some little ventures, as it were, on that vast ocean.

We all know with how womanly and serene a temper literature has been pursued by Joanna Baillie, by Miss Mitford,[13] and other women of admirable genius—with how absolutely no sacrifice or loss of feminine dignity they have cultivated the profession of authorship * * * Had that been opened for Miss Wordsworth, I am satisfied that she would have passed a more cheerful middle-age, and would not, at any period, have yielded to that nervous depression, (or is it, perhaps, nervous irritation?) which I grieve to hear, has clouded her latter days.

✤ Maria Jane Jewsbury
From Letter to Dora Wordsworth

The essayist, poet, and novelist Maria Jane Jewsbury (1800–1833) lived a life both parallel and counter to Dorothy's. Jewsbury had charge of her several siblings after her mother's untimely death. She wrote and traveled but also published. Like Dorothy she became ill. She married and went with her husband to India, where she died of cholera. Friendly with the entire Wordsworth family, Jewsbury became quite close to Dora, with whom she corresponded frequently. This text describing Dorothy as a visiting whirlwind is taken from one of her letters of 1828 printed by Eric Gillet in Maria Jane Jewsbury *(Oxford University Press, 1932), xlv.*

I think you would smile if you knew all she did and saw. "Panting Time" (that is myself) toiled after her in vain. Churches—Museums—Factories—Shopping-Institutions—Company—at home and abroad—not that I attempted to compete with her,—no I merely lay in bed and legislated—provided relays of friends and carriages—and had the pleasure of knowing that my visitor was pleased—and that she won all hearts before and around her. She is the very genius of Popularity—an embodied spell. I should be jealous of her for a continuance. I should be dethroned even on my own sofa—amidst my own circle.

---

[13] Joanna Baillie (1787–1855), playwright and poet. For Mitford see pp. 285–290.

Life in the Wordsworth Household

Choosing a life of poetry lived with her brother and then with his family, Dorothy Wordsworth did both the work of a typical nineteenth-century housekeeper and the work of a writer. William and Dorothy moved first to Alfoxden House, a very large dwelling with several outbuildings, all of which Dorothy managed. Describing a visit to Alfoxden in My First Acquaintance with Poets, *the essayist William Hazlitt (1778–1830) shows some details of that life choice.*[1]

"I arrived, and was well received. The country about Nether Stowey is beautiful, green and hilly, and near the sea-shore. I saw it but the other day, after an interval of twenty years, from a hill near Taunton. How was the map of my life spread out before me, as the map of the country lay at my feet! In the afternoon, Coleridge took me over to All-Foxden, a romantic old family-mansion of the St. Aubins, where Wordsworth lived. It was then in the possession of a friend of the poet's, who gave him the free use of it.[2] . . . Wordsworth himself was from home, but his sister kept house, and set before us a frugal repast; and we had free access to her brother's poems, the *Lyrical Ballads,* which were still in manuscript, or in the form of *Sybilline Leaves.*"

The "frugal repast" that Dorothy served Hazlitt was much different from a dinner she put together on July 23, 1797, to celebrate the move to Alfoxden House. Some fourteen people attended, including John Thelwell, the radical politician, lecturer, and poet. His presence, as well as the unconventional behavior of the household

---

[1] For the full text of this essay, see the *Longman Anthology of British Literature* (3rd ed.), vol. 2 (2a), 1029–1042.

[2] Actually, the Wordsworths paid £23 pounds a year in rent.

THE
ART OF COOKERY,

MADE

PLAIN and EASY;

Which far excels any Thing of the Kind yet publifhed.

CONTAINING,

I. A Lift of the various Kinds of Meat, Poultry, Fifh, Vegetables, and Fruit, in Seafon, in every Month of the Year.
II. Directions for Marketting.
III. How to Roaft and Boil to Perfection.
IV. Sauces for all plain Difhes.
V. Made Difhes.
VI. To drefs Poultry, Game, &c.
VII. How expenfive a French Cook's Sauce is.
VIII. To make a Number of pretty little Difhes for Suppers, or Side or Corner Difhes.
IX. To drefs Turtle, Mock-turtle, &c.
X. To drefs Fifh.
XI. Sauces for Fifh.
XII. Of Soups and Broths.
XIII. Of Puddings and Pies.
XIV. For a Lent Dinner; a Number of good Difhes, which may be made ufe of at any other Time.

XV. Directions for the Sick.
XVI. For Captains of Ships; how to make all ufeful Difhes for a Voyage; and fetting out a Table on board.
XVII. Of Hog's Puddings, Saufages, &c.
XVIII. To pot, make Hams, &c.
XIX. Of Pickling.
XX. Of making Cakes, &c.
XXI. Of Cheefecakes, Creams, Jellies, Whipt Syllabubs.
XXII. Of Made Wines, Brewing, Baking, French Bread, Muffins, Cheefe, &c.
XXIII. Jarring Cherries, Preferves, &c.
XXIV. To make Anchovies, Vermicelli, Catchup, Vinegar, and to keep Artichokes, French Beans, &c.
XXV. Of Diftilling.
XXVI. Directions for Carving.
XXVII. Ufeful and valuable Family Receipts.
XXVIII. Receipts for Perfumery, &c.

IN WHICH ARE INCLUDED,

One Hundred and Fifty new and ufeful RECEIPTS, not inferted in any former Edition.

WITH A COPIOUS INDEX.

By Mrs. GLASSE.

A NEW EDITION,
With all the MODERN IMPROVEMENTS:
And alfo the ORDER of a BILL of FARE for each Month; the Difhes arranged on the Table in the moft fafhionable Style.

LONDON:

Printed for T. Longman, B. Law, J. Johnfon, G. G. and J. Robinfon, H. Gardner, T. Payne, F. and C. Rivington, J. Sewell, W. Richardfon, W. Lane, W. Lowndes, G. and T. Wilkie, W. Nicoll, W. Fox, Ogilvy and Speare, J. Debrett, J. Scatcherd, Vernor and Hood, Clarke and Son, J. Nunn, J. Barker, B. Crofby, Cadell and Davies, and E. Newbery.

1796.

Title Page, 1796 Edition of Mrs. Glasse's *The Art of Cookery Made Plain and Easy.*

J U L Y.

FIRST COURSE.

Mackerel, &c.

Breaft of Veal a la Braife.   Tongue and Turnips.   Pulpeton.

Venifon Pafty.   Herb Soup.   Neck of Venifon.

Chickens.   Boiled Goofe and ftewed red Cabbage.   Mutton Cutlets.

Trout boiled.

SECOND COURSE.

Roaft Turkey.

Stewed Peas.   Apricot Tart.   Blanc-mange.

Sweetbreads.   Jellies.   Fricaffee of Rabbits.

Cuftards.   Green Codlin Tart.   Blaized Pippins.

Roaft Pigeons.

THIRD COURSE.

Fricaffee of Rabbits.

Apricots.   Pains à la Ducheffe.   Forced Cucumbers.

Crawfifh ragooed.   Morello Cherry Tart.   Lobfters à la Braife.

Jerufalem Artichokes.   Apricot Puffs.   Green Gage Plums.

Lamb Stones.

and friends, resulted in a spy's being sent from the Home Office to investigate. The Wordsworths and Coleridge finally had to leave Alfoxden.

❧ Hannah Glasse
From *The Art of Cookery*

Living on a tiny budget, the Wordsworths could not entertain lavishly, but friends chipped in. "My dear Poole," Coleridge writes to his neighbor, "we have taken a fore-quarter of lamb from your mother, which you will be so good, according to your word, or (as the wit said to the Minister of State) notwithstanding your promise, to send over to the Foxes [probably Alfoxden] to-morrow morning by a boy."[3]

To prepare the dinner, Dorothy, like almost every other woman in England, might have consulted Hannah Glasse's The Art of Cookery. *First published in 1747, the cookbook went through over twenty editions. The selection here is from the edition of 1796. Mutton cutlets and "lamb stone" are among the dishes on the sample July menus.*

RULES TO BE OBSERVED IN ROASTING MEAT, POULTRY, AND GAME.

I SHALL first begin with roast of all sorts, and must desire the cook to order her fire according to what she is to dress; if any thing very little or thin, then a pretty little brisk fire, that it may be done quick and nice; if a very large joint, then be sure a good fire be laid to cake. Let it be clear at the bottom: and when your meat is half done, move the dripping-pan and spit a little from the fire, and stir up a good brisk fire for according to the goodness of your fire, your meat will be done sooner or later. Take great care the spit be very clean; and be sure to clean it with nothing but sand and water. Wash it clean, and wipe it with a dry cloth; for oil, brick-dust, and such things, will spoil your meat.

Lamb

IF a large fore-quarter, an hour and a half; if a small one, an hour. The outside must be papered, basted with good butter, and you must have a very quick fire. If a leg, about three quarters of an hour; a neck, a breast, or shoulder, three quarters of an hour; if very small half an hour will do. These last-mentioned joints are not to be

[3] *Letters*, Griggs, I, 196, 332.

papered, or have the skin raised, but to be dressed like mutton, and garnished with cresses or small sallading.

From the Home Secretary's Investigation of the Wordsworths as Spies

By August of 1797, the daily routine that involved people like Coleridge and Thelwell had made the Wordsworths objects of suspicion and speculation. Charles Mogg, a servant at Alfoxden House, and the woman who had been cook there reported the Wordsworths' oddities to the cook's current employer, a Dr. Lysons, who contacted the Duke of Portland, the Home Secretary, with this letter.

Bath, 11 Aug 1797.

"'MY LORD DUKE—On the 8th instant I took the liberty to acquaint your Grace with a very suspicious business concerning an emigrant family, who have contrived to get possession of a Mansion House at Alfoxton, late belonging to the Revd. Mr. St. Albyn, under Quantock Hills. I am since informed, that the Master of the house has no wife with him, but only a woman who passes for his Sister. The man has Camp Stools, which he and his visitors take with them when they go about the country upon their nocturnal or diurnal excursions, and have also a Portfolio in which they enter their observations, which they have been heard to say were almost finished. They have been heard to say they should be rewarded for them, and were—very attentive to the River near them—probably the River coming within a mile or two of Alfoxton from Bridgewater. These people may possibly be under Agents to some principal at Bristol.

Having got these additional anecdotes which were dropt by the person mentioned in my last I think it necessary to acquaint your Grace with them, and have the honor to be &c.

"D. LYSONS."[4]

The Home Office sent out a spy, G. Walsh, whom Coleridge reports encountering in a very funny passage in Biographia Literaria, *(I, 10). In the following letter, G. Walsh reports in to Mr. J. King,*

---

[4] Source: A. J. Eagleston, "Wordsworth, Coleridge and the Spy" in *Coleridge: studies by several hands on the hundredth anniversary of his death*, eds. Edmund Blunden and Earl Leslie Griggs (Constable & Co., 1934), 71–88.

Under-Secretary of State for the Home Office, relaying the observations of Charles Mogg.

Bear Inn, Hungerford, Berks: 11 Aug 1797

SIR,—Charles Mogg says that he was at Alfoxton last Saturday was a week, that he there saw Thomas Jones who lives in the Farm House at Alfoxton, who informed Mogg that some French people had got possession of the Mansion House and that they were washing and Mending their cloaths all Sunday, that He Jones would not continue their as he did not like It. That Christopher Trickie and his Wife who live at the Dog pound at Alfoxton, told Moggs that the French people had taken the plan of Their House, and that They had also taken the plan of all the places round that part of the Country, that a Brook runs in the front of Trickie's House and the French people inquired of Trickie wether the Brook was Navigable to the Sea, and upon being informed by Trickie that It was not, They were afterwards seen examining the Brook quite down *to* the Sea. That Mrs. Trickie confirmed everything her husband had said. Mogg spoke to some other persons inhabitants of that Neighbourhood, who all told him they thought these French people very suspicious persons and that They were doing no good there. And that was the general opinion of that part of the country. The French people kept no Servant, but They were visited by a number of persons, and were frequently out upon the heights most part of the Night.

Mogg says that Alfoxton lays about Twelve miles below Bridgewater and within Two Miles of the Sea. Mogg says that he never spoke to Doctor Lysons, but that a Woman who is Cook to the Doctor had lived fellow Servant with Mogg at Alfoxton, and that in his way from Thence home, he called upon her at the Doctor's House in Bath last Monday, when talking about Alfoxton, He mentioned these circumstances to her.

As Mr. Mogg is by no means the most intelligent Man in the World, I thought It my duty to send You the whole of his Story as he related It.

I shall wait here Your further Orders and am

Sir,

Your most obedient Humble Servt.

G. WALSH.

Mr. King immediately sent instructions to the detective.

Whitehall Aug 12th, 1797.

SIR,—I have considered the contents of your letter to me from the Bear Inn, Hungerford, of yesterday's date. You will immediately proceed to Alfoxton or its neighbourhood yourself, taking care on your arrival so to conduct yourself as to give no cause of suspicion to the Inhabitants of the Mansion house there. You will narrowly watch their proceedings, and observe how they coincide with Mogg's account and that contained in the within letter from Mr. Lysons to the Duke of Portland. If you are in want of further information or assistance, you will call on Sir P. Hale Bart. of Boymore near Bridgewater, and upon showing him this letter you will I am confident receive it. You will give me a precise account of all the circumstances you observe, with your sentiments thereon; you will of course ascertain if you can the names of the persons, and will add their descriptions—and above all you will be careful not to give them any cause of alarm, that if necessary they may be found on the spot. Should they however move you must follow their track and give me notice thereof, and of the place to which they have betaken themselves. I herewith transmit you a bank note for £20.

J. KING.

Mr. Walsh continues his quest. The last two letters on record describe the "Sett of violent Democrats" and their July dinner party.

Globe Inn, Stowey, Somerset: 15th August 1797

SIR,—In consequence of Your orders which I read Yesterday, I immediately set off for this Place, which altho it is five Miles from Alfoxton, is the nearest house I can get any accommodation at.

I had not been many minutes in this house before I had an opportunity of entering upon my Business, By a Mr Woodhouse asking the Landlord, If he had seen any of those Rascalls from Alfoxton. To which the Landlord reply'd, He had seen Two of them Yesterday, Upon which Woodhouse asked the Landlord, If Thelwall was gone. I then asked if they meant the famous Thelwall. They said Yes. That he had been down some time, and that there were a Nest of them at Alfoxton House who were protected by a Mr. Poole a Tanner of this Town, and that he supposed Thelwall was there (Alfoxton House) at this time. I told Woodhouse that I had heard somebody say at Bridgewater that They were French people at the

Manor House. The Landlord and Woodhouse answered No, No. They are not French, But they are people that will do as much harm, as All the French can do.

I hope To-morrow to be able to give you some information, in the mean time I shall be very attentive to your instructions.

I think this will turn out no French affair, but a mischiefuous gang of disaffected Englishmen. I have just procured the Name of the person who took the House. His name is Wordsworth, a name I think known to Mr. Ford.

> I have the honor to be Sir
> Your most obedient Humble Sert.
> G. WALSH

Stowey: 16th August 1797.

SIR,—The inhabitants of Alfoxton House are a Sett of violent Democrats. The House was taken for a Person of the name of Wordsworth, who came to It from a Village near Honiton in Devonshire, about five Weeks since. The Rent of the House is secured to the Landlord by a Mr Thomas Poole of this Town. Mr Poole is a Tanner and a Man of some property. He is a most Violent Member of the Corresponding Society[5] and a strenuous supporter of Its Friends, He has with him at this time a Mr Coldridge and his wife both of whom he has supported since Christmas last. This Coldridge came last from Bristol and is reckoned a Man of superior Ability. He is frequently publishing, and I am told is soon to produce a new work. He has a Press in the House and I am informed He prints as well as publishes his own productions.

Mr Poole with his disposition, is the more dangerous from his having established in this Town, what He stiles The Poor Man's Club, and placing himself at the head of It, By the Title of the Poor Man's Friend. I am told that there are 150 poor Men belonging to this Club, and that Mr Poole has the intire command of every one of them, When Mr Thelwall was here, he was continually with Mr Poole.

By the direction on a letter that was going to the Post Yesterday, It appears that Thelwall is now at Bristol.

---

[5] Founded in 1792, the Corresponding Society addressed itself to concerns of the working class, activities the government tried to suppress with the 1795 Gagging Acts.

I last Night saw Thomas Jones who lives at Alfoxton House. He exactly confirms Mogg of Hungerford, with this addition that the Sunday after Wordsworth came, he Jones was desired to wait at table, that there were 14 persons at Dinner Poole and Coldridge were there, And there was a little Stout Man with dark cropt Hair and wore a White Hat and Glasses (Thelwall) who after Dinner got up and talked so loud and was in such a passion that Jones was frightened and did not like to go near them since. That Wordsworth has lately been to his former House and brought back with him a Woman Servant, that Jones has seen this Woman who is very Chatty, and that she told him that Her Master was a Phylosopher. That the Night before last Two men came to Alfoxton House, And that the Woman Servant Yesterday Morning told Jones that one of the Gentlemen was a Great Counsellor from London, and the other a Gentleman from Bristol.

Jones had been apply'd to by the Servant to weed the Garden, but had declined going, as he was afraid of the people. But upon my applying a few shillings Mr Jones has got the better of his fears and is this Day weeding the Garden, and in the evening is to bring me the Name of the Great Counsellor and every other information he can Collect. It is reported here that Thelwall is to return soon to this Place and that he is to occupy a part of Alfoxton House.

> I have the honor to be Sir
> Your most obedient Humble Servt.
> G. WALSH.

❧ Richard Woodhouse
"A Conversation about Incest" from his *Cause Book*

Speculations about the Wordsworths followed them wherever they went. In a legal notebook, begun September 1821, Richard Wood-house includes an account from De Quincey about the persistent rumor of an incestuous relationship between Dorothy and William.[6]

F. W. Bateson's Wordsworth: A Reinterpretation *(London, 1954) reopened the question, arguing that Wordsworth married to cure himself of his love for his sister, but sacrificed poetic power in the bargain.*

---

[6] Source: Robert Morrison, "Richard Woodhouse's *Cause Book:* The Opium-Eater, the Magazine Wars, and the London Literary Scene in 1821," *Harvard Library Bulletin,* 9.3 (Fall, 1998), my source for this excerpt.

In a 1970 essay, reproduced in Essays by Divers Hands *(37 [1972]: 75–94), Mary Moorman contends that there was no decline of poetic power after 1802, and refuted the theory of sibling sexual attraction. The controversy flared again in the* TLS *from August through December 1974, sparked by remarks in Molly Lefebure's* Samuel Taylor Coleridge: A Bondage of Opium *and then again in* TLS *during April and May 1976. De Quincey, for one, thought: "There is no harm in sexual intercourse between a brother and a sister" (Diary, 1803).*

Speaking of the characters of minds of different people, & indeed of various whole classes, he took notice that he considered the minds of the people in his own neighbourhood as being particularly gross & uncharitable; that they were fond of retailing anecdotes, however horrible, as true, without ever taking the trouble to ascertain their foundation, or caring at all whether they were true or not. This he attributes to the want of novelty & stimulus operating upon the vacant & inactive minds of people having no worldly cares to occupy them, rather than to any inherent maliciousness: the worst was that these tales, tho' they always cease to be current when any newer scandal is imported to supply their place, are yet liable at any time to be recalled from their temporary oblivion; and indeed are so; & they often acquire more effect in their revised state than they had originally: for at that time, tho' all repeated them, yet they were recent, & easily proved if true, & the very circumstance, that everyone had the same story, yet no one could vouch for it, or personally knew anything of it, satisfied all the world that there was nothing in it. Yet when a story was revived, it was always mentioned with an on dit[7] & as having been "well known, & the common talk at the time it happened"—so that the rumour had thus more chance of meeting belief than when it was first sent abroad, and "the last state" of the lie "is worse than the first." The Opium-Eater mentioned several stories, entirely groundless, & carrying in their very horror an assurance of their falsehood & absurdity. Among these was one, that he was himself the father of Mrs. Wordsworth's child that died; & who has already been alluded to—the grounds for this fiction, were the plainness of the child's appearance, the comparative want of fondness, or rather indifference of most people, even Wordsworth himself for the little thing, and the Opium-Eater's partiality for it, & grief for its death. The gross-minded vulgar could find no solution for these to them marvelous appearances but in the

---

[7] "They say," thus a kind of disclaimer.

supposition that the child was his. Again there was an unnatural tale current, & which the Opium-Eater had heard even in London, of Wordsworth having been intimate with his own sister. The reason for this story having birth seemed to be that Wordsworth was very much in the habit of taking long rambles among the mountains, & romantic scenes near his habitation. His sister, who is also a great walker, used very frequently to accompany him, and indeed does so still. It is Wordsworth's custom whenever he meets or parts with any of the female part of his own relations to kiss them. This he has frequently done when he has met his sister on her rambles or parted from her, and that in roads or on mountains, or elsewhere, without heeding whether he was observed or not. And he has been perhaps seen by hinds & Clowns[8] or other persons, who have repeated what they have seen; & this simple fact, occurring probably under the eyes of those (and the Opium-Eater says he has met many such, even in the upper & better-informed classes) who have not the slightest idea of pure love for anyone, or of that fine tie which forms the affection between a brother & a Sister, has been made up into the abominable accusation bruited about, to his prejudice, amongst his coarse–minded neighbours.

The Opium-Eater thought that possibly this love of hearing & repeating what is to the prejudice of another was stronger in Westmoreland than in any other part of England. But I thought from the specimens I had had of the reports rife in Staffordshire, & from the glee with which they were narrated; & with which the faults & misfortunes of persons were attended to in the Company of the parties themselves; & from the brutalities mental as well as corporeal that were mentioned as good jokes or with approbation by Staffordshire folks, that that County would far exceed anything Westmoreland could have to boast of in that very enviable department of traditional erudition.

♣ Samuel Rogers
From *Table Talk*

A telling phrase in Dorothy's Grasmere journal of May 11, 1802, details a morning's work: "he completely finished his poems I finished Derwent's frocks." Dorothy cooks, cleans, sews, washes, irons, writes; William writes. Their travels repeated this dynamic. In his Table Talk,

---

[8] Words connoting servants, farmhands, rustics.

Samuel Rogers describes meeting Dorothy, William, and Coleridge in Scotland.[9]

Early in the present century, I set out on a tour in Scotland, accompanied by my sister; but an accident which happened to her, prevented us from going as far as we had intended. During our excursion we fell in with Wordsworth, Miss Wordsworth, and Coleridge, who were, at the same time, making a tour in a vehicle that looked very like a cart. Wordsworth and Coleridge were entirely occupied in talking about poetry; and the whole care of looking out for cottages where they might get refreshment and pass the night, as well as of seeing their poor horse fed and littered, devolved upon Miss Wordsworth. She was a most delightful person,— so full of talent, so simple-minded, and so modest! If I am not mistaken, Coleridge proved so impracticable a travelling-companion, that Wordsworth and his sister were at last obliged to separate from him. During that tour they met with Scott, who repeated to them a portion of his then unpublished *Lay* which Wordsworth, as might be expected, did not greatly admire.

I do indeed regret that Wordsworth has printed only fragments of his sister's *Journal:* it is most excellent, and ought to have been published entire.

I was walking with Lord Lonsdale on the terrace at Lowther Castle, when he said, "I wish I could do something for poor Campbell." My rejoinder was, "I wish you would do something for poor Wordsworth, who is in such straitened circumstances, that he and his family deny themselves animal food several times a week." Lord Lonsdale was the more inclined to assist Wordsworth, because the Wordsworth family had been hardly used by the preceding Lord Lonsdale; and he eventually proved one of his kindest friends.

---

[9] *Recollections of the Table Talk of Samuel Rogers,* Ed. Alexander Dyce (Appleton, 1856), p. 205–207.

Literary Contexts

Dorothy Wordsworth was a member of a household, of Grasmere, and of a writing community that included her brother, Coleridge, De Quincey (who would live in Dove Cottage after the growing Wordsworth family moved to Allan Bank), and her many correspondents. Both William's and Coleridge's poems took shape in relation to her records of people and places in her journals. Here are some of the shorter poems by William related to passages in Dorothy's journals, and De Quincey's imaginative account of the Green family, constructed many years later.

Appearing in different versions, De Quincey's account originally was part of an essay titled "Recollections of Grasmere." The Greens's story was published in Tait's Edinburgh Magazine *in 1839 in a series begun five years earlier called both "Sketches of Life and Manners from the Autobiography of an English Opium-Eater" and "Lake Reminiscences from 1807 to 1830." In his 1854 collected works, De Quincey put the piece in the second volume as part of "Early Memorials of Grasmere."*

Wordsworth's poems are from the Cambridge Riverside *edition of 1904. The dates are those of the first publication. De Quincey's narrative is from* The Collected Writings of Thomas De Quincey, *edited by David Masson (Edinburgh, 1889–1890), vol. 13, 125–149. For longer poems, such as "The Thorn," "Resolution and Independence," and "Christabel," see* The Romantics and Their Contemporaries (*volume 2a of* The Longman Anthology of British Literature).

♣ William Wordsworth

"I WANDERED LONELY AS A CLOUD" (1807, SEE PP. 60–61)

(1807, SEE PP. 60–61)

> I wandered lonely as a cloud
> That floats on high o'er vales and hills,
> When all at once I saw a crowd,
> A host, of golden daffodils;

Beside the lake, beneath the trees,
Fluttering and dancing in the breeze.

Continuous as the stars that shine
And twinkle on the milky way,
They stretched in never-ending line
Along the margin of a bay: 10
Ten thousand saw I at a glance,
Tossing their heads in sprightly dance.

The waves beside them danced; but they
Out-did the sparkling waves in glee:
A poet could not but be gay,
In such a jocund company:
I gazed—and gazed—but little thought
What wealth the show to me had brought:

For oft, when on my couch I lie,
In vacant or in pensive mood,   20
They flash upon the inward eye
Which is the bliss of solitude;
And then my heart with pleasure fills,
And dances with the daffodils.

THE REDBREAST CHASING THE BUTTERFLY
(1807, SEE P. 63)

ART thou the bird whom Man love best,
The pious bird with the scarlet breast,
    Our little English Robin;
The bird that comes about our doors
When Autumn-winds are sobbing?   5
Art thou the Peter of Norway Boors?
    Their Thomas in Finland,[1]
    And Russia far inland?
The bird, that by some name or other
All men who know thee call their brother,   10
The darling of children and men?

---

[1] Perhaps a reference to a thirteenth-century English bishop who worked in Finland as a religious and political proselytizer.

Could Father Adam[2] open his eyes
And see this sight beneath the skies,
He'd wish to close them again.

—If the Butterfly knew but his friend,   15
Hither his flight he would bend;
And find his way to me,
Under the branches of the tree:
In and out, he darts about;
Can this be the bird, to man so good,   20
That, after their bewildering,
Covered with leaves the little children,
     So painfully in the wood?
What ailed thee, Robin, that thou could'st pursue
     A beautiful creature,   25
That is gentle by nature?
Beneath the summer sky
From flower to flower let him fly;
'T is all that he wishes to do.
The cheerer Thou of our in-door sadness,   30
He is the friend of our summer gladness:
What hinders, then, that ye should be
Playmates in the sunny weather,
And fly about in the air together!
His beautiful wings in crimson are drest,   35
A crimson as bright as thine own:
Would'st thou be happy in thy nest,
O pious Bird! whom man loves best,
Love him, or leave him alone!

BEGGARS (1807, SEE PP. 30–31)

Written at Town-end, Grasmere. Met, and described to me by my Sister, near the quarry at the head of Rydal lake, a place still a chosen resort of vagrants travelling with their families

---

[2] In Book XI of Milton's *Paradise Lost*, Adam despairingly shows Eve animals pursuing one another.

She had a tall man's height or more;
Her face from summer's noontide heat
No bonnet shaded, but she wore
A mantle to her very feet.
Descending with a graceful flow,   5
And on her head a cap as white as new-fallen snow.

Her skin was of Egyptian brown:
Haughty, as if her eye had seen
Its own light to a distance thrown,
She towered, fit person for a Queen   10
To lead those ancient Amazonian files;
Or ruling Bandit's wife among the Grecian isles.

Advancing, forth she stretched her hand
And begged an alms with doleful plea
That ceased not; on our English land   15
Such woes, I knew, could never be;
And yet a boon I gave her, for the creature
Was beautiful to see—a weed of glorious feature.

I left her, and pursued my way;
And soon before me did espy   20
A pair of little Boys at play,
Chasing a crimson butterfly;
The taller followed with his hat in hand,
Wreathed round with yellow flowers the gayest of the land.

The other wore a rimless crown   25
With leaves of laurel stuck about;
And, while both followed up and down,
Each whooping with a merry shout,
In their fraternal features I could trace
Unquestionable lines of that wild Suppliant's face.   30

Yet *they* so blithe of heart, seemed fit
For finest tasks of earth or air:
Wings let them have, and they might flit

Precursors to Aurora's car,
Scattering fresh flowers; though happier far, I ween,   35
To hunt their fluttering game o'er rock and level green.

They dart across my path—but lo,
Each ready with a plaintive whine!
Said I, "not half an hour ago
Your Mother has had alms of mine."   40
"That cannot be," one answered—"she is dead:"—
I looked reproof—they saw—but neither hung his head

"She has been dead, Sir, many a day."—
"Hush, boys! You're telling me a lie;
It was your mother as I say!   45
And, in the twinkling of an eye,
"Come! Come!" cried one, and without more ado,
Off to some other play the joyous Vagrants flew!

♣ Thomas De Quincey
Early Memorials of Grasmere

Soon after my return to Oxford in 1807–8, I received a letter from
Miss Wordsworth, asking for any subscriptions I might succeed in
obtaining amongst my college friends in aid of the funds then raising on behalf of an orphan family, who had become such by an
affecting tragedy that had occurred within a few weeks from my
visit to Grasmere.[3] Miss Wordsworth's simple but fervid memoir
not being within my reach at this moment, I must trust to my own
recollections and my own impressions to retrace the story; which,
after all, is not much of a story to excite or to impress, unless for
those who can find a sufficient interest in trials and calamities of
hard-working peasants, and can reverence the fortitude which,
being lodged in so frail a tenement as the person of a little girl, not
much, if anything, above nine years old, could face an occasion of
sudden mysterious abandonment, and could tower up, during one
night, into the perfect energies of womanhood, under the mere

---

[3] De Quincey, an early fan of William's, wrote to him in 1803 and finally got up
enough nerve to present himself to the family in 1807.

pressure of difficulty, and under the sense of new-born possibilities awfully bequeathed to her, and in the most lonely, perhaps, of English habitations.

The little valley of Easedale,—which, and the neighbourhood of which, were the scenes of these interesting events,—is on its own account one of the most impressive solitudes amongst the mountains of the Lake district; and I must pause to describe it. Easedale is impressive as a solitude; for the depth of its seclusion is brought out and forced more pointedly upon the feelings by the thin scattering of houses over its sides, and over the surface of what may be called its floor. These are not above six at the most; and one, the remotest of the whole, was untenanted for all the thirty years of my acquaintance with the place. *Secondly,* it is impressive from the excessive loveliness which adorns its little area. This is broken up into small fields and miniature meadows, separated, not—as too often happens, with sad injury to the beauty of the Lake country—by stone walls, but sometimes by little hedgerows, sometimes by little sparkling, pebbly "becks,"[4] lustrous to the very bottom, and not too broad for a child's flying leap, and sometimes by wild self-sown woodlands of birch, alder, holly, mountain ash, a hazel, that meander through the valley, intervening the different estates with natural sylvan marches, and giving cheerfulness in winter by the bright scarlet of their berries. It is the character of all the northern English valleys, as I have already remarked,—and it is a character first noticed by Wordsworth—that they assume, in their bottom areas, the level, floor-like shape, making everywhere a direct angle with the surrounding hills, and definitely marking out the margin of their outlines; whereas the Welsh valleys have too often the glaring imperfection of the basin shape, which allows no sense of any flat area or valley surface: the hills are already commencing at the very centre of what is called the level area. The little valley of Easedale is, in this respect, as highly finished as in every other; and in the Westmorland spring, which may be considered May and the earlier half of June, whilst the grass in the meadows is yet short from the habit of keeping the sheep on it until a much later period than elsewhere, (viz. until the mountains are far cleared of snow and the probability of storms as to make it safe to send them out on their summer migration), it follows naturally that the little fields in

[4] Small brooks.

Easedale have the most lawny appearance, and, from the humidity of the Westmorland[5] climate, the most verdant that it is possible to imagine. But there is a third advantage possessed by this Easedale, above other rival valleys, in the sublimity of mountain barriers. In one of its many rocky recesses is seen a "force" (such is the local name for a cataract), white with foam, descending at all seasons with considerable strength, and, after the melting of snows, with an Alpine violence. Follow the leading of this "force" for three quarters of a mile, and you come to a little mountain lake, locally termed a "tarn"[6] the very finest and most gloomily sublime of its class. From this tarn it was, I doubt not, though applying it to another, that Wordsworth drew the circumstances of his general description. And far beyond this "enormous barrier" that thus imprisons the very winds, tower upwards the aspiring heads (usually enveloped in cloud and mist) of Larimore, Bow Fell, and the other fells of Langdale Head and Borrowdale. Easedale, in its relation to Grasmere, is a chamber within a chamber, or rather a closet within a chamber— a chapel within a cathedral—a little private oratory within a chapel. The sole approach, as I have mentioned, is from Grasmere; and some *one* outlet there must inevitably be in every vale that can be interesting to a human occupant, since without water it would not be habitable, and running water must force an egress for itself, and, consequently, an ingress for the reader and myself. But, properly speaking, there is no other. For, when you explore the remoter end of the vale, at which you suspect some communication with the world outside, you find before you a most formidable amount of climbing, the extent of which can hardly be measured where there is no solitary object of human workmanship or vestige of animal life,—not a sheep-track, not a shepherd's hovel, but rock and heath,

---

[5] [De Quincey] It is pretty generally known, perhaps, that Westmorland and Devonshire are the two rainiest counties in England. At Kirby Lonsdale, lying just on the outer margin of the Lake district, one-fifth more rain is computed to fall than in the adjacent counties on same western side of England. But it is also notorious that the western side of the island universally is more rainy than the east; Collins called it the showery west.

[6] [De Quincey] A tarn is a lake, generally (perhaps always) a small one, and always, as I think (but this I have heard disputed), lying above the level of the inhabited valleys and the large lakes; and subject to this farther restriction, first noticed by Wordsworth, that it has no main feeder. Now, this latter accident of the *thing* at once explains and authenticates my account of the word, viz. that it is the Danish word taaren a trickling of tears, a deposit of waters from the weeping of rain down the smooth faces of the rocks.

heath and rock, tossed about in monotonous confusion. And, after the ascent is mastered, you descend into a second vale—long, narrow, sterile—known by the name of "Far Easedale": from which point, if you could drive a tunnel *under* the everlasting hills, perhaps six or seven miles might bring you to the nearest habitation of man, in Borrowdale; but, going *over* the mountains, the road cannot be less than twelve or fourteen, and, in point of fatigue, at the least twenty. This long valley, which is really terrific at noonday, from its utter loneliness and desolation, completes the defences of little sylvan Easedale. There is one door into it from the Grasmere side; but that door is obscure; and on every other quarter there is no door at all; not any, the roughest, access, but such as would demand a day's walking.

Such is the solitude—so deep and so rich in miniature beauty—of Easedale; and in this solitude it was that George and Sarah Green, two poor and hard-working peasants, dwelt, with a numerous family of small children. Poor as they were, they had won the general respect of the neighbourhood, from the uncomplaining firmness with which they bore the hardships of their lot, and from the decent attire in which the good mother of the family contrived to send out her children to the Grasmere parish-school. It is a custom, and a very ancient one, in Westmorland—the same custom (resting on the same causes) I have witnessed also in southern Scotland—that any sale by auction of household furniture (and seldom a month passes without something of the sort) forms an excuse for the good women, throughout the whole circumference of perhaps four or five valleys, to assemble at the place of sale, with the nominal purpose of buying something they may happen to want. A sale, except it were of the sort exclusively interesting to farming men, is a kind of general intimation to the country, from the owner of the property, that he will, on that afternoon, be "at home"[7] to all comers, and hopes to see as large an attendance as possible. Accordingly, it was the almost invariable custom—and often, too, when the parties were far too poor for such an effort of hospitality—to make ample provision, not of eatables, but of liquor, for all who came. Even a gentleman who should happen to present himself on such a festal occasion, by way of seeing the "humours" of the scene, was certain of meeting the most cordial welcome. The good woman of the house more particularly testified her sense of the honour done to her, and was sure to seek out some

[7] Hospitality of an "open house."

cherished and solitary article of china—a wreck from a century back—in order that he, being a porcelain man among so many delf[8] men and women, might have a porcelain cup to drink from.

The main secret of attraction at these sales—many of which I have attended—was the social rendezvous thus effected between parties so remote from each other (either by real distance or by virtual distance resulting from the separation effected by mountains 3000 feet high) that, in fact, without some such common object, they would not be likely to hear of each other for months, or actually to meet for years. This principal charm of the "gathering," seasoned, doubtless, to many by the certain anticipation that the whole budget of rural gossip would then and there be opened, was not assuredly diminished to the men by the anticipation of excellent ale (usually brewed six or seven weeks before, in preparation for the event), and possibly of still more excellent powsowdy (a combination of ale, spirits, and spices); nor to the women by some prospect, not so inevitably fulfilled, but pretty certain in a liberal house, of communicating their news over excellent tea. Even the auctioneer was always a character in the drama: he was always a rustic old humourist, and a jovial drunkard, privileged in certain good-humoured liberties and jokes with all bidders, gentle or simple, and furnished with an ancient inheritance of jests appropriate to the articles offered for sale,—jests that had, doubtless, done their office from Elizabeth's golden days, but no more, on that account, failing of their expected effect, with either man or woman of this nineteenth century, than the sun fails to gladden the heart because it is that same old superannuated sun that has gladdened it for thousands of years.

One thing, however, in mere justice to the Dalesmen of Westmorland and Cumberland, I am bound in this place to record. Often as I have been at these sales, and years before even a scattering of gentry began to attend, yet so true to the natural standard of politeness was the decorum uniformly maintained that even the old buffoon of an auctioneer never forgot himself so far as to found upon any article of furniture a jest fitted to call up a painful blush in any woman's face. He might, perhaps, go so far as to awaken a little rosy confusion upon some young bride's countenance, when pressing a cradle upon her attention; but never did I hear him utter, nor would he have been tolerated in uttering, a scurrilous or disgusting

---

[8] A glazed blue pottery from Delft, Holland, or a brown earthenware pottery glazed white and then decorated. "Porcelain" is white, translucent earthenware.

jest, such as might easily have been suggested by something offered at a house-hold sale. Such jests as these I heard for the first time at a sale in Grasmere in 1814; and, I am ashamed to say it, from some "gentlemen" of a great city. And it grieved me to see the effect, as it expressed itself upon the manly faces of the grave Dalesman—a sense of insult offered to their women, who met in confiding reliance upon the forbearance of the men, and upon their regard for the dignity of the female sex; this feeling struggling with the habitual respect they are inclined to show towards what they suppose gentle blood and superior education. Taken, generally, however, these were the most picturesque and festal meetings which the manners of the country produced. There you saw all ages and both sexes assembled; there you saw old men whose heads would have been studies for Guido;[9] there you saw the most colossal and stately figures amongst the young men that England has to show; there the most beautiful young women. There it was that the social benevolence, the innocent mirth, and the neighbourly kindness of the people, most delightfully expanded, and expressed themselves with the least reserve.

To such a scene it was,—to a sale of domestic furniture at the house of some proprietor in Langdale—that George and Sarah Green set forward in the forenoon of a day fated to be their last on earth. The sale was to take place in Langdalehead; to which, from their own cottage in Easedale it was possible in daylight, and supposing no mist upon the hills, to find out a short cut of not more than five or six miles. By this route they went; and, notwithstanding the snow lay on the ground, they reached their destination in safety. The attendance at the sale must have been diminished by the rigorous state of the weather; but still the scene was a gay one as usual. Sarah Green, though a good and worthy woman in her maturer years, had been imprudent, and—as the merciful judgment of the country is apt to express it—"unfortunate" in her youth. She had an elder daughter, who was illegitimate; and I believe the father of this girl was dead. The girl herself was grown up; and the peculiar solicitude of poor Sarah's maternal heart was at this time called forth on her behalf: she wished to see her placed in a very respectable house, where the mistress was distinguished for her notable qualities, and for success in forming good servants. This object,—as important to Sarah Green in the narrow range of her cares as, in a more exalted family, it might be to obtain a ship for a lieutenant that had passed

---

[9] Probably Italian painter Guido Reni (1575–1642).

as master and commander, or to get him "posted,"—occupied her almost throughout the sale. A doubtful answer had been given to her application; and Sarah was going about the crowd, and weaving her person in and out, in order to lay hold of this or that intercessor who might have, or might seem to have, some weight with the principal person concerned.

This I think it interesting to notice, as the last occupation which is known to have stirred the pulses of her heart. An illegitimate child is everywhere, even in the indulgent society of Westmorland Dalesmen, under some cloud of discountenance;[10] so that Sarah Green might consider her duty to be the stronger towards this child of her "misfortune." And she probably had another reason for her anxiety—as some words dropped by her on this evening led people to presume—in her conscientious desire to introduce her daughter into a situation less perilous than that which had compassed her own youthful steps with snares. If so, it is painful to know that the virtuous wish, whose

> "vital warmth
> Gave the last human motion to her heart,"[11]

should not have been fulfilled. She was a woman of ardent and affectionate spirit; of which Miss Wordsworth gave me some circumstantial and affecting instances. This ardour it was, and her impassioned manner, that drew attention to what she did; for, otherwise, she was too poor a person to be important in the estimation of strangers, and, of all possible situations, to be important at a sale, where the public attention was naturally fixed upon the chief purchasers, and the attention of the purchasers fixed upon the chief competitors. Hence it happened that, after she ceased to challenge notice by the emphasis of her solicitations for her daughter, she ceased to be noticed at all; and nothing was recollected of her subsequent behaviour until the time arrived for general separation. This time was considerably after sunset; and the final recollections of the crowd with respect to George and Sarah Green were that, upon

[10] [De Quincey] But still nothing at all in England by comparison with its gloomy excess in Scotland. In the present generation the rancorous bigotry of this feeling has been considerably mitigated. But, if the reader wishes to view it in its ancient strength, I advise him to look into the "Life of Alexander Alexander" (2 vols. 1830). He was a poor outcast, whose latter days were sheltered from ruin by the munificence of the late Mr. Blackwood, senior.

[11] "The hope whose vital anxiousness / Gives the last human interest to his heart," (177–178), a late version of "The Old Cumberland Beggar."

their intention being understood to retrace their morning path, and to attempt the perilous task of dropping down into Easedale from the mountains above Langdalehead, a sound of remonstrance arose from many quarters. However, at such a moment, when everybody was in the hurry of departure, and to such persons (persons, I mean, so mature in years and in local knowledge), the opposition could not be very obstinate: party after party rode off; the meeting melted away, or, as the northern phrase is, scaled;[12] and at length nobody was left of any weight that could pretend to influence the decision of elderly people. They quitted the scene, professing to obey some advice or other upon the choice of roads; but, at as early a point as they could do so unobserved, began to ascend the hills everywhere open from the rude carriage-way. After this they were seen no more. They had disappeared into the cloud of death. Voices were heard, some hours afterwards, from the mountains—voices, as some thought, of alarm: others said, No,—that it was only the voices of jovial people, carried by the wind into uncertain regions. The result was that no attention was paid to the sounds.

That night, in little peaceful Easedale, six children sat by a peat fire, expecting the return of their parents, upon whom they depended for their daily bread. Let a day pass, and they were starving. Every sound was heard with anxiety; for all this was reported many hundred times to Miss Wordsworth, and to those who, like myself, were never wearied of hearing the details. Every sound, every echo amongst the hills, was listened to for five hours, from seven to twelve. At length the eldest girl of the family—about nine years old—told her little brothers and sisters to go to bed. They had been trained to obedience; and all of them, at the voice of their eldest sister, went off fearfully to their beds. What could be their fears it is difficult to say; they had no knowledge to instruct them in the dangers of the hills; but the eldest sister always averred that they had as deep a solicitude as she herself had about their parents. Doubtless she had communicated her fears to them. Some time in the course of the evening—but it was late, and after midnight—the moon arose, and shed a torrent of light upon the Langdale fells, which had already, long hours before, witnessed in darkness the death of their parents.

---

[12] [De Quincey] "Scaled":—Scale is a verb both active and neuter. I use it here as a neuter verb, in the sense (a Cumberland sense) of separating to all the points of the compass. But by Shakespeare it is used in an active or transitive sense. Speaking of some secret news, he says, "We'll scale it a little more" i.e. spread it in all directions, and disentangle its complexities.

That night, and the following morning, came a further and a heavier fall of snow; in consequence of which the poor children were completely imprisoned, and cut off from all possibility of communicating with their next neighbours. The brook was too much for them to leap; and the little, crazy wooden bridge could not be crossed, or even approached with safety, from the drifting of the snow having made it impossible to ascertain the exact situation of some treacherous hole in its timbers, which, if trod upon, would have let a small child drop through into the rapid waters. Their parents did not return. For some hours of the morning the children clung to the hope that the extreme severity of the night had tempted them to sleep in Langdale; but this hope forsook them as the day wore away. Their father, George Green, had served as a soldier, and was an active man, of ready resources, who would not, under any circumstances, have failed to force a road back to his family, had he been still living; and this reflection, or rather semi-conscious feeling, which the awfulness of their situation forced upon the minds of all but the mere infants, awakened them to the whole extent of their calamity. Wonderful it is to see the effect of sudden misery, sudden grief, or sudden fear, in sharpening (where they do not utterly upset) the intellectual perceptions. Instances must have fallen in the way of most of us. And I have noticed frequently that even sudden and intense bodily pain forms part of the machinery employed by nature for quickening the development of the mind. The perceptions of infants are not, in fact, excited by graduated steps and continuously, but per saltum,[13] and by unequal starts. At least, within the whole range of my own experience, I have remarked that, after any very severe fit of those peculiar pains to which the delicate digestive organs of most infants are liable, there always became apparent on the following day a very considerable increase of vital energy and of quickened attention to the objects around them. The poor desolate children of Blentarn Ghyll,[14] hourly becoming more

[13] Latin: "by a leap" (by fits and starts).

[14] [De Quincey] Wordsworth's conjecture as to the origin of the name is probably the true one. There is, at a little elevation above the place, a small concave tract of ground, shaped like the bed of a tarn. Some causes having diverted the supplies of water, at some remote period, from the little reservoir, the tarn has probably disappeared; but, the bed, and other indications of a tarn (particularly a little gyhll or steep rocky cleft for discharging the water), having remained as memorials that it once existed, the country people have called it the Blind Tarn—the tarn which wants its eye, in wanting the luminous sparkle of the waters of right belonging to it.

pathetically convinced that they were orphans, gave many evidences of this awaking power as lodged, by a providential arrangement, in situations of trial that most require it. They huddled together, in the evening, round their hearth-fire of peats, and held their little family councils upon what was to be done towards any chance—if chance remained—of yet giving aid to their parents; for a slender hope had sprung up that some hovel or sheepfold might have furnished them a screen (or, in Westmorland phrase, a bield) against the weather quarter of the storm, in which hovel they might even now be lying snowed up; and, secondly, as regarded themselves, in what way they were to make known their situation, in case the snow should continue or should increase; for starvation stared them in the face if they should be confined for many days to their house.

Meantime, the eldest sister, little Agnes, though sadly alarmed, and feeling the sensation of *eeriness* as twilight came on and she looked out from the cottage-door to the dreadful fells on which, too probably, her parents were lying corpses (and possibly not many hundred yards from their own threshold), yet exerted herself to take all the measures which their own prospects made prudent. And she told Miss Wordsworth that, in the midst of the oppression on her little spirit from vague ghostly terrors, she did not fail, however, to draw some comfort from the consideration that the very same causes which produced their danger in one direction sheltered them from danger of another kind,—such dangers as she knew, from books that she had read, would have threatened a little desolate flock of children in other parts of England; for she considered thankfully that, if *they* could not get out into Grasmere, on the other hand bad men, and wild seafaring foreigners, who sometimes passed along the high road even in that vale, could not get to them; and that, as to their neighbours, so far from having anything to fear in that quarter, their greatest apprehension was lest they might not be able to acquaint them with their situation; but that, if this could be accomplished, the very sternest amongst them were kind-hearted people, that would contend with each other for the privilege of assisting them. Somewhat cheered with these thoughts, and having caused all her brothers and sisters—except the two little things, not yet of a fit age—to kneel down and say the prayers which they had been taught, this admirable little maiden turned herself to every household task that could have proved useful to them in a long captivity. First of all, upon some recollection that the clock was nearly going down, she wound it up. Next, she took all the milk which remained from what her mother had provided for the children's consumption during her absence and for the breakfast of the following morning,—this luckily was still in sufficient plenty for two days' consumption (skimmed or "blue" milk being only one halfpenny a quart, and the quart a most redundant one, in Grasmere),—this she took and scalded, so as to save it from turning sour. That done, she next examined the meal chest; made the common oatmeal porridge of the country (the "burgoo" of the Royal Navy); but put all of the children, except the two youngest, on short allowance; and, by way of reconciling them in some measure to this stinted meal, she found out a little hoard of flour, part of which she baked for them upon the hearth into little cakes; and this unusual delicacy persuaded them to think that they had been celebrating a feast. Next, before night coming on should make it too trying to her own feelings, or before fresh snow coming on might make it impossible, she issued out of doors. There her first task was, with the assistance of two younger brothers, to carry in from the peat-stack as many peats as might serve them for a week's consumption. That done, in the second place she examined the potatoes, buried in "brackens" (that is, withered fern): these were not many; and she thought it better to leave them where they were, excepting as many as would make a single meal, under a fear that the heat of their cottage would spoil them if removed.

Having thus made all the provision in her power for supporting their own lives, she turned her attention to the cow. Her she milked; but, unfortunately, the milk she gave, either from being badly fed, or from some other cause, was too trifling to be of much consideration towards the wants of a large family. Here, however, her chief anxiety was to get down the hay for the cow's food from a loft above the outhouse; and in this she succeeded but imperfectly, from want of strength and size to cope with the difficulties of the case,— besides that the increasing darkness by this time, together with the gloom of the place, made it a matter of great self-conquest for her to work at all; but, as respected one night at any rate, she placed the cow in a situation of luxurious warmth and comfort. Then, retreating into the warm house, and "barring" the door, she sat down to undress the two youngest of the children; them she laid carefully and cosily in their little nests upstairs, and sang them to sleep. The rest she kept up to hear her company until the clock should tell them it was midnight; up to which time she had still a lingering hope that some welcome shout from the hills above, which they were all to strain their ears to catch, might yet assure them that they were not wholly orphans, even though one parent should have perished. No shout, it may be supposed, was ever heard; nor could a shout, in any case, have been heard, for the night was one of tumultuous wind. And, though, amidst its ravings, sometimes they fancied a sound of voices, still, in the dead lulls that now and then succeeded, they heard nothing to confirm their hopes. As last services to what she might now have called her own little family, Agnes took precautions against the drifting of the snow *within* the door and *within* the imperfect window, which had caused them some discomfort on the preceding day; and, finally, she adopted the most systematic and elaborate plans for preventing the possibility of their fire being extinguished,—which, in the event of their being thrown upon the ultimate resource of their potatoes, would be absolutely indispensable to their existence, and in any case a main element of their comfort.

The night slipped away, and morning came, bringing with it no better hopes of any kind. Change there had been none but for the worse. The snow had greatly increased in quantity; and the drifts seemed far more formidable. A second day passed like the first,— little Agnes still keeping her young flock quiet, and tolerably comfortable, and still calling on all the elders in succession to say their prayers, morning and night.

A third day came; and, whether on that or on the fourth I do not now recollect, but on one or other, there came a welcome gleam of hope. The arrangement of the snow-drifts had shifted during the night; and, though the wooden bridge was still impracticable, a low wall had been exposed, over which, by a circuit which evaded the brook, it seemed possible that a road might be found into Grasmere. In some walls it was necessary to force gaps; but this was effected without much difficulty, even by children; for the Westmorland field walls are "open,"—that is, uncemented with mortar; and the push of a stick will generally detach so much from the upper part of any old crazy fence as to lower it sufficiently for female, or even for childish, steps to pass. The little boys accompanied their sister until she came to the other side of the hill; which, lying more sheltered from the weather, offered a path onwards comparatively easy. Here they parted; and little Agnes pursued her solitary mission to the nearest house she could find accessible in Grasmere.

No house could have proved a wrong one in such a case. Miss Wordsworth and I often heard the description renewed of the horror which, in an instant, displaced the smile of hospitable greet-ing, when little weeping Agnes told her sad tale. No tongue can express the fervid sympathy which travelled through the vale, like fire in an American forest, when it was learned that neither George nor Sarah Green had been seen by their children since the day of the Langdale sale. Within half an hour, or little more, from the remotest parts of the valley—some of them distant nearly two miles from the point of rendezvous—all the men of Grasmere had assembled at the little cluster of cottages called "Kirktown," from its adjacency to the venerable parish-church of St. Oswald. There were at the time I settled in Grasmere—viz. in the spring of 1809, and, therefore, I suppose, in 1807–8, fifteen months previously—about sixty-three households in the vale; and the total number of souls was about 265 to 270; so that the number of fighting men would be about sixty or sixty-six, according to the common way of computing the proportion; and the majority were athletic and powerfully built. Sixty, at least, after a short consultation as to the plan of operations, and for arranging the kind of signals by which they were to commu-nicate from great distances, and in the perilous events of mists or snow-storms, set off with the speed of Alpine hunters to the hills. The dangers of the undertaking were considerable, under the uneasy and agitated state of the weather; and all the women of the vale were in the greatest anxiety until night brought them back, in a body, unsuccessful. Three days at the least, and I rather think five, the search was ineffectual: which arose partly from the great extent of the ground to be examined, and partly from the natural mistake made of ranging almost exclusively during the earlier days on that part of the hills over which the path of Easedale might be presumed to have been selected under any reasonable latitude of circuitous-ness. But the fact is, when the fatal accident (for such it has often proved) of a permanent mist surprises a man on the hills, if he turns and loses his direction, he is a lost man; and, without doing this so as to lose the power of s'orienter[15] all at once, it is yet well known how difficult it is to avoid losing it insensibly and by degrees. Baf-fling snow-showers are the worst kind of mists. And the poor Greens had, under that kind of confusion, wandered many a mile out of their proper track; so that to search for them upon any line indicated by the ordinary probabilities would perhaps offer the slen-derest chance for finding them.

---

[15] French: "orienting oneself."

The zeal of the people, meantime, was not in the least abated, but rather quickened, by the wearisome disappointments; every hour of daylight was turned to account; no man of the valley ever came home to meals; and the reply of a young shoemaker, on the fourth night's return, speaks sufficiently for the unabated spirit of the vale. Miss Wordsworth asked what he would do on the next morning. "Go up again, of course," was his answer. But what if to-morrow also should turn out like all the rest? "Why, go up in stronger force on the day after." Yet this man was sacrificing his own daily earnings, without a chance of recompense. At length sagacious dogs were taken up; and, about noonday, a shout from an aerial height, amongst thick volumes of cloudy vapour, propagated through repeating bands of men from a distance of many miles, conveyed as by telegraph into Grasmere the news that the bodies were found. George Green was lying at the bottom of a precipice from which he had fallen. Sarah Green was found on the summit of the precipice; and, by laying together all the indications of what had passed, and reading into coherency the sad hieroglyphics of their last agonies, it was conjectured that the husband had desired his wife to pause for a few minutes, wrapping her, meantime, in his own greatcoat, whilst he should go forward and reconnoitre the ground, in order to catch a sight of some object (rocky peak, or tarn, or peat-field) which might ascertain their real situation. Either the snow above, already lying in drifts, or the blinding snowstorms driving into his eyes, must have misled him as to the nature of the circumjacent ground; for the precipice over which he had fallen was but a few yards from the spot in which he had quitted his wife. The depth of the descent and the fury of the wind (almost always violent on these cloudy altitudes) would prevent any distinct communication between the dying husband below and his despairing wife above; but it was believed by the shepherds best acquainted with the ground, and the range of sound as regarded the capacities of the human ear under the probable circumstances of the storm, that Sarah might have caught, at intervals, the groans of her unhappy partner, supposing that his death were at all a lingering one. Others, on the contrary, supposed her to have gathered this catastrophe rather from the *want* of any sounds, and from his continued absence, than from any one distinct or positive expression of it; both because the smooth and unruffled surface of the snow where he lay seemed to argue that he had died without a struggle, perhaps without a groan, and because that tremendous sound of "hurtling" in the upper chambers of the air which often accompanies a snow-storm, when combined with heavy gales of wind, would utterly suppress and stifle (as they conceived) any sounds so feeble as those from a dying man. In any case, and by whatever sad language of sounds or signs, positive or negative, she might have learned or guessed her loss, it was generally agreed that the wild shrieks heard towards midnight in Langdalehead[16] announced the agonizing moment which brought to her now widowed heart the conviction of utter desolation and of final abandonment to her own solitary and fast-fleeting energies. It seemed probable that the sudden disappearance of her husband from her pursuing eyes would teach her to understand his fate, and that the consequent indefinite apprehension of instant death lying all around the point on which she sat had kept her stationary to the very attitude in which her husband left her, until her failing powers, and the increasing bitterness of the cold to one no longer in motion, would soon make those changes of place impossible which too awfully had made themselves known as dangerous. The footsteps in some places, wherever drifting had not obliterated them, yet traceable as to the outline, though partially filled up with later falls of snow, satisfactorily showed that, however much they might have rambled, after crossing and doubling upon their own tracks, and many a mile astray from their right path, they must have kept together to the very plateau or shelf of rock at which (i.e. on which, and below which) their wanderings had terminated; for there were evidently no steps from this plateau in the retrograde order.

By the time they had reached this final stage of their erroneous course, all possibility of escape must have been long over for both alike; because their exhaustion must have been excessive before they could have reached a point so remote and high; and, unfortunately, the direct result of all this exhaustion had been to throw them farther off their home, or from "any dwelling-place of man,"[17] than

---

[16] [De Quincey] I once heard, also, in talking with a Langdale family upon this tragic tale, that the sounds had penetrated into the valley of Little Langdale; which is possible enough. For, although this interesting recess of the entire Langdale basin (which bears somewhat of the same relation to the Great Langdale that Easedale bears to Grasmere) does, in fact, lie beyond Langdalehead by the entire breadth of that dale, yet, from the singular accident of having its area raised far above the level of the adjacent vales, one most solitary section of Little Langdale (in which lies a tiny lake, and on the banks of that lake dwells one solitary family), being exactly at right angles both to Langdalehead and to the other complementary section of the Lesser Langdale, is brought into a position and an elevation virtually much nearer to objects (especially to audible objects) on the Easedale Fells.

[17] Quoting William's poem (p. 276).

they were at starting. Here, therefore, at this rocky pinnacle, hope was extinct for the wedded couple, but not perhaps for the husband. It was the impression of the vale that perhaps, within half-an-hour before reaching this fatal point, George Green might, had his conscience or his heart allowed him in so base a desertion, have saved himself singly, without any very great difficulty. It is to be hoped, however—and, for my part, I think too well of human nature to hesitate in believing—that not many, even amongst the meaner-minded and the least generous of men, could have reconciled themselves to the abandonment of a poor fainting female companion in such circumstances. Still, though not more than a most imperative duty, it was such a duty as most of his associates believed to have cost him (perhaps consciously) his life. It is an impressive truth that sometimes in the very lowest forms of duty, less than which would rank a man as a villain, there is, nevertheless, the sublimest ascent of self-sacrifice. To do less would class you as an object of eternal scorn: to do so much presumes the grandeur of heroism. For his wife not only must have disabled him greatly by clinging to his arm for support; but it was known, from her peculiar character and manner, that she would be likely to rob him of his coolness and presence of mind, by too painfully fixing his thoughts, where her own would be busiest, upon their helpless little family. "Stung with the thoughts of home"— to borrow the fine expression of Thomson[18] in describing a similar case—alternately thinking of the blessedness of that warm fireside at Blentarn Ghyll which was not again to spread its genial glow through her freezing limbs, and of those darling little faces which, in this world, she was to see no more; unintentionally, and without being aware even of that result, she would rob the brave man (for such he was) of his fortitude, and the strong man of his animal resources. And yet (such, in the very opposite direction, was equally the impression universally through Grasmere), had Sarah Green foreseen, could her affectionate heart have guessed, even the tenth part of that love and neighbourly respect for herself which soon afterwards expressed themselves in showers of bounty to her children; could she have looked behind the curtain of destiny sufficiently to learn that the very desolation of these poor children which wrung her maternal heart, and doubtless constituted to her the sting of

---

[18] James Thomson's *Winter*, describing a doomed shepherd caught in a mountain snowstorm (l. 286).

death, would prove the signal and the pledge of such anxious guardianship as not many rich men's children receive, and that this overflowing offering to her own memory would not be a hasty or decaying tribute of the first sorrowing sensibilities, but would pursue her children steadily until their hopeful settlement in life: anything approaching this, known or guessed, would have caused her (so said all who knew her) to welcome the bitter end by which such privileges were to be purchased, and solemnly to breathe out into the ear of that holy angel who gathers the whispers of dying mothers torn asunder from their infants a thankful Nunc dimittis (Lord, now lettest thou thy servant depart in peace), as the farewell ejaculation rightfully belonging to the occasion.

The funeral of the ill-fated Greens was, it may be supposed, attended by all the Vale. It took place about eight days after they were found; and the day happened to be in the most perfect contrast to the sort of weather which prevailed at the time of their misfortune. Some snow still remained here and there upon the ground; but the azure of the sky was unstained by a cloud; and a golden sunlight seemed to sleep, so balmy and tranquil was the season, upon the very hills where the pair had wandered,—then a howling wilderness, but now a green pastoral lawn in its lower ranges, and a glittering expanse of virgin snow in its higher. George Green had, I believe, an elder family by a former wife; and it was for some of these children, who lived at a distance, and who wished to give their attendance at the grave, that the funeral was delayed. At this point, because really suggested by the contrast of the funeral tranquillity with the howling tempest of the fatal night, it may be proper to remind the reader of Wordsworth's memorial stanzas:—[19]

> Who weeps for strangers? Many wept
> For George and Sarah Green;
> Wept for that pair's unhappy fate
> Whose graves may here be seen,
>
> By night upon these stormy fells
> Did wife and husband roam;
> Six little ones at home had left,
> And could not find that home.

[19] The first publication of the poem.

For *any* dwelling-place of man
　　As vainly did they seek:
He perished; and a voice was heard—
　　The widow's lonely shriek.

Not many steps, and she was left
　　A body without life—
A few short steps were the chain that bound
　　The husband to the wife.

Now do these sternly-featured hills
　　Look gently on this grave;
And quiet *now* are the depths of air,
　　As a sea without a wave.

But deeper lies the heart of peace,
　　In quiet more profound;
　　The heart of quietness is here
Within this churchyard bound.

And from all agony of mind
　　It keeps them safe, and far
From fear and grief, and from all need
　　Of sun or guiding star.

O darkness of the grave! how deep,
　　After that living night—
That last and dreary living one
　　Of sorrow and affright!

O sacred marriage-bed of death!
　　That keeps them side by side
In bond of peace, in bond of love,
　　That may not be untied!

　　After this solemn ceremony of the funeral was over—at which, by the way, I heard Miss Wordsworth declare that the grief of Sarah's illegitimate daughter was the most overwhelming she had ever witnessed—a regular distribution of the children was made amongst the wealthier families of the Vale. There had already, and before the funeral, been a perfect struggle to obtain one of the children amongst all who had any facilities for discharging the duties of such a trust; and even the poorest had put in their claim to bear some part in the expenses of the case. But it was judiciously decided that none of the children should be intrusted to any persons who seemed likely, either from old age or from slender means, or from nearer and more personal responsibilities, to be under the necessity of devolving the trust, sooner or later, upon strangers who might have none of that interest in the children which, attached, in the minds of the Grasmere people, to the circumstances that made them orphans, Two twins, who had naturally played together and slept together from their birth, passed into the same family: the others were dispersed; but into such kind-hearted and intelligent families, with continued opportunities of meeting each other on errands, or at church, or at sales, that it was hard to say which had the more comfortable home. And thus, in so brief a period as one fortnight, a household that, by health and strength, by the humility of poverty and by innocence of life, seemed sheltered from all attacks but those of time, came to be utterly broken up. George and Sarah Green slept in Grasmere churchyard, never more to know the want of "sun or guiding star." Their children were scattered over wealthier houses than those of their poor parents, through the Vales of Grasmere or Rydal; and Blentarn Ghyll, after being shut up for a season, and ceasing for months to send up its little slender column of smoke at morning and evening, finally passed into the hands of a stranger.

The Wordsworths, meantime, acknowledged a peculiar interest in the future fortunes and education of the children. They had taken by much the foremost place in pushing the subscriptions on behalf of the family,—feeling, no doubt, that, when both parents, in any little sequestered community like that of Grasmere, are suddenly cut off by a tragical death, the children in such a case devolve by a sort of natural right and providential bequest on the other members of this community. They energetically applied themselves to the task of raising funds by subscription; most of which, it is true, might not be wanted until future years should carry one after another of the children successively into different trades or occupations; but they well understood that more by tenfold would be raised under an immediate appeal to the sympathies of men whilst yet burning fervently towards the sufferers in this calamity than if the application were delayed until the money should be needed. The Royal Family were made acquainted with the details of the case; they were powerfully affected by the story, especially by the account of little Agnes, and her premature assumption of the maternal character; and they contributed most munificently, Her Majesty, and three at least of her august daughters, were amongst the subscribers to the fund. For my part, I could have obtained a good deal from the careless liberality of Oxonian friends towards such a fund. But, knowing previously how little, in such an application, it would aid me to plead the name of Wordsworth as the founder of the subscription (a name that *now* would stand good for some thousands of pounds in that same Oxford: so passes the injustice, as well as the glory, of this world!)— knowing this, I did not choose to trouble anybody; and the more so as Miss Wordsworth, upon my proposal to write to various ladies upon whom I could have relied for their several contributions, wrote back to me desiring that I would not, and upon this satisfactory reason—that the fund had already swelled, under the Royal patronage, and the interest excited by so much of the circumstances as could be reported in hurried letters, to an amount beyond what was likely to be wanted for persons whom there was no good reason for pushing out of the sphere to which their birth had called them. The parish even was liable to give aid; and, in the midst of Royal bounty, this aid was not declined. Perhaps this was so far a solitary and unique case that it might be the only one in which some parochial Mr. Bumble found himself pulling in joint harness with the denizens of Windsor Castle, and a coadjutor of "Majesties" and "Royal Highnesses." Finally, to complete their own large share in the charity, the Wordsworths took into their own family one of the children, a girl; the least amiable, I believe, of the whole; slothful and sensual; so, at least, I imagined; for this girl it was, that in years to come caused by her criminal negligence the death of little Kate Wordsworth.[20] From a gathering of years far ahead of the events, looking back by accident to this whole little cottage romance of Blentarn Ghyll, with its ups and downs, its lights and shadows, and its fitful alternations of grandeur derived from mountain solitude and of humility derived from the very lowliest poverty,—its little faithful Agnes keeping up her records of time in harmony with the mighty world outside, and feeding the single cow, the total "estate" of the new-made orphans,— I thought of that beautiful Persian apologue where some slender drop or crystallizing filament within the shell of an oyster fancies itself called upon to bewail its own obscure lot, consigned apparently and irretrievably to the gloomiest depths of the Persian Gulf.

---

[20] Particularly close to William's child, De Quincey tells the story of her death in "Lake Reminiscences."

But changes happen; good and bad luck will fall out, even in the darkest depths of the Persian Gulf; and messages of joy can reach those that wait in silence, even where no post-horn has ever sounded. Behold! the slender filament has ripened into the most glorious of pearls. In a happy hour for himself, some diver from the blossoming forests of Ceylon brings up to heavenly light the matchless pearl; and very soon that solitary crystal drop, that had bemoaned its own obscure lot, finds itself glorifying the central cluster in the tiara bound upon the brow of him who signed himself "King of Kings," the Shah of Persia, and that shook all Asia from the Indus to the Euphrates. Not otherwise was the lot of little Agnes: faithful to duties so suddenly revealed amidst terrors ghostly as well as earthly; paying down her first tribute of tears to an affliction that seemed past all relief, and such that at first she, with her brothers and sisters, seemed foundering simultaneously with her parents in one mighty darkness. And yet, because, under the strange responsibilities which had suddenly surprised her, she sought counsel and strength from God, teaching her brothers and sisters to do the same, and seemed (when alone at midnight) to hear her mother's voice calling to her from the hills above, one moon had scarcely finished its circuit before the most august ladies on our planet were reading, with sympathizing tears, of Agnes Green, and from the towers of Windsor Castle[21] came gracious messages of inquiry to little, lowly Blentarn Ghyll.

In taking leave of this subject I may mention, by the way, that accidents of this nature are not by any means so uncommon in the mountainous districts of Cumberland and Westmorland as the reader might infer from the intensity of the excitement which waited on the catastrophe of the Greens. In that instance it was not the simple death by cold upon the hills, but the surrounding circumstances, which invested the case with its agitating power. The fellowship in death of a wife and husband; the general impression that the husband had perished in his generous devotion to his wife (a duty, certainly, and no more than a duty, but still, under the instincts of self-preservation, a generous duty); sympathy with their long agony, as expressed by their long ramblings, and the earnestness of their efforts to recover their home; awe for the long concealment which rested upon their fate; and pity for the helpless condition of the children,—so young and so

[21] Seat of the royal family.

instantaneously made desolate, and so nearly perishing through the loneliness of their situation, co-operating with stress of weather, had they not been saved by the prudence and timely exertions of a little girl not much above eight years old;—these were the circumstances and necessary adjuncts of the story which pointed and sharpened the public feelings on that occasion. Else the mere general case of perishing upon the mountains is not, unfortunately, so rare, in *any* season of the year, as for itself alone to command a powerful tribute of sorrow from the public mind.

Viewing the World: The Picturesque and Travel

Seeing the details of the natural world and writing of what William calls "the ennobling interchange" of the mind and nature often depend, for descriptive power, on the aesthetic of the picturesque. Reports of daily walks as well as extended tours speak the language of this way of viewing the landscape. The excerpts presented here parallel the forms of Dorothy's writing as she moves through the world. They also highlight the discourse that she and William develop as they explore the world as romantic writers.[1]

❧ William Gilpin
From Observations Relative to Picturesque Beauty

An important writer on the subject was the Reverend William Gilpin (1724–1804). In such works as Three Essays: On Picturesque Beauty; On Picturesque Travel; *and* On Sketching Landscape *(1794), Gilpin defined picturesque elements of landscape: "variety," "irregularity," "ruggedness," "rusticity," "intricacy," "singularity," and "chiaroscuro." He thus placed the picturesque between the tamer, smoother "beautiful" and the overwhelming "sublime." This excerpt from* Gilpin's Observations Relative to Picturesque Beauty Made in the Year 1772 on

---

[1] For example, Molly Lefebure notes: "By 1797, William and Dorothy Wordsworth had established themselves, in the eyes of a still very small, but highly selective circle, as notable personalities in the vanguard of the fashion of picturesque taste and Romantic sensibility" (214). Walking and touring as central enterprises of the nineteenth century have been studied in a number of books: Roger Gilbert, *Walks in the World* (Princeton UP, 1991); Jeffrey Robinson, *The Walk: Notes on a Romantic Image* (U Oklahoma P, 1989); Ann D. Wallace, *Walking, Literature, and English Culture* (Oxford UP, 1993). Robin Jarvis's *Romantic Writing and Pedestrian Travel* (St. Martin's, 1997) contains a particularly insightful chapter on Dorothy as walker.

Several Parts of England; particularly the Mountains, and Lakes of Cumberland, and Westmoreland *describes Grasmere. Other countries, Gilpin writes in the preceding section, may have "grander" scenes, but mountains and lakes are nowhere "better proportioned" than in Cumberland and Westmorland.*

FROM VOLUME I SECTION X

Ambleside is an ordinary village; but delightfully seated. A cove of lofty mountains half incircles it on the north; and the lake of Wynander opens in front; near the shores of which it stands.

The ground between it and the mountains, which are at least two miles distant, is various, broken, and woody. A mountain-torrent, about half a mile from the village, forms a grand cascade; but it was so overgrown with thickets, that we had no point of view to see it from, but the top; which is the most unpicturesque we could have.

From this fall the stream rustles along a narrow valley, or gill, luxuriantly adorned with rock, and wood: and winding through it about a mile, emerges near the head of the lake, into which it enters. This gill was so overgrown with wood, that it appeared almost impervious: but if a path could be carried through it, and the whole a little opened, it might be made very beautiful. A scene in itself so pleasing, with a noble cascade at one end, and an extensive lake at the other, could not fail, to strike the imagination in the most forcible manner.

From Ambleside we set out for Bowness, to take a view of the lake. Part of the road we had traversed, the day before, from Kendal; and were a second time amused by the woody landscape it afforded; and it's[2] sudden, interrupted openings to the lake, before the whole burst of that magnificent scene was presented.—From the higher grounds, above Bowness, we had an elevated view of it's whole extent.

Windermere, or Winander-water, as it is sometimes called, extends from north to south, about twelve or fourteen miles. In breadth, it rarely exceeds two; and is seldom narrower than one. The southern end winds a little towards the west. The northern, and western coasts are wild, and mountainous—the eastern and southern are more depressed; in some parts cultivated, in others woody. Opposite to Bowness, the lake is divided into two parts by a cluster of islands, one of which is larger than the rest.

[2] *It's* for the possessive is common nineteenth-century usage.

Bowness is the capital port-town on the lake; if we may adopt a dignified style, which the grandeur of the country naturally suggests. It is the great mart for fish, and charcoal; both which commodities are largely imported here and carried by land into the country. It's harbour is crowded with vessels of various kinds; some of which are used merely as pleasure-boats in navigating the lake,—In one of these we embarked, and standing out to sea; made for the great island; which we were informed was a very interesting scene.

We soon arrived at it; and standing at the south end, we ordered our boat to meet us at the north point; meaning to traverse it's little boundaries.

A more sequestered spot cannot easily be conceived. Nothing can be more excluded from the noise, and interruption of life or abound with a greater variety of those circumstances, which make retirement pleasing. . . .

He who would take upon him to ornament such a scene as this, would have only to conduct his walk and plantations, so as to take advantage of the grand parts of the continent around him;—to hide what is offensive—and, amidst a choice of great and picturesque scenes, to avoid shewing too much. As he would have, at all times, an exuberance of water, he should not be ostentatious in displaying it. It would be a relief to the eye sometimes to exclude it wholly; and to introduce a mere sylvan scene, with distant mountains rising above it. A transient glance of the water, with some well-chosen objects beyond it, would often also have a good effect and sometimes a grand expansion of the whole.—Thus the objects around, tho unmanageable in themselves, might be brought under command by the assistance of an insular situation.

With regard to the ornamenting of such a scene, an elegant *neatness* is all the improver should aim at. Amidst these grand objects of nature, it would be absurd to catch the eye with the affected decorations of art. The simple idea he would desire to preserve, is, what the place itself suggests, a sequestered retreat. The boundaries should in a great measure be thickets—on the eastern coast especially, which is opposed to the only cultivated part of the country: and if there be any thing in that part worth giving to the eye, it might be given through some unaffected opening.

For thickets, the wild wood of the country would abundantly suffice. It grows luxuriantly, and would soon produce it's effect.

The middle parts of the island, with a few clumps properly disposed, might be neat pasturage, with flocks, and herds which would contrast agreeably with the rough scenery around.

The house, at present, stands too formally in the middle of the island. It might stand better near the southern promontory. The air of this sweet retreat is said to be very pure.*

This island belonged formerly to the Philipsons, a family of note in Westmoreland. During the civil wars, two of them, an elder, and a younger brother, served the king. The former, who was the proprietor of it, commanded a regiment: the latter was a major.

The major, whose name was Robert, was a man of great spirit, and enterprise and for his many feats of personal bravery, had obtained, among the Oliverians[3] of those parts, the appellation of Robin the Devil.

After the war subsided, Col. Briggs, a steady friend to the usurpation, residing at Kendal, under the double character of a leading magistrate (for he was a justice of the peace) and an active commander, held the country in awe. This person having heard, that Major Philipson was at his brother's house on the island in Windermere, resolved, if possible, to seize, and punish a man, who had made himself so particularly obnoxious. With this view he mustered a party, which he thought sufficient; and went himself on the enterprise. How it was conducted, my authority** does not inform us—whether he got together the navigation of the lake, and blockaded the place by sea; or whether, he landed, and carried on his approaches in form. Neither do we learn the strength of the garrison within nor of the works without: tho every gentleman's house was, at that time, in some degree a fortress. All we learn, is, that Major Philipson endured a siege of eight, or ten days with great gallantry; till his brother, the colonel, hearing of his distress, raised a party, and relieved him.

It was now the major's turn to make reprizals. He put himself therefore at the head of a little troop of horse, and rode to Kendal,

---

* [Gilpin's notes indicated with.*] Since this view of Windermere island was taken, it hath been under the hands of improvement. The proprietor I have been told, spent six thousand pounds upon it; with which sum he has contrived to do almost every thing, that one would wish had been left undone. It is now in other hands, which may probably restore it's beauty.

[3] Supporters of Oliver Cromwell, leader of the Puritan faction.

** Dr. Bourn's history of Westmoreland.

where Col. Briggs resided. Here being informed, that the colonel was at prayers, (for it was on a Sunday morning) he stationed his men properly in the avenues; and himself, armed, rode directly into the church. It is said, he intended to seize the colonel, and carry him off: but as this seems to have been totally impracticable, it is rather probable that his intention was to kill him on the spot; and in the midst of the confusion, to escape. Whatever his intention was, it was frustrated; for Briggs happened to be elsewhere.

The congregation, as might be expected, was thrown into great confusion on seeing an armed man, on horseback, enter the church; and the major taking the advantage of their astonishment, turned his horse round, and rode quietly out. But having given an alarm he was presently assaulted as he left the church and being seized; his girths were cut; and he was unhorsed.

At this instant, his party made a furious attack on the assailants; and the major, killing with his own hand, the man, who had seized him, clapped the saddle, ungirthed as it was, upon his horse; and vaulting into it rode full speed through the streets of Kendal calling to his men to follow him; and with his whole party made a safe retreat to his asylum in the lake.—The action marked the man. Many knew him and they who did not, knew as well from the exploit, that it could be nobody, but *Robin the Devil*.—Such are the calamities of civil war! After the direful effects of public opposition cease; revenge, and private malice long keep alive the animosity of individuals.

✤ Mary Russell Mitford
Nutting

Dorothy's journal descriptions of life in Alfoxden and Grasmere may be viewed in the context of the work of Mary Russell Mitford (1787–1855), whose accounts of life in a country village depend on the picturesque aesthetic. One of Mitford's editors, Henry Chorley, compared her to the French landscape painter Claude Lorraine (1600–1682). The "Claude" glass, named after the painter, was used by advocates of the picturesque to frame natural scenes.

Mitford's success as a poet and dramatist was not enough to allow support of her family, ruined by her father's gambling addiction. So, in 1819 she began publishing stories of life in Three Mile Cross, the village to which reduced circumstances had forced her family to move. Thomas Campbell rejected her pieces for New Monthly Magazine, *but they were accepted at the* Lady's Magazine, *where they boosted the circulation from 250 to over 2000, and domestic scenes became the vogue. The pieces were collected and published from 1824 to 1832, and a full edition appeared in 1843. The following essay describes a familiar pastime to readers of the Wordsworths—"Nutting."*

SEPTEMBER 26th.—One of those delicious autumnal days, when the air, the sky, and the earth seem lulled into a universal calm, softer and milder even than May. We sallied forth for a walk, in a mood congenial to the weather and the season, avoiding, by mutual consent, the bright and sunny common, and the gay high-road, and stealing through shady, unfrequented lanes, where we were not likely to meet any one,—not even the pretty family procession which in other years we used to contemplate with so much interest—the father, mother, and children, returning from the wheat-field, the little ones laden with bristling close-tied bunches of wheat-ears, their own gleanings, or a bottle and a basket which had contained their frugal dinner, whilst the mother would carry her babe hushing and lulling it, and the father and an elder child trudged after with the cradle, all seeming weary, and all happy. We shall not see such a procession as this to-day; for the harvest is nearly over, the fields are deserted, the silence may almost be felt. Except the wintry notes of the red-breast, nature herself is mute. But how beautiful, how gentle, how harmonious, how rich! The rain has preserved to the herbage all the freshness and verdure of spring, and the world of leaves has lost nothing of its midsummer brightness, and the hare-bell is on the banks, and the woodbine in the hedges, and the low furze, which the lambs cropped in the spring, has burst again into its golden blossoms.

All is beautiful that the eye can see; perhaps the more beautiful for being shut in with a forest-like closeness. We have no prospect in this labyrinth of lanes, cross-roads, mere cart-ways, leading to the innumerable little farms into which, this part of the parish is divided. Up-hill or down, these quiet woody lanes scarcely give us a peep at the world, except when, leaning over a gate, we look into one of the small enclosures, hemmed in with hedge-rows, so closely set with growing timber, that the meady opening looks almost like a glade in a wood; or when some cottage, planted at a corner of one of the little greens formed by the meeting of these cross-ways, almost startles us by the unexpected sight of the dwellings of men in such a solitude. But that we have more of hill and; dale, and that our cross-roads are excellent in their kind, this side of our parish would resemble the description given of La Vendee, in Madame Laroche-Jacquelin's most interesting book.[4] I am sure if wood can entitle a country to be called Le Bocage, none can have a better right to the name. Even this pretty snug farm-house on the hill-side, with its front covered with the rich vine, which goes wreathing up to the very top of the clustered chimney, and its sloping orchard full of fruit—even this pretty quiet nest can hardly peep out of its leaves. Ah! they are gathering in the orchard harvest. Look at that young rogue in the old mossy apple-tree—that great tree, bending with the weight of its golden-rennets—see how he pelts his little sister beneath with apples as red and as round as her own cheeks, while she, with her outstretched frock, is trying to catch them, and laughing and offering to pelt again as often as one bobs against her; and look at that still younger imp, who, as grave as a judge, is creeping on hands and knees under the tree, picking up the apples as they fall so deedily,[5] and depositing them so honestly in the great basket on the grass, already fixed so firmly and opened so widely, and filled almost to overflowing by the brown rough fruitage of the golden-rennet's next neighbour the russeting; and see that smallest urchin of all, seated apart in infantine state on the turfy bank, with that toothsome piece of deformity a crumpling in each hand now biting from one sweet, hard, juicy morsel and now from another.— Is not that a pretty English picture? And then, farther up the orchard, that bold hardy lad, the eldest-born, who has scaled (Heaven knows how!) the tall, straight upper branch of that great pear-tree, and is sitting there as securely and as fearlessly, in as much real safety and apparent danger, as a sailor on the top-mast. Now he shakes the tree with a mighty swing that brings down a pelting shower of stony bergamots, which the father gathers rapidly up, whilst the mother can hardly assist for her motherly fear—a

---

[4] [Mitford] An almost equally interesting account of that very peculiar and interesting scenery, may be found in "The Mind of La Vendee," an English novel, remarkable for its simplicity and truth of painting, written by Mrs. Le Noir, the daughter of Christopher Smart, an inheritrix of much of his talent. Her works deserve to be better known.

[5] [Mitford] "Deedily,"—I am not quite sure that this word is good English; but it is genuine Hampshire, and is used by the most correct of female writers, Miss Austen. It means (and it is no small merit that it has no exact synonyme) any thing done with a profound and plodding attention, an action which engrosses all the powers of mind and body.

fear which only spurs the spirited boy to bolder ventures. Is not that a pretty picture? And they are such a handsome family too, the Brookers. I do not know that there is any gipsy blood, but there is the true gipsy complexion, richly brown, with cheeks and lips so deeply red, black hair curling close to their heads in short crisp rings, white shining teeth—and such eyes!—That sort of beauty entirely eclipses your mere roses and lilies. Even Lizzy, the prettiest of fair children, would look poor and watery by the side of Willy Brooker, the sober little personage who is picking up the apples with his small chubby hands, and filling the basket so orderly, next to his father the most useful man in the field. "Willy!" He hears without seeing; for we are quite hidden by the high bank, and a spreading hawthorn bush that overtops it, though between the lower branches and the grass we have found a convenient peephole. "Willy!" The voice sounds to him like some fairy dream, and the black eyes are raised from the ground with sudden wonder, the long silky eye-lashes thrown back till they rest on the delicate brow, and a deeper blush is burning on those dark cheeks, and a smile is dimpling about those scarlet lips. But the voice is silent now, and the little quiet boy, after a moment's pause, is gone coolly to work again. He is indeed a most lovely child, I think some day or other he must marry Lizzy; I shall propose the match to their respective mammas. At present the parties are rather too young for a wedding— the intended bridegroom being, as I should judge, six, or thereabout, and the fair bride barely five,—but at least we might have a betrothment after the royal fashion,—there could be no harm in that. Miss Lizzy, I have no doubt, would be as demure and coquettish as if ten winters more had gone over her head, and poor Willy would open his innocent black eyes, and wonder what was going forward. They would be the very Oberon and Titania of the village, the fairy king and queen.

Ah! here is the hedge along which the periwinkle wreathes and twines so profusely, with its ever-green leaves shining like the myrtle, and its starry blue flowers. It is seldom found wild in this part of England; but, when we do meet with it, it is so abundant and so welcome,—the very robin-redbreast of flowers, a winter friend. Unless in those unfrequent frosts which destroy all vegetation, it blossoms from September to June, surviving the last lingering crane's-bill, forerunning the earliest primrose, hardier even than the mountain daisy,—peeping out from beneath the snow, looking at itself in the ice, smiling through the tempests of life, and yet welcoming and enjoying the sun-beams. Oh, to be like that flower!

The little spring that has been bubbling under the hedge all along the hill-side, begins, now that we have mounted the eminence and are imperceptibly descending, to deviate into a capricious variety of clear deep pools and channels, so narrow and so choked with weeds, that a child might overstep them. The hedge has also changed its character. It is no longer the close compact vegetable wall of hawthorn, and maple, and brier-roses, intertwined with bramble and woodbine, and crowned with large elms or thickly-set saplings. No! the pretty meadow which rises high above us, backed and almost surrounded by a tall coppice, needs no defence on our side but its own steep bank, garnished with tufts of broom, with pollard oaks wreathed with ivy, and here and there with long patches of hazel overhanging the water. "Ah, there are still nuts on that bough!" and in an instant my dear companion, active and eager and delighted as a boy, has hooked down with his walking-stick one of the lissome hazel stalks, and cleared it of its tawny clusters, and in another moment he has mounted the bank, and is in the midst of the nuttery, now transferring the spoil from the lower branches into that vast variety of pockets which gentlemen carry about them, bending the tall tops into the lane, holding them down by main force, so that I might reach them and enjoy the pleasure of collecting some of the plunder myself. A very great pleasure he knew it would be. I doffed my shawl, tucked up my flounces, turned my straw bonnet into a basket, and began gathering and scrambling—for, manage it how you may, nutting is scrambling work,—those boughs, however tightly you may grasp them by the young fragrant twigs and the bright green leaves, will recoil and burst away; but there is a plea-sure even in that: so on we go, scrambling and gathering with all our might and all our glee. Oh what an enjoyment! My life long I have had a passion for that sort of seeking which implies finding, (the secret, I believe, of the love of field-sports, which is in man's mind a natural impulse,)—therefore I love violeting,—therefore, when we had a fine garden, I used to love to gather strawberries, and cut asparagus, and, above all, to collect the filberts from the shrubberies: but this hedge-row nutting beats that sport all to nothing. That was a make-believe thing, compared with this; there was no surprise, no suspense, no unexpectedness—it was as inferior to this wild nutting, as the turning out of a bag-fox is to unearthing the fellow, in the eyes of a staunch fox-hunter. Oh what enjoyment this nut-gathering is! They are in such abundance, that it seems as if there were not a boy in the parish, nor a young man, nor a young woman,—for a basket of nuts is the universal tribute of country gallantry; our pretty damsel Harriet has had at least half-a-dozen this season; but no one has found out these. And they are so full too, we lose half of them from over-ripeness; they drop from the socket at the slightest motion. If we lose, there is one who finds. May is as fond of nuts as a squirrel, and cracks the shell and extracts the kernel with equal dexterity. Her white glossy head is upturned now to watch them as they fall. See how her neck is thrown back like that of a swan, and how beautifully her folded ears quiver with expectation, and how her quick eye follows the rustling noise, and her light feet dance and pat the ground, and leap up with eagerness, seeming almost sustained in the air, just as I have seen her when Brush is beating a hedge-row, and she knows from his questing that there is a hare afoot. See, she has caught that nut just before it touched the water; but the water would have been no defence,—she fishes them from the bottom, she delves after them amongst the matted grass—even my bonnet—how beggingly she looks at that! "Oh what a pleasure nutting is!—Is it not, May?" But the pockets are almost full, and so is the basket-bonnet, and that bright watch the sun says it is late; and after all it is wrong to rob the poor boys—"Is it not, May?"—May shakes her graceful head denyingly, as if she understood the question—"And we must go home now—must we not? But we will come nutting again some time or other—shall we not, my May?"

✤ Ann Radcliffe
From *A Journey Made in the Summer of 1794 Through Holland* . . .

Best known for her Gothic novels such as The Romance of the Forest *(1791) or* The Mysteries of Udolpho *(1794), Ann Radcliffe (1764–1823) was also a writer of travel literature. A* Journey Made in the Summer of 1794 Through Holland and the Western Frontier of Germany with a Return Down the Rhine to Which are Added Observations During a Tour to the Lakes of Lancashire, Westmoreland, and Cumberland *(1795) covers much of the same ground that Dorothy explores in her journals. Like many tourists, Radcliffe is happy to greet the cliffs of Dover on her return and to extol the superiority of the English way of life. Her English*

tour takes her through such places as Ullswater, Penrith, Threlkeld, Derwentwater, Skiddaw, Hawkeshead, Ambleside, and Grasmere—the scenes of Dorothy's life.
[Return to England]

At length, the breeze wafting us more to the north, we discriminated the bolder features of the English coast, and, about noon, found ourselves nearly in the middle of the channel, having Picardy on our left and Kent on the right, its white cliffs aspiring with great majesty over the flood. The sweeping bay of Dover, with all its chalky heights, soon after opened. The town appeared low on the shore within, and the castle, with round and massy towers, crowned the vast rock, which advancing into the sea, formed the eastern point of the crescent, while Shakespeare's cliffy boulder still and sublime as the eternal name it bears, was the western promontory of the bay. The height and grandeur of this cliff were particularly striking, when a ship was seen sailing at its base, diminished by comparison to an inch. From hence the cliffs towards Folkstone, though still broken and majestic, gradually decline. There are, perhaps, few prospects of sea and shore more animated and magnificent than this. The vast expanse of water, the character of the cliffs, that guard the coast, the ships of war and various merchantmen moored in the Downs, the lighter vessels skimming along the channel, and the now distant shore of France, with Calais glimmering faintly, and hinting of different modes of life and a new world, all these circumstances formed a scene of pre-eminent combination, and led to interesting reflection. Our vessel was bound to Deal, and leaving Dover on the fourth, we entered that noble bay, which the rich shores of Kent open for the sea. Gentle hills, swelling all round from the water, green with woods, or cultivation, and speckled with towns and villages, with now and then the towers of an old fortress, offered a landscape particularly cheering to eyes accustomed to the monotonous flatness of Dutch views. And we landed in England under impressions of delight more varied and strong than can be conceived, without referring to the joy of an escape from districts where there was scarcely an home for the natives, and to the love of our own country, greatly enhanced by all that had been seen of others.

Between Deal and London, after being first struck by the superior appearance and manners of the people to those of the countries we had been lately accustomed to, a contrast too obvious as well as too often remarked to be again insisted upon, but which made all the ordinary circumstances of the journey seem new and delightful, the difference between the landscapes of England and Germany occurred forcibly to notice. The large scale, in which every division of land appeared in Germany, the long corn grounds, the huge stretches of hills, the vast plains and the wide vallies could not but be beautifully opposed by the varieties and undulations of English surface, with gently swelling slopes, rich in verdure, thick inclosures, woods, bowery hop grounds, flickered mansions, announcing the wealth, and substantial farms, with neat villages, the comfort of the country, which landscape may be compared to cabinet pictures, delicately beautiful and highly finished; German scenery to paintings for a vestibule, of bold outline and often sublime, but coarse and to be viewed with advantage only from a distance. On our way over these wilds, parts of which are called Endmoor and Cowbrows, we overtook only long trains of coal carts, and, after ten miles of bleak mountain road, began to desire a temporary home, somewhat sooner than we perceived Kendal, white-smoking in the dark vale. As we approached, the outlines of its ruinous castle were just distinguishable through the gloom, scattered in masses over the top of a small round hill, on the right. At the entrance of the town, the river Kent dashed in foam down a weir; beyond it, on a green slope, the gothic tower of the church was half hid by a cluster of dark trees; gray fells glimmered in the distance.

Radcliffe's Description of Gowbarrow Park
Where Dorothy Sees the Daffodils
(See DW60–61, WmW255–256).

Leaving the hamlet of Watermillock at some distance on the left, and passing the seat of Mr. Robinson, sequestered in the gloom of beech and sycamores, there are fine views over the second reach, as the road descends the common towards Gowbarrow. Among the boldest fells, that breast the lake on the left shore, are Holling-fell and Swarth-fell, now no longer boasting any part of the forest of Martindale, but shewing huge walls of naked rock, and scars which many torrents have inflicted. One channel only in this dry season retained its shining stream; the chasm was dreadful, parting the mountain from the summit to the base; and its waters in winter, leaping in foam from precipice to precipice, must be infinitely sublime;

not, however, even then from their mass, but from the length and precipitancy of their descent.

The perspective as the road descends into Gowbarrow-park is perhaps the very finest on the lake. The scenery of the first reach is almost tame when compared with this, and it is difficult to say where it can be equalled for Alpine sublimity, and for effecting wonder and awful elevation. The lake, after expanding at a distance to great breadth, once more loses itself beyond the enormous pile of rock called Place-fell, opposite to which the shore, seeming to close upon all further progress, is bounded by two promontories covered with woods, that shoot their luxuriant foliage to the water's edge. The shattered mass of gray rock, called Yew-crag, rises immediately over these, and, beyond, a glen opens to a chaos of mountains more solemn in their aspect, and singular in their shapes, than any which have appeared, point crowding over point in lofty succession. Among these is Stone-cross-pike and huge Helvellyn, scowling over all; but though this retains its preeminence, its dignity is lost in the mass of alps around and below it. A fearful gloom involved them, the shadows of a stormy sky upon mountains of dark rock and heath. All this is seen over the woody fore-ground of the park, which, soon shrouding us in its bowery lanes, allowed the eye and the fancy to repose, while venturing, towards new forms and assemblages of sublimity. Meantime, the green shade, under which we passed, where the sultry low of cattle, and the sound of streams hurrying from the heights through the copses of Gowbarrow to the lake below, were all that broke the stillness; these, with gleamings of the water, close on the left, between the foliage and which, was ever changing its hue, sometimes assuming the soft purple of a pigeon's neck, at others the silvery tint of sunshine—these circumstances of imagery were in soothing and beautiful variety with the gigantic visions we had.

From Keswick to Windemere

The road from Keswick to Ambelside commences by the ascent of Castle-rigg, the mountain, which the Penrith road descends, and which, on that side, is crowned by a Druid's temple. The rise is now very laborious, but the views it affords over the vale of Keswick are not dearly purchased by the fatigue. All Bassenthwaite, its mountains softening away in the perspective, and terminating, on the west, in the sister woods of Wythorp-brows, extends from the eye and, immediately beneath, the northern end of Derwentwater, with Cawfey-pike, Thornthwaite-fell, the rich upland vale of Newland peeping from between their bases, and the fairy woods of Foepark jutting into the lake below. But the finest prospect is from a gate about halfway up the hill, whence you look down upon the head of Derwentwater, with all the alps of Borrowdale, opening darkly.

After descending Castle-rigg and crossing the top of St. John's vale, we seemed as if going into banishment from society, the road then leading over a plain, closely surrounded by mountains so wild, that neither a cottage, or a wood soften their rudeness, and so steep and barren, that not even sheep appear upon their sides. From this plain the road enters Legberwaite, a narrow valley, running at the back of Borrowdale, green at the bottom, and varied with a few farms, but without wood, and with fells of gray precipices, rising to great height and nearly perpendicular on either hand, whose fronts are marked only by the torrents, that tumble from their utmost summits, and perpetually occur. We often stopped to listen to their hollow sounds amidst the solitary greatness of the scene, and to watch their headlong fall down the rocky chasms, their white foam and silver line contrasting with the dark hue of the clefts. In sublimity of descent these were frequently much superior to that of Lowdore, but as much inferior to it in mass of water and picturesque beauty.

As the road ascended towards Helvellyn, we looked back through this vast rocky vista to the sweet vale of St. John, lengthening the perspective, and saw, as through a telescope, the broad broken steeps of Saddleback and the points of Skiddaw, darkly blue, closing it to the north. The grand rivals of Cumberland were now seen together; and the road, soon winding high over the skirts of Helvellyn, brought us to Leathes-water, to which the mountain forms a vast side skreen, during its whole length. This is a long, but narrow and unadorned lake, having little else than walls of rocky fells, starting from its margin. Continuing on the precipice, at some height from the shore, the road brought us, after three miles, to the poor village of Wythburn, and soon after to the foot of Dunmail Rays, which, though a considerable ascent, forms the dip of two lofty mountains, Steel-fell and Seat Sandle, that rise with finely sweeping lines, on each side, and shut up the vale. . . . Beyond Dunmail Rays, one of the grand passes from Cumberland into Westmoreland, Helm-crag rears its crest, a strange fantastic summit round, yet jagged and splintered, like the wheel of a water-mill, overlooking Grasmere, which, soon after, opened below. A green spreading circle of mountains embosoms this small lake, and, beyond, a wider range rises in amphitheatre, whose rocky tops are rounded and scolloped, yet are great, wild, irregular, and were then over-spread with a tint of faint purple. The softest verdure margins the water, and mingles with corn enclosures and woods, that wave up the hills; but scarcely a cottage any where appears, except at the northern end of the lake, where the village of Grasmere and its very neat white church stand among trees, near the shore, with Helm-crag and a multitude of fells, rising over it and beyond each other in the perspective. The lake was clear as glass, reflecting the headlong mountains, with every feature of every image on its tranquil banks; and one green island varies, but scarcely adorns its surface, bearing only a rude and now shadeless hut. At a considerable height above the water, the road undulates for a mile, till, near the southern end of Grasmere, it mounts the crags of a fell, and seemed carrying us again into such scenes of ruin and privation as we had quitted with Legberthwaite and Leathes-water. But, descending the other side of the mountain, we were soon cheered by the view of plantations, enriching the banks of Rydal-water, and by thick woods, mingling among cliffs above the narrow lake, which winds through a close valley, for about a mile. This lake is remarkable for the beauty of its small round islands, luxuriant with elegant trees and shrubs, and whole banks are green to the water's edge. Rydal-hall stand's finely on an eminence, somewhat withdrawn from the east end; in a close romantic nook, among old woods, that feather the fells which rise over their summits, and spread widely along the neighbouring eminences. This antient white mansion looks over a rough grassy descent, screened by groves of oak and majestic planes, towards the head of Windermere, about two miles distant, a small glimpse of which is caught beyond the wooded steeps of a narrow valley. In the woods and in the disposition of the ground round Rydal-hall there is a charming wildness, that suits the character of the general scene; and, wherever art appears, it is with graceful plainness and meek subjection to nature.

The taste, by which a cascade in the pleasure–grounds, pouring under the arch of a rude bridge, amidst the green tint of woods, is shewn through a darkened garden–house, and, therefore, with all the effect, which the opposition of light and shade can give, is even not too artificial; so admirably is the intent accomplished of making all the light, that is admitted, fall upon the objects, which are chiefly meant to be observed.

The road to Ambleside runs through the valley in front of Rydal-hall, and for some distance among the grounds that belong to it, where again the taste of the owner is conspicuous in the disposition of plantations among pastures of extraordinary richness, and where pure rivulets are suffered to wind without restraint over their dark rocky channels. Woods mantle up the cliffs on either side of this sweet valley, and, higher still, the craggy summits of the fells crowd over the scene. Two miles among its pleasant shades, near the banks of the murmuring Rotha, brought us to Ambleside, a black and very antient little town, hanging on the lower steeps of a mountain, where the vale opens to the head of Windermere.

❧ Henry Crabb Robinson
From *Diaries, Reminiscences, and Correspondence*

While he may have been a barrister-at-law by profession, Henry Crabb Robinson (1775–1867) devoted himself to romantic writers, painters, and musicians, whose art and lives he appreciated and described in his journals and letters. His Diaries, Reminiscences, and Correspondence, *from which this excerpt is taken, was edited and published posthumously in 1869 by Thomas Sadler. Accompanying the Wordsworths to the continent, Robinson presents a version very different from Dorothy's account. Scenery, he observes, has been written about extensively; "I abstain" he writes, "from descriptions of the usual sights." He wants to chronicle people and gossip. He also references William's poetic version of the tour:* Memorials of a Tour on the Continent 1820 *(1822). All poems mentioned are from this consecutively numbered collection.*

Swiss Tour with the Wordsworths.—This account of my first tour in Switzerland may not improperly be compared to the often-cited performance of "Hamlet," with the character of Hamlet left out. The fact being that every place in Switzerland is known to every one, or may be, from the innumerable books that have been published, the names are sufficient, and I shall therefore content myself with relating the few personal incidents of the journey, and a very few particulars about places. What I have to say will probably disappoint the reader, who may be aware that the journey was made in the company of no less a person than the poet Wordsworth.

He came to London with Mrs. and Miss Wordsworth in the month of June, partly to be present at the marriage of Mrs. Wordsworth's kinsman, Mr. Monkhouse, with Miss Horrocks, of Preston, in Lancashire, and to accompany them in a marriage tour. I was very much gratified by a proposal to be their companion on as much of the journey as my circuit would permit. It was a part of their plan to go by way of the Rhine and it was calculated (justly, as the event showed) that I might, by hastening through France, reach them in time to see with them a large portion of the beauties of Switzerland.

Mr. Wordsworth published on his return a small volume, entitled, "Memorials of a Tour on the Continent," one of the least popular of his works. Had it appeared twenty years afterwards, when his fame was established, the reception would have been very different.

[. . . . .]

On the 14th I went to Berne. I rose before five, and saw the greater part of the town before breakfast. It is one of the most singular places I ever saw. It stands on a sort of peninsular elevation formed by the River Aare, and consists of two or three long streets, with a few others intersecting them. The houses are of freestone, and are built in part on arches, under which there is a broad passage, with shops within. No place, therefore, can be cooler in summer or warmer in winter. In the middle of the streets there is a channel with a rapid stream of water. About the town there are fountains in abundance, crowned with statues of armed men, Swiss heroes. And there are gross and whimsical representations of bears[6] on several of the public buildings. Two living bears are kept in a part of the fosse[7] of the town. I walked to the Enge Terrace, from which the view of the Bernese Alps is particularly fine. The people are as picturesque as the place. The women wear black caps fitting the head closely, with prodigious black gauze wings: Miss Wordsworth calls it the butterfly cap. In general, I experienced civility enough from the people I spoke to, but one woman, carrying a burthen on her head, said sharply, on my asking the way, "Ich kann kein Welsch" (I can't speak any foreign language)." And on my pressing the question, being curious to see more of her, and at last saying, "Sie ist dumm" (she is, stupid), she screamed out, "Fort, fort" (go along).

---

[6] Bears appear on the town's coat of arms.
[7] Moat.

On the 15th I went to Solothurn, and an acquaintance began out of which a catastrophe sprang. In the stage between Berne and Solothurn, which takes a circuit through an unpicturesque, flat country, were two very interesting young men, who I soon learned were residing with a Protestant clergyman at Geneva, and completing their education. The elder was an American, aged twenty-one, named Goddard. He had a sickly air, but was intelligent, and not ill-read in English poetry. The other was a fine handsome lad, aged sixteen, of the name of Trotter, son of the then, or late, Secretary to the Admiralty. He was of Scotch descent. They were both genteel and well-behaved young men, with the grace communicated by living in good company. We became at once acquainted,—I being then, as now, young in the facility of forming acquaintance. We spent a very agreeable day and evening together, partly in a walk to a hermitage in the neighbourhood, and took leave of each other at night,—I facing bound for Lucerne, they for Zurich. But in the morning I saw, to my surprise, my young friends with their knapsacks in their hands ready to accompany me. Goddard said, with a very amiable modesty, "If you will permit us, we wish to go with you. I am an admirer of Wordsworth's poems, and I should be delighted merely to see him. Of course I expect no more." I was gratified by this proposal, and we had a second day of enjoyment, and this through a very beautiful country. My expectations were not disappointed. I had heard of the Wordsworth party from travellers with whom we met. I found my friends at the Cheval Blanc. From them I had a most cordial reception, and I was myself in high spirits. Mrs. Wordsworth wrote in her journal: "H. C. R. was drunk with pleasure, and made us drunk too." [1] My companions also were kindly received.

I found that there was especial good luck attending my arrival. Wordsworth had met with an impudent fellow, a guide, who, because he would not submit to extortion, had gone off with the ladies' cloaks to Sarnen. Now it so happened that one of our fellow travellers this day was the Statthalter[8] of Sarnen. I spoke to him before we went to bed, and we arranged to go to Sarnen the next day. We rose at four o'clock, had a delightful walk to Winkel, embarked there on the lake, sailed to Alpnach, and then proceeded on foot. The judge was not betrayed into any impropriety. He had heard Mr. Wordsworth's story, and on going to the inn, he, without suffering Mr. Wordsworth to say a word, most judiciously

---

[8] Governor-general of a region.

interrogated the landlord, who was present when the bargain was made. He confirmed every part of Mr. Wordsworth's statement. On this, the Statthalter said, "I hear the man has not returned, a fact which shows that he is in the wrong. I know him to be a bad fellow. He will be home this evening, you may rely on it, and you shall have the cloaks to-morrow." Next day the man came, and was very humble.

Wordsworth and I returned to dinner, and found my young friends already in great favour with the ladies. After dinner we walked through the town, which has no other remarkable feature than the body of water flowing through it, and the several covered wooden bridges. In the angles of the roof of these bridges there are paintings on historical and allegorical subjects. One series from the Bible, another from the Swiss war against Austria, a third called the Dance of Death. The last is improperly called, for Death does not force his partner to an involuntary waltz, as in the famous designs which go by Holbein's[9] name, but appears in all the pictures an unwelcome visitor. There are feeling and truth in many of the conceptions, but the expression is too often ludicrous, and too often coarsely didactic.

August 18th—Proceeded on our journey. I purchased a knapsack, and sent my portmanteau to Geneva. All the party were, in like manner, put on short commons as to luggage, and our plan of travelling was this: in the plains and level valleys we had a char-a-banc,[10] and we walked up and down the mountains. Once only we hired mules, and these, the guides only used. Our luggage was so small, even for five (Mrs. Monkhouse and Miss Horrocks did not travel about with the rest of the party), that a single guide could carry the whole.

We sailed on the lake as far as Kusnacht, the two young men being still our companions; and between two and three we began to ascend the Rigi, an indispensable achievement in a Swiss tour. We engag'd beds at the Staffel, and went on to see the sun set, but we were not fortunate in the weather. Once or twice there were gleams of light on some of the lakes, but there was little charm of colouring. After an early and comfortable supper we enjoyed the distant

[9] As court painter to Henry VIII, Hans Holbein (1497–1543) became known for his portraits. The Bavarian painter also created a series of 41 woodcuts entitled "Dance of Death."

[10] Tour bus.

lightning; but it soon became very severe, and some of the rooms in the hotel were flooded with rain. Our rest was disturbed by a noisy party, who, unable to obtain beds for themselves, resolved that no one else should enjoy his. The whole night was spent by them in an incessant din of laughing, singing, and shouting. We were called up between three and four A.M., but had a very imperfect view from this "dread summit of the Queen of Mountains"[11]—Regina montium. The most beautiful part of the scene was that which arose from the clouds below us. They rose in succession, sometimes concealing the country, and then opening to our view dark lakes, and gleams of very brilliant green. They sometimes descended as if into an abyss beneath us. We saw a few of the snow-mountains illuminated by the first rays of the sun.

My journal simply says: "After breakfast our young gentlemen left us." I afterwards wrote, "We separated at a spot well suited to the parting of those who were to meet no more. Our party descended through the valley of our 'Lady of the Snow,' and our late companions went to Arth. We hoped to meet in a few weeks at Geneva."

I will leave the order of time, and relate now all that appertains to this sad history. The young men gave us their address, and we promised to inform them when we should be at Geneva, on our return. But on that return we found that poor Goddard had perished in the lake of Zurich, on the third day after our leave-taking on the Rigi.

I heard the story from Trotter on the 23rd of September. They had put themselves in a crazy boat and a storm arising, the boat overset. It righted itself to no purpose. Trotter swam to the shore, but Goddard was not seen again. Trotter was most hospitably received by a Mr. Keller, near whose house the catastrophe took place. The body was cast ashore next day, and afterwards interred in the neighbouring churchyard of Kusnacht. An inscription was placed near the spot where the body was found, and a mural monument erected in the church. At the funeral a pathetic address was delivered by the Protestant clergyman, which I read in the Zurich paper. We were all deeply impressed by the event. Wordsworth, I knew, was not fond of drawing the subjects of his poems from occurrences in themselves interesting, and therefore, though I urged

---

[11] *Memorials of a Tour on the Continent:* "XXXIII Elegiac Stanzas." Subsequent roman-numbered identifications are cited in the text.

him to write on this tragic incident, I little expected he would. There is, however, a beautiful elegiac poem by him on the subject. (To the later editions there is prefixed a prose introduction. This I wrote. Mr. Wordsworth wrote to me for information, and I drew up the account in the first person.)

> "And we were gay, our hearts at ease;
> With pleasure dancing through the frame
> We journeyed; all we knew of care—
> Our path that straggled here and there;
> Of trouble—but the fluttering breeze;
> Of Winter—but a name.
> If foresight could have rent the veil
> Of three short days—but hush—no more!
> Calm is the grave, and calmer none
> Than that to which thy cares are gone,
> Thou victim of the stormy gale;
> Asleep on Zurich's shore.
> Oh, Goddard!—what art thou?—a name—
> A sunbeam follow'd by a shade." (XXXIII: *Elegaic Stanzas*)

In a subsequent visit to Switzerland I called at Mr. Keller's, and saw some of the ladies of the house, who gave me full particulars. I afterwards became acquainted, in Italy, with Goddard's nearest surviving relative, a sister, then married to a Mr.———. The winter preceding I was at Rome, when a Mrs. Kirkman, the wife of an American gentleman, once Principal of Harvard College, asked me whether I had ever known a Mr. Goddard, her countryman. On my answering in the affirmative, she said, "I am sorry to hear it, for there has been a lady here in search of you. However, she will be here again on her return from Naples." And in a few months I did see her. It was Goddard's sister. She informed me that Wordsworth's poem had afforded her mother great comfort, and that she had come to Europe mainly to collect all information still to be had about her poor brother; that she had seen the Kellers with whom she was pleased, and that she had taken notes of all the circumstances of her brother's fate; that she had seen Trotter, had been to Rydal Mount, and learned from Wordsworth of my being in Italy. She was a woman of taste, and of some literary pretensions.

On my return to England, I was very desirous to renew my acquaintance with Trotter, but I inquired after him in vain. After a time, when I had relaxed my inquiries, I heard of him accidentally— that he was a stock-broker, and had married a Miss Otter, daughter of the Bishop of Chichester. I had learned this just before one of the balloting evenings at the Athenaeum[12]—when, seeing Strutt there, and beginning my inquiries about his brother-in-law, he stopped them by saying, "You may ask himself, for there he is. He has been a member of the Athenaeum these twelve years!" He called to Trotter, "Here is a gentleman who wants to speak with you."—"Do you recollect me?"—"No, I do not."—"Do you recollect poor Goddard?"—"You can be no one but Mr. Robinson." We were glad to see each other, and our acquaintance was renewed. The fine youth is now the intelligent man of business. He has written a pamphlet on the American State Stocks. Many years ago he came up from the country, travelling fifty miles to have the pleasure of breakfasting with Mr. and Mrs. Wordsworth at my apartments.

To go back to the 19th of August, after parting from our young companions we proceeded down the valley in which is the chapel dedicated to our Lady of the Snow, the subject of Wordsworth's nineteenth poem. The preceding eighteen have to do with objects which had been seen before I joined the party. The elegiac stanzas are placed near the end of the collection, I know not for what reason. The stanzas on the chapel express poetically the thoughts which a prosaic mind like mine might receive from the numerous votive offerings hung on the walls. There are pictures representing accidents,—such as drowning, falling from a horse, and the Mother and the Child are in the clouds,—it being understood that the escape proceeded from her aid. Some crutches with painted inscriptions bear witness to the miracles wrought on the lame.

> "To thee, in this aerial cleft,
> As to a common centre, tend
> All sufferers that no more rely
> On mortal succour—all who sigh
> And pine, of human hope bereft,
> Nor wish for earthly friend.
>
> * * * * * *
>
> Thy very name, O Lady! flings
> O'er blooming fields and gushing springs
> A tender sense of shadowy fear,
> And chastning sympathies!" (XIX: *Our Lady of the Snow*).

---

[12] An elite gentleman's club founded in 1823. Women were admitted in 2002.

We passed the same day through Goldau, a desolate spot, once a populous village, overwhelmed by the slip from the Rossberg.

On the 20th at Schwyz, which Wordsworth called the "heart" of Switzerland, as Berne is the "head" (XXI). Passing through Brunnen, we reached Altorf on the 21st, the spot which suggested Wordsworth's twentieth effusion. My prose remark on the people shows the sad difference between observation and fancy. I wrote: "These patriotic recollections are delightful when genuine, but the physiognomy of the people does not speak in favour of their ancestors. The natives of the district have a feeble and melancholy character. The women are afflicted by goiter.[13] The children beg, as in other Catholic cantons. The little children, with cross-bows in their hands, sing unintelligible songs. Probably Wilhelm Tell serves, like Henri Quatre, as a name to beg by. But what says the true poet?—

> "Thrice happy burghers, peasants, warriors old,
> Infants in arms, and ye, that as ye go
> Homeward or schoolward, ape what ye behold;
> Heroes before your time, in frolic fancy bold!"
> "And when that calm Spectatress from on high
> Looks down—the bright and solitary moon,
> Who never gazes but to beautify;
> And snow-fed torrents, which the blaze of noon
> Roused into fury, murmur a soft tune
> That fosters peace, and gentleness recalls;
> *Then* might the passing monk receive a boon
> Of saintly pleasure from these pictured walls,
> While, on the warlike groups, the mellowing lustre falls" (XX:
> *Effusion in Presence of the Painted Tower of Tell at Altorf*).

We next crossed the St. Gotthard. Wordsworth thinks this pass more beautiful than the more celebrated [a blank here]. We slept successively at Amsteg on the 22nd, Hospenthal on the 23rd, and Airolo on the 24th. On the way we were overtaken by a pedestrian, a young Swiss, who had studied at Heidelberg, and was going to Rome. He had his flute, and played the Ranz des Vaches. Wordsworth begged me to ask him to do this, which I did on condition that he wrote a sonnet on it. It is XXII. of the collection. The young man was intelligent, and expressed pleasure in our company. We were sorry when he took French leave. We were English, and I

---

[13] Enlarged thyroid gland, that appears as swelling of the neck front. Often occurs owing to lack of iodine in the diet.

have no doubt he feared the expense of having such costly companions. He gave a sad account of the German Universities, and said that Sand, the murderer of Kotzebue, had many apologists among the students.[14]

We then proceeded on our half-walk and half-drive, and slept on the 25th at Bellinzona, the first decidedly Italian town. We walked to Locarno, where we resisted the first, and indeed almost the only, attempt at extortion by an innkeeper on our journey. Our landlord demanded twenty-five francs for a luncheon, the worth of which could scarcely be three. I tendered a ducat (twelve francs), and we carried away our luggage. We had the good fortune to find quarters in a new house, the master of which had not been spoiled by receiving English guests.

On the 27th we had a row to Luino, on the Maggiore, a walk to Ponte Tresa, and then a row to Lugano, where we went to an excellent hotel, kept by a man of the name of Rossi, a respectable man.

Our apartments consisted of one handsome and spacious room, in which were Mr. and Mrs. Wordsworth (this room fronted the beautiful lake); a small, back room, occupied by Miss Wordsworth, with a window looking into a dirty yard, and having an internal communication with a two-bedded room, in which Monkhouse and I slept. I had a very free conversation with Rossi about the Queen,[15] who had been some time in his house. It is worth relating here, and might have been worth making known in England, had the trial then going on had another issue. He told me, but not emphatically, that when the Queen came, she first slept in the large room, but not liking that, she removed to the back room. "And Bergami" said Rossi, "had the room in which you and the other gentleman slept."—"And was there," I asked, "the same communications then that there is now between the two rooms?"—"Of course," he replied. "It was in the power, certainly, of the Queen

---

[14] In 1819, Karl Ludwig Sand, a student, murdered the playwright August von Kotzebue, a conservative critic of the growing democratic student movements. Metternich used the assassination as justification for the repressive Carlsbad Decrees.

[15] The marriage of Caroline of Brunswick to George Prince of Wales was disastrous from the start. She so repulsed him that he refused to be near her; she lived a notorious life in England and abroad. The House of Lords tried her for adultery with (among others) Bartolomeo Bergami, not only foreign but also lower class. The trial lasted over fifty days, but partly owing to Caroline's popularity with the people and the brilliance of her lawyer, Lord Brougham, the case was dropped. She tried to be crowned at George's coronation, but was barred from Westminster Abbey; she died two and a half weeks later.

and Bergami to open the door: whether it was opened or not, no one can say." He added, "I know nothing; none of my servants know anything." The most favourable circumstance related by Rossi was, that Bergami's brother did not fear to strike off much from the bill. He added, too, that the Queen was surrounded by *cattiva gente*.[16]

On the 28th, we took an early walk up the mountain San Salvador, which produced No. XXIV of Wordsworth's Memorial Poems. Though the weather was by no means favourable, we enjoyed a much finer view than from the Rigi. The mountains in the neighbourhood are beautiful, but the charm of the prospect lies in a glimpse of distant mountains. We saw a most elegant pyramid, literally in the sky, partly black, and partly shining like silver. It was the Simplon. Mont Blanc and Monte Rosa were seen in parts. Clouds concealed the bases, and too soon also the summits. This splendid vision lasted but a few minutes. The plains of Piedmont were hardly visible, owing to the black clouds which covered this part of the horizon. We could, however, see in the midst of a dark surface a narrow ribbon of white, which we were told was the Po. We were told the direction in which Milan lay, but could not see the cathedral.

The same day we went on to Menaggio, on the Lake Como. This, in Wordsworth's estimation, is the most beautiful of the lakes. On the 29th and 30th we slept at Cadenabbia, and "fed our eyes"—

> "in paths sun-proof
> With purple of the trellis roof,
> That through the jealous leaves escapes
> From Cadenabbia's pendent grapes" (XXV: *The
> Italian Itinerary and the Swiss Goatherd*).

The beds in which Monkhouse and I slept at Menaggio were intolerable, but we forgot the sufferings of night in the enjoyment of the morning. I wrote in my journal: "This day has been spent on the lake, and so much exquisite pleasure I never had on water. The tour, or rather excursion, we have been making surpassed in scenery all that I have ever made; and Wordsworth asserts the same. I write now from an inn where we have been served with all the promptitude of an English hotel, and with neatness equal to that of Holland. But the pleasure can hardly be recorded. It consists in the contemplation of scenes absolutely indescribable by words, and in

---

[16] Naughty or bad people.

sensations for which no words have been even invented. We were lucky in meeting two honest fellows of watermen, who have been attentive and not extortionate. I will not enumerate the points of view and villas we visited. We saw nothing the guide-books do not speak of."

. . . .

On the 5th of September the Wordsworths went back to the lake of Como in order to gratify Miss Wordsworth, who wished to see every spot which her brother saw in his first journey,—a journey made when he was young.

On the 7th, Monkhouse and I went to Varese. As we approached the town we drew nigh the mountains. Varese is most delightfully situated. There is on a mountain, 2,000 feet high, a church with fifteen appendant chapels. To this we found peasants were flocking in great numbers, it being the eve of the birthday of the Virgin. We resolved to witness this scene of devotion, and our walk afforded me more delight than any single excursion I have yet made. For two miles the mountain is very steep. The fifteen chapels are towards the top, and beautiful, containing representations of the Passion of Christ in carved and painted wood. The figures are as large as life, and at least very expressive. Though so closely resembling wax figures, they excited no disgust. On the contrary, I was highly pleased with the talent of the artists. The dragging of the cross, and the crucifixion, are deeply affecting. The spectator looks through iron grates, the apertures of which are purposely small. My view was imperfect, on account of the number of pious worshippers. Towards the top the crowd was immense. We sometimes had to jump over the bodies of men and women. The church I could scarcely enter. Hundreds of women were lying about with their provisions in baskets. The hats of the peasantry were covered with holy gingerbread mingled with bits of glass. Bands of people came up chanting after a sort of leader. This scene of devotion would have compensated for the walk; but we had, in addition, a very fine prospect. On one side the plains of Lombardy, studded with churches and villages, on another five or six pieces of water. In another direction we saw a mass of Alpine hills and valleys, glens, rocks, and precipices. A part of the lake of Lugano was prominently visible. To enjoy this view I had to ascend an eminence beyond the church. Our walk home, Monkhouse thought, was hardly less than six miles. We found our inn rather uncomfortable from the number of guests, and from the singing in the streets.

We rejoined the Wordsworths at Baveno on the 8th. Then we crossed the Simplon, resting successively on the 9th at Domo d'Ossola, 10th Simplon, 11th Turtman, and the 12th and 13th at the baths of Leuk. From this place we walked up the Gemmi, by far the most wonderful of all the passes of Switzerland I had ever, or have now ever, crossed. The most striking part is a mountain wall 1,600 feet in perpendicular height, and having up it a zigzag path broad enough to enable a horse to ascend. The road is hardly visible from below. A parapet in the more dangerous parts renders it safe. Here my journal mentions our seeing men employed in picking up bees in a torpid state from the cold. The bees had swarmed four days before. It does not mention what I well recollect, and Wordsworth has made the subject of a sonnet, the continued barking of a dog *irritated by the echo of his own voice*. In human life this is perpetually occurring. It is said that a dog has been known to contract an illness by the continued labour of barking at his own echo. In the present instance the barking lasted while we were on the spot.

> "A solitary wolf-dog, ranging on
> Through the bleak concave, wakes this wondrous chime
> Of airy voices lock'd in unison,—
> Faint—far off—near—deep—solemn and sublime!
> So from the body of one guilty deed
> A thousand ghostly fears and haunting thoughts proceed!"
> (XXXI: *Echo Upon the Gemmi*).

On the 14th we slept at Martigny, having passed through the most dismal of all the valleys in Switzerland—the valley of the Rhone, and Sion, the most ugly of all the towns. A barren country, and a town of large and frightful edifices. An episcopal town too. It looked poverty-struck.

I say nothing of Chamouni, where we slept two nights, the 15th and 16th; nor of the roads to it, but that the Tete Noire, by which we returned, is still more interesting than the Col de Balme, by which we went. Again at Martigny on the 17th. I should not have omitted to mention that, to add to the sadness produced by the Valais, Wordsworth remarked that the Alps themselves were in a state of decay—crumbled to pieces. . . .

[. . . . .]

At Paris I renewed my old acquaintance, and saw the old sights. On the 8th I left the Wordsworths, who were intending to prolong their stay. On the 9th I slept at Amiens; on the 10th was on the road; on the 11th reached Dover; and on the 12th of October slept in my own chambers.

"And so," my journal says, "I concluded my tour in excellent health and spirits, having travelled farther, and seen a greater number and a greater variety of sublime and beautiful objects, and in company better calculated to make me feel the worth of these objects, than any it has been my good fortune to enjoy." Of that journal I must now say that it is the most meagre and defective I ever wrote—perhaps from want of time. The most interesting details, and not the least true, have been written from memory, the journal giving me only the outlines. The fidelity of what I have written from recollection might be doubted; but that would be unjust.

❧ Mary Wordsworth
From Her Journal of 1820 Tour of the Continent

> *William Wordsworth recalls the 1820 tour in a letter to Robinson, March 12, 1821. "You will be pleased to hear," William writes, "that the two ladies are busy transcribing their journals." Living in the Wordsworth household, Mary Wordsworth, too, was occupied with writing. She describes this particular text to her daughter Dora in a letter of February 20th, 1821 as coming from "hasty notes made by snatches during our journey." What follows are excerpts from her version of the 1820 tour, selected to correspond with the passages printed from Dorothy's journal. My text is Knight's 1884 edition of William's poems, volume 6; ellipses are Knight's.[17]*

Calais—Passing through the gates of the city, we had before us a line of white-capped Fish-women, with thin brown faces. The fish very foul, yet at dinner the same sort proved excellent.

Thursday, 13th July. . . .—Bruges. What a place. D. and I walked out as soon as we could after our arrival. . . . Went into the old church. The nuns, the different worshippers, the pictures, the place, the quiet stately streets, grand buildings, graceful nun-like women

---

[17] The full text of Mary's journal has never been published. Having worked with the manuscripts, however, Helen Boden has written a notable comparison of Mary's journal to Dorothy's: "Matrilineal Journalism: Mary and Dorothy Wordsworth's 1820 Continental Tours and the Female Sublime." *Women's Writing* 5:3 (1998), 329–352.

in their long cloaks, treading with swan-like motions those silent avenues of majestic architecture, I must leave to D. to describe. My own mind was uplifted by a sort of devotional elevation as if striving to fit itself to become worthy of what these temples would lead to.

Friday, 14th.—At Bruges all is silence, grace, and unmixed dignity. . . . You felt a sort of veneration for everything you looked upon. Nothing of this here [at Ghent]; yet what a splendid place! The evening too suited its character, for the sun went down in brightness. Yesterday was not a sunny day, and Bruges wanted no sunshine, its own outline in the gloom of evening needed no golden lustre. Yet *this* William witnessed, when D. and I were not with him, the great Tower of the Market House bathed in gold!

Namur, Tuesday 18th.—Our ride yesterday, except for the intervention of Waterloo, and its interests, which were so melancholy that I do not like to touch upon them, was a dull one, though the road was pleasant through the forest of Soigny. Waterloo, its pretty chapel, the walls within covered with monuments, recording the fall of many of our brave countrymen, and some few others as brave, La Haye Sainte, La Belle Alliance, Quatre Bras. Dined at Geneppe; two bullet shots in the wainscot of the room, which, during the battle, had been heaped with dead and dying.

Thursday, 20th July.— . . . Descend towards the town of Aix-la-Chapelle, a chapel on the opposite side of the vale upon a high knoll, overlooking the spires and towers. . . . Wm. T. M., and myself walked to the chapel we had seen on the heights, said to be built by Charlemagne: a very interesting view of the town, and over a large space of the country beyond, and *into* the country looking the other way. Wm. went higher to a monument recording that Buonaparte visited the spot with one attendant. We were too late to be satisfied here, the darkness only allowing us to form a notion of the outline, and to catch here and there a spire or a tower in the distance. The chapel here alluded to was not larger in appearance than the tiny rocky edifice at Buttermere. A Christ under the branches of a spreading oak, brought to my mind by contrast, a gay image of a brightly painted fox, on a sign board, among the branches of a flowing chestnut tree, which William and I saw gleaming in the setting sun when walking through the village of Souldren.

Friday, July 21. Cologne.— . . . The Cathedral, a most magnificent edifice. Tower unfinished (this I perceived, but took it for a ruin at ten miles distance), built 700 years ago. The outside reminds you of Westminster Abbey in parts and, had the Projector's wish been fulfilled, within and without, this would have been a much more sumptuous pile. It affectingly called to my mind William's lines—

> 'Things incomplete and purposes betrayed
> Make sadder transits o'er truth's mystic glass,[18]
> Than noblest objects utterly decayed.

Within the fluted Pillars are very grand; the dimensions, 1180 German feet high, 700 long, and 500 broad. A curious old picture, 450 years old. Subject, the 3 Kings of Cologne in the centre (for it was divided into three parts, and kept shut up to protect it), and on the sides Ursula and the 11,000 virgins, by Ralfe; mounted 250 steps to the top of the unfinished Tower, and had a fine prospect of the river winding its way towards Dusseldorf. . . . The cathedral—that august and solemnly impressive Temple. . . . William in his musing way.

Monday, July 31st.— . . . We drew towards the town of Villengen, a foreign looking place standing in the descent, and lifting up its metallic dome-like spires, without the accompaniment of a single tree. . . . The Church with its two-fold spire glittered in the hot sunshine, like pewter in a melting state. Our guide had told us that near this place the Danube took its rise; but not so. . . . At Donaueschingen changed horses again. Here we laved in the water which flowed from the source of the majestic Danube, a little, clear, bright, black rill, that issuing from a capacious stone fountain, into which it springs, crosses the road, and glides rapidly along the side of a beautiful pleasure-ground. . . . We washed, drank, and luxuriated in the cool and pure waters of this rill, unwilling to quit what we were not again to see—a reality very different from the stately Danube, so long an image to the imagination.

Monday, August 14.—At sunset we reached the edge of the flat green area, sublimely guarded; from its head rose Engleberg (whence the angels sang), Tittlesberg, the highest of these Alps. But

---

[18] [Knight] This reference is to the sonnet on *Malham Cove;* but the second line of the quotation should have been—"Make sadder transits o'er thought's optic glass" unless Mrs. Wordsworth was quoting from another written version of the sonnet.

between these two stood another more fantastically shaped rocky hill with a broken jagged crest, and without snow. . . . All around the Vale is completely enclosed by lofty barriers, piercing or supporting the clouds. From the eminence whence we first had a sight of the mists curling in the glowing sun upon the heights of Engleberg, the white convent with its own, and its lesser attendant chapels; the pensive moving figures, in their gay attire, that as we approached saluted us; and before we gained our harbour for the night, the convent bell calling to vespers, seemed to summon my ears to listen for the angels' voices from that celestial mount. All these impressions could not but excite in us thankfulness that we had been led to this Abyssinian Vale (as D. appropriately termed it).

Thursday, Aug. 24.—. . .On the banks of the infant Ticino, which has its source in the pools above, within a few hundred yards of that which gives birth to the Reuss, D. and I resolved to reject all political boundaries, and thenceforth consider ourselves in Italy. With the pure stream we descended; but first were joined by Mr R., J. M., and Wm., with a young German, whom Mr R. had picked up in the morning; a Heidelberg student, travelling on foot to Rome. He sang and played to us upon the flute, airs from Rossini, the Swiss Cow Song, &c. Then on we went, wending our way over the grass between the paved road and the brook wherever we could. The Brook dashing down its stony channel, now over rocks, now under shelving snow, and its banks seen clothed with underwood and pines. Passed by its first wooden bridge, leading to the cottages, not unmindful of our own Duddon; and presently did it grace such an assemblage of rocks, dells, and woods, forming waterfalls, pools, and all the various charms that a mountain stream can show.

Sunday, Sept. 17, Chamouny.—. . . As we passed one of the little clustering villages in the Vale of Chamouny, standing at the foot of one of the five glaciers (the Argentiere I believe), its pretty white Church at that moment was encircled by a most interesting procession—bare-headed men first carried the symbols or banners, who were followed by a train of females: two and two winding round the building; white garments thrown over their heads and covering their shoulders, like so many nuns; but in that romantic place, the situation of the Church, and the costume so peculiar, it was quite impossible not to connect the moving belt of white pyramids with the snowy ones immediately above them. We were afterwards told by a young priest, as we passed along the green meadows of Orsina, whither he was going to do duty, and with whom D. fell into conversation, that it was sacrament day, and that the ceremony we had seen occurs once a month in all the vallies, and that those pure vestments do not belong to the Church, but to the Individuals who wear them. Our genial companion told D. that he lived upon the Triant, in a village high above its banks, and where, had he been at home, he would have been glad to have received us as his guests.

Sunday, Sept. 20.— . . . We had great pleasure in discovering traces of a more difficult ascent (in one instance, with the remains of an oratory[19]), down which William and Jones came thirty years ago. William pointed out to us an ancient, high, many windowed edifice, by the roadside, at the Hospital where they had lodged; a wild and solemn harbour! On the opposite side of the road, a neat little church, as clean as any English chapel, standing in its tiny enclosure of burial ground; below, the Tusa; but its murmur, or rather raving, could not be heard for the riotous din of a torrent, tumbling from the stupendous mountain above, a tumultuous sound, distinctly remembered by William, an unchangeable object! Bonaparte's words, "Be thou fettered," would have been of no avail here. . . . As we advance, Pines climbing up to the skies, in some places clothing the very pinnacles of the highest rocks. The road cut and carried through masses of the solid rock. . . . Symptoms of desolation as we advance. Mountains crumbling gradually, or brought down by force of waters. Blasted pines standing or torn up, and lying in a decaying state, in the torrent's bed. In the midst of such scenes to come in view of one of those lovely green Prairies is an enlivening sight, with its little cottage. . . . Watching as we did all the way snatches of the old road, we traced it as we thought across the river and up the ascent on the other side; and afterwards Wm. told us that there was the very point where he and Jones had committed the same mistake, had taken that road (as recorded in his poem) and had to retrace their steps—and bend downwards with the stream, under a sort of depression from the feeling that he had crossed the Alps.

Paris, Monday, Oct. 2d— . . . I shall here close these very imperfect notices, commenced at D's request; and with a notion, on my part,

---

[19] Small chapel for private prayer.

that they might be useful when she wrote her Journal: but soon finding, that, with such a view, mine was a superfluous labour, I should not have had the resolution to go on, except at Wm's desire and from the feeling that my Daughter, and perhaps her brothers, might one day find pleasure, should they ever have the good fortune to trace our steps, in reconising objects their Mother had seen.

[*Like Dorothy, however, Mary continues to describe the journey home.*]

Boulogne—Embarked in a small vessel; wind contrary. The vessel struck upon a sandbank. Then was driven with violence upon a rocky road in the harbour. Tide was ebbing very fast.

Dover, Wed. 8th Nov.—At 11 o'clock we took coach and thoroughly enjoyed our journey between the green pastures of Kent, besprinkled with groups of trees, and bounded by hedgerows. The scatterd cattle quietly selecting their own food was a cheering and a home-feeling sight.

Social and Political

If magnificent individualism formed a basis for the writings of Romanticism, so did social and political activity. From engagement in the lives of her neighbors to consideration of national politics, Dorothy's life and work address issues such as those represented by the following texts about education, aid to the poor, and the changes in England's agricultural economy.

✣ Dorothy Wordsworth
Letter to Jane Pollard

When she was 17, Dorothy moved to Forncett with the Cooksons. The influence of the evangelical Anglican Clapham Sect, which emphasized saving individuals through helping the poor and downtrodden, can be seen in the ways in which Reverend Cookson and his household functioned in his parish. In a letter of January 25, 1790, written to Jane Pollard, Dorothy describes a "little school" for local girls that she has helped the Cooksons establish.

Did I ever tell you that I had got a little school? . . . ; I have only kept it six months. I have nine scholars . . . Our hours in winter are, on Sunday mornings from nine till church time, at noon from half past one till three; and at night from four till half-past 5. Those who live near us come to me every Wednesday and Saturday evening. I only instruct them in reading and spelling and they get off prayers hymns and catechisms. I have one very bright scholar, some very tolerable, and one or two very bad. I intend in a little time to have a school upon a more extensive plan . . .

❧ Sarah Trimmer
From *Œconomy of Charity*

On December 7, 1791, Dorothy writes to Jane again of expanding their efforts to establish "a sort of School of Industry." She writes, too, of the frequent visits to Forncett of William Wilberforce, Cookson's college friend, whose influence is evident in the plans for these schools. Wilberforce gave Dorothy money "to distribute in what manner I think best to the poor." He also suggested reading material, including work by Mrs. Sarah Trimmer (1741–1810).

Mrs. Trimmer's Œconomy of Charity set the pattern for both Sunday schools and schools of industry. The work is "Addressed to Ladies." All women—rich, poor, young, old, married, single—will benefit, Trimmer insists, from becoming involved in educational undertakings. A special dedication to the Queen, who at Windsor has supported both a Sunday School and a school for girls, "which may properly be denominated a School of industry," indicates Trimmer's ideology. The full title of the 1801 edition is: An address to ladies; adapted to the present state of charitable institutions in England: with a particular view to the cultivation of religious principles, among the lower orders of people.

[. . .] Wherever Sunday-schools are established, instead of seeing the streets filled on the Sabbath-day with ragged children engaged at idle sports, and uttering oaths and blasphemies, we behold them assembling in schools, neat in their persons and apparel, and receiving with the greatest attention instructions suited to their capacities and conditions. In the intervals of school-hours they walk quietly and regularly to church, where they join with the congregation in offering prayers and praises to the great Creator of high and low and are put into a course of piety and morality, which is likely to render them useful members of society. But it is, I believe, a general observation, founded on experience, that Sunday-schools, unless visited by persons of superior rank in life to the masters and mistresses, seldom answer the proposed ends. Something out of the common way is necessary to induce many parents to send their children; and many children would be averse to going if they were not assured of an exemption from that kind of discipline practised in weekly schools, and taught to expect pleasures superior to those they enjoy in the pursuit of idle amusements, to which, if at liberty, they usually devote the Sabbath-day.

Nothing is a greater excitement to them all than the hope of being noticed by their superiors. To use the words of an excellent advocate for this institution.[1] "Visitors are the very life and soul of the system, the veins through which the blood is daily circulating to the heart, and by that heart sent back to the remotest member." [15–16].

. . . .

[. . .] The task of early education in all families naturally devolves upon mothers; and those who discharge this duty are consequently particularly qualified to open the understandings of poor children, which frequently are even in those of twelve and fourteen, as destitute of cultivation as the minds of new-born infants.

Accustomed to instruct their own families, women acquire a pleasing and easy method of communicating knowledge, which is more engaging to the young and ignorant than the graver methods generally employed by learned and scientific men. Women are besides acquainted with a variety of particulars that fall peculiarly within their own province, which enable them to advise the bigger girls in respect to decorum of behaviour and propriety of dress—points of very essential consequence to young females of every denomination. . . .

I must not forbear to mention that by kindly interesting themselves in the instruction of poor girls, mothers may bring down the blessing of Heaven on their own families. The Almighty Father often repays his children for the duties they perform in kind, and with the most bountiful interest. She, therefore, who extends the practice of maternal tenderness towards poor destitute children, may humbly hope an hundred fold return of happiness in the improvement of her own immediate offspring, at least in their eternal welfare; especially if her first cares are directed to training her daughters in that way in which Christians should go.

But not to matrons only would I confine the interesting, the satisfactory office of visiting Sunday-schools. Could unmarried ladies be prevailed on to give their kind assistance, they would find occasions for exercising those amiable qualities, which are partly lost to the world for want of their forming matrimonial connections. Providence has exempted them from family cares; some of them live in affluence; numbers in easy circumstances; their hours often hang heavy on their hands—how then can they apply their

[1] [Trimmer's note] See preface to a sermon on the advantages of Sunday-schools, by the Rev. John Bennet of Manchester.

superfluities both of time and money to more advantages than in affording instruction and employment to poor children? Few people are so inconsiderable as not to be able to contribute to the welfare of a neighbourhood in some way or other; though it frequently happens that assistance is withheld by women in particular, for want of each individual considering what services are required of them, or what it is possible for them to perform: others are restrained by modesty and diffidence from taking an active part. But I am persuaded that, would single ladies condescend to become nursing mothers to the poor of the rising generation, their happiness would be greatly increased.[2]

Young ladies may also, with peculiar propriety, assist in Sunday-schools and it is particularly incumbent on them to do so, since it is for them chiefly that we are endeavouring to train up to religion and virtue, servants, labourers, and mechanics: the rising generation of poor are instructed by us, that our children may be better served than their parents have been, and that, when they have households of their own, they may lie down in peace and take their rest, without the dread of being disturbed by the nightly robber; and travel the road free from the painful apprehension of being molested by the daring highwayman.

It is a general complaint that domestic servants are not attached to their masters and mistresses, but act towards them from fearful and mercenary motives; and that no confidence is to be placed in the lower kinds of labourers and workmen. This may justly be imputed to their being sent into the world without proper sense of the duties of their station. It is certainly of consequence to have good principled servants. Has not our age produced instances of some who have been in league with robbers?—of others who have set fire to their masters' houses—eloped with considerable sums of money, and betrayed many important trusts? And does not almost every mistress of a family complain that the expenses of housekeeping are greatly increased by the wastefulness of servants? And is it not generally lamented that the immoralities practised by the lower orders of people, keep their employers in a constant state of suspicion and uneasiness; and that it is scarcely possible to engage their gratitude by any act of kindness?

---

[2] [Trimmer] I would beg leave to recommend to the perusal of ladies in general, a little work which has been long neglected, but which every woman of education ought to peruse. It is entitled THE LADIES CALLING; a new edition of it has been lately advertised.

An opportunity now presents itself for preventing the increase of these evils, if, as is supposed, they originate from the want of early instruction. The education of poor children is no longer entirely left to their ignorant and corrupted parents; it is in many places become a public business and if they are not in general better taught for the future, the fault will lie with ourselves. Do we wish our daughters to have modest, discreet, trusty maid-servants?—let us unanimously resolve to give a helping hand towards infusing good principles into the minds of poor girls. Do we desire they should be served with affectionate esteem?—let us take them to Sunday-schools, where, by a thousand little attentions which they will be happy to shew, they may engage the gratitude of those whom they will probably here-after have occasion to employ, and make them ambitious of being received into the service of persons whose friendship and humanity they have already experienced; instead of forsaking their native places and exposing themselves to a variety of temptations. [21–28].

. . . .

. . . But to return to the subject of young ladies acting as visitors in Sunday-schools. It may be asked—Are girls, whose own education is not yet completed, qualified for such an employment? In order to answer this question, I entreat that the object and nature of the instructions in Sunday-schools may be considered. It is not intended that the children of the poor should be instructed in languages, geography, history, and other articles that constitute a polite educa-tion; but merely in such a knowledge of the English language as shall enable them to read the scriptures; in the plain duties of chris-tianity; and in those modes of conduct which their station requires.

—Few girls, in the middling classes of life, are so neglected in the first of these articles as not to be able to examine into the improve-ments of the Sunday-scholars; . . . It may also be required of young ladies to exercise their own minds in considering the various articles of Christian faith and practice: they may likewise instruct Sunday-scholars in the duties of obedience to parents, submission to teachers, reverence of the clergy, modesty of behaviour, propriety of dress, &c.—These instructions will at the same time serve to recal to their minds what their own station requires; and, I should think, will operate as the most effectual antidote against the immoralities and follies of the age: for it must be ascribed to a want of proper reflection that our young people are frequently so disrespectful to those whom they are bound to honour, and that they run into such ridiculous modes of dress, and levity of conduct, as cannot render them pleasing in any station.

It is a common observation, that women are apt to indulge an inclination for adorning their persons. This propensity is allowable, nay laudable, within proper bounds; for a total neglect of appearances may be justly reckoned an indecorum. But the present age runs into a contrary extreme. It is now the mode to affect distortion. Ladies of fortune, except on extraordinary occasions, instead of being distinguished by the richness of their dress, frequently wear their clothes of such materials that people much beneath them can follow their fashions. Those who set these modes will scarcely look into my unfashionable book; but should they honour it with a perusal, I hope they will pardon me for saying it seems as if they had entered into a conspiracy against persons in the middling and lower classes of life, to make experiment how far a desire of aping their betters will lead them in the paths of vanity and extravagance; how much more honourable would it be to set them an example of propriety—then would the outward appearance of every woman secure the respect due to her particular station; regard would be paid to circumstances, and character and we should no longer see the modest virgin, with disheveled hair, inviting the insults of libertines, and lessening herself in the esteem of the worthy and good. I shall not take upon me to satirize more particularly the extravagancies of the present age in respect to dress, they have been sufficiently ridiculed and exposed, and those who are regardless of propriety are proof against derision. I will only observe that it is certainly requisite for every visitor of a Sunday-school to dress in such a manner as may give weight to her lessons on this head; and evince that they really pay more attention to the inward adornings of the mind than to a fashionable appearance; for there would be great inconsistency in recommending moderation to the poor when they themselves practice excess. [37–41]

. . . .

It is impossible to conceive a more deplorable set of children than those of this place were before the establishment of Sunday-schools. They now come to church clean and tight, and have a pride in being so. But the girls have had great advantages: for not only the inhabitants of the town, but many other ladies in the neighbourhood, have given benefactions for the express purpose of procuring them necessaries.

I think it is scarcely possible for any lady to go among a set of ragged children without feeling an urgent desire to clothe them better, and make them look like human creatures and this may be done at a very little expense, as I shall endeavour to shew in its proper place. The duty of clothing the naked, ladies will be reminded of while they are hearing the New Testament read in Sunday-schools: and surely the precepts that recommend this branch of charity will strike the mind with double force when the immediate objects of it stand before them in tattered garments, that make silent but powerful claims on their humanity. In such an assembly, what lady can read the account of Dorcas without forming a resolution to imitate her example?[3] It certainly must be as pleasing in the sight of God to make coats and garments for children, whose parents are not capable of doing it, as for widows. Working for the poor is a species of charity which forms a part of the prerogative of our sex, and gives to those who have leisure for it an opportunity, of doing much good with very little trouble and expense. Were it more generally practised by young people it would moderate that inordinate love of dress, which renders many, who cannot afford to employ miliners and mantua-makers, literally slaves to fashion: they would be ashamed to covet such a variety of ornaments when they beheld what trifles gratify others of the same species with themselves. Besides, the having caps and other things, gratis, would be an inducement to the poor to dress suitably to their condition: and then people in the middling stations of life might support a sufficient degree of gentility to secure respect without being driven to extravagance. . . .

It is observable that the bigger girls, contrary to expectation, attend Sunday-schools with great readiness, and leave them with reluctance. The truth is, that too many of those who stay at home, find Sunday, so far from being a day of rest, the most uncomfortable day in the week: added to the fatigue of nursing a fretful humoursome child, a girl has perhaps the ill-nature of a morose father to endure; who, finding the expense of maintaining his family a restraint on his extravagance instead of rejoicing in his children, murmurs and repines at the burden of them, deals out blows instead of blessing and quarrels with his wife; so that all is discord

---

[3] [Trimmer] Act ix, 36. Trimmer's reference is to "a disciple named Tabitha, which means Dorcas or Gazelle. She was full of good works and acts of charity." She dies. Her grieving friends send for Peter who is in the vicinity. "All the widows stood beside him weeping, and showing coats and garments which Dorcas made while she was with them" (39). Peter sends everyone from the room and raises Dorcas from the dead.

and confusion: or a scolding drunken mother whose tongue is a perpetual scourge.... [46–52]

. . . .

. . . Extensive manufactories, I acknowledge, cannot be carried on in every place, nor is it desirable that they should, because they would often interfere with the interests of agriculture; but I humbly conceive that it would be very practicable to employ every woman who is industriously inclined, and to train up children from their early years, so that they should become habitually industrious.

It is a most lamentable sight to enter a cottage, and behold a poor woman sitting in rags, surrounded by a set of dirty children: we are shocked, and turn away with disgust, condemning her in our hearts for sloth and untidiness; but let us stop an instant, and hear her apology.

"I am ashamed to appear before you ladies in this condition, but indeed I have not the means of cleanliness—I have not so much as a mop or pail to clean my apartments—we have no change of apparel—look at the bed in which my dear babes must lie naked while I wash their linen—not so much as a single sheet—nor can I purchase even a bit of sope—nay, I have not a towel to wipe our faces and hands with; my husband labours hard in summer, but what he earns then is exhausted before winter is half over—he has been out of work for many weeks; and we have had so much sickness in the family that we have been obliged to sell our clothes, and the little furniture we were possessed of—I also go to haymaking, weeding, &c. when I possibly can, but have never been taught to do any in-doors work—nay, I cannot even mend the rags I have, for I have had no learning bestowed upon me—consider also, how my constitution is worn by frequent child-bearing and nursing my infants at the breast, without a proper supply of nourishment myself—consider how hardly I live—how uncomfortably I lie—how I am harrassed with incessant fatigue and corroding care—how I am overlooked by my superiors.—The parish it is true allows me as such as can be afforded to our share but that is barely sufficient to keep us from starving:—we may be admitted into the workplace, but that is already crowded with poor.—O that death would come and take from the world a set of abject wretches whom nobody regards." This apology and others of equal weight might, I am persuaded, be made by many a poor despised fellow creature.

But we will suppose a case not quite so bad.

A poor woman who has been taught both knitting and needle-work in her childhood, and knows also how to spin wool and flax, marries and removes with a family to a distant place where her husband can get higher wages, but where there is no employment for poor women, except in the labours of agriculture. The man is seldom out of work, and at first brings home his wages instead of spending them at an alehouse; but the expenses of rent and provisions demand the principal part of his earnings: his wife's talents are in a great measure useless; should she spin, he knows not where to get her yarn manufactured; she has nobody to recommend her to knitting or needle-work, and therefore is not able to earn any thing at home; all kinds of clothing are so very dear that she can seldom afford to purchase new; but has to be sure a great advantage over such a woman as I have before described, in being able to patch and mend, by which means she will keep her family tight, if she can only manage to buy,[4] rags by the pound. Her habitual industry makes her long to earn money; she cannot bear that the whole burden should be on her husband; she therefore goes into the fields and gardens to work, leaving her children for the day to the care of a woman who makes it her business to look after a number of little ones in the absence of their mothers. Instead of sitting down in peace and quietness in her own little neat apartment, surrounded by playful innocents, she finds in the fields or gardens a set of reprobates, who shock her ears, with oaths, blasphemies, and indecency. Her mind is filled with anxiety for her children's safety; she is not at liberty to return home to prepare a comfortable dinner, nay not even a supper for her husband. He may be enticed for the sake of a good fire, and other refreshments which if she had spinning or knitting he could provide, to go to an alehouse; she may herself be prevailed on, when overcome with fatigue or faintness, to drink destructive spirits, and by degrees become a dramdrinker. She must become a Sabbath breaker, by either continuing her occupation, or washing, ironing, or cleaning house. In short, innumerable evils may be the consequence of her removal to a place where she is excluded from the employments of her early days. I have great reason to believe from observation, that many men, who when they first marry are soberly inclined, gradually become sots from their wives working out of doors.

[4] [Trimmer] I have seen a little girl at a Sunday-school very neatly dressed, whose gown, apron, shift, and cap, were entirely made of pieces of white and coloured linen, purchased in this manner. This influence shews the great charity of schools for needle work.

It may perhaps be necessary and even proper, for women and girls to assist at hay–making, and harvest work because at such times a great number of hands are required; and these employments make a very agreeable variety to those who live a great deal within doors; and if performed by a set of neighbours who know one another, may be carried on without any ill consequences. The little children may be looked after at that time of the year, in the fields, by the bigger ones, and it is usual to allow such refreshments to hay-makers, &c. as supersede any excuse for going to an alehouse; but I am confident that the promiscuous intercourse of good and bad men and women, boys and girls, which prevails in the environs of London particularly, is the cause of many irregularities and vices; and I cannot help thinking that there are enough of the other sex to perform the usual business of agriculture, and that it is invading their province for women to forsake their spinning, needle-work, and knitting, to work the whole summer long, and in winter also, in the fields and gardens; yet what can they do if there is no suitable employment to be had I observed before, that wherever manufactories are established, and fully employed, parishes have an internal resource against the miseries of extreme Indigence: in order to drive poverty away then, labour must be universally introduced.

I have been informed that Houses of Industry have been established in some counties with very great success; but it is not practicable nor indeed expedient, to collect all the poor of a parish into these seminaries: they are proper receptacles for vagabonds who must be compelled to work, but will not answer for whole families; besides, they are at first very expensive to erect, and in this land of liberty lay too great a restraint, in many instances, on the freedom of the poor; numbers of whom would work with greater alacrity if delivered from the idea of restraint, and under no compulsion but what arises from pecuniary wants. I could therefore wish to see established in every parish, Schools of Industry for poor girls.

If, for instance, there was a school for spinning flax, girls of five years of age might be employed at it; and the yarn might easily be manufactured in white or striped linen and checks; and by the time each little spinstress had worn out the clothes with which the parish or private benefactors should at first furnish her, she might earn sufficient to entitle her to linen and other necessaries.

Another school, for carding and spinning wool, would furnish materials for linseywoolsey, serge, stuffs, baize, yarn and worsted for knitting.

At a third school girls might be taught needle-work of the useful kind: and at a fourth school they might learn to knit stockings.

These schools, if properly conduced, would reflect benefits on each other; they might easily be set on foot by voluntary benefactions and in a short time would support themselves, and yield a surplus; and would require no further aid than inspection to see that the produce was properly applied; which would be a very agreeable employment for ladies, and very easy too, if the task was divided among a number of visitors, to attend these little manufactories in rotation. Young ladies might assist in this office with the greatest propriety; by which means they would obtain an early insight into domestic œconomy, and acquire a habit of calculating expenses; a strong impression would be made on their minds in favour of industry, they would be ashamed to be idle, and would consider it as a duty to reward diligence in others.

I am happy in being able to inform my readers of a little manufactory, which has benefited a neighbourhood for upwards of fourteen years, that exactly agrees with my idea of Schools of Industry. . . . [62–71]

✢ A Country Farmer
Cursory Remarks on Inclosures

If, as Robert Frost proposed, "Good fences make good neighbors," maybe no fences make better neighbors. Enclosure, the fencing off of common property for private use, began in England in the Middle Ages and increased dramatically at the end of the eighteenth century; from 1793 to 1815, over 2000 enclosure acts were passed. In the following pamphlet, a farmer describes from his perspective much of what Dorothy notes in her Grasmere journal: people driven off the land that has supported them for generations; the effect on the general economy when small cottage industries go under; families torn apart by forced migration. Rural parishes such as Grasmere witnessed a brain and money drain.[5]

Agricultural innovations such as the seed planting-drill and the four-field crop rotation system necessitated larger pieces of land than had

[5] Enclosure, or inclosure, in Britain is the topic of many studies. Among them are: J. L. and Barbara Hammond, *The Village Labourer* (Longmans, 1911); J. M. Neeson, *Commoners: Common Right, Enclosure and Social Change in England, 1700–1820* (Cambridge UP, 1993); James Alfred Yelling, *Common Field and Enclosure in England, 1450–1650* (Macmillan, 1977). In *Romanticism, Lyricism and History* (State University of New York Press, 1999), Sarah M. Zimmerman not only discusses Dorothy and her relationship to the rhetoric of Romanticism but also the ways in which John Clare writes against enclosure.

previously been farmed. Most farms were small, and plots owned by the same family were usually not contiguous. By dividing up a community's common land and redistributing ownership of pieces of land, Enclosure Acts created large plots that could be farmed more efficiently with new technologies. Furthermore, the new holdings had to be enclosed, or surrounded by costly fences erected at the owner's expense. And, these fences ensured that the poor could no longer glean, or gather, what was left behind after the harvest. Subsistence farmers had used the common land, which no longer existed, as a source of firewood and as a place to graze animals. They simply could not support themselves and their families. Food production did increase, and fewer farm workers were needed, so people migrated to centers of industrialization where their labor was necessary. In a Grasmere journal entry of May 19, 1800, Dorothy records this exchange with John Fisher, who "observed that in a short time there would be only two ranks of people, the very rich and the very poor, 'for those who have small estates,' says he, 'are forced to sell, and all the land goes into one hand.'"

Enclosure was a hot political issue, and the government took a number of steps to deal with it. In 1793, George III established the "Board or Society for the Encouragement of Agriculture and Internal Improvement." Volumes of Communications to the Board of Agriculture on subjects relative to The Husbandry and Internal Improvement of the Country *take up various elements of country life from sheds, cottages, cow barns and chicken houses to air and its effects on butter and cream, to irrigation ditches, to putting bells on horses, and of course to building walls. The topic of turning grasslands into tillage generates essay after essay. Numerous pamphlets, such as* Political Enquiry in the Consequences of Enclosing Waste Lands, and the High Cost of Butcher's Meat, *appeared.*

Dealing with the land, especially the procedures relating to enclosure, became so complicated that in 1801, 1836, and 1835, General Enclosure Acts were passed to simplify the process. But as both Dorothy and the country farmer tell it, enclosure is fraught with contraries.

Cursory Remarks on Inclosures

Shewing the pernicious and destructive consequences of inclosing common fields, &c.

By A COUNTRY FARMER

London

Printed and Sold by John Abraham, St. Swithin's Lane, Lombard-Street; Also by J. Debbett, Piccadilly; and J. Bew, Paternoster-Row, 1786.

The practice of inclosing common fields, has been pursued with unremitting ardour for about sixty years last past, under the specious pretence of improvement, but in fact to the great injury of the public in general, and the utter ruin of thousands of individuals in particular, and an advantage to none, except a few land-owners, and they often disappointed in their hope of gain by the vast experience attending the putting their project into execution.

Our forefathers fell into the same practice, and pursued it for some time, till convinced by experience of the inutility of the proceeding, they wisely stopt short, and ordered all the lands that had not been inclosed upwards of fifty years, to be laid open again, and that no lands in future should be included except such as should be made appear by two creditable witnesses was not worth ploughing.

Therefore, to obtain an act of parliament to inclose a common field two witnesses are produced to swear that the lands thereof, in their present state, are not worth occupying; though at the same time they are lands of the best soil in the kingdom, and produce corn, in the greatest abundance, and of the best quality. And by inclosing such lands, they are generally prevented from producing any corn at all, as the land-owner converts twenty small farms into about four large ones, and at the same time the tenants of these large farms are tied down in their leases not to plough any of the premises left to farm, by which means several hundred villages, that forty years ago contained between four and five hundred inhabitants, very few now will be found to exceed eighty, and some not half that number; nay some contain only one poor old decripid man or woman, hired by the occupiers of the lands who live in another parish to prevent their being obliged to pay towards the support of the next parish.

Therefore, if the riches of a country consists in the number of its inhabitants, which I believe none the most sanguine for inclosures, will debase their judgement so low as to deny, it must then be acknowledged that every proceeding in depopulation, must in proportion destroy the riches and power of a country, as every diminution of magnitude brings it nearer to a point, though perhaps never on annihilation.

If those whose benefits it is would spare half the time and attention as they waste in fruitless and florid speeches, they might, and I dare say would, stop the progress of this powerful and growing evil. It may be here said, what method must be taken to reduce what is now said to a demonstration? The answer is plain and easy: Let an order be sent to the church-wardens and overseers of the poor of every parish that has been inclosed within sixty years, to make a return of the number of the present inhabitants, and also of the number of inhabitants prior to such inclosures taking place, and the deficiency of inhabitants will plainly and truly appear.

It may be said, that the inclosed parishes may shew a decrease of about two hundred thousand, yet the number of inhabitants in the whole kingdom may be as numerous as if no such inclosures had been affected, by the inhabitants of the inclosed parishes settling in other places. Indeed, this may be the case in a few instances where the parties have wherewithal to rent ten pounds a year or upwards, but those cannot bear but a small proportion of the whole, as not one of those families in fifty are able to pay that rent for the sake of a settlement, and most the inclosed parishes are so over burthened with poor, that they will neither receive nor give a certificate. From which it is easy to conceive what must be the fate of those poor destitute inhabitants.

The consequence is, the old and infirm fall a burthen to the parish they belong till Death's merciful hand puts a period to their miserable existence, and by degrees easeth the parish of its burthens, which in a few years is generally accomplished, as the young and healthy have dispersed themselves, those that could pay their passage having transported themselves to America, and many of those who could not pursue that method for want of money to answer the purpose, have actually sold themselves for three years to supply that deficiency, and to free themselves from a country where Hunger, the worst of human misfortunes, stared them in the face, and all means of satisfying their craving appetite, even in a land of plenty, totally obliterated.

The young that are left to be brought up by those parishes are, when grown to maturity, obliged to pursue the same course, or join their fellow parishioners (who had neither ability nor spirit to voluntarily transport themselves) in forming troops of the most abandoned thieves that ever disgraced any civilized country, and glut the gallows with food, and freighting our ships to the coast of Africa at every returning session, and leaving at the same time a crowded prison to be disposed of in the same manner, or for ballast heaving on the river Thames.

It may be said that inclosing does not produce *all* these direful effects, all which I am ready to own; but at the same time I believe no one will say that there is not many instances where the effect may not be traced to that cause, and many other latent ones lying hid in such a number of circumstances that it may be hard for the wisest and most penetrating searcher to trace back the effect to its original cause, yet in some measure or other that may be the first spring, in a great many instances, though not seen by the most penetrating observer.

Many of the small farmers who have been thus deprived of their livelihood, have sold their flock in trade, and have raised from fifty to five hundred pounds, with which they have procured themselves, their families, and money, a passage to America, with hearts full of resentment against a legislature who had thus cruelly deprived them of the means of providing for themselves and families in their native country. No wonder then that the British arms were so unsuccessful on that continent in the late impolitic contest there.

There are another kind of people which are generally greatly injured by inclosing: which are those who have small landed property in such parishes who are allured by the prospect of gain to enter readily into the measure, while others have been reluctant, foreseeing the consequence, yet, through promises, fair speeches, or threats, have been brought to comply with the rest in their own destruction; and having little or no money to prosecute such an undertaking, are obliged to have recourse to the pernicious practice of borrowing, and never fail of meeting with a lender in the chief proprieter of lands in the parish, whose sole view at first setting out was to get the land of the whole parish into his own hands.

The first step to this is to advance money on the mortgage of those small parcels of lands, which in a few years (principal and interest) never fails to eat them up, and turns the owners a-drift to shift for themselves how and where they can, without land or money, to procure them food, some of whom, who but a few years since lived comfortably, free, and early upon their small patrimony, are now by the above means driven to the earning of their bread by working for six shillings a week when they can get employment; others, who have had a little left over and above what has satisfied their avaricious lender, have ventured on the method of taking a voyage to America, hoping thereby to secure to themselves a patrimony in a more hospitable country.

Neither is this all the inconveniency and hurt to the country: the diminution of the specie which those emigrants take with them is a great injury to circulation, as there cannot be less than a deficiency of £2,500,000 caused by this means within fifty years last past, while that deficiency is replaced by nothing but what may be blown away like chaff before the wind, and very likely, sooner or later, may be of less value, unless to light a pipe. It cannot be supposed that emigration is confined to husbandmen alone, but some of our artificers must have pursued the same plan, and no doubt but in time we shall hear the bad effect of it, by finding that America will manufacture those goods for herself which she used to import from hence, to the great injury of the trade of Great Britain, if not the total ruin of it; as in that country a working man may live for about one third of what he could live for here, and must flourish many years, before their taxes in that part of the world rise to one fourth part of what they are here at this present time; so that in a short time they bid fair to out-strip all European nations, to in most kinds of manufactories, Nature having provided them with all the materials necessary for the purpose.

In some places the lands here inclosed do not answer the end of pasturage, and in that case tillage is still to be pursued because the rents cannot be raised so high as in respect of pasturage, therefore the land-owner has not the advantage as in case his land turns out fit for pasturage, and is oftener the looser by that proceeding than a gainer. The only advantage is to the farmer, by having his land fenced in so that he may make just what use he pleases of it to his own advantage (which is considerable, when it is considered he enjoys that fruit of his own labour and industry) for then his neighbor cannot claim a right to partake of the fruits of his expence and trouble, but this holds good in no other respect than on such lands that bear nothing but from the quantity of manure that is yearly laid upon them.

As to the quantity of corn that will grow on the same land, there cannot be much difference, provided the management is the same; but if there is any difference, the open fields must have the advantage, as corn, like all other plants, thrives in proportion to the fresh air which is communicated to it; and there is undoubtedly a great obstruction of fresh air in enclosures, from the number of hedges, the natural consequence of enclosing. To prove the truth of this, let a bushel of wheat or any other grain be weighed out of the corn that hath grown in each situation, and the weight will determine in favour of the open field, as that will have the advantage by about four pounds.

There is another disadvantage attending inclosed lands, that renders the corn growing on not so good in quality as that which grows in open fields, and especially wheat: all that which grows near the hedge is thin and weak, and liable to retain the wet, and grow after a shower of rain; nay, even the very dew in that situation is often hard to be dried out by the sun and wind,—a great disadvantage when compared with that which grows in open fields.

Every baker knows the consequence of having ever so few grown corns in a quantity of wheat: the bread made of that wheat, however good the other part may be, will be soft and unpleasing to their customers; to remedy which, they are obliged to have recourse to allum, or feed their hogs with the flour.

I shall now just lay before the public the particulars before and after, and the expense of inclosing one parish, the name of which I must beg leave to be excused naming, as I do not mean to give the least offence to any gentleman, by giving the least hint whereby a discovery may be made of any one concerned, but only to shew the impolicy of such practice to the public in general.

About forty years hence a certain parish contained eighty two houses; twenty of which were small farms, forty-two cottages, and twenty inmates, maintaining four hundred and twenty inhabitants, containing about one thousand eight hundred acres of common field land, and about two hundred acres of rich common swerd land;[6] on which were maintained about two hundred milch cows, and about sixty dry ones, from May day till the meadows were cleared of hay, which gave them two hundred acres more to range in; and the ground that the cows had made room for about one hundred horses; the fallow and ground left by the horses maintained one thousand two hundred sheep.

[6] Swerd or sward: mossy turf or meadowland.

	£.	s.	d.
The annual gross rent, before the Inclosure took place, including sixty cottages and inmates	1137	17	0
Hand-tax, at 4s. in the pound, To be deducted	110	0	0
The net rent, before inclosing	1027	17	0
The annual gross rent, after inclosing	1801	12	0
From which deduct the land-tax as before	110	0	0
Net rent, after inclosing,	1691	12	2
From whence take the old net rent	1027	17	0
The annual gain in rent by inclosing	663	15	2
Expenses attending the procuring an Act of Parliament, Commissioners, Surveying and letting out	924	14	0
Ditching and quickening	312	12	6
Staking and railing	927	17	6
Gates and Stiles	147	18	0
Incident expences	56	15	0
TOTAL EXPENCES	2369	17	0
The interest of 23691. 17s. at Five percent	118	9	10
The loss of rent in sixty cottages And inmates, at 40s. a year each	120	0	0
The rent of the land gained, by taking in the common land, erroneously called waste.	510	0	0
	748	9	10
From whence take the annual gain by including	663	15	2
Loss to the proprietor, if he had not Monopolized the common land	84	14	8

From whence it is evident that the sole inducement to inclose common fields is, to ingross the lands that lay dispersed about such fields, from the use and benefit of the poor, and for which increase of rent no land tax is paid.

As the parish from whence this is taken is a vicarage, the great tythes being unappropriated, are in the hands of the owner of the parish, and the glebe lands from whence the Vicar has his maintenance are improved to about double their former value, and accounted for in the gross of this calculation.

It is also necessary to take notice and examine the produce of the same lands in their two states, that is to say, before and after the inclosure thereof, to shew the advantage and disadvantage that arises therefrom. To ascertain which take the following calculation.

	£	s.	d.
The net rent before inclosing	1027	17	0
Ploughing and sowing	1200	0	0
Labour	780	0	0
Ending of harvest	190	0	0
Poor's rates	36	0	0
Church-rate	11	0	0
Highways	40	0	0
Cattle bought in	260	0	0
Interest of flock	200	0	0
Total expense to the Tenants, Before inclosing, rent included	3744	17	0
The net rent after inclosing	1691	10	2
Four Shepherds at 25l. a year each, board included	100	0	0
Eight maid-servants at 18l. a year each, board included,	144	0	0
The poor's rate for the first three or four years after the fields were discontinued ploughing, 95l. which may reasonably be computed at 50l upon an average	50	0	0
Church rate as before	11	0	0
Highways ditto	40	0	0
Cattle brought in	300	0	0
Interest of flock	200	0	0
Total expence, after inclosing, to be taken from the expence before enclosing	1208	6	10

But what does this difference arise from? Why, from there being no necessity of raising the rent from industry.

It is now proper to enquire into the produce of the same lands, in their different situations and strike a balance to see who are injured.

To begin with their produce before inclosure, which upon an average will be found as follows:

1100 Quarter of Wheat at 28 s. per quarter	1540	0	0
1200 Quarters of Barley at 16s per quarter	960	0	0
900 Quarters of Beans at 15s. per quarter	675	0	0
250 Todds of Wool at 16s. per todd	200	0	0
600 Lambs, which increased the flock Yearly, valued at 10s. each, when grown	300	0	0
5000 Pounds of Cheese, at one penny Half-penny per pound	31	5	0
6000 Pounds of Butter, at five pence Per pound	125	0	0
100 Calves at 20s. each	100	0	0
150 Pigs, sold upon an average for 12 s. each	90	0	0
Poultry and Eggs	80	0	0
The produce before inclosure, out of which the rent was paid.	4101	5	0

PRODUCE AFTER INCLOSURE

By Fat Beasts	960	0	0
Sheep and Lambs	760	0	0
Calves	165		
Wool	235	0	0
Butter	190	0	0
Cheese	100	0	0
Horses	250	0	0
The produce after inclosure out of which The rent is paid	2660	0	0
A yearly loss to the public of	1441	5	0
The money raised by the present Four occupiers	2660	0	0
The net rent, as it now stands	1691	10	2
The gain to be divided among The present occupiers	968	9	10

So that each occupier has two hundred and forty-two pounds two shillings and five-pence half-penny per annum to live upon, exclusive of maintaining their servants. Over and above the loss to three hundred and upwards of individuals, who are driven from their habitations, and many of them at this instant starving for want of bread, and the profits of their labours for ever lost to the public, as appears from the difference of the produce of the common field lands and those enclosed.

Here it may be said, let a law be made to enable every tenant to plough his land and sow it with what he pleases. This indeed might in some measure assist the public by the produce of the land when ploughed, but could by no means recompence the thousands whose rights have been taken from them.

From what has been said, I think no one can be at a loss to account for the rapid progress in the rise of all kinds of provisions which have increased in an arithmetical progression, according as the inclosures took place year by year. The cause of which is easily accounted for, as the lands in their former state were let to five times the number of tenants, and at about half their present rent, which rent was to be raised by dint of industry, as they were not opulent, and were obliged to make money of every thing they could sell; therefore the markets were fully stocked, and to supply the markets, the farmers wives used all their industry and care to raise all manner of poultry and eggs, and to make the most of their dairies, out of which they used to supply the house with all manner of goods from the shops, and the remainder used to sink into their own pockets as a kind of pin-money, to buy themselves and children such necessary little articles as they required, without applying to their husbands for every trifling penny they might want to lay out. And thus many hundred villages supported themselves for many hundred years, with content, happiness, and ease to themselves, and an abundance to spare to the public.

On the other hand, the farmers are reduced to one fourth of their number, and they very opulent, generally have enough to support themselves and families without any kind of business, but to raise fortunes for their families, take on of those large inclosed farms at more than double the rent it used to go at, and being rich, are not obliged to dispose of the produce of their farm till they can get what price they please, and by that means lay what burthen they think proper on the Public, or they would never be able to pay their advanced rents, and support that luxury which the present age has fallen into, and to which they are no small contributors, as they think themselves upon a footing with the squire, and actually have as much formality in receiving and returning visits. Their entertainments are as expensive as they are elegant; for it is no uncommon thing for one of their new-created farmers to spend ten or twelve pounds at one entertainment; and to wash down delicate food, must have the most expensive wines, and those the best of their kind; and to set off the entertainment in the greatest splendor, an elegant side-board of plate is provided of the newest fashion. As to dress no one that is not personally acquainted with the opulent farmer's daughter can distinguish her from the daughter of a Duke by her dress, both equally wishing to imitate something, but they know not what.

View the farmer before the land was inclosed; and you will find him entertaining his friends with a part of a hog of his own feeding, and a draught of ale brewed from his own malt presented in a brown jug, or a glass, if it would bear it, which was the utmost of his extravagance: in those happy days you might view the farmer in a coat of the growth of his flock, and spun by his industrious wife and daughter clad from their own hands of industry, and the growth of their own flock their best attire—their outward covering being a neat camblet, faced with a small quantity of silk in colour according to the choice of the wearer.

Thus it plainly appears from this false notion of improvement that many thousands of inhabitants are fenced out of their livelihood, and out of their native-country, and their labour entirely lost to the remaining community; and if this practice is suffered to continue, England must be content with about half its number of inhabitants, which will render them an easy prey to their ambitious and aspiring neighbors.

Here it may be observed, that as the number of inhabitants of any country decrease, the taxes must fall proportionably heavier on the remainder, and in the end must be intolerable, except with those inclosing gentlemen who have so well contrived their business as to pay no taxes at all, as, before their inclosures took place, when the land-tax was four shillings in the pound, they upon a medium calculation paid one shilling and nine pence; and considering the lands they incroach, and the advancement in rent, I think it may with justice be said they paid no land-tax, as the land of itself that has been incroached pays more than five times the old tax, and every one knows the land has not been saddled with any new tax for many years last past, but only altered or changed from two shillings to four, and from four to two shillings again, as occasion required, and this upon the most unequal terms that can be devised by a people that call themselves wise, generous, and disinterested.

It is well known that the trading part of this nation is overburdened with taxes, and a great part of the landed property is in the same situation, who pay from two shillings and six-pence to five shillings and three-pence in the pound, when, if all were made alike, and were to be taxed two shillings in the pound, it would raise more money to be paid into the Exchequer than the present nominal four-shilling tax; however, the experiment might be tried, and if two shillings should be found short to answer the purpose, six-pence or a shilling more might be added as occasion might require, and sure no one could complain, when they were all reduced upon an equitable footing.

It is natural to say, but how are the real rents of the lands to be come at? I must own that would be attended with some trouble and difficulty, and at first perhaps some inadvertent errors might arise, but time, and vigilance in the assessors would soon obviate that, when asked by a law, inflicting a penalty of four times the value of the tax upon the person who should give in a false return of his rent; and the same penalty might be inflicted upon the assessor or assessors for willingly making a false return, and to keep the assessors to their duty, supervisors might be appointed in each respective hundred, to inspect into and report what they should find amiss or wrong in the assessment to the Commissioners of the land tax for the time being. If this plan was pursued, I dare venture to affirm that the disgraceful and impolitic tax on female servants, and the oppressive and partial tax upon shops, might have been given up.

And as those who have inclosed have taken in large quantities of that which they could lay no just claim to, a tax or fine of so much per acre might be laid thereon, for all such quantities of land so taken in, as might raise large sums for the present necessities of Government, which might in some measure atone for the injury done to the public in general and individuals in particular.

Beside the inclosing of common fields, there is another kind of inclosure, the taking of large and extensive wastes, as they are called; and what pretence can be shewn for so doing, I cannot conceive, except it is to enrich or add more to some one individual, who perhaps before had too much or at least more than came to his share, at the expence and injury of thousands, whose livelihood almost entirely depended upon those commons or wastes.

For this kind of inclosure there might be some colour of justice, were those commons or wastes lotted out and given to the poor inhabitants who had a right of common thereon, they paying a small quit-rent to the lord of the manor, and after three years cultivation to pay a land tax at the rate of so much in the pound *ad valorem;* this would keep many people in England who would have the means of employing themselves, and be the cause of the earth yielding an abundance for the use of the public in general.

Here it will be said, this must be effected by including, and those poor people are not able to carry that into execution. What! Are things come to that pitch that nothing can be done without inclosing? How were the lands of many thousands of parishes laid out and cultivated for many hundred years, for seventy, eighty, or one hundred miles extent, with very few hedges to obstruct the circulation of the wholesome air, uncorrupted by stagnation; and I believe mankind are as capable of laying out common or open field-lands now as they were a thousand years ago.

It would be well if those whose province it is would look into, and exert their great abilities towards the real improvement of their country, which then would in a short time wear the face of the greatest plenty, and upon such reasonable terms, that the labourer and his useful offspring might enjoy a belly-full, which in their present state I am very certain many are obliged to go without.

There are many thousands of acres in this kingdom that are looked upon neither fit for tillage or pasture, therefore are entirely neglected, and turn out to little or no account even for common, where only a few sheep feed, or rather starve upon them. The different soils that are found among those barren and uncultivated lands would require a large volume to enumerate them, and many years trial to find out what vegetation they are most adapted to, but there is no doubt but they might be brought to some degree of perfection, if proper encouragement were given.

FINIS

Further Reading

Dorothy Wordsworth's Writings

Journals of Dorothy Wordsworth. Ed. William Knight. 2 vols. London: Macmillan and Co. Ltd., 1897.

Journals of Dorothy Wordsworth. Ed. Ernest de Selincourt. 2 vols. Hamden, Conn.: Archon, 1970.

Journals of Dorothy Wordsworth. Ed. Mary Moorman. Oxford: Oxford UP, 1971.

The Grasmere Journals. Ed. Pamela Woof. Oxford: Oxford UP, 1991.

Recollections of a tour made in Scotland A.D. *1803*. Ed. J. C. Shairp. Edinburgh: Edmonston and Douglas, 1874.

The Collected Poems of Dorothy Wordsworth. Ed. Susan M. Levin in *Dorothy Wordsworth and Romanticism*. New Brunswick: Rutgers UP, 1987.

Wordsworth, William. *Poetical Works*. Ed. William Knight. Edinburgh: William Patterson, 1884.

Major anthologies now present Dorothy's work. See, among the best:

The Longman Anthology of British Literature. Vol 2a (3rd ed.). Eds. Susan Wolfson and Peter Manning. New York: Longman, 2006.

The Norton Anthology of English Literature. Eds. M. H. Abrams and Jack Stillinger. New York: W. W. Norton & Company, 2005.

British Literature: 1780–1830. Eds. Anne K. Mellor and Richard E. Matlak. New York: Harcourt Brace, 1995.

As yet, we have no complete scholarly edition of Dorothy Wordsworth's work, but some very interesting new editions based on older published versions do exist.

Carol Kyros Walker adds an introduction, notes, and her own stunning photographs to *Recollections of a Tour Made in Scotland A.D. 1803*. New Haven: Yale UP, 1997.

Under the title *The Continental Journals, 1798–1820* (London: Thoemmes, 1995), Helen Boden presents *Journal of Visit to Hamburgh and of Journey from Hamburgh to Goslar* and *Journal of a Tour on the Continent (1820)* in the *Her Write His Name* reprint series. Thoemmes Press started this project with a view to making "available the forgotten works of neglected writers whose literary contributions have been overshadowed by those of a more famous male relative. . . . New introductions provide the social context for these writings. . . ."

Biography and Letters

De Selincourt, Ernest. *Dorothy Wordsworth: A Biography*. Oxford: Clarendon, 1933.

Gittings, Robert, and Jo Manton. *Dorothy Wordsworth*. Oxford: Clarendon, 1985.

Wordsworth, Christopher. *Memoirs of William Wordsworth, poet laureate, D. C. L.* Boston: Ticknor, Reed, and Fields, 1851.

Wordsworth, Dorothy. *Letters of Dorothy Wordsworth/A Selection*. Ed. Alan G. Hill. Oxford: Clarendon, 1981.

Wordsworth, William. *Letters of the Wordsworth Family: From 1787–1855*. Ed. William Knight. Boston: Ginn, 1907.

Wordsworth, William and Dorothy. *The Letters of William and Dorothy Wordsworth*. Eds. Alan G. Hill, Mary Moorman, and Chester L. Shaver. Oxford: Clarendon, 1967–1982.

Critical Studies

The *Bulletin of Bibliography* 40:4 (1983): 252–255 contains a list of primary and secondary sources compiled by Elizabeth Russell Taylor. Approximately fifty critical studies are cited. The MLA bibliography for 2006 adds over one hundred studies. What follows is a brief selection of works NOT fully cited in our footnotes.

Alexander, Meena. *Women in Romanticism: Mary Wollstonecraft, Dorothy Wordsworth, and Mary Shelley*. Houndmills, Basingstoke, Hampshire: Macmillan Education, 1989.

Brownstein, Rachel. "The Private Life: Dorothy Wordsworth's Journals." *Modern Language Quarterly* 34 (1973): 48–63.

Cervelli, Kenneth. *Dorothy Wordsworth's Ecology.* London: Routledge, 2007.

Davis, Robert Con. "The Structure of the Picturesque: Dorothy Wordsworth's Journals." *The Wordsworth Circle* 9:1 (1978): 45–49.

Fay, Elizabeth. *Becoming Wordsworthian: A Performative Aesthetic.* Amherst: University of Massachusetts Press, 1995.

Heinzelman, Kurt. "'Household Laws': Dorothy Wordsworth's Grasmere Journal." *A/B: Autobiography Studies* 2:4 (1986–87): 21–26.

———. "Poetry and Real Estate: Wordsworth as Developer." *Southwest Review* 84:4 (1999): 573–588.

Homans, Margaret. *Women Writers and Poetic Identity.* Princeton: Princeton UP, 1980.

———. *Bearing the Word: Language and Female Experience in Nineteenth-Century Women's Writing.* Chicago: University of Chicago Press, 1986.

Kincaid-Ehlers, Elizabeth. *Blue Woman on a Green Field: A Consideration of Dorothy Wordsworth.* DAI 39 (1978): 2291A–2292A.

Lefebure, Molly. *Samuel Taylor Coleridge: A Bondage of Opium.* London: Gollancz, 1974.

Levy, Michelle. "The Wordsworths, the Greens, and the Limits of Sympathy." *Studies in Romanticism* 42 (2003): 543–563.

Liu, Alan. "On the Autobiographical Present: Dorothy Wordsworth's *Grasmere Journals.*" *Criticism* 26 (1984): 115–137.

McCormick, Anita H. "'I shall be beloved—I want no more': Dorothy Wordsworth's Rhetoric and the Appeal to Feeling in *The Grasmere Journals.*" *Philological Quarterly* 69:4 (1990): 471–493.

Mellor, Anne K. *Romanticism and Gender.* London and New York: Routledge, 1993.

Moorman, Mary. *William Wordsworth: A Biography.* Oxford: Clarendon, 1957.

Morley, F. V. *Dora Wordsworth, Her Book.* London: Oxford UP, 1924.

Nabholtz, John R. "Dorothy Wordsworth and the Picturesque." *Studies in Romanticism* 3 (1964): 118–128.

Rogers, John. *"Dearest Friend": A Study of Dorothy Wordsworth's Journals*. DAI 35 (1974): 1632A–1633A.

Tomlinson, Bernard. "Editing Dorothy Wordsworth." *Contemporary Review* 262 (1993): 44–46.

Wolfson, Susan. "Individual in Community: Dorothy Wordsworth in Conversation with William." *Romanticism and Feminism*. Ed. Anne Mellor. Bloomington: Indiana UP, 1988, 139–166.

Woof, Pamela. "Dorothy Wordsworth's Journals: The Patterns and Pressures of Composition." *Romantic Revisions*. Eds. Robert Brinkley and Keith Hanley. Cambridge: Cambridge UP, 1992: 169–190.

Wordsworth, Mary. *The Letters of Mary Wordsworth, 1800–1855*. Ed. Mary E. Burton. Oxford: Clarendon, 1958.

Wordsworth, William, and Samuel Taylor Coleridge. *Lyrical Ballads*. Ed. W. J. B. Owen. London: Oxford UP, 1969.

Worthen, John. *The Gang: Coleridge, the Hutchinsons and the Wordsworths in 1802*. New Haven: Yale UP, 2001.

Web Sites

The Dove Cottage/Wordsworth Trust Website: www.wordsworth.org.uk

www.thecumbriadirectory.com

Film

Ken Russell: *Clouds of Glory*, 1978.